BOOK ONE

RESEARCH OF FAMILY NAMES

Cramer - Watson - Husted - Levick - Sutton

Joyce Sutton

Order this book online at www.trafford.com
or email orders@trafford.com

Most Trafford titles are also available at major online book retailers.

Printed in the United States of America.

ISBN:978-1-4269-6985-0 (sc)

Library of Congress Control Number: 2011916977

Trafford rev. 10/12/2011

www.trafford.com

North America & international
toll-free: 1 888 232 4444 (USA & Canada)
phone: 250 383 6864 • fax: 812 355 4082

Introduction

BOOK 1

THIS IS A RESEARCH BOOK ON BOTH SIDES OF MY FAMILY. MY HUSBANDS SIDE STARTS WITH THE FAMILY NAME OF CRAMER AND INCLUDES WATSON AND SUTTON INCLUDING WHO THEY MARRIED AND THEIR CHILDREN. MOST OF MY RESEARCH IS BACKED UP WITH PAPER DOCUMENTATION .

BOOK 2

IS ON MY SIDE OF THE FAMILY, MOST OF IT IS DOCUMENTED. SOME OF MY COUSINS HAVE SENT ME INFORMATION ON THEIR DIRECT LINE WHICH IS ADDED BUT NOT DOCUMENTED. MY FAMILY NAMES ARE HOFFMAN/HUFFMAN, SHEEHAN/SHAHAN, HOVATTER, SHUMATE, SMITH, JONES, MANCUSO AND SUTTON, WHO THEY MARRIED AND THEIR CHILDREN.

IN SHARING THE INFORMATION WE HAVE ABOUT OUR ANCESTRY WE HOPE THAT IT MAY BE OF HELP TO OTHERS THAT ARE TRYING TO FIND THEIR FAMILY TREE.

IF I HAVE MADE ANY MISTAKES PLEASE SEND ME THE CORRECTED INFORMATION AND I WILL ADD IT UNDER SEPERATE COVER. I ENDEAVORED TO MAKE THE FAMILY TREES AS TRUE AS POSSIBLE. I CONSIDER IT MY FAMILY BIBLE.

JOYCE SUTTON
jsutton639@aol.com

THIS IS A RESEARCH BOOK ON THE NAMES OF:

CRAMER
WATSON
SUTTON
FROM THE NEW JERSEY AREA

HOFFMAN
HOVATTER
SUMMERS
SHAHAN
FROM PA, MD, VA AND WV AREA

SHUMATE
SMITH
JONES
FROM THE AL AND MS AREA

THERE ARE MANY OTHER NAMES THAT HAVE MARRIED INTO THESE FAMILIES, YOURS MIGHT BE ONE OF THEM.

GOOD LUCK WITH YOUR FAMILY RESEARCH. I HOPE I WAS OF SOME HELP.

JOYCE

Preface

Starting with the first Cramers/Cramners known to arrive in the Americas to where we are today. This basically is our family line. A lot of research has gone into this family by several other researchers. We are indebted to them for all the hard work they put into researching the family.
I will refer to Cramer/Cramner as Cramer from here on. You will notice that it seems like history is repeating it's self in a few family lines but that is because there are Cramers that married Cramers. Remember there were three Cramer sons to make three separate lines to the present day Cramers.
My research will continue from Cramer to Watson. Watson to Sutton.

The other half the Sutton family will be on my side of the family. My ancestry began in Germany and came to this country before the Revolutionary War. I have proven my ancestry back to that period and I am a Daughter of the American Revolution.
My family names are Hoffman, Summers, Shahan/Sheehan, Hovatter. My father was a first generation to this country from Italy, his name was Mancuso and that leads to me who married Robert T. Sutton.

Descendants of William Cramer 1st Wm. Cramer

1 William Cramer - 1689
+Elizabeth Carwithy
2 Elizabeth Cramer
+George Pack
2 Thomas Cramer 1662 -
+Deborah
2 William Cramer 1664 -
+Rachel
3 William Cramer 1691 -
+Ruth Southwick
4 William Cramer 1717 - 1799
+Miriam Stockham
5 William Cramer 1756 -
+Nancy Somers
6 William B. Cramer 1792 -
+Mary Adams - 1825
7 Charles A. Cramer 1821 - 1892
+Elizabeth Adams 1825 - 1914
8 [2] George F. Cramer 1854 - 1915
+[1] Mary E. Cramer 1868 - 1899
9 [3] Dora Cramer 1891 - 1961
+[4] Grover Maxwell 1884 - 1939
10 [5] Carlton Maxwell 1908 - 1967
10 [6] Baby Estelle Maxwell May -
9 [7] Norris C. Cramer 1886 - 1936
+[8] Elsie Mick 1888 - 1963
9 [9] Mary Edna Cramer 1888 - 1928
+[10] Thomas S. Watson 1882 - 1964
10 [11] Hilma Watson 1910 -
+[12] Lindley Llewellyn Newcomer 1906 - 1992
11 [13] John Newcomer
+[14] Barbara Lee Boffemmyer
12 [15] John Whitney Newcomer 1959 -
+[16] Joan Lida Luby
13 [17] Leah Eliza Newcomer
13 [18] Adam Samuel Newcomer
12 [19] Thomas England Newcomer 1966 -
11 [20] Ronald Newcomer 1944 - 1963
10 [21] Dora Watson 1915 - 1965
+[22] Robert O. Sutton 1906 - 1987
11 [23] Twin Baby Sutton 1930 - 1930
11 [24] Twin Baby Sutton 1930 - 1930
11 [25] Robert Thomas Sutton 1932 -
+[26] Joyce F.. Mancuso 1934 -
12 [27] Dolores Lea Sutton 1958 -
12 [28] Susan Joyce Sutton 1964 -
+[29] Christopher Keating
13 [30] Christopher Keating Jr.
13 [31] Benjamin Keating
12 [32] Bobbi Lynn Sutton 1968 -
+[33] Karl Frank Chase
13 [34] Shawn Joseph Chase 1995 -
13 [35] Samantha Joyce Chase 1997 -
*Partner of [32] Bobbi Lynn Sutton:
+[36] Mr. McHenry
13 [37] Dani-Lynn McHenry 2006 -
11 [38] Edna May Sutton 1937 -
+[39] George Borton 1940 - 2000
11 [40] Marjorie Louise Sutton 1940 -
+[41] Lawrence Rose
12 [42] Lawrence Rose
10 [43] Marjorie Watson 1921 -
+[44] Frank Cuifolo
8 Elwood Cramer
+Sarah Stackhouse
8 William H. Cramer 1846 - 1870
8 Albert Allen Cramer
8 Sarah M. Cramer 1857 - 1860
8 Mary O. Cramer 1859 -
8 Charles A. Cramer 1863 -
8 Howard H. Cramer 1864 - 1941
+Clara Bozarth 1868 - 1959
9 Earle C. Cramer 1895 - 1975
+Elizabeth French 1904 - 1977
10 Norman Earle Cramer 1930 -

+Delilah Crowley
11 Douglas Cramer
+Margarite Keating
12 James Cramer
12 Laura Cramer
11 Gregory Cramer
11 Jeff Cramer
11 Joan Cramer
11 Harold Cramer
11 Charles Robert Cramer 1967 - 1982
11 Douglas Cramer
+Margarite Keating
12 James Cramer
12 Laura Cramer
9 Casper Cramer 1901 - 1901
9 Julia E. Cramer
+John A. Herman
7 Isaacc Cramer
+Abigail Cobb
7 William A. Cramer
+Sarah Louisa Cavileer
6 Borden Cramer
+Martha Morris
6 Emily Cramer
+Joseph Ridgway Esq.
6 Clarinda Cramer
+John Somers
6 Mary Cramer
+Jonothan Cawley
5 Andrew Cramer
5 Samuel Cramer
+Mary Gale
5 Josiah Cramer
5 Amariah Cramer
+Hannah Rogers
5 Athalania Cramer
+Amos Southard
5 Miriam Cramer
5 Ruth Cramer
+James Pharo
4 James Cramer
4 Josiah Cramer
+Sarah Wilkinson
4 Ruth Cramer
4 Elizabeth Cramer
4 Abraham Cramer
+Abigail Willits Birdsall
3 Elizabeth Cramer
+John Corbet, Jr.
3 John Cramer
3 Thomas Cramer
+[46] Mary Ridgway
3 Sarah Cramer
+Timothy Ridgway
3 Andrew Cramer
+Sarah
3 Levi Cramer
+Ester Horner/Horne
3 John Cramer 1696 -
+Mary Andrews
*2nd Wife of John Cramer:
+Rebecca Stout
4 John Cramer, Jr. 1730 - 1790
+Margaret Smith 1735 - 1811
5 John Cramer 1758 - 1815
+Hannah Johnson 1765 - 1827
6 Daniel S. Cramer 1785 - 1853
+Charlotte Loveland 1794 - 1869
7 [73] John Smith Cramer 1818 - 1880
+[45] Dorcas Tabitha Cramer 1818 - 1853
8 [74] Mary E. Cramer 1840 - 1841
8 [75] Margaret Ann Cramer
+[76] Theodore C. Allen
8 [77] Sarah Jane Cramer 1843 - 1865
8 [78] William Asbury Cramer
+[79] Phebe Ann Mingin
8 [80] Mary Eliza Cramer 1848 - 1848

8 [81] Uriah Burris Cramer 1850 - 1917
+[82] Electa Throckmorton 1845 - 1919
9 [83] Uriah Smith Cramer
+[84] Helen Louise Driscoll
9 [85] Lettie E. Cramer
+[86] Benjamin F. Driscoll
9 [87] Theodore E. Cramer
+[88] Ella Camille Martin
9 [89] Renard Ethyl Cramer 1865 - 1927
+[90] Mary Emma Prince 1871 - 1937
10 [91] Olive Cramer
+[92] John Wiseman
10 [93] Ada May Cramer 1897 - 1933
+[94] Merrill Cleveland Mathis 1884 - 1934
11 [95] Ida May Mathis
+[96] Elsworth Butler
*2nd Husband of [95] Ida May Mathis:
+[97] Fillmore Shinn
12 [98] Percy Shinn
+[99] Barbara Stevenson
13 [100] Robert Shinn
13 [101] Jeanne Shinn
13 [102] Kathryn Shinn
12 [103] Grace Shinn
11 [104] Mary Mathis 1918 -
+[105] George Filling, Jr.
11 [106] Irene Mathis 1921 -
11 [107] Sarah Mathis 1925 -
11 [108] Mildred Mathis 1928 -
11 [109] Merriell Cleveland Mathis, Jr. 1931 -
10 [110] Jefferson Cramer
+[111] Mary Ann Gallagher
9 [112] Sarah Eliza Cramer
+[113] Ephraim Ford
9 [114] Rhoda Amelia Cramer
+[115] Nathaniel C. Jones
9 [116] Sidney Uriah Cramer 1880 - 1880
9 [117] Eva L. Cramer
+[118] Samuel E. Cramer
8 [119] Edith Eliza Cramer
+[120] Wilson Bodine Cramer
7 [48] Sarah Ann Cramer 1816 - 1897
+[47] Darius Cramer 1808 - 1858
8 [49] Lavinia Cramer 1833 - 1895
+[50] Chalkley S. Cramer 1833 - 1855
8 [51] William G. Cramer 1837 - 1912
+[52] Mary Frances Maxwell 1847 - 1907
9 [1] Mary E. Cramer 1868 - 1899
+[2] George F. Cramer 1854 - 1915
10 [3] Dora Cramer 1891 - 1961
+[4] Grover Maxwell 1884 - 1939
11 [5] Carlton Maxwell 1908 - 1967
11 [6] Baby Estelle Maxwell May -
10 [7] Norris C. Cramer 1886 - 1936
+[8] Elsie Mick 1888 - 1963
10 [9] Mary Edna Cramer 1888 - 1928
+[10] Thomas S. Watson 1882 - 1964
11 [11] Hilma Watson 1910 -
+[12] Lindley Llewellyn Newcomer 1906 - 1992
12 [13] John Newcomer
+[14] Barbara Lee Boffemmyer
13 [15] John Whitney Newcomer 1959 -
+[16] Joan Lida Luby
14 [17] Leah Eliza Newcomer
14 [18] Adam Samuel Newcomer
13 [19] Thomas England Newcomer 1966 -
12 [20] Ronald Newcomer 1944 - 1963
11 [21] Dora Watson 1915 - 1965
+[22] Robert O. Sutton 1906 - 1987
12 [23] Twin Baby Sutton 1930 - 1930
12 [24] Twin Baby Sutton 1930 - 1930
12 [25] Robert Thomas Sutton 1932 -
+[26] Joyce F.. Mancuso 1934 -
13 [27] Dolores Lea Sutton 1958 -
13 [28] Susan Joyce Sutton 1964 -
+[29] Christopher Keating
14 [30] Christopher Keating Jr.

.... 14 [31] Benjamin Keating
.... 13 [32] Bobbi Lynn Sutton 1968 -
.... +[33] Karl Frank Chase
.... 14 [34] Shawn Joseph Chase 1995 -
.... 14 [35] Samantha Joyce Chase 1997 -
.... *Partner of [32] Bobbi Lynn Sutton:
.... +[36] Mr. McHenry
.... 14 [37] Dani-Lynn McHenry 2006 -
.... 12 [38] Edna May Sutton 1937 -
.... +[39] George Borton 1940 - 2000
.... 12 [40] Marjorie Louise Sutton 1940 -
.... +[41] Lawrence Rose
.... 13 [42] Lawrence Rose
.... 11 [43] Marjorie Watson 1921 -
.... +[44] Frank Cuifolo
.... 9 [53] Estella Cramer 1870 - 1942
.... +[54] Winfield Peterson 1864 - 1917
.... 9 [55] William F. Cramer 1875 - 1936
.... +[56] Elizabeth J. Headley 1881 - 1968
.... 8 [57] Charles Henry "Spide" Cramer 1839 -
.... +[58] Sarah Jane Maxwell
.... 8 [59] Mary Elizabeth Cramer 1842 -
.... +[60] William H. Mathis
.... 8 [61] Calab Smith "Swampy" Cramer 1844 -
.... +[62] Mary Jane Robbins
.... 8 [63] Ellis S. Cramer 1845 -
.... 8 [64] Sarah Ann Cramer 1847 -
.... +[65] John Hickman
.... 8 [66] Emma M. Cramer 1852 -
.... +[67] Carlisle Gaskill
.... 8 [68] Chalkley Sears Cramer 1856 -
.... +[69] Frances Caroline Johnson
.... 8 [70] Daniel D. Cramer 1858 -
.... +[71] Anna M. Adams
.... 7 Charles Fletcher Cramer
.... +Eliza Cale
.... 7 [72] John Smith Cramer
.... +[45] Dorcas Tabitha Cramer 1818 - 1853
.... 7 Joseph Cramer
.... 7 Mary Cramer
.... 7 Esther Ann Cramer
.... +Abraham Cramer
.... 7 Hannah Ann Cramer
.... +Charles Brewer
.... 7 Elizabeth Cramer
.... 6 Elizabeth Cramer
.... +Thomas Smith
.... 6 John Cramer
.... +Nancy Jenkins
.... 6 Isaiah Cramer
.... +Rachel Randolph
.... 6 Jonathan Cramer
.... +Ann Brewer
.... 6 Margaret Cramer
.... +John Randolph
.... 6 Asa Smith Cramer
.... +Catherine Hall
.... 6 Hannah Cramer
.... +Isaiah Weeks
.... 6 Mary Cramer
.... +Samuel Weeks
.... 6 Jane Cramer
.... +John Hall
.... 6 William Cramer
.... +Elizabeth Jordan
.... 6 Elizabeth S. Cramer
.... +Benjamin B. Doughty
.... 5 Amy Cramer
.... 5 Mary Cramer
.... +Samuel Goldsmith
.... 5 Jacob Cramer
.... +Elizabeth ?
.... 5 Sylvanus Cramer
.... +Sarah Jane Gifford
.... 5 Ruth Cramer - 1793
.... 4 Jacob Cramer
.... +Phoebe Valentine

4 Seymour/Semon Cramer
+Mary Smith
4 Rachel Cramer
+Edward Allen, Sr.
4 Elizabeth Cramer
+Nehemiah Mathis
4 Rebecca Cramer
+William Carter
4 Hannah Cramer
+Joseph Burns
3 Elizabeth Cramer
+John Coret, Jr.
3 William Cramer
+Ruth Southwick
3 Thomas Cramer
+[46] Mary Ridgway
2 John Cramer 1666 -
+Sarah Osborne 1663 -
3 John Cramer
+Hannah Potter
3 Thomas Cramer
+Abigail Willets
3 Jeremiah Cramer
+Abiah Tuttle
3 Stephen Cramer 1700 - 1777
+Sarah Andrews 1701/02 - 1748
4 Caleb Cramer 1732/33 - 1818
+Sara
5 Isaac Cramer 1756 - 1839
+Dorcas Adams 1766 - 1848
6 Charles Cramer 1789 - 1872
+Mary Gaskill 1791 - 1873
7 [47] Darius Cramer 1808 - 1858
+[48] Sarah Ann Cramer 1816 - 1897
8 [49] Lavinia Cramer 1833 - 1895
+[50] Chalkley S. Cramer 1833 - 1855
8 [51] William G. Cramer 1837 - 1912
+[52] Mary Frances Maxwell 1847 - 1907
9 [1] Mary E. Cramer 1868 - 1899
+[2] George F. Cramer 1854 - 1915
10 [3] Dora Cramer 1891 - 1961
+[4] Grover Maxwell 1884 - 1939
11 [5] Carlton Maxwell 1908 - 1967
11 [6] Baby Estelle Maxwell May -
10 [7] Norris C. Cramer 1886 - 1936
+[8] Elsie Mick 1888 - 1963
10 [9] Mary Edna Cramer 1888 - 1928
+[10] Thomas S. Watson 1882 - 1964
11 [11] Hilma Watson 1910 -
+[12] Lindley Llewellyn Newcomer 1906 - 1992
12 [13] John Newcomer
+[14] Barbara Lee Boffemmyer
13 [15] John Whitney Newcomer 1959 -
+[16] Joan Lida Luby
14 [17] Leah Eliza Newcomer
14 [18] Adam Samuel Newcomer
13 [19] Thomas England Newcomer 1966 -
12 [20] Ronald Newcomer 1944 - 1963
11 [21] Dora Watson 1915 - 1965
+[22] Robert O. Sutton 1906 - 1987
12 [23] Twin Baby Sutton 1930 - 1930
12 [24] Twin Baby Sutton 1930 - 1930
12 [25] Robert Thomas Sutton 1932 -
+[26] Joyce F.. Mancuso 1934 -
13 [27] Dolores Lea Sutton 1958 -
13 [28] Susan Joyce Sutton 1964 -
+[29] Christopher Keating
14 [30] Christopher Keating Jr.
14 [31] Benjamin Keating
13 [32] Bobbi Lynn Sutton 1968 -
+[33] Karl Frank Chase
14 [34] Shawn Joseph Chase 1995 -
14 [35] Samantha Joyce Chase 1997 -
*Partner of [32] Bobbi Lynn Sutton:
+[36] Mr. McHenry
14 [37] Dani-Lynn McHenry 2006 -
12 [38] Edna May Sutton 1937 -

+[39] George Borton 1940 - 2000
12 [40] Marjorie Louise Sutton 1940 -
+[41] Lawrence Rose
13 [42] Lawrence Rose
11 [43] Marjorie Watson 1921 -
+[44] Frank Cuifolo
9 [53] Estella Cramer 1870 - 1942
+[54] Winfield Peterson 1864 - 1917
9 [55] William F. Cramer 1875 - 1936
+[56] Elizabeth J. Headley 1881 - 1968
8 [57] Charles Henry "Spide" Cramer 1839 -
+[58] Sarah Jane Maxwell
8 [59] Mary Elizabeth Cramer 1842 -
+[60] William H. Mathis
8 [61] Calab Smith "Swampy" Cramer 1844 -
+[62] Mary Jane Robbins
8 [63] Ellis S. Cramer 1845 -
8 [64] Sarah Ann Cramer 1847 -
+[65] John Hickman
8 [66] Emma M. Cramer 1852 -
+[67] Carlisle Gaskill
8 [68] Chalkley Sears Cramer 1856 -
+[69] Frances Caroline Johnson
8 [70] Daniel D. Cramer 1858 -
+[71] Anna M. Adams
7 Charles Burris Cramer 1828 - 1879
+Ellen S. Adams 1832 -
7 William Sears Cramer
+Catherine Leek
7 Aaron G. Cramer
+Ann Mott
7 Thomas Allen Cramer
+Rebecca Ann Cramer
7 Isaac F. Cramer
+Elizabeth Haines
7 Lavinia Cramer
+John Carter
7 Edith Eliza Cramer
+John W. Cramer
7 [45] Dorcas Tabitha Cramer 1818 - 1853
+[72] John Smith Cramer
*2nd Husband of [45] Dorcas Tabitha Cramer:
+[73] John Smith Cramer 1818 - 1880
8 [74] Mary E. Cramer 1840 - 1841
8 [75] Margaret Ann Cramer
+[76] Theodore C. Allen
8 [77] Sarah Jane Cramer 1843 - 1865
8 [78] William Asbury Cramer
+[79] Phebe Ann Mingin
8 [80] Mary Eliza Cramer 1848 - 1848
8 [81] Uriah Burris Cramer 1850 - 1917
+[82] Electa Throckmorton 1845 - 1919
9 [83] Uriah Smith Cramer
+[84] Helen Louise Driscoll
9 [85] Lettie E. Cramer
+[86] Benjamin F. Driscoll
9 [87] Theodore E. Cramer
+[88] Ella Camille Martin
9 [89] Renard Ethyl Cramer 1865 - 1927
+[90] Mary Emma Prince 1871 - 1937
10 [91] Olive Cramer
+[92] John Wiseman
10 [93] Ada May Cramer 1897 - 1933
+[94] Merrill Cleveland Mathis 1884 - 1934
11 [95] Ida May Mathis
+[96] Elsworth Butler
*2nd Husband of [95] Ida May Mathis:
+[97] Fillmore Shinn
12 [98] Percy Shinn
+[99] Barbara Stevenson
13 [100] Robert Shinn
13 [101] Jeanne Shinn
13 [102] Kathryn Shinn
12 [103] Grace Shinn
11 [104] Mary Mathis 1918 -
+[105] George Filling, Jr.
11 [106] Irene Mathis 1921 -

.... 11 [107] Sarah Mathis 1925 -
.... 11 [108] Mildred Mathis 1928 -
.... 11 [109] Merriell Cleveland Mathis, Jr. 1931 -
.... 10 [110] Jefferson Cramer
.... +[111] Mary Ann Gallagher
.... 9 [112] Sarah Eliza Cramer
.... +[113] Ephraim Ford
.... 9 [114] Rhoda Amelia Cramer
.... +[115] Nathaniel C. Jones
.... 9 [116] Sidney Uriah Cramer 1880 - 1880
.... 9 [117] Eva L. Cramer
.... +[118] Samuel E. Cramer
.... 8 [119] Edith Eliza Cramer
.... +[120] Wilson Bodine Cramer
.... 7 Samuel B. Cramer
.... +Ruth Elmy Lamson
.... 7 Mary Ann Cramer
.... +William G. Adams
.... 7 Uriah Cramer
.... +Sarah S. Haines
.... 6 George A. Cramer
.... +Lucy Cale
.... 6 Bethiah Cramer
.... +Archibald Sooy
.... 6 Uriah Cramer
.... +Maria Franklin
.... 6 Mary Cramer
.... +Isaiah Robbins
.... 6 Isaac Cramer 1796 - 1831
.... 6 Lavinia Cramer
.... +William French
.... 6 Hope Cramer 1801 - 1859
.... 6 Lucy Ann Cramer
.... +Edward Johnson
.... *2nd Wife of John Cramer:
.... +Sarah Osborne

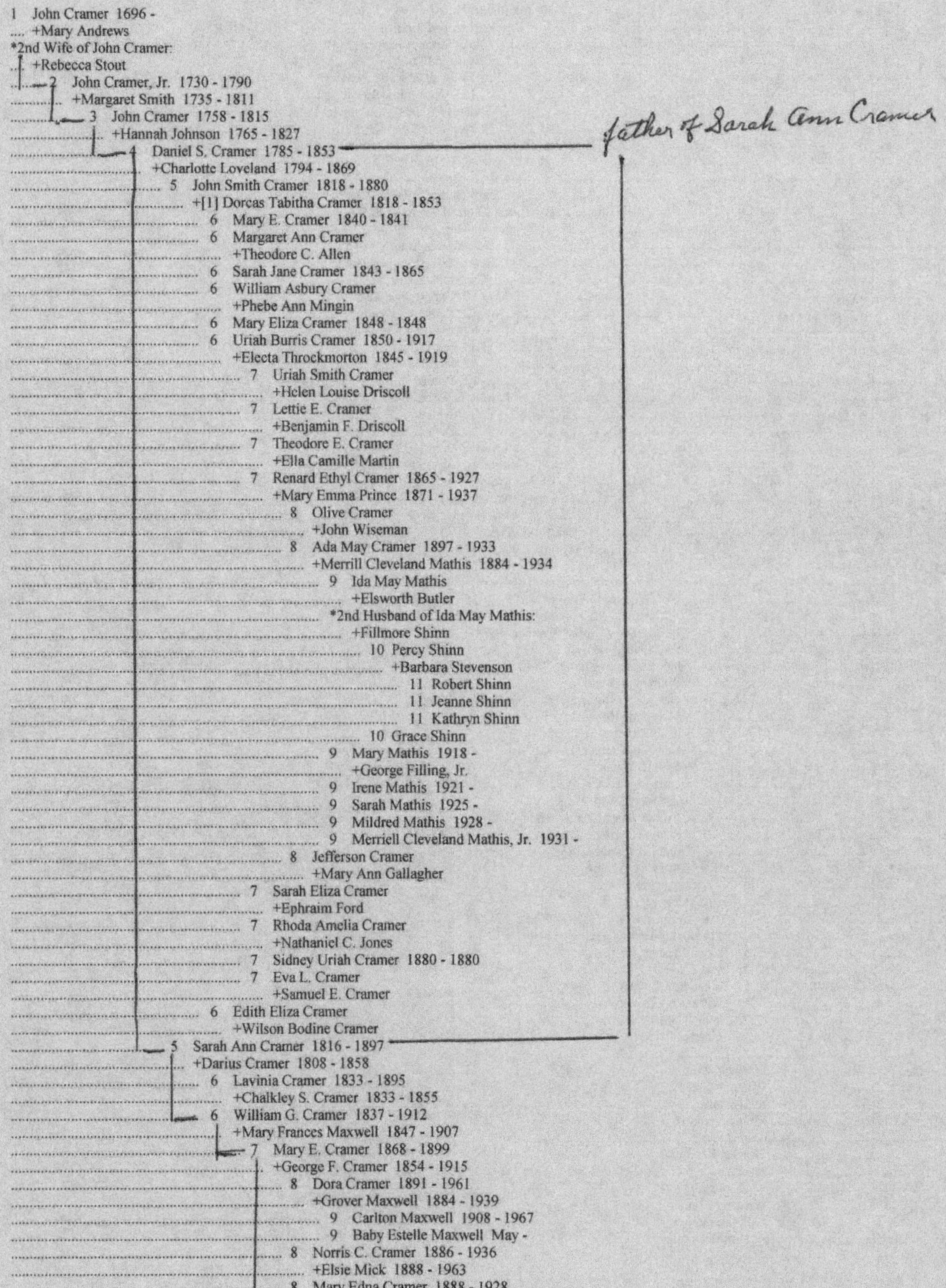

Descendants of John Cramer Son of 2nd William

1 John Cramer 1696 -
+Mary Andrews
*2nd Wife of John Cramer:
+Rebecca Stout
2 John Cramer, Jr. 1730 - 1790
+Margaret Smith 1735 - 1811
3 John Cramer 1758 - 1815
+Hannah Johnson 1765 - 1827
4 Daniel S. Cramer 1785 - 1853 — father of Sarah Ann Cramer
+Charlotte Loveland 1794 - 1869
5 John Smith Cramer 1818 - 1880
+[1] Dorcas Tabitha Cramer 1818 - 1853
6 Mary E. Cramer 1840 - 1841
6 Margaret Ann Cramer
+Theodore C. Allen
6 Sarah Jane Cramer 1843 - 1865
6 William Asbury Cramer
+Phebe Ann Mingin
6 Mary Eliza Cramer 1848 - 1848
6 Uriah Burris Cramer 1850 - 1917
+Electa Throckmorton 1845 - 1919
7 Uriah Smith Cramer
+Helen Louise Driscoll
7 Lettie E. Cramer
+Benjamin F. Driscoll
7 Theodore E. Cramer
+Ella Camille Martin
7 Renard Ethyl Cramer 1865 - 1927
+Mary Emma Prince 1871 - 1937
8 Olive Cramer
+John Wiseman
8 Ada May Cramer 1897 - 1933
+Merrill Cleveland Mathis 1884 - 1934
9 Ida May Mathis
+Elsworth Butler
*2nd Husband of Ida May Mathis:
+Fillmore Shinn
10 Percy Shinn
+Barbara Stevenson
11 Robert Shinn
11 Jeanne Shinn
11 Kathryn Shinn
10 Grace Shinn
9 Mary Mathis 1918 -
+George Filling, Jr.
9 Irene Mathis 1921 -
9 Sarah Mathis 1925 -
9 Mildred Mathis 1928 -
9 Merriell Cleveland Mathis, Jr. 1931 -
8 Jefferson Cramer
+Mary Ann Gallagher
7 Sarah Eliza Cramer
+Ephraim Ford
7 Rhoda Amelia Cramer
+Nathaniel C. Jones
7 Sidney Uriah Cramer 1880 - 1880
7 Eva L. Cramer
+Samuel E. Cramer
6 Edith Eliza Cramer
+Wilson Bodine Cramer
5 Sarah Ann Cramer 1816 - 1897
+Darius Cramer 1808 - 1858
6 Lavinia Cramer 1833 - 1895
+Chalkley S. Cramer 1833 - 1855
6 William G. Cramer 1837 - 1912
+Mary Frances Maxwell 1847 - 1907
7 Mary E. Cramer 1868 - 1899
+George F. Cramer 1854 - 1915
8 Dora Cramer 1891 - 1961
+Grover Maxwell 1884 - 1939
9 Carlton Maxwell 1908 - 1967
9 Baby Estelle Maxwell May -
8 Norris C. Cramer 1886 - 1936
+Elsie Mick 1888 - 1963
8 Mary Edna Cramer 1888 - 1928

+Thomas S. Watson 1882 - 1964
9 Hilma Watson 1910 -
+Lindley Llewellyn Newcomer 1906 - 1992
10 John Newcomer
+Barbara Lee Boffemmyer
11 John Whitney Newcomer 1959 -
+Joan Lida Luby
12 Leah Eliza Newcomer
12 Adam Samuel Newcomer
11 Thomas England Newcomer 1966 -
10 Ronald Newcomer 1944 - 1963
9 Dora Watson 1915 - 1965
+Robert O. Sutton 1906 - 1987
10 Twin Baby Sutton 1930 - 1930
10 Twin Baby Sutton 1930 - 1930
10 Robert Thomas Sutton 1932 -
+Joyce F.. Mancuso 1934 -
11 Dolores Lea Sutton 1958 -
11 Susan Joyce Sutton 1964 -
+Christopher Keating
12 Christopher Keating Jr.
12 Benjamin Keating
11 Bobbi Lynn Sutton 1968 -
+Karl Frank Chase
12 Shawn Joseph Chase 1995 -
12 Samantha Joyce Chase 1997 -
*Partner of Bobbi Lynn Sutton:
+Mr. McHenry
12 Dani-Lynn McHenry 2006 -
10 Edna May Sutton 1937 -
+George Borton 1940 - 2000
10 Marjorie Louise Sutton 1940 -
+Lawrence Rose
11 Lawrence Rose
9 Marjorie Watson 1921 -
+Frank Cuifolo
7 Estella Cramer 1870 - 1942
+Winfield Peterson 1864 - 1917
7 William F. Cramer 1875 - 1936
+Elizabeth J. Headley 1881 - 1968
6 Charles Henry "Spide" Cramer 1839 -
+Sarah Jane Maxwell
6 Mary Elizabeth Cramer 1842 -
+William H. Mathis
6 Calab Smith "Swampy" Cramer 1844 -
+Mary Jane Robbins
6 Ellis S. Cramer 1845 -
6 Sarah Ann Cramer 1847 -
+John Hickman
6 Emma M. Cramer 1852 -
+Carlisle Gaskill
6 Chalkley Sears Cramer 1856 -
+Frances Caroline Johnson
6 Daniel D. Cramer 1858 -
+Anna M. Adams
5 Charles Fletcher Cramer
+Eliza Cale
5 John Smith Cramer
+[1] Dorcas Tabitha Cramer 1818 - 1853
5 Joseph Cramer
5 Mary Cramer
5 Esther Ann Cramer
+Abraham Cramer
5 Hannah Ann Cramer
+Charles Brewer
5 Elizabeth Cramer
4 Elizabeth Cramer
+Thomas Smith
4 John Cramer
+Nancy Jenkins
4 Isaiah Cramer
+Rachel Randolph
4 Jonathan Cramer
+Ann Brewer
4 Margaret Cramer
+John Randolph
4 Asa Smith Cramer

.... +Catherine Hall
.... 4 Hannah Cramer
.... +Isaiah Weeks
.... 4 Mary Cramer
.... +Samuel Weeks
.... 4 Jane Cramer
.... +John Hall
.... 4 William Cramer
.... +Elizabeth Jordan
.... 4 Elizabeth S. Cramer
.... +Benjamin B. Doughty
.... 3 Amy Cramer
.... 3 Mary Cramer
.... +Samuel Goldsmith
.... 3 Jacob Cramer
.... +Elizabeth ?
.... 3 Sylvanus Cramer
.... +Sarah Jane Gifford
.... 3 Ruth Cramer - 1793
.... 2 Jacob Cramer
.... +Phoebe Valentine
.... 2 Seymour/Semon Cramer
.... +Mary Smith
.... 2 Rachel Cramer
.... +Edward Allen, Sr.
.... 2 Elizabeth Cramer
.... +Nehemiah Mathis
.... 2 Rebecca Cramer
.... +William Carter
.... 2 Hannah Cramer
.... +Joseph Burns

Descendants of John Cramer Son of 1st William

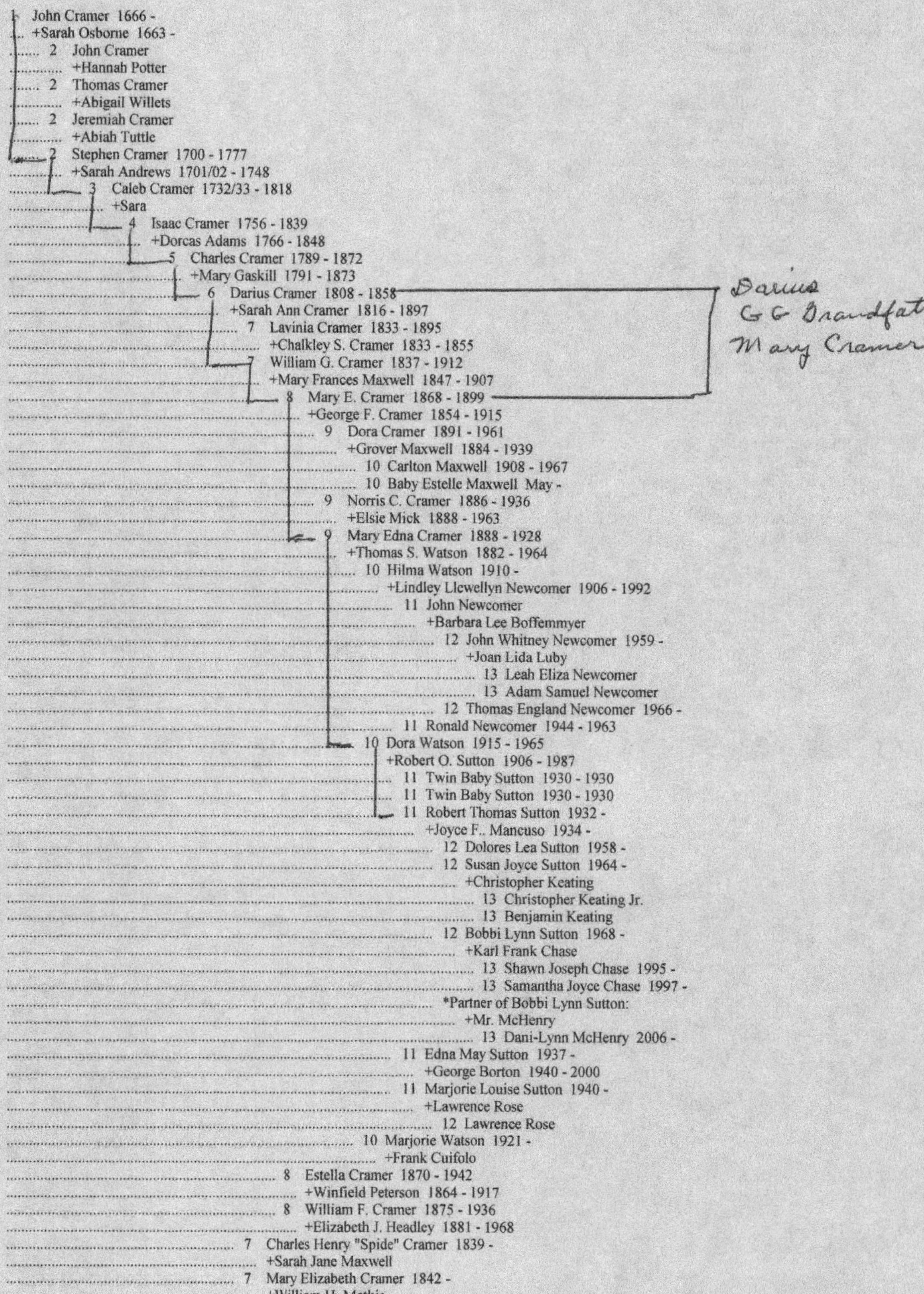

1 John Cramer 1666 -
+Sarah Osborne 1663 -
2 John Cramer
+Hannah Potter
2 Thomas Cramer
+Abigail Willets
2 Jeremiah Cramer
+Abiah Tuttle
2 Stephen Cramer 1700 - 1777
+Sarah Andrews 1701/02 - 1748
3 Caleb Cramer 1732/33 - 1818
+Sara
4 Isaac Cramer 1756 - 1839
+Dorcas Adams 1766 - 1848
5 Charles Cramer 1789 - 1872
+Mary Gaskill 1791 - 1873
6 Darius Cramer 1808 - 1858
+Sarah Ann Cramer 1816 - 1897
7 Lavinia Cramer 1833 - 1895
+Chalkley S. Cramer 1833 - 1855
7 William G. Cramer 1837 - 1912
+Mary Frances Maxwell 1847 - 1907
8 Mary E. Cramer 1868 - 1899
+George F. Cramer 1854 - 1915
9 Dora Cramer 1891 - 1961
+Grover Maxwell 1884 - 1939
10 Carlton Maxwell 1908 - 1967
10 Baby Estelle Maxwell May -
9 Norris C. Cramer 1886 - 1936
+Elsie Mick 1888 - 1963
9 Mary Edna Cramer 1888 - 1928
+Thomas S. Watson 1882 - 1964
10 Hilma Watson 1910 -
+Lindley Llewellyn Newcomer 1906 - 1992
11 John Newcomer
+Barbara Lee Boffemmyer
12 John Whitney Newcomer 1959 -
+Joan Lida Luby
13 Leah Eliza Newcomer
13 Adam Samuel Newcomer
12 Thomas England Newcomer 1966 -
11 Ronald Newcomer 1944 - 1963
10 Dora Watson 1915 - 1965
+Robert O. Sutton 1906 - 1987
11 Twin Baby Sutton 1930 - 1930
11 Twin Baby Sutton 1930 - 1930
11 Robert Thomas Sutton 1932 -
+Joyce F.. Mancuso 1934 -
12 Dolores Lea Sutton 1958 -
12 Susan Joyce Sutton 1964 -
+Christopher Keating
13 Christopher Keating Jr.
13 Benjamin Keating
12 Bobbi Lynn Sutton 1968 -
+Karl Frank Chase
13 Shawn Joseph Chase 1995 -
13 Samantha Joyce Chase 1997 -
*Partner of Bobbi Lynn Sutton:
+Mr. McHenry
13 Dani-Lynn McHenry 2006 -
11 Edna May Sutton 1937 -
+George Borton 1940 - 2000
11 Marjorie Louise Sutton 1940 -
+Lawrence Rose
12 Lawrence Rose
10 Marjorie Watson 1921 -
+Frank Cuifolo
8 Estella Cramer 1870 - 1942
+Winfield Peterson 1864 - 1917
8 William F. Cramer 1875 - 1936
+Elizabeth J. Headley 1881 - 1968
7 Charles Henry "Spide" Cramer 1839 -
+Sarah Jane Maxwell
7 Mary Elizabeth Cramer 1842 -
+William H. Mathis

Darius GG Grandfather to Mary Cramer

7 Calab Smith "Swampy" Cramer 1844 -
+Mary Jane Robbins
7 Ellis S. Cramer 1845 -
7 Sarah Ann Cramer 1847 -
+John Hickman
7 Emma M. Cramer 1852 -
+Carlisle Gaskill
7 Chalkley Sears Cramer 1856 -
+Frances Caroline Johnson
7 Daniel D. Cramer 1858 -
+Anna M. Adams
6 Charles Burris Cramer 1828 - 1879
+Ellen S. Adams 1832 -
6 William Sears Cramer
+Catherine Leek
6 Aaron G. Cramer
+Ann Mott
6 Thomas Allen Cramer
+Rebecca Ann Cramer
6 Isaac F. Cramer
+Elizabeth Haines
6 Lavinia Cramer
+John Carter
6 Edith Eliza Cramer
+John W. Cramer
6 Dorcas Tabitha Cramer 1818 - 1853
+John Smith Cramer
*2nd Husband of Dorcas Tabitha Cramer:
+John Smith Cramer 1818 - 1880
7 Mary E. Cramer 1840 - 1841
7 Margaret Ann Cramer
+Theodore C. Allen
7 Sarah Jane Cramer 1843 - 1865
7 William Asbury Cramer
+Phebe Ann Mingin
7 Mary Eliza Cramer 1848 - 1848
7 Uriah Burris Cramer 1850 - 1917
+Electa Throckmorton 1845 - 1919
8 Uriah Smith Cramer
+Helen Louise Driscoll
8 Lettie E. Cramer
+Benjamin F. Driscoll
8 Theodore E. Cramer
+Ella Camille Martin
8 Renard Ethyl Cramer 1865 - 1927
+Mary Emma Prince 1871 - 1937
9 Olive Cramer
+John Wiseman
9 Ada May Cramer 1897 - 1933
+Merrill Cleveland Mathis 1884 - 1934
10 Ida May Mathis
+Elsworth Butler
*2nd Husband of Ida May Mathis:
+Fillmore Shinn
11 Percy Shinn
+Barbara Stevenson
12 Robert Shinn
12 Jeanne Shinn
12 Kathryn Shinn
11 Grace Shinn
10 Mary Mathis 1918 -
+George Filling, Jr.
10 Irene Mathis 1921 -
10 Sarah Mathis 1925 -
10 Mildred Mathis 1928 -
10 Merriell Cleveland Mathis, Jr. 1931 -
9 Jefferson Cramer
+Mary Ann Gallagher
8 Sarah Eliza Cramer
+Ephraim Ford
8 Rhoda Amelia Cramer
+Nathaniel C. Jones
8 Sidney Uriah Cramer 1880 - 1880
8 Eva L. Cramer
+Samuel E. Cramer
7 Edith Eliza Cramer
+Wilson Bodine Cramer

.... 6 Samuel B. Cramer

.... +Ruth Elmy Lamson

.... 6 Mary Ann Cramer

.... +William G. Adams

.... 6 Uriah Cramer

.... +Sarah S. Haines

.... 5 George A. Cramer

.... +Lucy Cale

.... 5 Bethiah Cramer

.... +Archibald Sooy

.... 5 Uriah Cramer

.... +Maria Franklin

.... 5 Mary Cramer

.... +Isaiah Robbins

.... 5 Isaac Cramer 1796 - 1831

.... 5 Lavinia Cramer

.... +William French

.... 5 Hope Cramer 1801 - 1859

.... 5 Lucy Ann Cramer

.... +Edward Johnson

Descendants of William Cramer 5th Gen. Wm. Cramer

G G Grandfather to George F. Cramer

1 William Cramer 1756 -
+Nancy Somers
.... 2 William B. Cramer 1792 -
.... +Mary Adams - 1825
.... 3 Charles A. Cramer 1821 - 1892
.... +Elizabeth Adams 1825 - 1914
.... 4 George F. Cramer 1854 - 1915
.... +Mary E. Cramer 1868 - 1899
.... 5 Dora Cramer 1891 - 1961
.... +Grover Maxwell 1884 - 1939
.... 6 Carlton Maxwell 1908 - 1967
.... 6 Baby Estelle Maxwell May -
.... 5 Norris C. Cramer 1886 - 1936
.... +Elsie Mick 1888 - 1963
.... 5 Mary Edna Cramer 1888 - 1928
.... +Thomas S. Watson 1882 - 1964
.... 6 Hilma Watson 1910 -
.... +Lindley Llewellyn Newcomer 1906 - 1992
.... 7 John Newcomer
.... +Barbara Lee Boffemmyer
.... 8 John Whitney Newcomer 1959 -
.... +Joan Lida Luby
.... 9 Leah Eliza Newcomer
.... 9 Adam Samuel Newcomer
.... 8 Thomas England Newcomer 1966 -
.... 7 Ronald Newcomer 1944 - 1963
.... 6 Dora Watson 1915 - 1965
.... +Robert O. Sutton 1906 - 1987
.... 7 Twin Baby Sutton 1930 - 1930
.... 7 Twin Baby Sutton 1930 - 1930
.... 7 Robert Thomas Sutton 1932 -
.... +Joyce F.. Mancuso 1934 -
.... 8 Dolores Lea Sutton 1958 -
.... 8 Susan Joyce Sutton 1964 -
.... +Christopher Keating
.... 9 Christopher Keating Jr.
.... 9 Benjamin Keating
.... 8 Bobbi Lynn Sutton 1968 -
.... +Karl Frank Chase
.... 9 Shawn Joseph Chase 1995 -
.... 9 Samantha Joyce Chase 1997 -
.... *Partner of Bobbi Lynn Sutton:
.... +Mr. McHenry
.... 9 Dani-Lynn McHenry 2006 -
.... 7 Edna May Sutton 1937 -
.... +George Borton 1940 - 2000
.... 7 Marjorie Louise Sutton 1940 -
.... +Lawrence Rose
.... 8 Lawrence Rose
.... 6 Marjorie Watson 1921 -
.... +Frank Cuifolo
.... 4 Elwood Cramer
.... +Sarah Stackhouse
.... 4 William H. Cramer 1846 - 1870
.... 4 Albert Allen Cramer
.... 4 Sarah M. Cramer 1857 - 1860
.... 4 Mary O. Cramer 1859 -
.... 4 Charles A. Cramer 1863 -
.... 4 Howard H. Cramer 1864 - 1941
.... +Clara Bozarth 1868 - 1959
.... 5 Earle C. Cramer 1895 - 1975
.... +Elizabeth French 1904 - 1977
.... 6 Norman Earle Cramer 1930 -
.... +Delilah Crowley
.... 7 Douglas Cramer
.... +Margarite Keating
.... 8 James Cramer
.... 8 Laura Cramer
.... 7 Gregory Cramer
.... 7 Jeff Cramer
.... 7 Joan Cramer
.... 7 Harold Cramer
.... 7 Charles Robert Cramer 1967 - 1982
.... 7 Douglas Cramer
.... +Margarite Keating

.... 8 James Cramer
.... 8 Laura Cramer
.... 5 Casper Cramer 1901 - 1901
.... 5 Julia E. Cramer
.... +John A. Herman
.... 3 Isaacc Cramer
.... +Abigail Cobb
.... 3 William A. Cramer
.... +Sarah Louisa Cavileer
.... 2 Borden Cramer
.... +Martha Morris
.... 2 Emily Cramer
.... +Joseph Ridgway Esq.
.... 2 Clarinda Cramer
.... +John Somers
.... 2 Mary Cramer
.... +Jonothan Cawley

Descendants of Isaac Cramer

1 Isaac Cramer 1756 - 1839
+Dorcas Adams 1766 - 1848
2 Charles Cramer 1789 - 1872
+Mary Gaskill 1791 - 1873
3 Darius Cramer 1808 - 1858
+Sarah Ann Cramer 1816 - 1897
4 Lavinia Cramer 1833 - 1895
+Chalkley S. Cramer 1833 - 1855
4 William G. Cramer 1837 - 1912
+Mary Frances Maxwell 1847 - 1907
5 Mary E. Cramer 1868 - 1899
+George F. Cramer 1854 - 1915
6 Dora Cramer 1891 - 1961
+Grover Maxwell 1884 - 1939
7 Carlton Maxwell 1908 - 1967
7 Baby Estelle Maxwell May -
6 Norris C. Cramer 1886 - 1936
+Elsie Mick 1888 - 1963
6 Mary Edna Cramer 1888 - 1928
+Thomas S. Watson 1882 - 1964
7 Hilma Watson 1910 -
+Lindley Llewellyn Newcomer 1906 - 1992
8 John Newcomer
+Barbara Lee Boffemmyer
9 John Whitney Newcomer 1959 -
+Joan Lida Luby
10 Leah Eliza Newcomer
10 Adam Samuel Newcomer
9 Thomas England Newcomer 1966 -
8 Ronald Newcomer 1944 - 1963
7 Dora Watson 1915 - 1965
+Robert O. Sutton 1906 - 1987
8 Twin Baby Sutton 1930 - 1930
8 Twin Baby Sutton 1930 - 1930
8 Robert Thomas Sutton 1932 -
+Joyce F.. Mancuso 1934 -
9 Dolores Lea Sutton 1958 -
9 Susan Joyce Sutton 1964 -
+Christopher Keating
10 Christopher Keating Jr.
10 Benjamin Keating
9 Bobbi Lynn Sutton 1968 -
+Karl Frank Chase
10 Shawn Joseph Chase 1995 -
10 Samantha Joyce Chase 1997 -
*Partner of Bobbi Lynn Sutton:
+Mr. McHenry
10 Dani-Lynn McHenry 2006 -
8 Edna May Sutton 1937 -
+George Borton 1940 - 2000
8 Marjorie Louise Sutton 1940 -
+Lawrence Rose
9 Lawrence Rose
7 Marjorie Watson 1921 -
+Frank Cuifolo
5 Estella Cramer 1870 - 1942
+Winfield Peterson 1864 - 1917
5 William F. Cramer 1875 - 1936
+Elizabeth J. Headley 1881 - 1968
4 Charles Henry "Spide" Cramer 1839 -
+Sarah Jane Maxwell
4 Mary Elizabeth Cramer 1842 -
+William H. Mathis
4 Calab Smith "Swampy" Cramer 1844 -
+Mary Jane Robbins
4 Ellis S. Cramer 1845 -
4 Sarah Ann Cramer 1847 -
+John Hickman
4 Emma M. Cramer 1852 -
+Carlisle Gaskill
4 Chalkley Sears Cramer 1856 -
+Frances Caroline Johnson
4 Daniel D. Cramer 1858 -
+Anna M. Adams
3 Charles Burris Cramer 1828 - 1879

.... +Ellen S. Adams 1832 -
.... 3 William Sears Cramer
.... +Catherine Leek
.... 3 Aaron G. Cramer
.... +Ann Mott
.... 3 Thomas Allen Cramer
.... +Rebecca Ann Cramer
.... 3 Isaac F. Cramer
.... +Elizabeth Haines
.... 3 Lavinia Cramer
.... +John Carter
.... 3 Edith Eliza Cramer
.... +John W. Cramer
.... 3 Dorcas Tabitha Cramer 1818 - 1853
.... +John Smith Cramer
.... *2nd Husband of Dorcas Tabitha Cramer:
.... +John Smith Cramer 1818 - 1880
.... 4 Mary E. Cramer 1840 - 1841
.... 4 Margaret Ann Cramer
.... +Theodore C. Allen
.... 4 Sarah Jane Cramer 1843 - 1865
.... 4 William Asbury Cramer
.... +Phebe Ann Mingin
.... 4 Mary Eliza Cramer 1848 - 1848
.... 4 Uriah Burris Cramer 1850 - 1917
.... +Electa Throckmorton 1845 - 1919
.... 5 Uriah Smith Cramer
.... +Helen Louise Driscoll
.... 5 Lettie E. Cramer
.... +Benjamin F. Driscoll
.... 5 Theodore E. Cramer
.... +Ella Camille Martin
.... 5 Renard Ethyl Cramer 1865 - 1927
.... +Mary Emma Prince 1871 - 1937
.... 6 Olive Cramer
.... +John Wiseman
.... 6 Ada May Cramer 1897 - 1933
.... +Merrill Cleveland Mathis 1884 - 1934
.... 7 Ida May Mathis
.... +Elsworth Butler
.... *2nd Husband of Ida May Mathis:
.... +Fillmore Shinn
.... 8 Percy Shinn
.... +Barbara Stevenson
.... 9 Robert Shinn
.... 9 Jeanne Shinn
.... 9 Kathryn Shinn
.... 8 Grace Shinn
.... 7 Mary Mathis 1918 -
.... +George Filling, Jr.
.... 7 Irene Mathis 1921 -
.... 7 Sarah Mathis 1925 -
.... 7 Mildred Mathis 1928 -
.... 7 Merriell Cleveland Mathis, Jr. 1931 -
.... 6 Jefferson Cramer
.... +Mary Ann Gallagher
.... 5 Sarah Eliza Cramer
.... +Ephraim Ford
.... 5 Rhoda Amelia Cramer
.... +Nathaniel C. Jones
.... 5 Sidney Uriah Cramer 1880 - 1880
.... 5 Eva L. Cramer
.... +Samuel E. Cramer
.... 4 Edith Eliza Cramer
.... +Wilson Bodine Cramer
.... 3 Samuel B. Cramer
.... +Ruth Elmy Lamson
.... 3 Mary Ann Cramer
.... +William G. Adams
.... 3 Uriah Cramer
.... +Sarah S. Haines
.... 2 George A. Cramer
.... +Lucy Cale
.... 2 Bethiah Cramer
.... +Archibald Sooy
.... 2 Uriah Cramer
.... +Maria Franklin

.... 2 Mary Cramer
.... +Isaiah Robbins
.... 2 Isaac Cramer 1796 - 1831
.... 2 Lavinia Cramer
.... +William French
.... 2 Hope Cramer 1801 - 1859
.... 2 Lucy Ann Cramer
.... +Edward Johnson

Descendants of William Cramer

Generation No. 1

1. WILLIAM[1] CRAMER died Abt. 1689. He married ELIZABETH CARWITHY Bef. 1665, daughter of DAVID CARWITHY and GRACE.

Notes for WILLIAM CRAMER:
Descendants of William Cranmer/Cramer of Elizabethtown, NJ as researched and recorded by Jean Shropshire Harris and Murray Thomas Harris. Published by the Groucester County Historical Society, Woodbury, NJ. Reference #0000
William Cranmer, the progenitor of the Cranmer/Cramer families of the Jersey shore, first appears as one of the early settlers of Southhold, long Island, NY. Before 1665 he married Elizabeth Carwithy, daughter of David and Grace Carwithy of Southold. David Carwithy's will written 30 Agugust 1665 mentions his daughter Elizabeth Cramer. William and his family must have already moved to Elizabethtown, NJ because William Cramer is recorded as having taken an oath of allegiance and fidelity to the King of England at Elizabeth on 19 February 1665., and was probably one of the original settlers. He gave his occupation as carpenter, and paid quitrents on 209 acres of land at Elizabethtown in 1670, the same year he was appointed town constable there. In 1677 William sold several parcels of upland, together with his dwelling house and house lot to John Tow and traveled to Lewes,Delaware with Luke Watson, another Elizabethtown's founders. He died before 4 December 1689, when the administration of his estate was granted to his son Thomas Cramer of Elizabethtown. There are accounts of William Cramers relation to the famous Archbishop of Canterbury who was burned at the stake in England, but to date no evidence has come to light which would prove or disprove this connection.

Children of WILLIAM CRAMER and ELIZABETH CARWITHY are:

i. ELIZABETH[2] CRAMER, m. GEORGE PACK.

Notes for ELIZABETH CRAMER:
Reference #5000

ii. THOMAS CRAMER, b. Abt. 1662; m. DEBORAH.

Notes for THOMAS CRAMER:
Reference #1000

2. iii. WILLIAM CRAMER, b. Abt. 1664.
3. iv. JOHN CRAMER, b. Abt. 1666.

Generation No. 2

2. WILLIAM[2] CRAMER *(WILLIAM[1])* was born Abt. 1664. He married RACHEL Abt. 1688.

Notes for WILLIAM CRAMER:
Reference #2000

Children of WILLIAM CRAMER and RACHEL are:

4. i. WILLIAM[3] CRAMER, b. June 12, 1691.
ii. ELIZABETH CRAMER, m. JOHN CORBET, JR..
iii. JOHN CRAMER.
iv. THOMAS CRAMER, m. MARY RIDGWAY.
v. SARAH CRAMER, m. TIMOTHY RIDGWAY.
vi. ANDREW CRAMER, m. SARAH.
vii. LEVI CRAMER, m. ESTER HORNER/HORNE.
5. viii. JOHN CRAMER, b. Abt. 1696.
ix. ELIZABETH CRAMER, m. JOHN CORET, JR..
x. WILLIAM CRAMER, m. RUTH SOUTHWICK.
xi. THOMAS CRAMER, m. MARY RIDGWAY.

3. JOHN[2] CRAMER *(WILLIAM[1])* was born Abt. 1666. He married (1) SARAH OSBORNE, daughter of STEPHEN OSBORNE and SARAH STANBOROUGH. She was born Abt. 1663. He married (2) SARAH OSBORNE.

Notes for JOHN CRAMER:
Reference #4000
John was a member of the Society of Friends and is listed in the Rahway and Plainfield Monthly Meeting Minutes, and in the minutes of the Woodbridge Monthly Meeting. John Cramer of Elizabethtown bought land at Barnagate on 9 May 1702. John and Sarah later owned land and settled in Whippany. The text "Along the Whippanong", by Myrose & Kitchell describes John's property with a map and descriptiuon. His will was probated in Essex County on 22 June 1716. The will left his sons Thomas and John each 4 pounds and his lawful wife the rest of his estate to bring up his children.

Children of JOHN CRAMER and SARAH OSBORNE are:

i. JOHN[3] CRAMER, m. HANNAH POTTER.
ii. THOMAS CRAMER, m. ABIGAIL WILLETS.
iii. JEREMIAH CRAMER, m. ABIAH TUTTLE.
6. iv. STEPHEN CRAMER, b. Abt. 1700; d. April 1777.

Generation No. 3

4. WILLIAM[3] CRAMER *(WILLIAM[2], WILLIAM[1])* was born June 12, 1691. He married RUTH SOUTHWICK September 15, 1716.

Notes for WILLIAM CRAMER:
Reference #2001

Children of WILLIAM CRAMER and RUTH SOUTHWICK are:

7. i. WILLIAM[4] CRAMER, b. Bet. 1717 - 1725, Northamton; d. Bef. 1799.
ii. JAMES CRAMER.
iii. JOSIAH CRAMER, m. SARAH WILKINSON.
iv. RUTH CRAMER.
v. ELIZABETH CRAMER.
vi. ABRAHAM CRAMER, m. ABIGAIL WILLITS BIRDSALL.

5. JOHN[3] CRAMER *(WILLIAM[2], WILLIAM[1])* was born Abt. 1696. He married (1) MARY ANDREWS April 08, 1721. He married (2) REBECCA STOUT 1726.

Children of JOHN CRAMER and REBECCA STOUT are:

8. i. JOHN[4] CRAMER, JR., b. Abt. 1730; d. 1790.
ii. JACOB CRAMER, m. PHOEBE VALENTINE.
iii. SEYMOUR/SEMON CRAMER, m. MARY SMITH.
iv. RACHEL CRAMER, m. EDWARD ALLEN, SR..
v. ELIZABETH CRAMER, m. NEHEMIAH MATHIS.
vi. REBECCA CRAMER, m. WILLIAM CARTER.
vii. HANNAH CRAMER, m. JOSEPH BURNS.

6. STEPHEN[3] CRAMER *(JOHN[2], WILLIAM[1])* was born Abt. 1700, and died April 1777. He married SARAH ANDREWS, daughter of EDWARD ANDREWS and SARAH ONG. She was born January 08, 1701/02, and died Abt. 1748.

Notes for STEPHEN CRAMER:
Reference #4004

Child of STEPHEN CRAMER and SARAH ANDREWS is:

9. i. CALEB[4] CRAMER, b. February 16, 1732/33; d. March 12, 1818.

Generation No. 4

7. WILLIAM^4 CRAMER *(WILLIAM^3, WILLIAM^2, WILLIAM^1)* was born Bet. 1717 - 1725 in Northamton, and died Bef. 1799. He married MIRIAM STOCKHAM November 21, 1746.

Notes for WILLIAM CRAMER:
Reference #2006

Children of WILLIAM CRAMER and MIRIAM STOCKHAM are:

10. i. WILLIAM^5 CRAMER, b. Abt. 1756.
 ii. ANDREW CRAMER.
 iii. SAMUEL CRAMER, m. MARY GALE.
 iv. JOSIAH CRAMER.
 v. AMARIAH CRAMER, m. HANNAH ROGERS.
 vi. ATHALANIA CRAMER, m. AMOS SOUTHARD.
 vii. MIRIAM CRAMER.
 viii. RUTH CRAMER, m. JAMES PHARO.

8. JOHN^4 CRAMER, JR. *(JOHN^3, WILLIAM^2, WILLIAM^1)* was born Abt. 1730, and died 1790. He married MARGARET SMITH July 23, 1757. She was born 1735, and died 1811.

Notes for JOHN CRAMER, JR.:
John served in the Revolution in the Contineltal line and, according to the DAR Patriot index, died in 1790

Children of JOHN CRAMER and MARGARET SMITH are:

11. i. JOHN^5 CRAMER, b. July 28, 1758; d. March 01, 1815.
 ii. AMY CRAMER.
 iii. MARY CRAMER, m. SAMUEL GOLDSMITH.
 iv. JACOB CRAMER, m. ELIZABETH ?.
 v. SYLVANUS CRAMER, m. SARAH JANE GIFFORD.
 vi. RUTH CRAMER, d. 1793.

Notes for RUTH CRAMER:
In the Little Egg Harbor monthly meeting minutes she applied for assistance on the 14th of the second month of 1788, and reported to have been aided on the 13th of the third month of 1788, and this relief continued through 1793.

9. CALEB^4 CRAMER *(STEPHEN^3, JOHN^2, WILLIAM^1)* was born February 16, 1732/33, and died March 12, 1818. He married SARA Abt. 1755.

Notes for CALEB CRAMER:
Reference #4011

Child of CALEB CRAMER and SARA is:

12. i. ISAAC^5 CRAMER, b. September 01, 1756; d. November 17, 1839.

Generation No. 5

10. WILLIAM^5 CRAMER *(WILLIAM^4, WILLIAM^3, WILLIAM^2, WILLIAM^1)* was born Abt. 1756. He married NANCY SOMERS.

Notes for WILLIAM CRAMER:
Reference #2025

Children of WILLIAM CRAMER and NANCY SOMERS are:

13. i. WILLIAM B.^{6} CRAMER, b. April 16, 1792; d. West Creek, NJ.
 ii. BORDEN CRAMER, m. MARTHA MORRIS.
 iii. EMILY CRAMER, m. JOSEPH RIDGWAY ESQ..
 iv. CLARINDA CRAMER, m. JOHN SOMERS.

v. MARY CRAMER, m. JONOTHAN CAWLEY.

11. JOHN[5] CRAMER *(JOHN[4], JOHN[3], WILLIAM[2], WILLIAM[1])* was born July 28, 1758, and died March 01, 1815. He married HANNAH JOHNSON. She was born September 16, 1765, and died October 16, 1827.

More About JOHN CRAMER:
Burial: Lost at Sea

More About HANNAH JOHNSON:
Burial: Lower Bank NJ

Children of JOHN CRAMER and HANNAH JOHNSON are:
14. i. DANIEL S.[6] CRAMER, b. December 13, 1785; d. July 14, 1853.
ii. ELIZABETH CRAMER, m. THOMAS SMITH.
iii. JOHN CRAMER, m. NANCY JENKINS.
iv. ISAIAH CRAMER, m. RACHEL RANDOLPH.
v. JONATHAN CRAMER, m. ANN BREWER.
vi. MARGARET CRAMER, m. JOHN RANDOLPH.
vii. ASA SMITH CRAMER, m. CATHERINE HALL.
viii. HANNAH CRAMER, m. ISAIAH WEEKS.
ix. MARY CRAMER, m. SAMUEL WEEKS.
x. JANE CRAMER, m. JOHN HALL.
xi. WILLIAM CRAMER, m. ELIZABETH JORDAN.
xii. ELIZABETH S. CRAMER, m. BENJAMIN B. DOUGHTY.

12. ISAAC[5] CRAMER *(CALEB[4], STEPHEN[3], JOHN[2], WILLIAM[1])*[1] was born September 01, 1756, and died November 17, 1839. He married DORCAS ADAMS[1] Abt. 1783. She was born November 23, 1766, and died August 06, 1848.

Notes for ISAAC CRAMER:
Reference #4030
Isaac served in the Revolutionary War. Served in NJ War time Residence Burlington County Militia Certificate # 192 some of No Pounds, Sixteen shilling and eight peace, signed by James Fenimore 5/1/1784

More About ISAAC CRAMER:
Burial: Isaac Cemetery in New Gretna

More About DORCAS ADAMS:
Burial: Isaac Cemetery in New Gretna

Children of ISAAC CRAMER and DORCAS ADAMS are:
15. i. CHARLES[6] CRAMER, b. 1789, Bass River, NJ; d. July 29, 1872, Bridgeport, NJ.
ii. GEORGE A. CRAMER, m. LUCY CALE.
iii. BETHIAH CRAMER, m. ARCHIBALD SOOY.
iv. URIAH CRAMER, m. MARIA FRANKLIN.
v. MARY CRAMER, m. ISAIAH ROBBINS.
vi. ISAAC CRAMER, b. February 05, 1796; d. December 23, 1831.
vii. LAVINIA CRAMER, m. WILLIAM FRENCH.
viii. HOPE CRAMER, b. December 12, 1801; d. February 26, 1859.
ix. LUCY ANN CRAMER, m. EDWARD JOHNSON.

Generation No. 6

13. WILLIAM B.[6] CRAMER *(WILLIAM[5], WILLIAM[4], WILLIAM[3], WILLIAM[2], WILLIAM[1])* was born April 16, 1792, and died in West Creek, NJ. He married MARY ADAMS March 15, 1818. She died January 07, 1825 in West Creek, NJ.

Notes for WILLIAM B. CRAMER:
Reference #2077

DORCAS

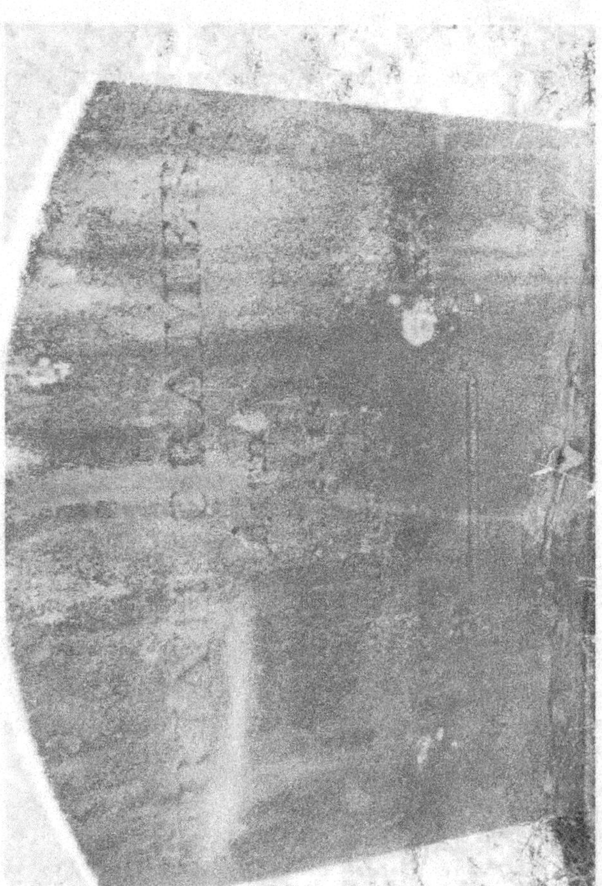

CUBA
ARMY
UNITED
NAVY
U.S.A.

BROTHER
JOHN H
CRAMER
BORN MAY 20

1852
JAN 24 1926

William B. Died at West Creek at age 73 on 7/23/1862. He was a Blacksmith. The information on the children of William B. Was obtained from his family Bible in the possession of his 3rd Great-grand daughter Dana (Dombroski) Maher.

Children of WILLIAM CRAMER and MARY ADAMS are:

16. i. CHARLES A.^{7} CRAMER, b. June 15, 1821; d. September 01, 1892.
ii. ISAACC CRAMER, m. ABIGAIL COBB.
iii. WILLIAM A. CRAMER, m. SARAH LOUISA CAVILEER.

14. DANIEL S.^{6} CRAMER *(JOHN^{5}, JOHN^{4}, JOHN^{3}, WILLIAM^{2}, WILLIAM^{1})* was born December 13, 1785, and died July 14, 1853. He married CHARLOTTE LOVELAND March 25, 1810, daughter of CHARLELS LOVELAND and SARAH GRANT. She was born April 03, 1794, and died February 11, 1869.

More About DANIEL S. CRAMER:
Burial: Lower Bank NJ

More About CHARLOTTE LOVELAND:
Burial: Lower Bank NJ

Children of DANIEL CRAMER and CHARLOTTE LOVELAND are:

17. i. JOHN SMITH^{7} CRAMER, b. December 15, 1818; d. September 24, 1880.
18. ii. SARAH ANN CRAMER, b. June 29, 1816; d. May 27, 1897.
iii. CHARLES FLETCHER CRAMER, m. ELIZA CALE.
iv. JOHN SMITH CRAMER, m. DORCAS TABITHA CRAMER; b. September 16, 1818; d. October 04, 1853.
v. JOSEPH CRAMER.
vi. MARY CRAMER.
vii. ESTHER ANN CRAMER, m. ABRAHAM CRAMER.
viii. HANNAH ANN CRAMER, m. CHARLES BREWER.
ix. ELIZABETH CRAMER.

15. CHARLES^{6} CRAMER *(ISAAC^{5}, CALEB^{4}, STEPHEN^{3}, JOHN^{2}, WILLIAM^{1})*[1] was born 1789 in Bass River, NJ[1], and died July 29, 1872 in Bridgeport, NJ[1]. He married MARY GASKILL[1] April 06, 1809. She was born January 01, 1791 in West Creek, NJ[1], and died March 16, 1873 in Bridgeport, NJ[1].

Notes for CHARLES CRAMER:
Reference #4072
At one time he and his wife lived next to the Isaac Cramer Cemetery on Rloute 542 in New Gretna, NJ.

More About CHARLES CRAMER:
Burial: Hillside Cemetary[1]

More About MARY GASKILL:
Burial: Hillside Cemetary[1]

Children of CHARLES CRAMER and MARY GASKILL are:

19. i. DARIUS^{7} CRAMER, b. December 08, 1808; d. September 13, 1858.
ii. CHARLES BURRIS CRAMER[1], b. March 14, 1828[1]; d. May 24, 1879[1]; m. ELLEN S. ADAMS[1]; b. April 19, 1832[1].
iii. WILLIAM SEARS CRAMER, m. CATHERINE LEEK.
iv. AARON G. CRAMER, m. ANN MOTT.
v. THOMAS ALLEN CRAMER, m. REBECCA ANN CRAMER.
vi. ISAAC F. CRAMER, m. ELIZABETH HAINES.
vii. LAVINIA CRAMER, m. JOHN CARTER.
viii. EDITH ELIZA CRAMER, m. JOHN W. CRAMER.
20. ix. DORCAS TABITHA CRAMER, b. September 16, 1818; d. October 04, 1853.
x. SAMUEL B. CRAMER, m. RUTH ELMY LAMSON.
xi. MARY ANN CRAMER, m. WILLIAM G. ADAMS.
xii. URIAH CRAMER, m. SARAH S. HAINES.

Generation No. 7

16. CHARLES A.[7] CRAMER *(WILLIAM B.[6], WILLIAM[5], WILLIAM[4], WILLIAM[3], WILLIAM[2], WILLIAM[1])* was born June 15, 1821, and died September 01, 1892. He married ELIZABETH ADAMS, daughter of WILLIAM ADAMS and ELIZABETH TAYLOR. She was born September 03, 1825, and died October 16, 1914.

Notes for CHARLES A. CRAMER:
Reference #2217

More About CHARLES A. CRAMER:
Burial: Miller Cemetery, New Gretna, NJ

More About ELIZABETH ADAMS:
Burial: Miller Cemetery, New Gretna, NJ

Children of CHARLES CRAMER and ELIZABETH ADAMS are:

21. i. GEORGE F.[8] CRAMER, b. August 11, 1854; d. October 14, 1915.

ii. ELWOOD CRAMER, m. SARAH STACKHOUSE.

Notes for ELWOOD CRAMER:
Reference #2541

iii. WILLIAM H. CRAMER, b. 1846; d. April 1870.

iv. ALBERT ALLEN CRAMER.

Notes for ALBERT ALLEN CRAMER:
Reference #2542

v. SARAH M. CRAMER, b. April 06, 1857; d. July 28, 1860.

vi. MARY O. CRAMER, b. October 21, 1859.

vii. CHARLES A. CRAMER, b. September 11, 1863.

22. viii. HOWARD H. CRAMER, b. September 1864; d. 1941.

17. JOHN SMITH[7] CRAMER *(DANIEL S.[6], JOHN[5], JOHN[4], JOHN[3], WILLIAM[2], WILLIAM[1])* was born December 15, 1818, and died September 24, 1880. He married DORCAS TABITHA CRAMER June 14, 1840, daughter of CHARLES CRAMER and MARY GASKILL. She was born September 16, 1818, and died October 04, 1853.

Notes for JOHN SMITH CRAMER:
Reference #2383

Children of JOHN CRAMER and DORCAS CRAMER are:

i. MARY E.[8] CRAMER, b. November 13, 1840; d. January 20, 1841.

ii. MARGARET ANN CRAMER, m. THEODORE C. ALLEN.

iii. SARAH JANE CRAMER, b. November 10, 1843; d. March 13, 1865.

iv. WILLIAM ASBURY CRAMER, m. PHEBE ANN MINGIN.

v. MARY ELIZA CRAMER, b. July 07, 1848; d. October 30, 1848.

23. vi. URIAH BURRIS CRAMER, b. March 27, 1850, Bass River; d. December 08, 1917, Port Republic, NJ.

vii. EDITH ELIZA CRAMER, m. WILSON BODINE CRAMER.

18. SARAH ANN[7] CRAMER *(DANIEL S.[6], JOHN[5], JOHN[4], JOHN[3], WILLIAM[2], WILLIAM[1])*[1] was born June 29, 1816[1], and died May 27, 1897[1]. She married DARIUS CRAMER[1] January 03, 1833[1], son of CHARLES CRAMER and MARY GASKILL. He was born December 08, 1808[1], and died September 13, 1858[1].

More About SARAH ANN CRAMER:
Burial: Hillside Cemetary[1]

Notes for DARIUS CRAMER:
Reference #4142

More About DARIUS CRAMER:

Burial: Hillside Cemetary[1]

Children of SARAH CRAMER and DARIUS CRAMER are:

- i. LAVINIA[8] CRAMER[1], b. November 27, 1833[1]; d. 1895[1]; m. CHALKLEY S. CRAMER[1], May 16, 1854[1]; b. 1833[1]; d. December 13, 1855[1].
- 24. ii. WILLIAM G. CRAMER, b. August 10, 1837; d. November 29, 1912.
- iii. CHARLES HENRY "SPIDE" CRAMER[1], b. October 30, 1839[1]; m. SARAH JANE MAXWELL.
- iv. MARY ELIZABETH CRAMER[1], b. 1842[1]; m. WILLIAM H. MATHIS.
- v. CALAB SMITH "SWAMPY" CRAMER[1], b. November 29, 1844[1]; m. MARY JANE ROBBINS.
- vi. ELLIS S. CRAMER[1], b. 1845[1].
- vii. SARAH ANN CRAMER[1], b. May 16, 1847[1]; m. JOHN HICKMAN.
- viii. EMMA M. CRAMER[1], b. September 17, 1852[1]; m. CARLISLE GASKILL.
- ix. CHALKLEY SEARS CRAMER[1], b. May 02, 1856[1]; m. FRANCES CAROLINE JOHNSON.
- x. DANIEL D. CRAMER[1], b. March 1858[1]; m. ANNA M. ADAMS.

19. DARIUS[7] CRAMER *(CHARLES[6], ISAAC[5], CALEB[4], STEPHEN[3], JOHN[2], WILLIAM[1])*[1] was born December 08, 1808[1], and died September 13, 1858[1]. He married SARAH ANN CRAMER[1] January 03, 1833[1], daughter of DANIEL CRAMER and CHARLOTTE LOVELAND. She was born June 29, 1816[1], and died May 27, 1897[1].

Notes for DARIUS CRAMER:
Reference #4142

More About DARIUS CRAMER:
Burial: Hillside Cemetary[1]

More About SARAH ANN CRAMER:
Burial: Hillside Cemetary[1]

Children are listed above under (18) Sarah Ann Cramer.

20. DORCAS TABITHA[7] CRAMER *(CHARLES[6], ISAAC[5], CALEB[4], STEPHEN[3], JOHN[2], WILLIAM[1])* was born September 16, 1818, and died October 04, 1853. She married (1) JOHN SMITH CRAMER, son of DANIEL CRAMER and CHARLOTTE LOVELAND. She married (2) JOHN SMITH CRAMER June 14, 1840, son of DANIEL CRAMER and CHARLOTTE LOVELAND. He was born December 15, 1818, and died September 24, 1880.

Notes for JOHN SMITH CRAMER:
Reference #2383

Children are listed above under (17) John Smith Cramer.

Generation No. 8

21. GEORGE F.[8] CRAMER *(CHARLES A.[7], WILLIAM B.[6], WILLIAM[5], WILLIAM[4], WILLIAM[3], WILLIAM[2], WILLIAM[1])*[1] was born August 11, 1854[1], and died October 14, 1915[1]. He married MARY E. CRAMER[1] 1886[1], daughter of WILLIAM CRAMER and MARY MAXWELL. She was born June 27, 1868[1], and died June 23, 1899[1].

Notes for GEORGE F. CRAMER:
Reference #2543

More About GEORGE F. CRAMER:
Burial: Hillside Cemetary[1]

More About MARY E. CRAMER:
Burial: Hillside Cemetary[1]

Children of GEORGE CRAMER and MARY CRAMER are:

- 25. i. DORA[9] CRAMER, b. September 1891; d. 1961.
- ii. NORRIS C. CRAMER[1], b. December 20, 1886[1]; d. April 17, 1936[1]; m. ELSIE MICK[1], May 09, 1910[1]; b. September 08, 1888[1]; d. September 13, 1963[1].

More About NORRIS C. CRAMER:
Burial: Hillside Cemetary[1]

More About ELSIE MICK:
Burial: Hillside Cemetary[1]

26. iii. MARY EDNA CRAMER, b. May 06, 1888; d. July 22, 1928.

22. HOWARD H.[8] CRAMER *(CHARLES A.[7], WILLIAM B.[6], WILLIAM[5], WILLIAM[4], WILLIAM[3], WILLIAM[2], WILLIAM[1])* was born September 1864, and died 1941. He married CLARA BOZARTH October 1895 in Washington twp, daughter of CHARLES BOZARTH and JULIA WEEKS. She was born November 30, 1868, and died July 31, 1959 in Elwood, NJ.

More About HOWARD H. CRAMER:
Burial: Miller Cemetery, New Gretna, NJ

More About CLARA BOZARTH:
Burial: Miller Cemetery, New Gretna, NJ

Children of HOWARD CRAMER and CLARA BOZARTH are:

27. i. EARLE C.[9] CRAMER, b. December 25, 1895; d. May 17, 1975.
ii. CASPER CRAMER, b. March 1901; d. May 1901, Leektown, NJ.
iii. JULIA E. CRAMER, m. JOHN A. HERMAN.

23. URIAH BURRIS[8] CRAMER *(JOHN SMITH[7], DANIEL S.[6], JOHN[5], JOHN[4], JOHN[3], WILLIAM[2], WILLIAM[1])* was born March 27, 1850 in Bass River, and died December 08, 1917 in Port Republic, NJ. He married ELECTA THROCKMORTON August 28, 1870. She was born July 23, 1845 in Tuckerton, NJ, and died March 28, 1919 in Bass River.

More About ELECTA THROCKMORTON:
Burial: Hillside Cemetery

Children of URIAH CRAMER and ELECTA THROCKMORTON are:

i. URIAH SMITH[9] CRAMER, m. HELEN LOUISE DRISCOLL.
ii. LETTIE E. CRAMER, m. BENJAMIN F. DRISCOLL.
iii. THEODORE E. CRAMER, m. ELLA CAMILLE MARTIN.
28. iv. RENARD ETHYL CRAMER, b. October 29, 1865; d. May 28, 1927.
v. SARAH ELIZA CRAMER, m. EPHRAIM FORD.
vi. RHODA AMELIA CRAMER, m. NATHANIEL C. JONES.
vii. SIDNEY URIAH CRAMER, b. March 08, 1880; d. June 1880.
viii. EVA L. CRAMER, m. SAMUEL E. CRAMER.

24. WILLIAM G.[8] CRAMER *(DARIUS[7], CHARLES[6], ISAAC[5], CALEB[4], STEPHEN[3], JOHN[2], WILLIAM[1])*[1] was born August 10, 1837[1], and died November 29, 1912[1]. He married MARY FRANCES MAXWELL[1]. She was born April 03, 1847[1], and died August 28, 1907[1].

More About WILLIAM G. CRAMER:
Burial: Hillside Cemetary[1]

More About MARY FRANCES MAXWELL:
Burial: Hillside Cemetary[1]

Children of WILLIAM CRAMER and MARY MAXWELL are:

29. i. MARY E.[9] CRAMER, b. June 27, 1868; d. June 23, 1899.
ii. ESTELLA CRAMER[1], b. August 10, 1870[1]; d. June 07, 1942[1]; m. WINFIELD PETERSON[1], March 30, 1889[1]; b. March 30, 1864[1]; d. December 29, 1917[1].
iii. WILLIAM F. CRAMER[1], b. December 06, 1875[1]; d. June 27, 1936[1]; m. ELIZABETH J. HEADLEY[1]; b. October 1881[1]; d. October 28, 1968[1].

Generation No. 9

25. DORA[9] CRAMER *(GEORGE F.[8], CHARLES A.[7], WILLIAM B.[6], WILLIAM[5], WILLIAM[4], WILLIAM[3], WILLIAM[2], WILLIAM[1])*[1] was born September 1891, and died 1961. She married GROVER MAXWELL. He was born October 06, 1884, and died June 04, 1939.

More About DORA CRAMER:
Burial: Hillside Cemetary New Gretna, NJ

More About GROVER MAXWELL:
Burial: Hillside Cemetary, New Gretna, NJ

Children of DORA CRAMER and GROVER MAXWELL are:

i. CARLTON[10] MAXWELL, b. 1908; d. 1967.
ii. BABY ESTELLE MAXWELL, b. May.

26. MARY EDNA[9] CRAMER *(GEORGE F.[8], CHARLES A.[7], WILLIAM B.[6], WILLIAM[5], WILLIAM[4], WILLIAM[3], WILLIAM[2], WILLIAM[1])*[1] was born May 06, 1888[1], and died July 22, 1928[1]. She married THOMAS S. WATSON[1], son of JOHN WATSON and ELLA PIERCE. He was born August 06, 1882 in Gloucester County, NJ[1], and died May 03, 1965 [1].

Notes for MARY EDNA CRAMER:
Reference #2925
This should be a correction to the above reference.
Mary Edna Cramer had a daughter before she married Thomas Watson. Her daughter was named Maud Cramer born May 18, 1906, died June 6, 1923.
Maud Cramer is buried along side her mother Mary Edna Watson, at Hillside Cemetery, New Gretna, NJ.

More About MARY EDNA CRAMER:
Burial: Hillside Cemetary[1]

Notes for THOMAS S. WATSON:
Thomas Watson Listed the names of Sara and John in the family bible. I believe that Sara may have died as a child as nothing else can be found on her. We have been searching for a Walker Watson and found out that John's middle name is Walker.
Daniel E. Iszard resident of Mays Landing, Atlantic County, NJ was made legal gaurdian of Thomas, Rebecca and Alonzo On October 25, 1892 by Surrogate John S. Risley. (Ella remarried in 1891 and may have had to give up her children because of her new husband)??
Thomas died at the age of 81 years 8 months and 27 days old.

More About THOMAS S. WATSON:
Burial: Hillside Cemetary[1]

Children of MARY CRAMER and THOMAS WATSON are:

30. i. HILMA[10] WATSON, b. May 02, 1910.
31. ii. DORA WATSON, b. February 09, 1915; d. January 15, 1965.
iii. MARJORIE WATSON[1], b. 1921[1]; m. FRANK CUIFOLO[1].

27. EARLE C.[9] CRAMER *(HOWARD H.[8], CHARLES A.[7], WILLIAM B.[6], WILLIAM[5], WILLIAM[4], WILLIAM[3], WILLIAM[2], WILLIAM[1])* was born December 25, 1895, and died May 17, 1975. He married ELIZABETH FRENCH October 20, 1923 in Bass River, NJ, daughter of SUWARROW FRENCH and IDA ALLEN. She was born July 21, 1904, and died February 17, 1977.

More About EARLE C. CRAMER:
Burial: Miller Cemetery, New Gretna, NJ

More About ELIZABETH FRENCH:
Burial: Miller Cemetery, New Gretna, NJ

Child of EARLE CRAMER and ELIZABETH FRENCH is:

32. i. NORMAN EARLE[10] CRAMER, b. May 02, 1930, New Gretna.

28. RENARD ETHYL[9] CRAMER *(URIAH BURRIS[8], JOHN SMITH[7], DANIEL S.[6], JOHN[5], JOHN[4], JOHN[3], WILLIAM[2], WILLIAM[1])* was born October 29, 1865, and died May 28, 1927. He married MARY EMMA PRINCE. She was born October 12, 1871, and died May 17, 1937 in Tuckerton, NJ.

More About MARY EMMA PRINCE:
Burial: Miller Cemetery, New Gretna, NJ

Children of RENARD CRAMER and MARY PRINCE are:

i. OLIVE[10] CRAMER, m. JOHN WISEMAN.

33. ii. ADA MAY CRAMER, b. April 05, 1897; d. February 27, 1933.

iii. JEFFERSON CRAMER, m. MARY ANN GALLAGHER.

29. MARY E.[9] CRAMER *(WILLIAM G.[8], DARIUS[7], CHARLES[6], ISAAC[5], CALEB[4], STEPHEN[3], JOHN[2], WILLIAM[1])*[1] was born June 27, 1868[1], and died June 23, 1899[1]. She married GEORGE F. CRAMER[1] 1886[1], son of CHARLES CRAMER and ELIZABETH ADAMS. He was born August 11, 1854[1], and died October 14, 1915[1].

More About MARY E. CRAMER:
Burial: Hillside Cemetary[1]

Notes for GEORGE F. CRAMER:
Reference #2543

More About GEORGE F. CRAMER:
Burial: Hillside Cemetary[1]

Children are listed above under (21) George F. Cramer.

Generation No. 10

30. HILMA[10] WATSON *(MARY EDNA[9] CRAMER, GEORGE F.[8], CHARLES A.[7], WILLIAM B.[6], WILLIAM[5], WILLIAM[4], WILLIAM[3], WILLIAM[2], WILLIAM[1])*[1] was born May 02, 1910[1]. She married LINDLEY LLEWELLYN NEWCOMER[1] September 1934 in New York City, NY, son of WILLIAM NEWCOMER and HELEN THOMAS. He was born March 08, 1906 in Connellsville, PA, and died December 1992 in Tampa, Fl.

Children of HILMA WATSON and LINDLEY NEWCOMER are:

34. i. JOHN[11] NEWCOMER.

ii. RONALD NEWCOMER[1], b. 1944, Westville, NJ; d. 1963, Wyoming.

Notes for RONALD NEWCOMER:
Died young in automobile accident.

31. DORA[10] WATSON *(MARY EDNA[9] CRAMER, GEORGE F.[8], CHARLES A.[7], WILLIAM B.[6], WILLIAM[5], WILLIAM[4], WILLIAM[3], WILLIAM[2], WILLIAM[1])*[1] was born February 09, 1915[1], and died January 15, 1965[1]. She married ROBERT O. SUTTON[1], son of WILLIAM SUTTON and EMMA ROGERS. He was born October 24, 1906[2,2,2,2,2,2,2,2,2,2,2,2,2,2,3,4], and died August 1987[5,5,5,5,5,5,5,5,5,5,5,5,5,5,6,7].

Notes for DORA WATSON:
Reference #3180
The twins are buried behind Maud Cramer, there are two little stones sticking out of the ground to mark their graves.

More About DORA WATSON:
Burial: Hillside cemetery, New Gretna[8]

Notes for ROBERT O. SUTTON:
[Genealogy.com, Family Archive #110, Vol. 2 L-Z, Ed. 9, Social Security Death Index: U.S., Date of Import: Dec 30, 2000, Internal Ref. #1.112.9.111416.32]

Individual: Sutton, Robert
Social Security #: 148-07-6985
Issued in: New Jersey

Birth date: Oct 24, 1906
Death date: Aug 1987

Residence code: New Jersey

ZIP Code of last known residence: 08224
Location associated with this ZIP Code:

New Gretna, New Jersey

Robert Sutton told his childred that the O. in his name stood for Osborn but we have not been able to verify this. His grandfather's middle initial also was an O. (for some reason either lost in the mail, etc. his birth certificate has never been registered. I am going to try and register him through the family bible and other papers we have).

More About ROBERT O. SUTTON:
Burial: Hillside cemetery, New Gretna[8]
Social Security Number: Social Security #: 148-07-6985[9,10]

Children of DORA WATSON and ROBERT SUTTON are:

i. TWIN BABY[11] SUTTON, b. Abt. 1930; d. Abt. 1930.

More About TWIN BABY SUTTON:
Burial: Abt. 1930, Hillside cemetery, New Gretna

ii. TWIN BABY SUTTON, b. Abt. 1930; d. Abt. 1930.

More About TWIN BABY SUTTON:
Burial: Abt. 1930, Hillside cemetery, New Gretna

35. iii. ROBERT THOMAS SUTTON, b. December 07, 1932, Atlantic City, NJ.
iv. EDNA MAY SUTTON[10], b. November 20, 1937, Mt. Holly; m. GEORGE BORTON, December 22, 1984, St Pauls Medthodist Church, New Gretna, NJ; b. October 03, 1940; d. January 08, 2000, New Gretna.
36. v. MARJORIE LOUISE SUTTON, b. Abt. 1940.

32. NORMAN EARLE[10] CRAMER *(EARLE C.[9], HOWARD H.[8], CHARLES A.[7], WILLIAM B.[6], WILLIAM[5], WILLIAM[4], WILLIAM[3], WILLIAM[2], WILLIAM[1])* was born May 02, 1930 in New Gretna. He married (1) DELILAH CROWLEY, daughter of HAROLD CROWLEY and ALELE FALKINBURG.

Children of NORMAN CRAMER and DELILAH CROWLEY are:

37. i. DOUGLAS[11] CRAMER.
ii. GREGORY CRAMER.
iii. JEFF CRAMER.
iv. JOAN CRAMER.
v. HAROLD CRAMER.
vi. CHARLES ROBERT CRAMER, b. June 28, 1967; d. August 24, 1982.

More About CHARLES ROBERT CRAMER:
Burial: Miller Cemetery, New Gretna, NJ

Child of NORMAN EARLE CRAMER is:

38. vii. DOUGLAS[11] CRAMER.

33. ADA MAY[10] CRAMER *(RENARD ETHYL[9], URIAH BURRIS[8], JOHN SMITH[7], DANIEL S.[6], JOHN[5], JOHN[4], JOHN[3], WILLIAM[2], WILLIAM[1])* was born April 05, 1897, and died February 27, 1933. She married MERRILL CLEVELAND MATHIS 1911. He was born October 10, 1884, and died June 21, 1934.

More About ADA MAY CRAMER:
Burial: Miller Cemetery, New Gretna, NJ

More About MERRILL CLEVELAND MATHIS:
Burial: Miller Cemetery, New Gretna, NJ

Children of ADA CRAMER and MERRILL MATHIS are:

39. i. IDA MAY[11] MATHIS.
ii. MARY MATHIS, b. June 01, 1918; m. GEORGE FILLING, JR..
iii. IRENE MATHIS, b. September 21, 1921.
iv. SARAH MATHIS, b. February 02, 1925.
v. MILDRED MATHIS, b. August 29, 1928.
vi. MERRIELL CLEVELAND MATHIS, JR., b. September 04, 1931, New Gretna.

Generation No. 11

34. JOHN[11] NEWCOMER *(HILMA[10] WATSON, MARY EDNA[9] CRAMER, GEORGE F.[8], CHARLES A.[7], WILLIAM B.[6], WILLIAM[5], WILLIAM[4], WILLIAM[3], WILLIAM[2], WILLIAM[1])[10]*. He married BARBARA LEE BOFFEMMYER May 04, 1957 in Media, PA.

Children of JOHN NEWCOMER and BARBARA BOFFEMMYER are:

40. i. JOHN WHITNEY[12] NEWCOMER, b. January 01, 1959.
ii. THOMAS ENGLAND NEWCOMER, b. February 23, 1966.

35. ROBERT THOMAS[11] SUTTON *(DORA[10] WATSON, MARY EDNA[9] CRAMER, GEORGE F.[8], CHARLES A.[7], WILLIAM B.[6], WILLIAM[5], WILLIAM[4], WILLIAM[3], WILLIAM[2], WILLIAM[1])[10]* was born December 07, 1932 in Atlantic City, NJ[10]. He married JOYCE F.. MANCUSO October 19, 1957 in Pomona, NJ[10], daughter of THOMAS MANCUSO and LOIS HOVATTER. She was born May 11, 1934 in Bristol, PA.

Notes for ROBERT THOMAS SUTTON:
Bob was born on a Wednesday. His wife Joyce was born on a Friday two years later, each year their bithdays fall on the same day of the week.

Notes for JOYCE F.. MANCUSO:
DAR member number 831198, installed Oct. 16, 2004

Children of ROBERT SUTTON and JOYCE MANCUSO are:

i. DOLORES LEA[12] SUTTON[10], b. September 24, 1958[10].
41. ii. SUSAN JOYCE SUTTON, b. December 01, 1964.
42. iii. BOBBI LYNN SUTTON, b. November 09, 1968.

36. MARJORIE LOUISE[11] SUTTON *(DORA[10] WATSON, MARY EDNA[9] CRAMER, GEORGE F.[8], CHARLES A.[7], WILLIAM B.[6], WILLIAM[5], WILLIAM[4], WILLIAM[3], WILLIAM[2], WILLIAM[1])[10]* was born Abt. 1940. She married LAWRENCE ROSE.

Notes for MARJORIE LOUISE SUTTON:

Kenneth's father is Austin Gibbons.

Child of MARJORIE SUTTON and LAWRENCE ROSE is:

i. LAWRENCE[12] ROSE.

37. DOUGLAS[11] CRAMER *(NORMAN EARLE[10], EARLE C.[9], HOWARD H.[8], CHARLES A.[7], WILLIAM B.[6], WILLIAM[5], WILLIAM[4], WILLIAM[3], WILLIAM[2], WILLIAM[1])* He married MARGARITE KEATING.

Children of DOUGLAS CRAMER and MARGARITE KEATING are:
- i. JAMES[12] CRAMER.
- ii. LAURA CRAMER.

38. DOUGLAS[11] CRAMER *(NORMAN EARLE[10], EARLE C.[9], HOWARD H.[8], CHARLES A.[7], WILLIAM B.[6], WILLIAM[5], WILLIAM[4], WILLIAM[3], WILLIAM[2], WILLIAM[1])* He married MARGARITE KEATING, daughter of WILTON KEATING and MARGUERITE TOTH.

Children of DOUGLAS CRAMER and MARGARITE KEATING are:
- i. JAMES[12] CRAMER.
- ii. LAURA CRAMER.

39. IDA MAY[11] MATHIS *(ADA MAY[10] CRAMER, RENARD ETHYL[9], URIAH BURRIS[8], JOHN SMITH[7], DANIEL S.[6], JOHN[5], JOHN[4], JOHN[3], WILLIAM[2], WILLIAM[1])* She married (1) ELSWORTH BUTLER. She married (2) FILLMORE SHINN.

Children of IDA MATHIS and FILLMORE SHINN are:
- 43. i. PERCY[12] SHINN.
- ii. GRACE SHINN.

Generation No. 12

40. JOHN WHITNEY[12] NEWCOMER *(JOHN[11], HILMA[10] WATSON, MARY EDNA[9] CRAMER, GEORGE F.[8], CHARLES A.[7], WILLIAM B.[6], WILLIAM[5], WILLIAM[4], WILLIAM[3], WILLIAM[2], WILLIAM[1])* was born January 01, 1959. He married JOAN LIDA LUBY June 21, 1981 in Birmingham, Michigan.

Children of JOHN NEWCOMER and JOAN LUBY are:
- i. LEAH ELIZA[13] NEWCOMER.
- ii. ADAM SAMUEL NEWCOMER.

41. SUSAN JOYCE[12] SUTTON *(ROBERT THOMAS[11], DORA[10] WATSON, MARY EDNA[9] CRAMER, GEORGE F.[8], CHARLES A.[7], WILLIAM B.[6], WILLIAM[5], WILLIAM[4], WILLIAM[3], WILLIAM[2], WILLIAM[1])[10]* was born December 01, 1964[10]. She married CHRISTOPHER KEATING[10], son of WILTON KEATING and MARGUERITE TOTH.

Notes for SUSAN JOYCE SUTTON:
DAR member number 831199

Children of SUSAN SUTTON and CHRISTOPHER KEATING are:
- i. CHRISTOPHER KEATING[13] JR.[10].
- ii. BENJAMIN KEATING[10].

42. BOBBI LYNN[12] SUTTON *(ROBERT THOMAS[11], DORA[10] WATSON, MARY EDNA[9] CRAMER, GEORGE F.[8], CHARLES A.[7], WILLIAM B.[6], WILLIAM[5], WILLIAM[4], WILLIAM[3], WILLIAM[2], WILLIAM[1])[10]* was born November 09, 1968[10]. She married (1) KARL FRANK CHASE[10], son of KARL SR. and CATHY. She met (2) MR. MCHENRY.

Notes for BOBBI LYNN SUTTON:
DAR member number 831200, installed Oct. 16, 2004

Children of BOBBI SUTTON and KARL CHASE are:
- i. SHAWN JOSEPH[13] CHASE[10], b. March 14, 1995[10].
- ii. SAMANTHA JOYCE CHASE[10], b. April 06, 1997[10].

Child of BOBBI SUTTON and MR. MCHENRY is:

iii. DANI-LYNN[13] MCHENRY, b. June 08, 2006.

43. PERCY[12] SHINN *(IDA MAY[11] MATHIS, ADA MAY[10] CRAMER, RENARD ETHYL[9], URIAH BURRIS[8], JOHN SMITH[7], DANIEL S.[6], JOHN[5], JOHN[4], JOHN[3], WILLIAM[2], WILLIAM[1])* He married BARBARA STEVENSON.

Children of PERCY SHINN and BARBARA STEVENSON are:

i. ROBERT[13] SHINN.
ii. JEANNE SHINN.
iii. KATHRYN SHINN.

Endnotes

1. Mancuso.FTW, Date of Import: Sep 6, 2000.
2. Broderbund Family Archive #110, Vol. 2, Ed. 7, Social Security Death Index: U.S., Date of Import: May 20, 2000, Internal Ref. #1.112.7.115546.117
3. Mancuso.FTW, Date of Import: Sep 6, 2000.
4. Genealogy.com, Family Archive #110, Social Security Death Index: U.S. Ed. 9, Social Security Death Index, Release date: April 10, 2000, Internal Ref. #1.112.9.111416.32.
5. Broderbund Family Archive #110, Vol. 2, Ed. 7, Social Security Death Index: U.S., Date of Import: May 20, 2000, Internal Ref. #1.112.7.115546.117
6. Mancuso.FTW, Date of Import: Sep 6, 2000.
7. Genealogy.com, Family Archive #110, Social Security Death Index: U.S. Ed. 9, Social Security Death Index, Release date: April 10, 2000, Internal Ref. #1.112.9.111416.32.
8. Mancuso.FTW, Date of Import: Sep 6, 2000.
9. Broderbund Family Archive #110, Vol. 2, Ed. 7, Social Security Death Index: U.S., Date of Import: May 20, 2000, Internal Ref. #1.112.7.115546.117
10. Mancuso.FTW, Date of Import: Sep 6, 2000.

Descendants of William Cramer

Generation No. 1

1. WILLIAM[2] CRAMER *(WILLIAM[1])* was born Abt. 1664. He married RACHEL Abt. 1688.

Notes for WILLIAM CRAMER:
Reference #2000

Children of WILLIAM CRAMER and RACHEL are:
2. i. WILLIAM[3] CRAMER, b. June 12, 1691.
ii. ELIZABETH CRAMER, m. JOHN CORBET, JR..
iii. JOHN CRAMER.
iv. THOMAS CRAMER, m. MARY RIDGWAY.
v. SARAH CRAMER, m. TIMOTHY RIDGWAY.
vi. ANDREW CRAMER, m. SARAH.
vii. LEVI CRAMER, m. ESTER HORNER/HORNE.
3. viii. JOHN CRAMER, b. Abt. 1696.
ix. ELIZABETH CRAMER, m. JOHN CORET, JR..
x. WILLIAM CRAMER, m. RUTH SOUTHWICK.
xi. THOMAS CRAMER, m. MARY RIDGWAY.

Generation No. 2

2. WILLIAM[3] CRAMER *(WILLIAM[2], WILLIAM[1])* was born June 12, 1691. He married RUTH SOUTHWICK September 15, 1716.

Notes for WILLIAM CRAMER:
Reference #2001

Children of WILLIAM CRAMER and RUTH SOUTHWICK are:
4. i. WILLIAM[4] CRAMER, b. Bet. 1717 - 1725, Northamton; d. Bef. 1799.
ii. JAMES CRAMER.
iii. JOSIAH CRAMER, m. SARAH WILKINSON.
iv. RUTH CRAMER.
v. ELIZABETH CRAMER.
vi. ABRAHAM CRAMER, m. ABIGAIL WILLITS BIRDSALL.

3. JOHN[3] CRAMER *(WILLIAM[2], WILLIAM[1])* was born Abt. 1696. He married (1) MARY ANDREWS April 08, 1721. He married (2) REBECCA STOUT 1726.

Children of JOHN CRAMER and REBECCA STOUT are:
5. i. JOHN[4] CRAMER, JR., b. Abt. 1730; d. 1790.
ii. JACOB CRAMER, m. PHOEBE VALENTINE.
iii. SEYMOUR/SEMON CRAMER, m. MARY SMITH.
iv. RACHEL CRAMER, m. EDWARD ALLEN, SR..
v. ELIZABETH CRAMER, m. NEHEMIAH MATHIS.
vi. REBECCA CRAMER, m. WILLIAM CARTER.
vii. HANNAH CRAMER, m. JOSEPH BURNS.

Generation No. 3

4. WILLIAM[4] CRAMER *(WILLIAM[3], WILLIAM[2], WILLIAM[1])* was born Bet. 1717 - 1725 in Northamton, and died Bef. 1799. He married MIRIAM STOCKHAM November 21, 1746.

Notes for WILLIAM CRAMER:
Reference #2006

Children of WILLIAM CRAMER and MIRIAM STOCKHAM are:

6. i. WILLIAM[5] CRAMER, b. Abt. 1756.
   ii. ANDREW CRAMER.
   iii. SAMUEL CRAMER, m. MARY GALE.
   iv. JOSIAH CRAMER.
   v. AMARIAH CRAMER, m. HANNAH ROGERS.
   vi. ATHALANIA CRAMER, m. AMOS SOUTHARD.
   vii. MIRIAM CRAMER.
   viii. RUTH CRAMER, m. JAMES PHARO.

5. JOHN[4] CRAMER, JR. *(JOHN[3], WILLIAM[2], WILLIAM[1])* was born Abt. 1730, and died 1790. He married MARGARET SMITH July 23, 1757. She was born 1735, and died 1811.

Notes for JOHN CRAMER, JR.:
John served in the Revolution in the Contineltal line and, according to the DAR Patriot index, died in 1790

Children of JOHN CRAMER and MARGARET SMITH are:

7. i. JOHN[5] CRAMER, b. July 28, 1758; d. March 01, 1815.
   ii. AMY CRAMER.
   iii. MARY CRAMER, m. SAMUEL GOLDSMITH.
   iv. JACOB CRAMER, m. ELIZABETH ?.
   v. SYLVANUS CRAMER, m. SARAH JANE GIFFORD.
   vi. RUTH CRAMER, d. 1793.

   Notes for RUTH CRAMER:
   In the Little Egg Harbor monthly meeting minutes she applied for assistance on the 14th of the second month of 1788, and reported to have been aided on the 13th of the third month of 1788, and this relief continued through 1793.

Generation No. 4

6. WILLIAM[5] CRAMER *(WILLIAM[4], WILLIAM[3], WILLIAM[2], WILLIAM[1])* was born Abt. 1756. He married NANCY SOMERS.

Notes for WILLIAM CRAMER:
Reference #2025

Children of WILLIAM CRAMER and NANCY SOMERS are:

8. i. WILLIAM B.[6] CRAMER, b. April 16, 1792; d. West Creek, NJ.
   ii. BORDEN CRAMER, m. MARTHA MORRIS.
   iii. EMILY CRAMER, m. JOSEPH RIDGWAY ESQ..
   iv. CLARINDA CRAMER, m. JOHN SOMERS.
   v. MARY CRAMER, m. JONOTHAN CAWLEY.

7. JOHN[5] CRAMER *(JOHN[4], JOHN[3], WILLIAM[2], WILLIAM[1])* was born July 28, 1758, and died March 01, 1815. He married HANNAH JOHNSON. She was born September 16, 1765, and died October 16, 1827.

More About JOHN CRAMER:
Burial: Lost at Sea

More About HANNAH JOHNSON:
Burial: Lower Bank NJ

Children of JOHN CRAMER and HANNAH JOHNSON are:

9. i. DANIEL S.[6] CRAMER, b. December 13, 1785; d. July 14, 1853.
ii. ELIZABETH CRAMER, m. THOMAS SMITH.
iii. JOHN CRAMER, m. NANCY JENKINS.
iv. ISAIAH CRAMER, m. RACHEL RANDOLPH.
v. JONATHAN CRAMER, m. ANN BREWER.
vi. MARGARET CRAMER, m. JOHN RANDOLPH.
vii. ASA SMITH CRAMER, m. CATHERINE HALL.
viii. HANNAH CRAMER, m. ISAIAH WEEKS.
ix. MARY CRAMER, m. SAMUEL WEEKS.
x. JANE CRAMER, m. JOHN HALL.
xi. WILLIAM CRAMER, m. ELIZABETH JORDAN.
xii. ELIZABETH S. CRAMER, m. BENJAMIN B. DOUGHTY.

Generation No. 5

8. WILLIAM B.[6] CRAMER *(WILLIAM[5], WILLIAM[4], WILLIAM[3], WILLIAM[2], WILLIAM[1])* was born April 16, 1792, and died in West Creek, NJ. He married MARY ADAMS March 15, 1818. She died January 07, 1825 in West Creek, NJ.

Notes for WILLIAM B. CRAMER:
Reference #2077
William B. Died at West Creek at age 73 on 7/23/1862. He was a Blacksmith. The information on the children of William B. Was obtained from his family Bible in the possession of his 3rd Great-grand daughter Dana (Dombroski) Maher.

Children of WILLIAM CRAMER and MARY ADAMS are:

10. i. CHARLES A.[7] CRAMER, b. June 15, 1821; d. September 01, 1892.
ii. ISAACC CRAMER, m. ABIGAIL COBB.
iii. WILLIAM A. CRAMER, m. SARAH LOUISA CAVILEER.

9. DANIEL S.[6] CRAMER *(JOHN[5], JOHN[4], JOHN[3], WILLIAM[2], WILLIAM[1])* was born December 13, 1785, and died July 14, 1853. He married CHARLOTTE LOVELAND March 25, 1810, daughter of CHARLELS LOVELAND and SARAH GRANT. She was born April 03, 1794, and died February 11, 1869.

More About DANIEL S. CRAMER:
Burial: Lower Bank NJ

More About CHARLOTTE LOVELAND:
Burial: Lower Bank NJ

Children of DANIEL CRAMER and CHARLOTTE LOVELAND are:

11. i. JOHN SMITH[7] CRAMER, b. December 15, 1818; d. September 24, 1880.
12. ii. SARAH ANN CRAMER, b. June 29, 1816; d. May 27, 1897.
iii. CHARLES FLETCHER CRAMER, m. ELIZA CALE.
iv. JOHN SMITH CRAMER, m. DORCAS TABITHA CRAMER; b. September 16, 1818; d. October 04, 1853.
v. JOSEPH CRAMER.
vi. MARY CRAMER.
vii. ESTHER ANN CRAMER, m. ABRAHAM CRAMER.
viii. HANNAH ANN CRAMER, m. CHARLES BREWER.
ix. ELIZABETH CRAMER.

Generation No. 6

10. CHARLES A.[7] CRAMER *(WILLIAM B.[6], WILLIAM[5], WILLIAM[4], WILLIAM[3], WILLIAM[2], WILLIAM[1])* was born June 15, 1821, and died September 01, 1892. He married ELIZABETH ADAMS, daughter of WILLIAM ADAMS and ELIZABETH TAYLOR. She was born September 03, 1825, and died October 16, 1914.

Notes for CHARLES A. CRAMER:
Reference #2217

More About CHARLES A. CRAMER:
Burial: Miller Cemetery, New Gretna, NJ

More About ELIZABETH ADAMS:
Burial: Miller Cemetery, New Gretna, NJ

Children of CHARLES CRAMER and ELIZABETH ADAMS are:

13. i. GEORGE F.[8] CRAMER, b. August 11, 1854; d. October 14, 1915.
ii. ELWOOD CRAMER, m. SARAH STACKHOUSE.

Notes for ELWOOD CRAMER:
Reference #2541

iii. WILLIAM H. CRAMER, b. 1846; d. April 1870.
iv. ALBERT ALLEN CRAMER.

Notes for ALBERT ALLEN CRAMER:
Reference #2542

v. SARAH M. CRAMER, b. April 06, 1857; d. July 28, 1860.
vi. MARY O. CRAMER, b. October 21, 1859.
vii. CHARLES A. CRAMER, b. September 11, 1863.
14. viii. HOWARD H. CRAMER, b. September 1864; d. 1941.

11. JOHN SMITH[7] CRAMER *(DANIEL S.[6], JOHN[5], JOHN[4], JOHN[3], WILLIAM[2], WILLIAM[1])* was born December 15, 1818, and died September 24, 1880. He married DORCAS TABITHA CRAMER June 14, 1840, daughter of CHARLES CRAMER and MARY GASKILL. She was born September 16, 1818, and died October 04, 1853.

Notes for JOHN SMITH CRAMER:
Reference #2383

Children of JOHN CRAMER and DORCAS CRAMER are:

i. MARY E.[8] CRAMER, b. November 13, 1840; d. January 20, 1841.
ii. MARGARET ANN CRAMER, m. THEODORE C. ALLEN.
iii. SARAH JANE CRAMER, b. November 10, 1843; d. March 13, 1865.
iv. WILLIAM ASBURY CRAMER, m. PHEBE ANN MINGIN.
v. MARY ELIZA CRAMER, b. July 07, 1848; d. October 30, 1848.
15. vi. URIAH BURRIS CRAMER, b. March 27, 1850, Bass River; d. December 08, 1917, Port Republic, NJ.
vii. EDITH ELIZA CRAMER, m. WILSON BODINE CRAMER.

12. SARAH ANN[7] CRAMER *(DANIEL S.[6], JOHN[5], JOHN[4], JOHN[3], WILLIAM[2], WILLIAM[1])*[1] was born June 29, 1816[1], and died May 27, 1897[1]. She married DARIUS CRAMER[1] January 03, 1833[1], son of CHARLES CRAMER and MARY GASKILL. He was born December 08, 1808[1], and died September 13, 1858[1].

More About SARAH ANN CRAMER:
Burial: Hillside Cemetary[1]

Notes for DARIUS CRAMER:
Reference #4142

More About DARIUS CRAMER:
Burial: Hillside Cemetary[1]

Children of SARAH CRAMER and DARIUS CRAMER are:

i. LAVINIA[8] CRAMER[1], b. November 27, 1833[1]; d. 1895[1]; m. CHALKLEY S. CRAMER[1], May 16, 1854[1]; b. 1833[1]; d. December 13, 1855[1].

16. ii. WILLIAM G. CRAMER, b. August 10, 1837; d. November 29, 1912.

iii. CHARLES HENRY "SPIDE" CRAMER[1], b. October 30, 1839[1]; m. SARAH JANE MAXWELL.

iv. MARY ELIZABETH CRAMER[1], b. 1842[1]; m. WILLIAM H. MATHIS.

v. CALAB SMITH "SWAMPY" CRAMER[1], b. November 29, 1844[1]; m. MARY JANE ROBBINS.

vi. ELLIS S. CRAMER[1], b. 1845[1].

vii. SARAH ANN CRAMER[1], b. May 16, 1847[1]; m. JOHN HICKMAN.

viii. EMMA M. CRAMER[1], b. September 17, 1852[1]; m. CARLISLE GASKILL.

ix. CHALKLEY SEARS CRAMER[1], b. May 02, 1856[1]; m. FRANCES CAROLINE JOHNSON.

x. DANIEL D. CRAMER[1], b. March 1858[1]; m. ANNA M. ADAMS.

Generation No. 7

13. GEORGE F.[8] CRAMER *(CHARLES A.[7], WILLIAM B.[6], WILLIAM[5], WILLIAM[4], WILLIAM[3], WILLIAM[2], WILLIAM[1])*[1] was born August 11, 1854[1], and died October 14, 1915[1]. He married MARY E. CRAMER[1] 1886[1], daughter of WILLIAM CRAMER and MARY MAXWELL. She was born June 27, 1868[1], and died June 23, 1899[1].

Notes for GEORGE F. CRAMER:
Reference #2543

More About GEORGE F. CRAMER:
Burial: Hillside Cemetary[1]

More About MARY E. CRAMER:
Burial: Hillside Cemetary[1]

Children of GEORGE CRAMER and MARY CRAMER are:

17. i. DORA[9] CRAMER, b. September 1891; d. 1961.

ii. NORRIS C. CRAMER[1], b. December 20, 1886[1]; d. April 17, 1936[1]; m. ELSIE MICK[1], May 09, 1910[1]; b. September 08, 1888[1]; d. September 13, 1963[1].

More About NORRIS C. CRAMER:
Burial: Hillside Cemetary[1]

More About ELSIE MICK:
Burial: Hillside Cemetary[1]

18. iii. MARY EDNA CRAMER, b. May 06, 1888; d. July 22, 1928.

14. HOWARD H.[8] CRAMER *(CHARLES A.[7], WILLIAM B.[6], WILLIAM[5], WILLIAM[4], WILLIAM[3], WILLIAM[2], WILLIAM[1])* was born September 1864, and died 1941. He married CLARA BOZARTH October 1895 in Washington twp, daughter of CHARLES BOZARTH and JULIA WEEKS. She was born November 30, 1868, and died July 31, 1959 in Elwood, NJ.

More About HOWARD H. CRAMER:
Burial: Miller Cemetery, New Gretna, NJ

More About CLARA BOZARTH:
Burial: Miller Cemetery, New Gretna, NJ

Children of HOWARD CRAMER and CLARA BOZARTH are:

19. i. EARLE C.[9] CRAMER, b. December 25, 1895; d. May 17, 1975.

ii. CASPER CRAMER, b. March 1901; d. May 1901, Leektown, NJ.

iii. JULIA E. CRAMER, m. JOHN A. HERMAN.

15. URIAH BURRIS[8] CRAMER *(JOHN SMITH[7], DANIEL S.[6], JOHN[5], JOHN[4], JOHN[3], WILLIAM[2], WILLIAM[1])* was born

March 27, 1850 in Bass River, and died December 08, 1917 in Port Republic, NJ. He married ELECTA THROCKMORTON August 28, 1870. She was born July 23, 1845 in Tuckerton, NJ, and died March 28, 1919 in Bass River.

More About ELECTA THROCKMORTON:
Burial: Hillside Cemetery

Children of URIAH CRAMER and ELECTA THROCKMORTON are:

- i. URIAH SMITH^{9} CRAMER, m. HELEN LOUISE DRISCOLL.
- ii. LETTIE E. CRAMER, m. BENJAMIN F. DRISCOLL.
- iii. THEODORE E. CRAMER, m. ELLA CAMILLE MARTIN.
- 20. iv. RENARD ETHYL CRAMER, b. October 29, 1865; d. May 28, 1927.
- v. SARAH ELIZA CRAMER, m. EPHRAIM FORD.
- vi. RHODA AMELIA CRAMER, m. NATHANIEL C. JONES.
- vii. SIDNEY URIAH CRAMER, b. March 08, 1880; d. June 1880.
- viii. EVA L. CRAMER, m. SAMUEL E. CRAMER.

16. WILLIAM G.^{8} CRAMER *(SARAH ANN^{7}, DANIEL S.^{6}, JOHN^{5}, JOHN^{4}, JOHN^{3}, WILLIAM^{2}, WILLIAM^{1})*[1] was born August 10, 1837[1], and died November 29, 1912[1]. He married MARY FRANCES MAXWELL[1]. She was born April 03, 1847[1], and died August 28, 1907[1].

More About WILLIAM G. CRAMER:
Burial: Hillside Cemetary[1]

More About MARY FRANCES MAXWELL:
Burial: Hillside Cemetary[1]

Children of WILLIAM CRAMER and MARY MAXWELL are:

- 21. i. MARY E.^{9} CRAMER, b. June 27, 1868; d. June 23, 1899.
- ii. ESTELLA CRAMER[1], b. August 10, 1870[1]; d. June 07, 1942[1]; m. WINFIELD PETERSON[1], March 30, 1889[1]; b. March 30, 1864[1]; d. December 29, 1917[1].
- iii. WILLIAM F. CRAMER[1], b. December 06, 1875[1]; d. June 27, 1936[1]; m. ELIZABETH J. HEADLEY[1]; b. October 1881[1]; d. October 28, 1968[1].

Generation No. 8

17. DORA^{9} CRAMER *(GEORGE F.^{8}, CHARLES A.^{7}, WILLIAM B.^{6}, WILLIAM^{5}, WILLIAM^{4}, WILLIAM^{3}, WILLIAM^{2}, WILLIAM^{1})*[1] was born September 1891, and died 1961. She married GROVER MAXWELL. He was born October 06, 1884, and died June 04, 1939.

More About DORA CRAMER:
Burial: Hillside Cemetary New Gretna, NJ

More About GROVER MAXWELL:
Burial: Hillside Cemetary, New Gretna, NJ

Children of DORA CRAMER and GROVER MAXWELL are:

- i. CARLTON^{10} MAXWELL, b. 1908; d. 1967.
- ii. BABY ESTELLE MAXWELL, b. May.

18. MARY EDNA^{9} CRAMER *(GEORGE F.^{8}, CHARLES A.^{7}, WILLIAM B.^{6}, WILLIAM^{5}, WILLIAM^{4}, WILLIAM^{3}, WILLIAM^{2}, WILLIAM^{1})*[1] was born May 06, 1888[1], and died July 22, 1928[1]. She married THOMAS S. WATSON[1], son of JOHN WATSON and ELLA PIERCE. He was born August 06, 1882 in Gloucester County, NJ[1], and died May 03, 1964[1].

Notes for MARY EDNA CRAMER:
Reference #2925

ii. GRACE SHINN.

Generation No. 11

31. JOHN WHITNEY[12] NEWCOMER *(JOHN[11], HILMA[10] WATSON, MARY EDNA[9] CRAMER, GEORGE F.[8], CHARLES A.[7], WILLIAM B.[6], WILLIAM[5], WILLIAM[4], WILLIAM[3], WILLIAM[2], WILLIAM[1])* was born January 01, 1959. He married JOAN LIDA LUBY June 21, 1981 in Birmingham, Michigan.

Children of JOHN NEWCOMER and JOAN LUBY are:

i. LEAH ELIZA[13] NEWCOMER.
ii. ADAM SAMUEL NEWCOMER.

32. SUSAN JOYCE[12] SUTTON *(ROBERT THOMAS[11], DORA[10] WATSON, MARY EDNA[9] CRAMER, GEORGE F.[8], CHARLES A.[7], WILLIAM B.[6], WILLIAM[5], WILLIAM[4], WILLIAM[3], WILLIAM[2], WILLIAM[1])*[10] was born December 01, 1964[10]. She married CHRISTOPHER KEATING[10], son of WILTON KEATING and MARGUERITE TOTH.

Notes for SUSAN JOYCE SUTTON:
DAR member number 831199

Children of SUSAN SUTTON and CHRISTOPHER KEATING are:

i. CHRISTOPHER KEATING[13] JR.[10].
ii. BENJAMIN KEATING[10].

33. BOBBI LYNN[12] SUTTON *(ROBERT THOMAS[11], DORA[10] WATSON, MARY EDNA[9] CRAMER, GEORGE F.[8], CHARLES A.[7], WILLIAM B.[6], WILLIAM[5], WILLIAM[4], WILLIAM[3], WILLIAM[2], WILLIAM[1])*[10] was born November 09, 1968[10]. She married (1) KARL FRANK CHASE[10]. She met (2) MR. MCHENRY.

Notes for BOBBI LYNN SUTTON:
DAR member number 831200, installed Oct. 16, 2004

Children of BOBBI SUTTON and KARL CHASE are:

i. SHAWN JOSEPH[13] CHASE[10], b. March 14, 1995[10].
ii. SAMANTHA JOYCE CHASE[10], b. April 06, 1997[10].

Child of BOBBI SUTTON and MR. MCHENRY is:

iii. DANI-LYNN[13] MCHENRY, b. June 08, 2006.

34. PERCY[12] SHINN *(IDA MAY[11] MATHIS, ADA MAY[10] CRAMER, RENARD ETHYL[9], URIAH BURRIS[8], JOHN SMITH[7], DANIEL S.[6], JOHN[5], JOHN[4], JOHN[3], WILLIAM[2], WILLIAM[1])* He married BARBARA STEVENSON.

Children of PERCY SHINN and BARBARA STEVENSON are:

i. ROBERT[13] SHINN.
ii. JEANNE SHINN.
iii. KATHRYN SHINN.

Endnotes

1. Mancuso.FTW, Date of Import: Sep 6, 2000.
2. Broderbund Family Archive #110, Vol. 2, Ed. 7, Social Security Death Index: U.S., Date of Import: May 20, 2000, Internal Ref. #1.112.7.115546.117
3. Mancuso.FTW, Date of Import: Sep 6, 2000.
4. Genealogy.com, Family Archive #110, Social Security Death Index: U.S. Ed. 9, Social Security Death Index, Release date: April 10, 2000, Internal Ref. #1.112.9.111416.32.

Descendants of Thomas Cramer

Generation No. 1

1. THOMAS^{2} CRAMER *(WILLIAM^{1})* was born Abt. 1662. He married DEBORAH.

Notes for THOMAS CRAMER:
Reference #1000

Descendants of Elizabeth Cramer

Generation No. 1

1. ELIZABETH[2] CRAMER *(WILLIAM[1])* She married GEORGE PACK.

Notes for ELIZABETH CRAMER:
Reference #5000

Descendants of John Cramer

Generation No. 1

1. JOHN[2] CRAMER *(WILLIAM[1])* was born Abt. 1666. He married (1) SARAH OSBORNE, daughter of STEPHEN OSBORNE and SARAH STANBOROUGH. She was born Abt. 1663. He married (2) SARAH OSBORNE.

Notes for JOHN CRAMER:
Reference #4000
John was a member of the Society of Friends and is listed in the Rahway and Plainfield Monthly Meeting Minutes, and in the minutes of the Woodbridge Monthly Meeting. John Cramer of Elizabethtown bought land at Barnagate on 9 May 1702. John and Sarah later owned land and settled in Whippany. The text "Along the Whippanong", by Myrose & Kitchell describes John's property with a map and descriptiuon. His will was probated in Essex County on 22 June 1716. The will left his sons Thomas and John each 4 pounds and his lawful wife the rest of his estate to bring up his children.

Children of JOHN CRAMER and SARAH OSBORNE are:

i. JOHN[3] CRAMER, m. HANNAH POTTER.
ii. THOMAS CRAMER, m. ABIGAIL WILLETS.
iii. JEREMIAH CRAMER, m. ABIAH TUTTLE.
2. iv. STEPHEN CRAMER, b. Abt. 1700; d. April 1777.

Generation No. 2

2. STEPHEN[3] CRAMER *(JOHN[2], WILLIAM[1])* was born Abt. 1700, and died April 1777. He married SARAH ANDREWS, daughter of EDWARD ANDREWS and SARAH ONG. She was born January 08, 1701/02, and died Abt. 1748.

Notes for STEPHEN CRAMER:
Reference #4004

Child of STEPHEN CRAMER and SARAH ANDREWS is:
3. i. CALEB[4] CRAMER, b. February 16, 1732/33; d. March 12, 1818.

Generation No. 3

3. CALEB[4] CRAMER *(STEPHEN[3], JOHN[2], WILLIAM[1])* was born February 16, 1732/33, and died March 12, 1818. He married SARA Abt. 1755.

Notes for CALEB CRAMER:
Reference #4011

Child of CALEB CRAMER and SARA is:
4. i. ISAAC[5] CRAMER, b. September 01, 1756; d. November 17, 1839.

Generation No. 4

4. ISAAC[5] CRAMER *(CALEB[4], STEPHEN[3], JOHN[2], WILLIAM[1])*[1] was born September 01, 1756, and died November 17, 1839. He married DORCAS ADAMS[1] Abt. 1783. She was born November 23, 1766, and died August 06, 1848.

Notes for ISAAC CRAMER:

Reference #4030
Isaac served in the Revolutionary War. Served in NJ War time Residence Burlington County Militia Certificate # 192 some of No Pounds, Sixteen shilling and eight peace, signed by James Fenimore 5/1/1784

More About ISAAC CRAMER:
Burial: Isaac Cemetery in New Gretna

More About DORCAS ADAMS:
Burial: Isaac Cemetery in New Gretna

Children of ISAAC CRAMER and DORCAS ADAMS are:

5. i. CHARLES[6] CRAMER, b. 1789, Bass River, NJ; d. July 29, 1872, Bridgeport, NJ.
- ii. GEORGE A. CRAMER, m. LUCY CALE.
- iii. BETHIAH CRAMER, m. ARCHIBALD SOOY.
- iv. URIAH CRAMER, m. MARIA FRANKLIN.
- v. MARY CRAMER, m. ISAIAH ROBBINS.
- vi. ISAAC CRAMER, b. February 05, 1796; d. December 23, 1831.
- vii. LAVINIA CRAMER, m. WILLIAM FRENCH.
- viii. HOPE CRAMER, b. December 12, 1801; d. February 26, 1859.
- ix. LUCY ANN CRAMER, m. EDWARD JOHNSON.

Generation No. 5

5. CHARLES[6] CRAMER *(ISAAC[5], CALEB[4], STEPHEN[3], JOHN[2], WILLIAM[1])*[1] was born 1789 in Bass River, NJ[1], and died July 29, 1872 in Bridgeport, NJ[1]. He married MARY GASKILL[1] April 06, 1809. She was born January 01, 1791 in West Creek, NJ[1], and died March 16, 1873 in Bridgeport, NJ[1].

Notes for CHARLES CRAMER:
Reference #4072
At one time he and his wife lived next to the Isaac Cramer Cemetery on Rloute 542 in New Gretna, NJ.

More About CHARLES CRAMER:
Burial: Hillside Cemetary[1]

More About MARY GASKILL:
Burial: Hillside Cemetary[1]

Children of CHARLES CRAMER and MARY GASKILL are:

6. i. DARIUS[7] CRAMER, b. December 08, 1808; d. September 13, 1858.
- ii. CHARLES BURRIS CRAMER[1], b. March 14, 1828[1]; d. May 24, 1879[1]; m. ELLEN S. ADAMS[1]; b. April 19, 1832[1].
- iii. WILLIAM SEARS CRAMER, m. CATHERINE LEEK.
- iv. AARON G. CRAMER, m. ANN MOTT.
- v. THOMAS ALLEN CRAMER, m. REBECCA ANN CRAMER.
- vi. ISAAC F. CRAMER, m. ELIZABETH HAINES.
- vii. LAVINIA CRAMER, m. JOHN CARTER.
- viii. EDITH ELIZA CRAMER, m. JOHN W. CRAMER.

7. ix. DORCAS TABITHA CRAMER, b. September 16, 1818; d. October 04, 1853.
- x. SAMUEL B. CRAMER, m. RUTH ELMY LAMSON.
- xi. MARY ANN CRAMER, m. WILLIAM G. ADAMS.
- xii. URIAH CRAMER, m. SARAH S. HAINES.

Generation No. 6

6. DARIUS[7] CRAMER *(CHARLES[6], ISAAC[5], CALEB[4], STEPHEN[3], JOHN[2], WILLIAM[1])*[1] was born December 08, 1808[1], and died September 13, 1858[1]. He married SARAH ANN CRAMER[1] January 03, 1833[1], daughter of DANIEL CRAMER and CHARLOTTE LOVELAND. She was born June 29, 1816[1], and died May 27, 1897[1].

Subj: **DAR Patriot Lookup: Reference Code RZJAAABK**
Date: 3/11/2007 10:39:09 A.M. Atlantic Daylight Time
From: auto_reply@dar.org
To: Jsutton639@aol.com

Dear Robert Sutton,

PLEASE DO NOT REPLY TO THIS EMAIL. If you would like to send a follow up message, please select the 'Send a Follow Up Message' link on the right column of the PI Lookup Page or from http://www.dar.org/natsociety/pi_lookup.cfm?RT=SC&ID=RZJAAABK.

A search of our Patriot Index provided the information found below.

KRAMER, Isaac
Birth: 1 Sep 1756
Service: NJ
Rank: Pvt
Death: NJ 17 Nov 1839
Patriot Pensioned: No Widow Pensioned: No
Children Pensioned: No Heirs Pensioned: No
Spouse: (1) Dorcas Adams

Directions for ordering a record copy of the application submitted for this patriot can be found at http://www.dar.org/natsociety/content.cfm?ID=146&hd=n&FO=Y.

If you are interested in membership in SAR for yourself or DAR for a female relative please send a follow up message with your address and phone number.

If you need to respond to this message, please click the 'Send a Follow Up Message' link on the right-hand column of the DAR Patriot Lookup Page and enter your reference code (RZJAAABK) or by clicking http://www.dar.org/natsociety/pi_lookup.cfm?RT=SC&ID=RZJAAABK.

Thank you for your interest in the DAR Patriot Lookup Service.

Sincerely,
Joyce
Patriot Lookup Volunteer

Original Request
================
Reference Code: RZJAAABK
Requestor: Robert Sutton (Jsutton639@aol.com)
Patriot First Name: Isaac Patriot Last Name: CramerBirth: Sept. 1, 1756 NJDeath: NJWar Time Residence: Burlington County Militia NJ Comments: I have information that says Isaac received Certificate # 192 for the sum of No Pounds, Sixteen Shilling and eight Peace, signed by James Fenimore 5/1/1784

Please note, NSDAR is committed to maintaining accurate records. If you find that our records contain errors, please submit copies of primary documentation supporting these changes, to the attention of the Corrections Genealogist, NSDAR, Office of the Registrar General, 1776 D St NW, Washington, DC. 20006-5303. We appreciate your interest in the Society's records.

Reference #4142

More About DARIUS CRAMER:
Burial: Hillside Cemetary[1]

More About SARAH ANN CRAMER:
Burial: Hillside Cemetary[1]

Children of DARIUS CRAMER and SARAH CRAMER are:

- i. LAVINIA[8] CRAMER[1], b. November 27, 1833[1]; d. 1895[1]; m. CHALKLEY S. CRAMER[1], May 16, 1854[1]; b. 1833[1]; d. December 13, 1855[1].
- 8. ii. WILLIAM G. CRAMER, b. August 10, 1837; d. November 29, 1912.
- iii. CHARLES HENRY "SPIDE" CRAMER[1], b. October 30, 1839[1]; m. SARAH JANE MAXWELL.
- iv. MARY ELIZABETH CRAMER[1], b. 1842[1]; m. WILLIAM H. MATHIS.
- v. CALAB SMITH "SWAMPY" CRAMER[1], b. November 29, 1844[1]; m. MARY JANE ROBBINS.
- vi. ELLIS S. CRAMER[1], b. 1845[1].
- vii. SARAH ANN CRAMER[1], b. May 16, 1847[1]; m. JOHN HICKMAN.
- viii. EMMA M. CRAMER[1], b. September 17, 1852[1]; m. CARLISLE GASKILL.
- ix. CHALKLEY SEARS CRAMER[1], b. May 02, 1856[1]; m. FRANCES CAROLINE JOHNSON.
- x. DANIEL D. CRAMER[1], b. March 1858[1]; m. ANNA M. ADAMS.

7. DORCAS TABITHA[7] CRAMER *(CHARLES[6], ISAAC[5], CALEB[4], STEPHEN[3], JOHN[2], WILLIAM[1])* was born September 16, 1818, and died October 04, 1853. She married (1) JOHN SMITH CRAMER, son of DANIEL CRAMER and CHARLOTTE LOVELAND. She married (2) JOHN SMITH CRAMER June 14, 1840, son of DANIEL CRAMER and CHARLOTTE LOVELAND. He was born December 15, 1818, and died September 24, 1880.

Notes for JOHN SMITH CRAMER:
Reference #2383

Children of DORCAS CRAMER and JOHN CRAMER are:

- i. MARY E.[8] CRAMER, b. November 13, 1840; d. January 20, 1841.
- ii. MARGARET ANN CRAMER, m. THEODORE C. ALLEN.
- iii. SARAH JANE CRAMER, b. November 10, 1843; d. March 13, 1865.
- iv. WILLIAM ASBURY CRAMER, m. PHEBE ANN MINGIN.
- v. MARY ELIZA CRAMER, b. July 07, 1848; d. October 30, 1848.
- 9. vi. URIAH BURRIS CRAMER, b. March 27, 1850, Bass River; d. December 08, 1917, Port Republic, NJ.
- vii. EDITH ELIZA CRAMER, m. WILSON BODINE CRAMER.

Generation No. 7

8. WILLIAM G.[8] CRAMER *(DARIUS[7], CHARLES[6], ISAAC[5], CALEB[4], STEPHEN[3], JOHN[2], WILLIAM[1])*[1] was born August 10, 1837[1], and died November 29, 1912[1]. He married MARY FRANCES MAXWELL[1]. She was born April 03, 1847[1], and died August 28, 1907[1].

More About WILLIAM G. CRAMER:
Burial: Hillside Cemetary[1]

More About MARY FRANCES MAXWELL:
Burial: Hillside Cemetary[1]

Children of WILLIAM CRAMER and MARY MAXWELL are:

- 10. i. MARY E.[9] CRAMER, b. June 27, 1868; d. June 23, 1899.
- ii. ESTELLA CRAMER[1], b. August 10, 1870[1]; d. June 07, 1942[1]; m. WINFIELD PETERSON[1], March 30, 1889[1]; b. March 30, 1864[1]; d. December 29, 1917[1].
- iii. WILLIAM F. CRAMER[1], b. December 06, 1875[1]; d. June 27, 1936[1]; m. ELIZABETH J. HEADLEY[1]; b. October 1881[1]; d. October 28, 1968[1].

9. Uriah Burris[8] Cramer *(Dorcas Tabitha[7], Charles[6], Isaac[5], Caleb[4], Stephen[3], John[2], William[1])* was born March 27, 1850 in Bass River, and died December 08, 1917 in Port Republic, NJ. He married Electa Throckmorton August 28, 1870. She was born July 23, 1845 in Tuckerton, NJ, and died March 28, 1919 in Bass River.

More About Electa Throckmorton:
Burial: Hillside Cemetery

Children of Uriah Cramer and Electa Throckmorton are:

- i. Uriah Smith[9] Cramer, m. Helen Louise Driscoll.
- ii. Lettie E. Cramer, m. Benjamin F. Driscoll.
- iii. Theodore E. Cramer, m. Ella Camille Martin.
- 11. iv. Renard Ethyl Cramer, b. October 29, 1865; d. May 28, 1927.
- v. Sarah Eliza Cramer, m. Ephraim Ford.
- vi. Rhoda Amelia Cramer, m. Nathaniel C. Jones.
- vii. Sidney Uriah Cramer, b. March 08, 1880; d. June 1880.
- viii. Eva L. Cramer, m. Samuel E. Cramer.

Generation No. 8

10. Mary E.[9] Cramer *(William G.[8], Darius[7], Charles[6], Isaac[5], Caleb[4], Stephen[3], John[2], William[1])*[1] was born June 27, 1868[1], and died June 23, 1899[1]. She married George F. Cramer[1] 1886[1], son of Charles Cramer and Elizabeth Adams. He was born August 11, 1854[1], and died October 14, 1915[1].

More About Mary E. Cramer:
Burial: Hillside Cemetary[1]

Notes for George F. Cramer:
Reference #2543

More About George F. Cramer:
Burial: Hillside Cemetary[1]

Children of Mary Cramer and George Cramer are:

- 12. i. Dora[10] Cramer, b. September 1891; d. 1961.
- ii. Norris C. Cramer[1], b. December 20, 1886[1]; d. April 17, 1936[1]; m. Elsie Mick[1], May 09, 1910[1]; b. September 08, 1888[1]; d. September 13, 1963[1].

  More About Norris C. Cramer:
  Burial: Hillside Cemetary[1]

  More About Elsie Mick:
  Burial: Hillside Cemetary[1]

- 13. iii. Mary Edna Cramer, b. May 06, 1888; d. July 22, 1928.

11. Renard Ethyl[9] Cramer *(Uriah Burris[8], Dorcas Tabitha[7], Charles[6], Isaac[5], Caleb[4], Stephen[3], John[2], William[1])* was born October 29, 1865, and died May 28, 1927. He married Mary Emma Prince. She was born October 12, 1871, and died May 17, 1937 in Tuckerton, NJ.

More About Mary Emma Prince:
Burial: Miller Cemetery, New Gretna, NJ

Children of Renard Cramer and Mary Prince are:

- i. Olive[10] Cramer, m. John Wiseman.
- 14. ii. Ada May Cramer, b. April 05, 1897; d. February 27, 1933.
- iii. Jefferson Cramer, m. Mary Ann Gallagher.

(Cramer is from Kraumer (Holland Dutch.)

1 Gales built the

Capt ~~Krammer~~ married a Gale and moved into the Merrygold place—Gale homestead.

2. Sprag - Chisholm [illegible]

From whom the C - KRaumer - Dutch Spelling

decoys were bought - Brant, Blue bill & blackduck.

3 Gales migrated to America 1613 with slaves and settled on the Wadding river at Merrygold point - Merrygold Creek. this became part of Ocean County later Burlington County N.J.

4. the house was built in three sections
It is possible to identify the flooring
as yellow pine (swamp) tongue and
groove, random with in the two main
rooms. the timbers are hand hewn
swamp White Oak (Quercus alba) in
the basement while the ceiling timber
of the fireplace room are heart white
cedar [Chamaecyparis thyoides). the siding
and shingles were swamp white cedar
(Chamaecyparis thyoides) while the timbers
used in the frame work are all white
~~[illegible]~~ oak. they were mitred, pegged and
braced [illegible] as was done in the sailing
ships

This is the record as far as I
have been able to discover from
the many old families who have
visited and talked to me.

Wm [illegible] Sr. 1965

Matilda Cramer Tilton 841 Second St. Trenton, N.J.
Margaret Cramer Kloffer 6 Perkins ave Pleasantv[illegible]
" " " " N.J.
Fred Kloffer
Willard G. Tilton 841 Second St. Trenton N.J.
[illegible] Cromer from New Gretna 76 - Aug 14 1949
John T Cramer - 1873 - on Cramer Place - aug 14 -
Smith Cramer, bought from - Died 48
He built the tories place Built in 1872 -
Rier + Edy - Mararet Anne sold to Smith Cramer.
1 John 6 Henry
2 Tom 7 Elwood
3 Mary 8 Bill
4 Margaret
5 Phoebe 9 Dela
Gaskell bought a morgage -
B. Smith Cramer - Magie Bermunda a daughter of Bill S. Cramer.
Febie Mengie Cramer moved to
Clayton when B Smith Cramer died.

Gaskell sold to John + Tom [illegible]

building loan took it over.

~~Red~~ Guthapple - from Phila - Dr. Shoemaker bought

Berry + Scott. they sold to John B. Davignee Sr. 1948

Charles Cromer owned the Silcock's place.

~~John + Cro~~ William + Cromer son.

1. Sears -
2. Aren
3. Charles II

1. John Towers Cromer.
2. William Loyed. "
3. Jessie Cromer
4. Lewis "
5. Georgie Cromer is now Georgie Luty lives in Pleasantville

essey Johnson place was in the Charles Cromer property.

Georgie married a Hotel manager + glasstown.

Georgie Cromer Luty - Pleasantville N.J. Dakota Ave.

29

Jesse Johnson —

As told by Stan McCarten, Feb. 18, 1950

"Jesse Johnson was quite a local character: an old bachelor, he lived with his mother in a big house on what is known as "the Johnson place." He never wore shoes and he had rigged up a big box on the front half of a wagon. He fashioned a sort of harness which he fitted to himself and did a business of hauling "light" loads, such as sacks of flour etc., between [illegible] and Egg Harbor, and similar distances. Once he had his old mother in the box on the wagon — [illegible] along the road by the swamp, at one end place [illegible] out, "The horse is getting balky, Ma, he's out of control" — and so saying he shied off into the ditch. The cart upset, the old lady fell out and broke her leg. Johnson had two hobbies: collecting glass bottles and old clocks. At the time of his death he had collected a pile of bottles nearly as high as the house. Old glass collectors cashed in on many of these bottles as glass collecting became more popular. He had over 100 old clocks in his house at one time. They were set to strike all at different times so that a clock was striking at all times of the day."

told by Cart [illegible]

Jesse had a habit of filling the pits in the old road with bottles. Then he would whip up the horses and as the heavy carts would roll over the bottles they would crack and explode with a great noise and Jesse would laugh uproariously.

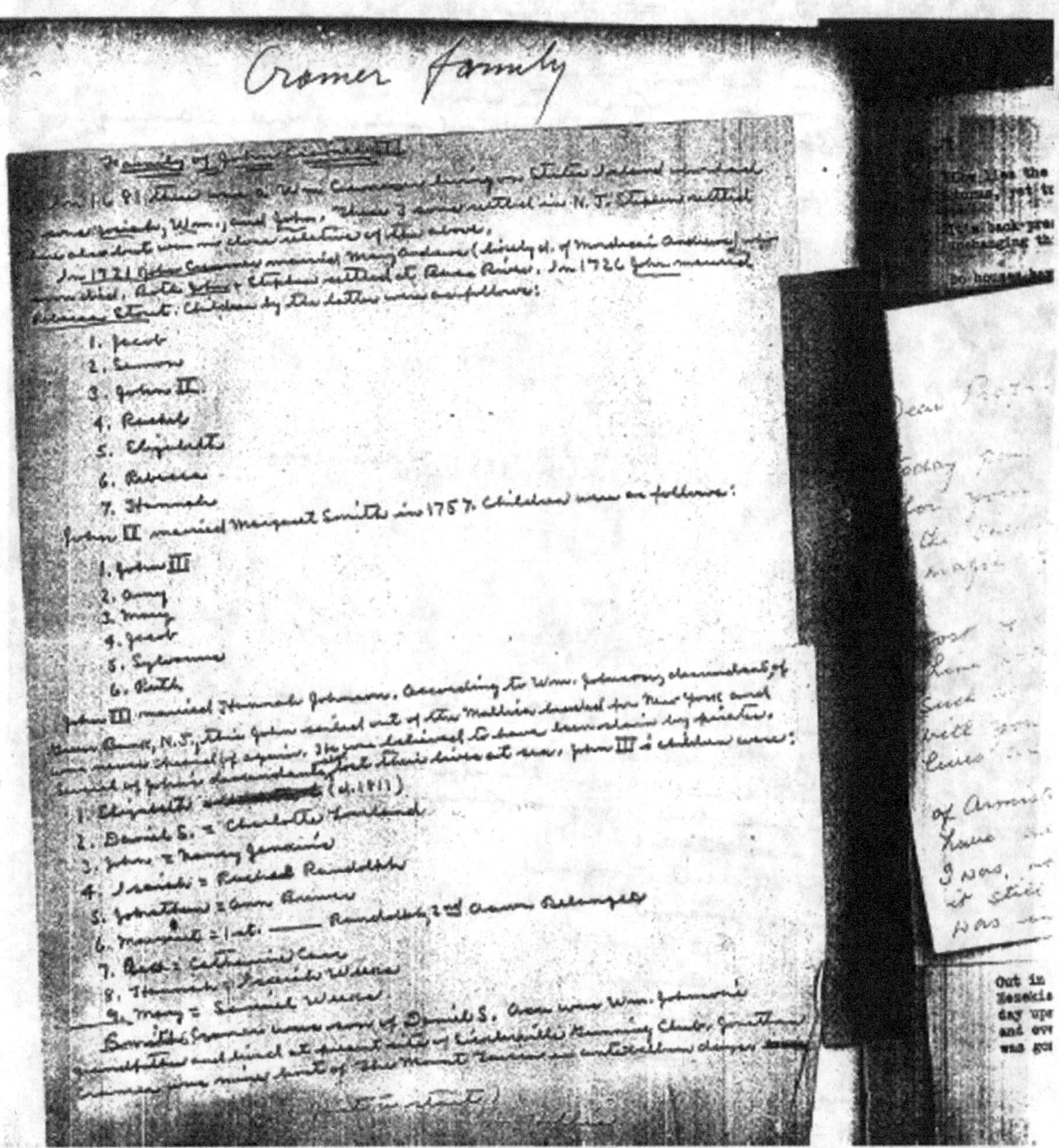

Cromer Family

Family of John [illegible]

In 1681 there was a Wm [illegible] living on Staten Island [illegible] [illegible] Wm, and John. These 3 were settled in N. J. Stephen settled [illegible] was no close relation of the above.

In 1721 John [illegible] married Mary Andrews (likely d. of Mordecai Andrews) [illegible] Both John & Stephen settled at [illegible] River. In 1726 John married [illegible]. Children by the latter were as follows:

1. Jacob
2. Simon
3. John II.
4. Rachel
5. Elizabeth
6. Rebecca
7. Hannah

John II married Margaret Smith in 1757. Children were as follows:

1. John III
2. Amy
3. Mary
4. Jacob
5. Sylvanus
6. Ruth

John III married Hannah Johnson. According to Wm. Johnson's descendant, of [illegible] N. J., this John sailed out of the [illegible] for New York and was never heard of again. He was believed to have been slain by pirates [illegible] lost their lives at sea. John III's children were: [illegible] (d. 1811)

1. Elizabeth [illegible]
2. Daniel S. = Charlotte [illegible]
3. John = Nancy Jennings
4. Isaiah = Rachel Randolph
5. Jonathan = Ann [illegible]
6. Margaret = 1st. —— Randolph, 2nd [illegible]
7. [illegible] = Catharine [illegible]
8. Hannah = Isaiah Weeks
9. Mary = Samuel Weeks

[illegible] Cromer was son of Daniel S. [illegible] Wm. Johnson's [illegible] grandfather [illegible]

[illegible]

Cromer Family

[illegible]

[illegible] 1681 there were Wm. Cromer [illegible] living on Staten Island [illegible] Josiah, Wm., and John. These 3 were settled in N.J. Stephen settled [illegible] but were no close relative of the above.

In 1721 John Cromer married Mary Andrews (likely d. of Mordecai Andrews) [illegible]. Both John & Stephen settled at [illegible] River. In 1726 John married [illegible] Stuart. Children by the latter were as follows:

1. Jacob
2. Simeon
3. John II
4. Rachel
5. Elizabeth
6. Rebecca
7. Hannah

John II married Margaret Smith in 1757. Children were as follows:

1. John III
2. Darcy
3. Mary
4. Sarah
5. Sylvanus
6. Ruth

John III married Hannah Johnson. According to Wm. Johnson, descendant of [illegible] Beach, N.J., this John sailed out of the Mullica headed for New York and was never heard of again. He was believed to have been slain by pirates. [illegible] of John's descendants lost their lives at sea. John III's children were:

(d. 1811)

1. Elizabeth
2. Daniel S. = Charlotte Loveland
3. John = Nancy Jenkins
4. Isaiah = Rachel Randolph
5. Jonathan = Ann Brewer
6. Margaret = 1st. —— Randolph, 2nd Aaron Belangee
7. [illegible] = Catherine Carr
8. Hannah = Isaiah Weeks
9. Mary = Samuel Weeks

Jonathan Cromer was son of Daniel S. Asa was Wm. Johnson's grandfather and lived at present site of [illegible] Gunning Club. Jonathan Cromer was [illegible] host of the Mount Tavern in antebellum days.

(Just a start)

— Hollis.

HOPE AT MERRYGOLD

Low lies the ground on which the old house stands. Half turned around as one who turns, yet turns again to watch the passing traveler and looks once more.

It's back pressed hard against the banks of Merrygold, this tidal stream the one unchanging thing, in all the passing years.

Do houses have a soul ? Do years of wind sun and rain leave their mark ? Do sound of voices long since stilled, sights now unseen; do they leave a void still unfilled ?

The timbers in this house once were living things. Mighty trees, citizens of a forest then unspoiled. Sap, the vital fluid, crept up and down the seasons through. Into the leaves, bark,roots and every thirsty fiber

Does not this force live on within the risen house ? Do houses have a soul ? I think they do.

Come stand within the door and listen to its voice. Down in the cellar depths the oven stands; here to and fro the silent baker walks, laying out the gleaming loaves that none shall eat.

Come with me to the west window. Here in the long ago, looking out, stood Hope, watching out wh ere stream and river meet. Watching for a sail that never came. Hope, loveless of all the flowers that Dorcas and Isaac grew.

Pass through the hallinto this roomwhere once the soft Quaker speech was heard. The voice of Isaac and his children, where are they now ?

The desk is there; the dusty ledgers stand in rows; the dim darkness of old portraits still look down. No sound now, only the haunting silence remains, silence that you can almost hear.

Here in this room, once long ago the builder of this house stood. Isaac the elder, sunken deep in reverie, thinking of Caleb his father and of his grandsire Stephen, they had laid wel? the family foundations; now they are gone.

Ara, his unseen mother came to mind. She had died when Isaac was so young that to him now she was a vision dim. A memory that was always therein the shadows of his mind; one that came and was gone.

Unbidden, as always, up from the heart wounds sorrow, came thoughts of Hope his daughter. The sad sweet thoughts; at first he could not bear them, but as the days, weeks and months passed by they became as a wound. A wound that has healed over, but deep below the hurt was there.

Seven other children yes, but Hope was gone.
Up in the burying ground, where the family laid their dead, the new grave still stood out among the old. Seven other children yes, but Hope has gone.

Out in the kitchen Dorcas, his wife, moves about. Dorcas, his beloved wife, old Hezekiah's daughter the Adams patriarch. To Dorcas it was still unreal, that awful day upstairs in the bedroom with its walls of blue. It was she that had found her, and even yet the horror of it still would not go. Seven other children yes, but Hope was gone.

continued -

Into that room no more would she go. To her it was though as if by not beliving it was not so. Isaac often walked alone here; he still could the words Hope had spoken standing by the window. " Without his father, I cannot live. " His words were, " Time will heal". It was not so.

Around the bier in silent sorrow the family sat. All were here, Cranmers, Adams, Leeks, Johnsons and all the others who made up the little place.
The old parson stood up and said " Let us pray, O God of love, look down and in thy mercy heal us all. Into thy forgiving hands we commit her spirt."

The old house still stands aslant out near the road, and in its walls the silent memories crowd. Sometimes when one is setting here the noiseless people come and walk the rooms. In cellar, the creak of oven door, upstairs the loose board in the floor, tell their story all too well.

And in the bedroom painted blue, there is a window yet to which rambling roses still climb. Looking in to see the place that once she knew. For here even yet while one remembers, Hope is not gone.

Do houses have a soul ?
Here is my clue,
Where still one loving heart remembers,
I think they do.

John Milton Adams 1958

Great, great , great grandson
of Isaac and Dorcas Cranmer of Merrygold

the cramer family seemed to have come from England. to England from Holland where the name was spelled Krammer. the Merrygold place was most likely built by golds from Holland. Margaret Gold married capt Cramer.

Isaac Cramer's Will 12th day July 1839

In the name of God Amen. I Isaac Cramer of the Township of Little Egg Harbor in the County of Burlington and the State of New Jersey, being weak in body but sound of mind and memory and understanding, do make and publish this last will and testament in maner [sic] and form folling [sic], that is to say, 1st - It is my will and I do order that all my just debts and funeral expenses be duly paid and satisfied as soon as can be conviently [sic] be done after my decease. 2nd - I give and bequeath unto my beloved wife Dorcas forever that plantation and farm where I now dwell, and all there unto belonging, such as is necessary for carrying on the farm business and all the household goods should she require them, together with my two horse wagon and her choice of as many cows as she may want. Also I bequeath unto her forever the salt meadow on the West side of the Throughfare [sic] except what I have disposed of and which I purchased of Hartshorn, and all the cash which I may have on hand together with all the money due me either on bonds or notes of hand at my decease after all my debts are satisfied, 3rd - I give and bequeath unto my son George Cramer forever the two lots of land and all thereunto belonging on which he now dwells, one of fifty acres which I purchased of my Uncle Isaac Cramer, and one of thirty six acres which I purchased of William Grant, and I also give him two lots of salt meadow lying on the East side of the Bass River, one lot containing twenty five acres and the other ten acres. 4th - I give and bequeath my son Charles Cramer, and to his heirs together the plantation and farm I purchased from my Father, and which is known by the Cavileer place, and I also give him all my land lying to the westward of a survey of twenty six acres which I took up in my own name and also the land I purchased of Samuel Sikes, bounded by land of William Allen Esq. I also give and bequeath unto him the following lots of salt meadow - one which I purchased of John (Melanafy?) of eleven acres and one of Jacob Barnhart of thirty acres and one lot of Robert Loveland of twelve acres. 5th - I give and bequeath my son Uriah Cramer and his heirs forever the plantation and Premises where he now dwells which I purchased of Maja Mathis containing eighty acres more or less. And I also give him all the upland on the Hartshorn place up to (William Pancoasts) line, then 1st east ten chains 2nd north fourteen chains along the line of the place where I now reside, then 3rd East eighteen chains, 4th - Northerly along the line of the place John Cramer purchased of Eli Mathis, to a green corner of the land I purchased of Samuel Sikes then, 5th - Five chains to a st - one cornder to the survey I purchased of same Sikes, 6th then Southeasterly along a line that was settled between me and Maja Mathis, about thirty chains to a corner standing in a swamp, 7th - then East eight chains to a cedar standing in the swamp, 8th - Southwesterly to a white oak corner to 4th lot, 9th - from said corner along John Sherman's line until it comes to aforesaid Hartshorn Survey. I give and bequeath unto him and his heirs all the salt meadows on the East side of Lovelands Throughfare [sic] which I purchased of my Father & Samuel and others. 6th - I bequeath to my Daughter Lusy [sic] Johnson and to her heirs forever the place and premises where she and her Husband now dwell, and I also give her and her heirs forever six acres of cedar swamp which I purchased of James Willetts, Which James sold for John Ridgeway and others, and I give her and her heirs forever eight acres more or less of salt meadows on Ditch point of Wading River, 7th - I give and bequeath unto my Daughter Bethia Sooy the sum of six hundred dollars to be paid to her by my executors hereafter to be named, which six hundred dollars to be made out of my real and personal property, not by thereto disposed of. 8th - It is my wish and I do order my executors to sell all my real and personal property as soon as can be conviently done after my decease. And out of the money arising therefrom to pay the legacies and other charges against my estate, and should there be a balance [sic] on hand after paying all demands against my estate, it is my will that my executors pay it to my wife. 9th - and lastly, I hereby appoint my worthy friends, Jesse Evans and Charles Adams my executors of this my last will and testament, in witness whereof I have hereto set my hand and seal this 12th day of July 1839.

Signed, sealed, published and declared by the same Isaac Cramer to be his testament and last will in presence of us. Edward Alloway, Nicholas Wentlings, John Forman,.
Charles Harker – surrogate.

Codical [sic] added to Isaac Cramer's will. July 27, 1839
I Isaac Cramer, of the Township of Little Egg Harbor in the County of Burlington and State of New Jersey, do this 27th day of July AD 1839, make and publish this Codical [sic] to my last will and testament in the manner following. That is to say whereas since making my last will and testament 12th of July 1839, I thought it proper to give and bequeath to my grandson Marmaduke, son of my daughter Hope, and to his heirs and assigns forever, all my house and lot of land thereunto belonging, now in the possession of Derias Cramer which is commonly called the Carlisle house. And I do hereby and request my executors to pay my daughter Bethiah Sooy five hundred dollars instead of six hundred dollars as it said in my last will and testament. – In witness I have set my hand and seal this day and year first above written.

His
Isaac Cramer
X
Mark

(note the X as he must have been too sick to write his name, his signature was on the first will.)

Witnessed by
Edward Alloways, Nicholas Wentlings, John Forman.
Book of Wills E page 411 in the Burlington County Surrogates Office Mt. Holly N.J.

Inventory of the goods or chattle weights and credits in part of Isaac Cramer
Dec. 9, 1839 by Jesse Evans and charles Adams, Executors & William Allen, Esq. & Micajah Mathis, two disinterested Freeholders Dec. 9, 1839

Purse	$125.46
Cash in hand Jesse Evans	500.00
Bedding & Bedsteds [sic]	70.00

One chest	2.00
One mahogany sideboard	15.00
One cherry Breakfast table	5.00
One Windsor chair	8.00
One Yanky [sic] clock	9.00
Two looking glasses & Old chest	6.50
One set of Crockery etc.	7.00
Indian corn in crib	450.00
Hay in Mows	250.00
15 head of cattle	165.00
2 scows one nearly new	15.00
Notes	
Maja Mathis for	49.17
Eli Mathis for	41.18
Charles Loveland for	18.00 (Doubtful)
Edward Johnson for	13.03
Job Weeks for	59.53
Marshall Mathis for	110.00
Samuel Loveland for	7.05 (Doubtful)
William W. Cramer for	36.25
William G. Leek for	17.83
Total of everything	$2,492.87

Descendants of John Cramer

1 John Cramer 1696 -
.... +Mary Andrews
*2nd Wife of John Cramer:
.... +Rebecca Stout
.... 2 John Cramer, Jr. 1730 - 1790
.... +Margaret Smith 1735 - 1811
.... 3 John Cramer 1758 - 1815
.... +Hannah Johnson 1765 - 1827
.... 4 Daniel S. Cramer 1785 - 1853
.... +Charlotte Loveland 1794 - 1869
.... 5 John Smith Cramer 1818 - 1880
.... +[1] Dorcas Tabitha Cramer 1818 - 1853
.... 6 Mary E. Cramer 1840 - 1841
.... 6 Margaret Ann Cramer
.... +Theodore C. Allen
.... 6 Sarah Jane Cramer 1843 - 1865
.... 6 William Asbury Cramer
.... +Phebe Ann Mingin
.... 6 Mary Eliza Cramer 1848 - 1848
.... 6 Uriah Burris Cramer 1850 - 1917
.... +Electa Throckmorton 1845 - 1919
.... 7 Uriah Smith Cramer
.... +Helen Louise Driscoll
.... 7 Lettie E. Cramer
.... +Benjamin F. Driscoll
.... 7 Theodore E. Cramer
.... +Ella Camille Martin
.... 7 Renard Ethyl Cramer 1865 - 1927
.... +Mary Emma Prince 1871 - 1937
.... 8 Olive Cramer
.... +John Wiseman
.... 8 Ada May Cramer 1897 - 1933
.... +Merrill Cleveland Mathis 1884 - 1934
.... 9 Ida May Mathis
.... +Elsworth Butler
.... *2nd Husband of Ida May Mathis:
.... +Fillmore Shinn
.... 10 Percy Shinn
.... +Barbara Stevenson
.... 11 Robert Shinn
.... 11 Jeanne Shinn
.... 11 Kathryn Shinn
.... 10 Grace Shinn
.... 9 Mary Mathis 1918 -
.... +George Filling, Jr.
.... 9 Irene Mathis 1921 -
.... 9 Sarah Mathis 1925 -
.... 9 Mildred Mathis 1928 -
.... 9 Merriell Cleveland Mathis, Jr. 1931 -
.... 8 Jefferson Cramer
.... +Mary Ann Gallagher
.... 7 Sarah Eliza Cramer
.... +Ephraim Ford
.... 7 Rhoda Amelia Cramer
.... +Nathaniel C. Jones
.... 7 Sidney Uriah Cramer 1880 - 1880
.... 7 Eva L. Cramer
.... +Samuel E. Cramer
.... 6 Edith Eliza Cramer
.... +Wilson Bodine Cramer
.... 5 Sarah Ann Cramer 1816 - 1897
.... +Darius Cramer 1808 - 1858
.... 6 Lavinia Cramer 1833 - 1895
.... +Chalkley S. Cramer 1833 - 1855
.... 6 William G. Cramer 1837 - 1912
.... +Mary Frances Maxwell 1847 - 1907
.... 7 Mary E. Cramer 1868 - 1899
.... +George F. Cramer 1854 - 1915
.... 8 Dora Cramer 1891 - 1961
.... +Grover Maxwell 1884 - 1939
.... 9 Carlton Maxwell 1908 - 1967
.... 9 Baby Estelle Maxwell May -
.... 8 Norris C. Cramer 1886 - 1936
.... +Elsie Mick 1888 - 1963
.... 8 Mary Edna Cramer 1888 - 1928

+Thomas S. Watson 1882 - 1964
9 Hilma Watson 1910 -
+Lindley Llewellyn Newcomer 1906 - 1992
10 John Newcomer
+Barbara Lee Boffemmyer
11 John Whitney Newcomer 1959 -
+Joan Lida Luby
12 Leah Eliza Newcomer
12 Adam Samuel Newcomer
11 Thomas England Newcomer 1966 -
10 Ronald Newcomer 1944 - 1963
9 Dora Watson 1915 - 1965
+Robert O. Sutton 1906 - 1987
10 Twin Baby Sutton 1930 - 1930
10 Twin Baby Sutton 1930 - 1930
10 Robert Thomas Sutton 1932 -
+Joyce F.. Mancuso 1934 -
11 Dolores Lea Sutton 1958 -
11 Susan Joyce Sutton 1964 -
+Christopher Keating
12 Christopher Keating Jr.
12 Benjamin Keating
11 Bobbi Lynn Sutton 1968 -
+Karl Frank Chase
12 Shawn Joseph Chase 1995 -
12 Samantha Joyce Chase 1997 -
*Partner of Bobbi Lynn Sutton:
+Mr. McHenry
12 Dani-Lynn McHenry 2006 -
10 Edna May Sutton 1937 -
+George Borton 1940 - 2000
10 Marjorie Louise Sutton 1940 -
+Lawrence Rose
11 Lawrence Rose
9 Marjorie Watson 1921 -
+Frank Cuifolo
7 Estella Cramer 1870 - 1942
+Winfield Peterson 1864 - 1917
7 William F. Cramer 1875 - 1936
+Elizabeth J. Headley 1881 - 1968
6 Charles Henry "Spide" Cramer 1839 -
+Sarah Jane Maxwell
6 Mary Elizabeth Cramer 1842 -
+William H. Mathis
6 Calab Smith "Swampy" Cramer 1844 -
+Mary Jane Robbins
6 Ellis S. Cramer 1845 -
6 Sarah Ann Cramer 1847 -
+John Hickman
6 Emma M. Cramer 1852 -
+Carlisle Gaskill
6 Chalkley Sears Cramer 1856 -
+Frances Caroline Johnson
6 Daniel D. Cramer 1858 -
+Anna M. Adams
5 Charles Fletcher Cramer
+Eliza Cale
5 John Smith Cramer
+[1] Dorcas Tabitha Cramer 1818 - 1853
5 Joseph Cramer
5 Mary Cramer
5 Esther Ann Cramer
+Abraham Cramer
5 Hannah Ann Cramer
+Charles Brewer
5 Elizabeth Cramer
4 Elizabeth Cramer
+Thomas Smith
4 John Cramer
+Nancy Jenkins
4 Isaiah Cramer
+Rachel Randolph
4 Jonathan Cramer
+Ann Brewer
4 Margaret Cramer
+John Randolph
4 Asa Smith Cramer

.... +Catherine Hall
.... 4 Hannah Cramer
.... +Isaiah Weeks
.... 4 Mary Cramer
.... +Samuel Weeks
.... 4 Jane Cramer
.... +John Hall
.... 4 William Cramer
.... +Elizabeth Jordan
.... 4 Elizabeth S. Cramer
.... +Benjamin B. Doughty
.... 3 Amy Cramer
.... 3 Mary Cramer
.... +Samuel Goldsmith
.... 3 Jacob Cramer
.... +Elizabeth ?
.... 3 Sylvanus Cramer
.... +Sarah Jane Gifford
.... 3 Ruth Cramer - 1793
.... 2 Jacob Cramer
.... +Phoebe Valentine
.... 2 Seymour/Semon Cramer
.... +Mary Smith
.... 2 Rachel Cramer
.... +Edward Allen, Sr.
.... 2 Elizabeth Cramer
.... +Nehemiah Mathis
.... 2 Rebecca Cramer
.... +William Carter
.... 2 Hannah Cramer
.... +Joseph Burns

Mr Darius Cramer Bible

1846

5 22 Turn ye.
5 25 A new Spirit.
5 30 God Eastward.
5 33 Leaf Heals.
5 60 Love Sincerely
412 Correction
411 Distant not Landmarks
411 Brawling Women
409 Seem Right
408 Back Slider
406 Dead Hell.
406 Fear Wisdom.

Proverbs.

34.4 Exodus Fourth Generation
Isaiah Chap 28. 1 to 6 V. Sick unto death.
Exodus. 14-14 Sabbath day P. 66.

Daniel S Cramer Departed this lief
July 14 1853 age 68 years 8 month 1 Day

Lorna

Family Record.

MARRIAGES.

Maried in jinuary
The 3 18 33.

Chalkley S. Cramer and
Lorina M. Cramer Were
Married May 16th 1854

William H Mathis
And Mary E Cramer
Were Married. Dec 25th 1864
~~Marriage of~~

MARRIAGES.

DARIUS CRAMER AND SARAH ANN
CRAMER WERE MARRIED,
JANUARY 3, A. D. 1833.

Family Record.

BIRTHS.	BIRTHS.
Darius Cramer Was Bornd in December the 8 day 1808	DARIUS CRAMER WAS BORN. DECEMBER 8, 1808
Sarah Ann Cramer Was Bornd in June the 29 day 1816	SARAH ANN CRAMER HIS WIFE. WAS BORN, JUNE 20, 1816.
	CHILDREN AGES.
Lovina Mariah Cramer Was Bornd in November the 27 day 1833	LOVINA MARIAH CRAMER WAS BORN, OCTOBER 27, 1833.
Hariet Bishup Cramer Was Bornd in Sepetember the 21 - 1835	
William G Cramer Was born August 10th day 1837	
Charles R Cramer Was Born in November the 26 day 1839	
Mary Elizabeth Cramer Was born September the 10 1842	

Family Record.

BIRTHS.	BIRTHS.
Caleb Smith Cramer Was Bornd in November The 29 day 1844	
Sarah Annah Cramer Was Bornd in May the 16 Day 1847	
Emma Matilda S Cramer was Born September the 17 1852	
[illegible]	

Family Record.

DEATHS.	DEATHS.
Deceased September the 19 1836 Darius Cramer Deceased September The 17. 1859. Mary E Mathis Departed This Life Nov 13th 1862 Lovina Mariah Mathis Deceased Jan. 19th. 1895	Chalkley S. Cramer Departed This Life Dec 13th 1855 Daniel S Cramer Departed This Life July 14 1853 age 68 years 8 Month 1 day Sarah Ann Mathis Departed this life May 23d 1897.

Descendants of Darius Cramer

Generation No. 1

1. DARIUS[7] CRAMER *(CHARLES[6], ISAAC[5], CALEB[4], STEPHEN[3], JOHN[2], WILLIAM[1])*[1] was born December 08, 1808[1], and died September 13, 1858[1]. He married SARAH ANN CRAMER[1] January 03, 1833[1], daughter of DANIEL CRAMER and CHARLOTTE LOVELAND. She was born June 29, 1816[1], and died May 27, 1897[1].

Notes for DARIUS CRAMER:
Reference #4142

More About DARIUS CRAMER:
Burial: Hillside Cemetary[1]

More About SARAH ANN CRAMER:
Burial: Hillside Cemetary[1]

Children of DARIUS CRAMER and SARAH CRAMER are:

i. LAVINIA[8] CRAMER[1], b. November 27, 1833[1]; d. 1895[1]; m. CHALKLEY S. CRAMER[1], May 16, 1854[1]; b. 1833[1]; d. December 13, 1855[1].
2. ii. WILLIAM G. CRAMER, b. August 10, 1837; d. November 29, 1912.
iii. CHARLES HENRY "SPIDE" CRAMER[1], b. October 30, 1839[1]; m. SARAH JANE MAXWELL.
iv. MARY ELIZABETH CRAMER[1], b. 1842[1]; m. WILLIAM H. MATHIS.
v. CALAB SMITH "SWAMPY" CRAMER[1], b. November 29, 1844[1]; m. MARY JANE ROBBINS.
vi. ELLIS S. CRAMER[1], b. 1845[1].
vii. SARAH ANN CRAMER[1], b. May 16, 1847[1]; m. JOHN HICKMAN.
viii. EMMA M. CRAMER[1], b. September 17, 1852[1]; m. CARLISLE GASKILL.
ix. CHALKLEY SEARS CRAMER[1], b. May 02, 1856[1]; m. FRANCES CAROLINE JOHNSON.
x. DANIEL D. CRAMER[1], b. March 1858[1]; m. ANNA M. ADAMS.

Generation No. 2

2. WILLIAM G.[8] CRAMER *(DARIUS[7], CHARLES[6], ISAAC[5], CALEB[4], STEPHEN[3], JOHN[2], WILLIAM[1])*[1] was born August 10, 1837[1], and died November 29, 1912[1]. He married MARY FRANCES MAXWELL[1]. She was born April 03, 1847[1], and died August 28, 1907[1].

More About WILLIAM G. CRAMER:
Burial: Hillside Cemetary[1]

More About MARY FRANCES MAXWELL:
Burial: Hillside Cemetary[1]

Children of WILLIAM CRAMER and MARY MAXWELL are:

i. MARY E.[9] CRAMER[1], b. June 27, 1868[1]; d. June 23, 1899[1]; m. GEORGE F. CRAMER[1], 1886[1]; b. August 11, 1854[1]; d. October 14, 1915[1].

More About MARY E. CRAMER:
Burial: Hillside Cemetary[1]

Notes for GEORGE F. CRAMER:
Reference #2543

More About GEORGE F. CRAMER:
Burial: Hillside Cemetary[1]

ii. ESTELLA CRAMER[1], b. August 10, 1870[1]; d. June 07, 1942[1]; m. WINFIELD PETERSON[1], March 30, 1889[1]; b. March 30, 1864[1]; d. December 29, 1917[1].

iii. WILLIAM F. CRAMER[1], b. December 06, 1875[1]; d. June 27, 1936[1]; m. ELIZABETH J. HEADLEY[1]; b. October 1881[1]; d. October 28, 1968[1].

Endnotes

1. Mancuso.FTW, Date of Import: Sep 6, 2000.

DARIUS CRAMER MARRIED SARAH ANN CRAMER SON OF CHARLES AND MARY GASKILL/CRAMER

SARAH ANN CRAMER IS DAUGHTER OF DANIEL S. CRAMER AND CHARLOTTE LOVELAND

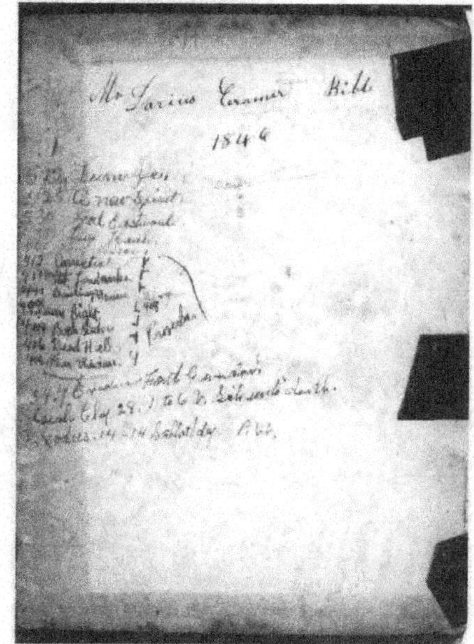

Darius Cramer

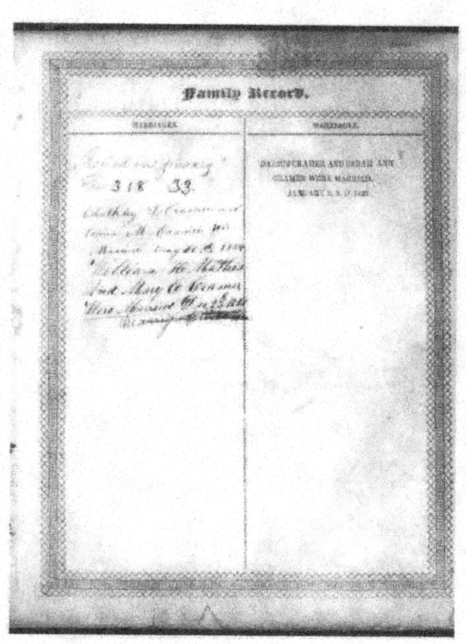

Family Record.

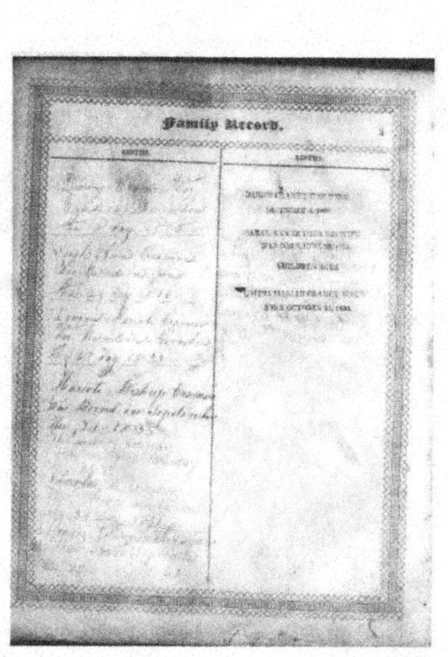

Family Record.

Descendants of Lavinia Cramer

Generation No. 1

1. LAVINIA[8] CRAMER *(DARIUS[7], CHARLES[6], ISAAC[5], CALEB[4], STEPHEN[3], JOHN[2], WILLIAM[1])*[1] was born November 27, 1833[1], and died 1895[1]. She married CHALKLEY S. CRAMER[1] May 16, 1854[1]. He was born 1833[1], and died December 13, 1855[1].

Endnotes

1. Mancuso.FTW, Date of Import: Sep 6, 2000.

LAVINIA CRAMER WIFE OF CHALKEY CRAMER

DAUGHTER OF DARIUS AND SARAH ANN CRAMER

CHALKEY FAMILY PICTURE

Descendants of Charles A. Cramer

Generation No. 1

1. CHARLES A.[7] CRAMER *(WILLIAM B.[6], WILLIAM[5], WILLIAM[4], WILLIAM[3], WILLIAM[2], WILLIAM[1])* was born June 15, 1821, and died September 01, 1892. He married ELIZABETH ADAMS, daughter of WILLIAM ADAMS and ELIZABETH TAYLOR. She was born September 03, 1825, and died October 16, 1914.

Notes for CHARLES A. CRAMER:
Reference #2217

More About CHARLES A. CRAMER:
Burial: Miller Cemetery, New Gretna, NJ

More About ELIZABETH ADAMS:
Burial: Miller Cemetery, New Gretna, NJ

Children of CHARLES CRAMER and ELIZABETH ADAMS are:

2. i. GEORGE F.[8] CRAMER, b. August 11, 1854; d. October 14, 1915.
ii. ELWOOD CRAMER, m. SARAH STACKHOUSE.

Notes for ELWOOD CRAMER:
Reference #2541

iii. WILLIAM H. CRAMER, b. 1846; d. April 1870.
iv. ALBERT ALLEN CRAMER.

Notes for ALBERT ALLEN CRAMER:
Reference #2542

v. SARAH M. CRAMER, b. April 06, 1857; d. July 28, 1860.
vi. MARY O. CRAMER, b. October 21, 1859.
vii. CHARLES A. CRAMER, b. September 11, 1863.
3. viii. HOWARD H. CRAMER, b. September 1864; d. 1941.

Generation No. 2

2. GEORGE F.[8] CRAMER *(CHARLES A.[7], WILLIAM B.[6], WILLIAM[5], WILLIAM[4], WILLIAM[3], WILLIAM[2], WILLIAM[1])*[1] was born August 11, 1854[1], and died October 14, 1915[1]. He married MARY E. CRAMER[1] 1886[1], daughter of WILLIAM CRAMER and MARY MAXWELL. She was born June 27, 1868[1], and died June 23, 1899[1].

Notes for GEORGE F. CRAMER:
Reference #2543

More About GEORGE F. CRAMER:
Burial: Hillside Cemetary[1]

More About MARY E. CRAMER:
Burial: Hillside Cemetary[1]

Children of GEORGE CRAMER and MARY CRAMER are:

i. DORA[9] CRAMER[1], b. September 1891; d. 1961; m. GROVER MAXWELL; b. October 06, 1884; d. June 04, 1939.

More About DORA CRAMER:

CHARLES A. CRAMER MARRIED ELIZABETH ADAMS

SON OF WILLIAM B. AND MARY ADAMS/CRAMER

Descendants of George F. Cramer

Generation No. 1

1. GEORGE F.[8] CRAMER *(CHARLES A.[7], WILLIAM B.[6], WILLIAM[5], WILLIAM[4], WILLIAM[3], WILLIAM[2], WILLIAM[1])*[1] was born August 11, 1854[1], and died October 14, 1915[1]. He married MARY E. CRAMER[1] 1886[1], daughter of WILLIAM CRAMER and MARY MAXWELL. She was born June 27, 1868[1], and died June 23, 1899[1].

Notes for GEORGE F. CRAMER:
Reference #2543

More About GEORGE F. CRAMER:
Burial: Hillside Cemetary[1]

More About MARY E. CRAMER:
Burial: Hillside Cemetary[1]

Children of GEORGE CRAMER and MARY CRAMER are:

2. i. DORA[9] CRAMER, b. September 1891; d. 1961.

ii. NORRIS C. CRAMER[1], b. December 20, 1886[1]; d. April 17, 1936[1]; m. ELSIE MICK[1], May 09, 1910[1]; b. September 08, 1888[1]; d. September 13, 1963[1].

More About NORRIS C. CRAMER:
Burial: Hillside Cemetary[1]

More About ELSIE MICK:
Burial: Hillside Cemetary[1]

3. iii. MARY EDNA CRAMER, b. May 06, 1888; d. July 22, 1928.

Generation No. 2

2. DORA[9] CRAMER *(GEORGE F.[8], CHARLES A.[7], WILLIAM B.[6], WILLIAM[5], WILLIAM[4], WILLIAM[3], WILLIAM[2], WILLIAM[1])*[1] was born September 1891, and died 1961. She married GROVER MAXWELL. He was born October 06, 1884, and died June 04, 1939.

More About DORA CRAMER:
Burial: Hillside Cemetary New Gretna, NJ

More About GROVER MAXWELL:
Burial: Hillside Cemetary, New Gretna, NJ

Children of DORA CRAMER and GROVER MAXWELL are:

i. CARLTON[10] MAXWELL, b. 1908; d. 1967.

ii. BABY ESTELLE MAXWELL, b. May.

3. MARY EDNA[9] CRAMER *(GEORGE F.[8], CHARLES A.[7], WILLIAM B.[6], WILLIAM[5], WILLIAM[4], WILLIAM[3], WILLIAM[2], WILLIAM[1])*[1] was born May 06, 1888[1], and died July 22, 1928[1]. She married THOMAS S. WATSON[1], son of JOHN WATSON and ELLA PIERCE. He was born August 06, 1882 in Gloucester County, NJ[1], and died May 03, 1964[1].

Notes for MARY EDNA CRAMER:
Reference #2925
This should be a correction to the above reference.

GEORGE F. CRAMER MARRIED TO MARY E. CRAMER

CHILDREN
DORA CRAMER
NORRIS CRAMER
MARY EDNA CRAMER

Hillside Cemetery

Cemetary marker

Descendants of Mary E. Cramer

Generation No. 1

1. MARY E.[9] CRAMER *(WILLIAM G.[8], DARIUS[7], CHARLES[6], ISAAC[5], CALEB[4], STEPHEN[3], JOHN[2], WILLIAM[1])*[1] was born June 27, 1868[1], and died June 23, 1899[1]. She married GEORGE F. CRAMER[1] 1886[1], son of CHARLES CRAMER and ELIZABETH ADAMS. He was born August 11, 1854[1], and died October 14, 1915[1].

More About MARY E. CRAMER:
Burial: Hillside Cemetary[1]

Notes for GEORGE F. CRAMER:
Reference #2543

More About GEORGE F. CRAMER:
Burial: Hillside Cemetary[1]

Children of MARY CRAMER and GEORGE CRAMER are:

2. i. DORA[10] CRAMER, b. September 1891; d. 1961.

ii. NORRIS C. CRAMER[1], b. December 20, 1886[1]; d. April 17, 1936[1]; m. ELSIE MICK[1], May 09, 1910[1]; b. September 08, 1888[1]; d. September 13, 1963[1].

More About NORRIS C. CRAMER:
Burial: Hillside Cemetary[1]

More About ELSIE MICK:
Burial: Hillside Cemetary[1]

3. iii. MARY EDNA CRAMER, b. May 06, 1888; d. July 22, 1928.

Generation No. 2

2. DORA[10] CRAMER *(MARY E.[9], WILLIAM G.[8], DARIUS[7], CHARLES[6], ISAAC[5], CALEB[4], STEPHEN[3], JOHN[2], WILLIAM[1])*[1] was born September 1891, and died 1961. She married GROVER MAXWELL. He was born October 06, 1884, and died June 04, 1939.

More About DORA CRAMER:
Burial: Hillside Cemetary New Gretna, NJ

More About GROVER MAXWELL:
Burial: Hillside Cemetary, New Gretna, NJ

Children of DORA CRAMER and GROVER MAXWELL are:

i. CARLTON[11] MAXWELL, b. 1908; d. 1967.

ii. BABY ESTELLE MAXWELL, b. May.

3. MARY EDNA[10] CRAMER *(MARY E.[9], WILLIAM G.[8], DARIUS[7], CHARLES[6], ISAAC[5], CALEB[4], STEPHEN[3], JOHN[2], WILLIAM[1])*[1] was born May 06, 1888[1], and died July 22, 1928[1]. She married THOMAS S. WATSON[1], son of JOHN WATSON and ELLA PIERCE. He was born August 06, 1882 in Gloucester County, NJ[1], and died May 03, 1964[1].

Notes for MARY EDNA CRAMER:
Reference #2925
This should be a correction to the above reference.

Wife of Thomas Watson

MARY E. CRAMER WIFE OF GEORGE F. CRAMER

DAUGHTER OF WILLIAM AND MARY FRANCES MAXWELL/CRAMER

Hillside Cemetery

Descendants of Dora Cramer

Generation No. 1

1. DORA[9] CRAMER *(GEORGE F.[8], CHARLES A.[7], WILLIAM B.[6], WILLIAM[5], WILLIAM[4], WILLIAM[3], WILLIAM[2], WILLIAM[1])*[1] was born September 1891, and died 1961. She married GROVER MAXWELL. He was born October 06, 1884, and died June 04, 1939.

More About DORA CRAMER:
Burial: Hillside Cemetary New Gretna, NJ

More About GROVER MAXWELL:
Burial: Hillside Cemetary, New Gretna, NJ

Children of DORA CRAMER and GROVER MAXWELL are:

i. CARLTON[10] MAXWELL, b. 1908; d. 1967.
ii. BABY ESTELLE MAXWELL, b. May.

Endnotes

1. Mancuso.FTW, Date of Import: Sep 6, 2000.

CARLTON MAXWELL
1906 — 1967

SON CARLTON

Hillside Cemetery

MAXWELL
GROVER S.
DORA C.
1891 — 1961

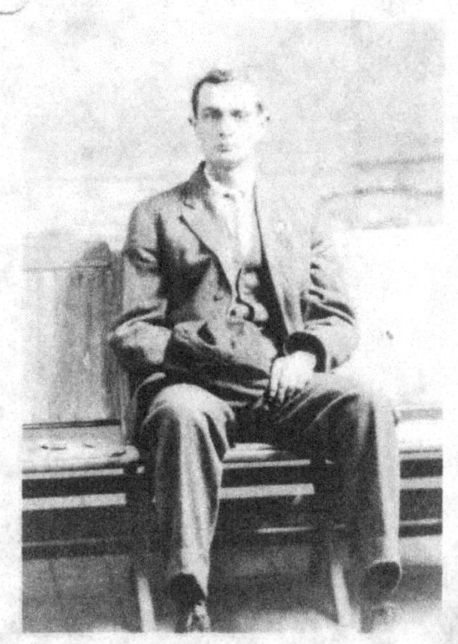

MAXWELL

DORA CRAMER/MAXWELL MARRIED GROVER MAXWELL

CHILDREN
CARLTON MAXWELL
ESTELLE MAXWELL DIED IN INFANCY

Descendants of Norris C. Cramer

Generation No. 1

1. NORRIS C.[9] CRAMER *(GEORGE F.[8], CHARLES A.[7], WILLIAM B.[6], WILLIAM[5], WILLIAM[4], WILLIAM[3], WILLIAM[2], WILLIAM[1])*[1] was born December 20, 1886[1], and died April 17, 1936[1]. He married ELSIE MICK[1] May 09, 1910[1]. She was born September 08, 1888[1], and died September 13, 1963[1].

More About NORRIS C. CRAMER:
Burial: Hillside Cemetary[1]

More About ELSIE MICK:
Burial: Hillside Cemetary[1]

Endnotes

1. Mancuso.FTW, Date of Import: Sep 6, 2000.

MARY E. CRAMER

JOHN S. CRAMER

GEORGE F. CRAMER
MOTHER
ELSIE M. CRAMER
1888 — 1963
CHARLES CRAMER'S SON
FATHER
CHARLES N. CRAMER
1886 — 1936

Millers' Cemetery

JOSEPH BAKER CRAMER

Millers Cemetery

Millers Cemetery

AUG 27 1861
CALEB L. CRAMER

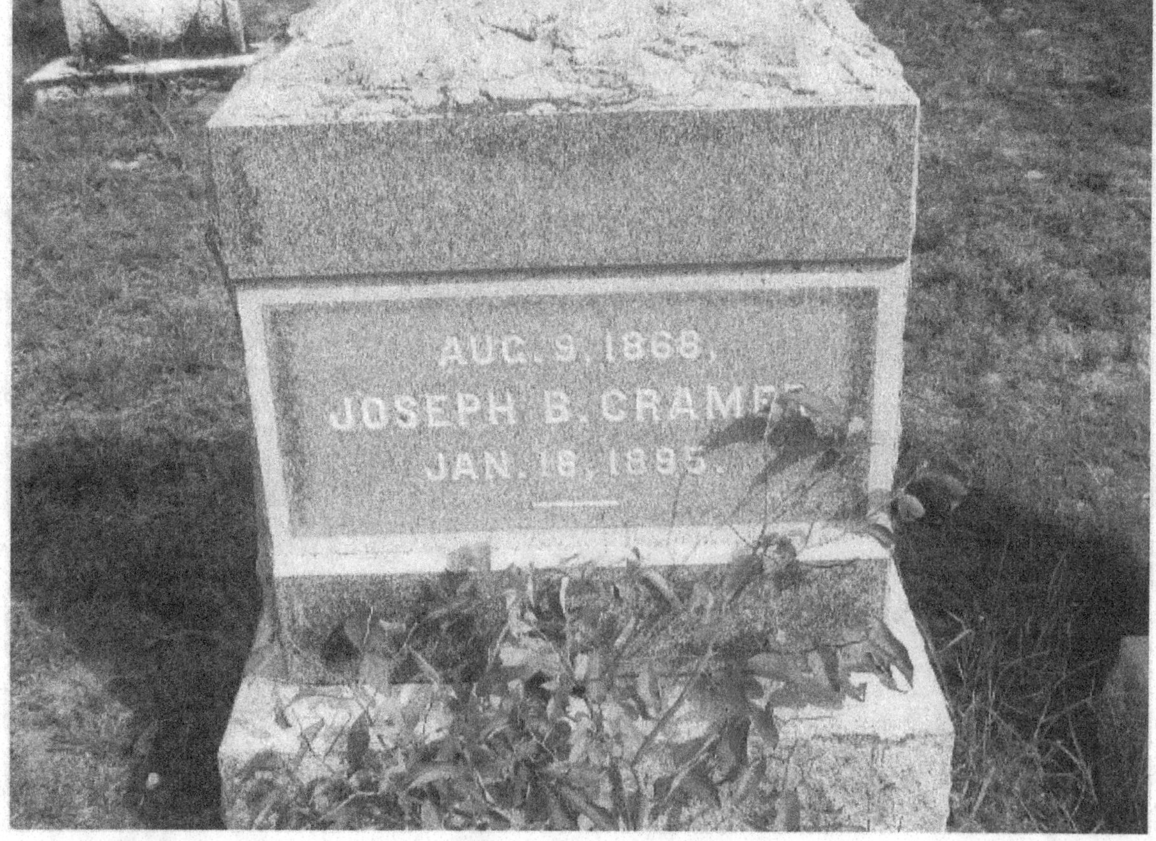
AUG. 9. 1868.
JOSEPH B. CRAME
JAN. 16. 1895.

Millers Cemetery

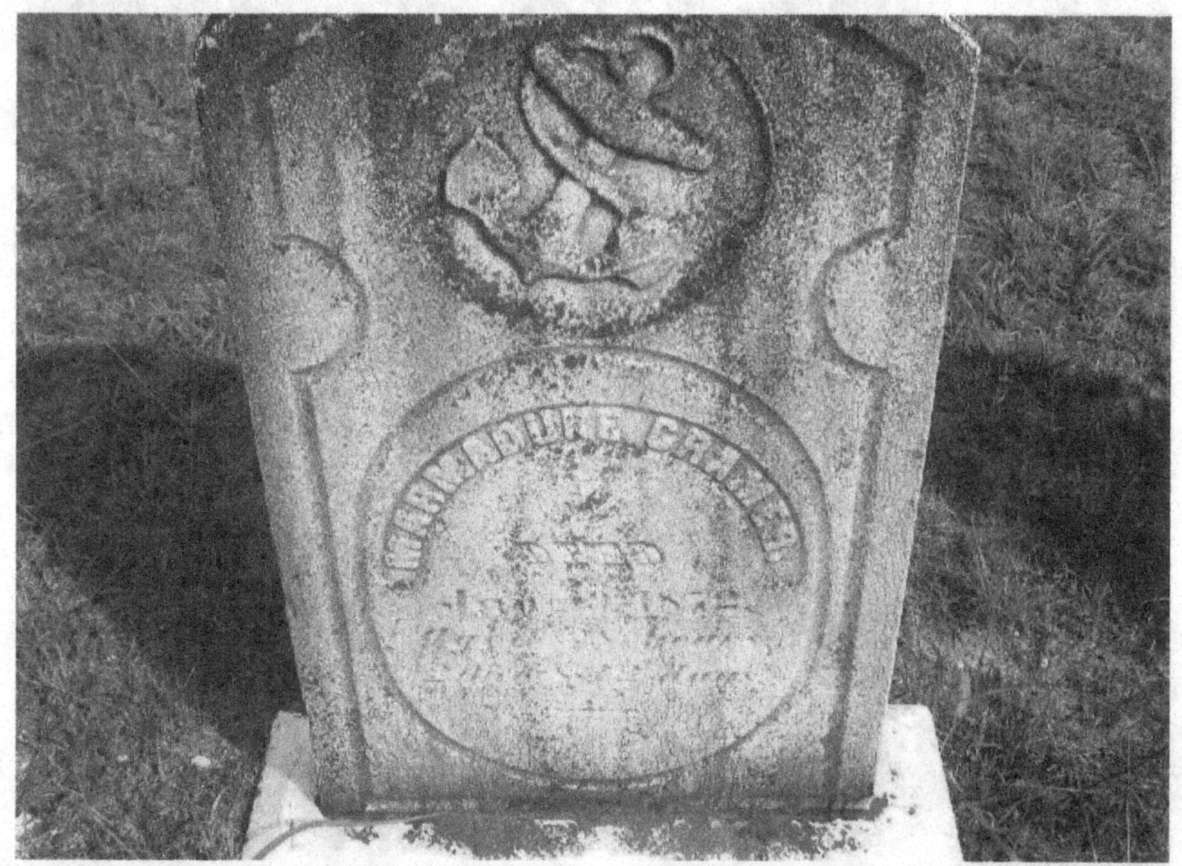

1828 — 1866

Millers Cemetery

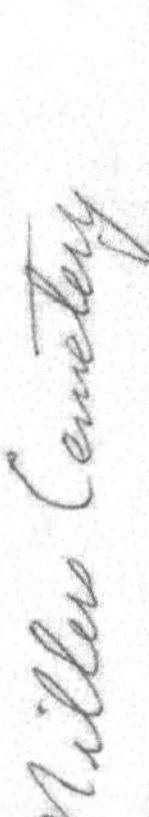
Miller Cemetery

CRAMER
Born 1850
Died 1923

SAMUEL P. CRAMER

Millers Cemetery

Miller Cemetery

Miller Cemetery

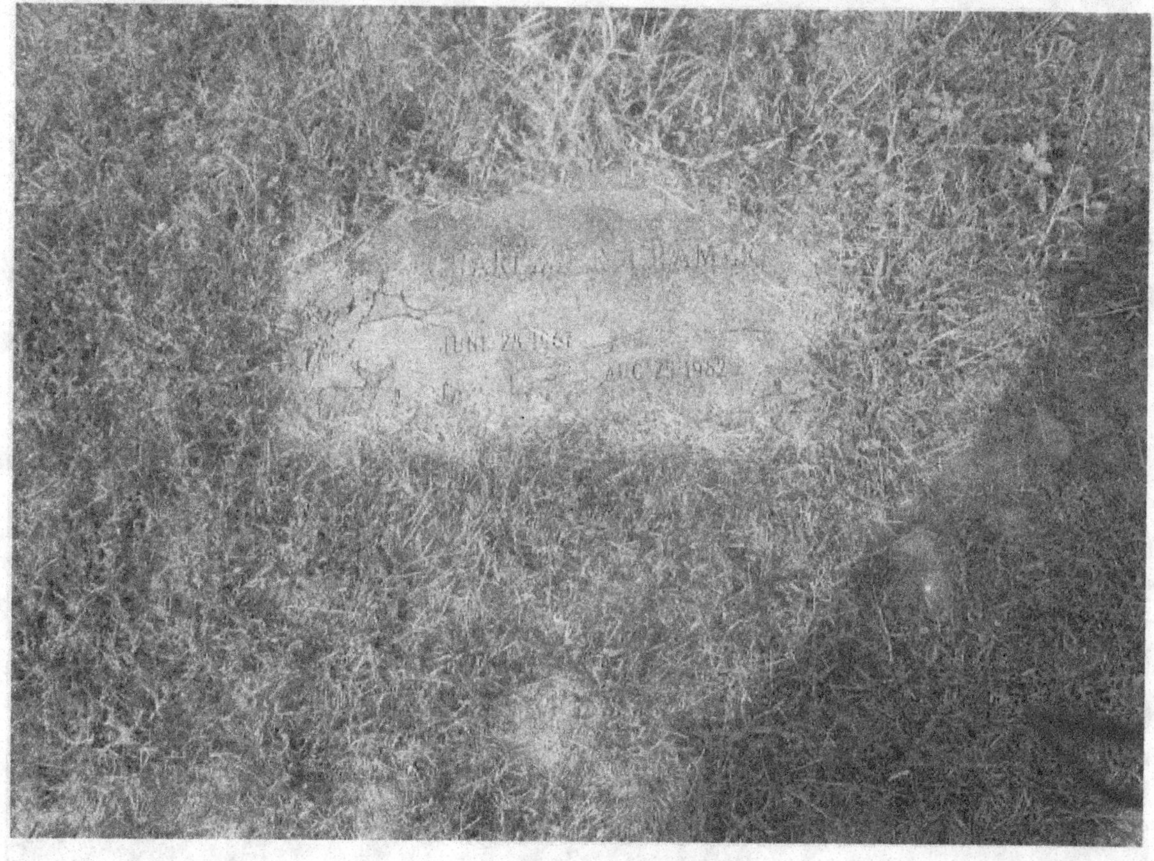

Millers Cemetery

pressofAtlanticCity.com
Life one page at a time

View/Sign Guestbook

Marguerite T. Keating Cramer

CRAMER, MARGUERITE T. KEATING, 48 - of Lower Bank, Washington Township, Burlington County, passed away on Sunday, November 11, 2007 at her home. She was born in Perth Amboy, formerly lived in Cherry Hill before moving to Lower Bank in 1974. She was a Barmaid at Lower Bank and Green Bank Taverns and sales clerk at Nesco Liquor Store. Marguerite was Washington Township Clean Community Coordinator, Planning and Zoning Board Member, Administrative council member of Lower Bank United Methodist Church, and trustee of Pinelands United Methodist Church. She is predeceased by her dad, Wilton Keating. She is survived by her husband, Douglas Cramer; her children, James Cramer and Laura Cramer; her mother, Marguerite Keating; her brothers, William, Keith, Eric, Mitchell, and Christopher. Marguerite's Viewing will be 10 a.m. to 12 Noon, Thursday, November 15, 2007 at Pinelands United Methodist Church of Lower Bank, River Rd., Lower Bank. Interment will follow at Lower Bank Cemetery. Memorials may be made to Green Bank Vol. Ambulance Squad, Lower Bank Vol. Fire Co., Pinelands United Methodist Church, or Atlanticare Hospice. Arrangements have been entrusted to Wimberg Funeral Home, 400 Liverpool Ave., Egg Harbor City, (609-965-0357) Condolences may be sent to www.wimbergfuneralhome.com

Published in The Press of Atlantic City on 11/13/2007.

Guest Book • Flowers • Gift Shop • Charities

Printer-friendly version E-mail to a friend

Guest Book Highlights

Marguerite T. Keating Cramer

November 13, 2007

You are all in our thoughts and prayers - Marguerite will be a missing link in the community! Keep your memories close, they'll guide you through the moments ahead!

Billie Sue (Dillon) Maclean (Laureldale, N

More »

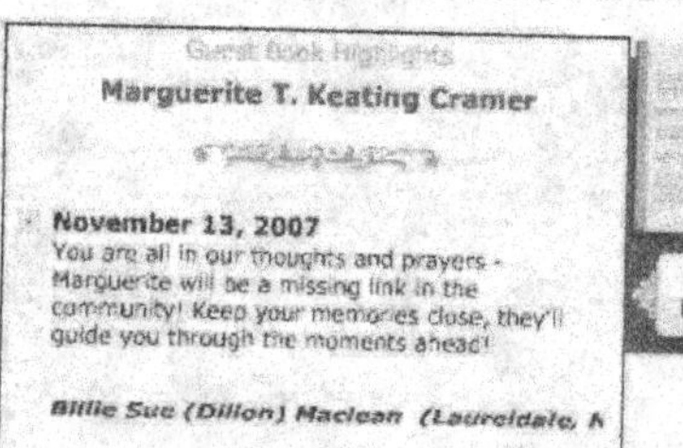

7 entries in this Guest Book.

Today's The Press of Atlantic City obituaries

Questions about obituaries or Guest Books?
Contact Legacy.com • Terms of use

Powered by Legacy.com
obituaries nationwide

MARY EDNA CRAMNER/CRAMER

MARRIED
THOMAS WATSON

THEIR THREE CHRILDREN ARE

HILMA, DORA AND MARJORY

Tom Watson

MARY EDNA CRAMNER/CRAMER

MARRIED
THOMAS WATSON

THEIR THREE CHRILDREN ARE

HILMA, DORA AND MARJORY

Tom Watson

EDNA CRAMER WATSON

EDNA CRAMER'S DAUGHTER

The Darius Cramer Bible is in the possession of Robert & Joyce Sutton, Lower Bank, N.J. The follow chart shows the family connections.

- **Darius Cramer (8 Dec 1808 - 13 Sep 1858)**
  & Sarah Ann Cramer (29 Jun 1816 - 27 May 1897)
  m. 3 Jan 1833
  - **Lavinia Cramer (1834 - 1895)**
    & Chalkley S. Cramer (1833 - 13 Dec 1855)
  - **Lavinia Cramer (1834 - 1895)**
    & Amasa Mathis (1831 - 17 Jan 1905)
  - **William G. Cramer (10 Aug 1837 - 29 Nov 1912)**
    & Mary Frances Maxwell (3 Apr 1847 - 28 Aug 1907)
    - **William Frank Cramer (6 Dec 1875 - 27 Jun 1936)**
      & Elizabeth J. Headley (Oct 1881 - 28 Oct 1968)
    - **Estella Cramer (10 Aug 1870 - 7 Jun 1942)**
      & Winfield Peterson (30 Mar 1864 - 29 Dec 1917)
      m. 30 Mar 1889
    - **Mary E. Cramer (27 Jun 1868 - 23 Jun 1899)**
      & George F. Cramer (11 Aug 1854 - 14 Oct 1915)
      m. 1886
      - **Norris C. Cramer (20 Dec 1886 - 17 Apr 1936)**
        & Elsie Mick (8 Sep 1888 - 13 Sep 1963)
        m. 9 May 1910
      - **Mary Edna Cramer (6 May 1888 - 22 Jul 1928)**
        & Thomas S. Watson (16 Aug 1882 - 3 May 1965)
        - **Hilma Watson (2 May 1910 -)**
          & Len Newcomer
          - **John Newcomer**
        - **Dora Watson (9 Feb 1915 - 15 Jan 1965)**
          & Robert O. Sutton (1907 - 13 Aug 1987)
          - **Robert Sutton Jr.**
            & Joyce Mancuso
        - **Marjorie Watson**
      - **Mary Edna Cramer (6 May 1888 - 22 Jul 1928)**
        & Unknown
        - **Maud Cramer (18 May 1906 - 6 Jun 1923)**
      - **Dora B. Cramer (Sep 1891 - 1961)**
        & Grover S. Maxwell (6 Oct 1884 - 4 Jun 1939)
        - **Charlton Maxwell**
        - **Estel Maxwell (20 Jun 1925 - 20 Jun 1925)**
      - **Unknown Cramer (12 Jan 1890 - 21 Jan 1890)**

Descendants of Alonzo Watson

1 Alonzo Watson
.. +Ann ?
.... 2 John Watson 1839 - 1889
.... +Ella Pierce 1843 -
.... 3 Sarah Watson 1869 -
.... 3 John Walker Watson 1870 - 1948
.... +Anna ? 1873 -
.... 4 Ervin Watson
.... 4 Emiline Watson
.... 3 Alonzo Watson 1878 -
.... +Stella ? - 1903
.... 3 Rebecca Watson 1880 - 1900
.... +George Vandergrife
.... 4 Edith Vandergrife 1900 -
.... +Robert Post
.... 3 Thomas S. Watson 1882 - 1964
.... +Mary Edna Cramer 1888 - 1928 } Watson M. Cramer
.... 4 Hilma Watson 1910 -
.... +Lindley Llewellyn Newcomer 1906 - 1992
.... 5 John Newcomer
.... +Barbara Lee Boffemmyer
.... 6 John Whitney Newcomer 1959 -
.... +Joan Lida Luby
.... 7 Leah Eliza Newcomer
.... 7 Adam Samuel Newcomer
.... 6 Thomas England Newcomer 1966 -
.... 5 Ronald Newcomer 1944 - 1963
.... 4 Dora Watson 1915 - 1965
.... +Robert O. Sutton 1906 - 1987
.... 5 Twin Baby Sutton 1930 - 1930
.... 5 Twin Baby Sutton 1930 - 1930
.... 5 Robert Thomas Sutton 1932 -
.... +Joyce F.. Mancuso 1934 -
.... 6 Dolores Lea Sutton 1958 -
.... 6 Susan Joyce Sutton 1964 -
.... +Christopher Keating
.... 7 Christopher Keating Jr.
.... 7 Benjamin Keating
.... 6 Bobbi Lynn Sutton 1968 -
.... +Karl Frank Chase
.... 7 Shawn Joseph Chase 1995 -
.... 7 Samantha Joyce Chase 1997 -
.... *Partner of Bobbi Lynn Sutton:
.... +Mr. McHenry
.... 7 Dani-Lynn McHenry 2006 -
.... 5 Edna May Sutton 1937 -
.... +George Borton 1940 - 2000
.... 5 Marjorie Louise Sutton 1940 -
.... +Lawrence Rose
.... 6 Lawrence Rose
.... 4 Marjorie Watson 1921 -
.... +Frank Cuifolo

Descendants of Alonzo Watson

Generation No. 1

1. ALONZO[1] WATSON He married ANN ?.

Child of ALONZO WATSON and ANN ? is:

2. i. JOHN[2] WATSON, b. Abt. 1839; d. September 13, 1889.

Generation No. 2

2. JOHN[2] WATSON *(ALONZO[1])* was born Abt. 1839, and died September 13, 1889. He married ELLA PIERCE August 16, 1863, daughter of JOSIAH PIERCE and HANNAH NASH. She was born Abt. 1843.

Notes for JOHN WATSON:
Received from the National Archives are 83 Pages of facts about John Watson, they have been numbered 1 to 83 and the page number will be inserted as references for each person.
According to the Birth Certificate of Thomas Watson, his father John Watsons' occupation was called Colier,(as far as we can determine from what Tom Watson told his grandson Robert Sutton,) this could be the term used for the maker of Charcoal. The word Colier was used in mining Coal, etc.
John enlisted in the Army Sept. 2, 1862 at Beverly NJ. Company G 25th Regiment, discharged July 20, 1863 he served as a private.
John died of Chronic Diareah contracted in the Army. There is an affidavit signed by J. Gaunt Ewards or Edwards M.D, stating this fact.
John's children received minors pension #566424, filed 6/13/1895, Certificate #282983. Each child received $2.00 per month.

Pg 22, 23, 27, 54, 70,

Notes for ELLA PIERCE:
The name Pierce is also spelled Pearce on a few of the documents received.

Page 54, 46,82

Children of JOHN WATSON and ELLA PIERCE are:

i. SARAH[3] WATSON, b. Abt. 1869.

Notes for SARAH WATSON:

3. ii. JOHN WALKER WATSON, b. August 16, 1870; d. July 25, 1948.

iii. ALONZO WATSON, b. April 09, 1878; m. STELLA ?; d. December 09, 1903.

Notes for STELLA ?:
Page in family bible says: Etta watson, wife of A. H. Watson departed this life Dec. 9, 1903.

4. iv. REBECCA WATSON, b. May 22, 1880; d. March 19, 1900.

5. v. THOMAS S. WATSON, b. August 06, 1882, Gloucester County, NJ; d. May 03, 1964.

Generation No. 3

3. JOHN WALKER[3] WATSON *(JOHN[2], ALONZO[1])* was born August 16, 1870, and died July 25, 1948. He married ANNA ?. She was born 1873.

More About JOHN WALKER WATSON:
Burial: Piney Hollow Cemetary

Notes for ANNA ?:
Census of 1930 shows John and Anna with 2 children, Erwin and Emiline

Children of JOHN WATSON and ANNA ? are:
i. ERVIN[4] WATSON.
ii. EMILINE WATSON.

4. REBECCA[3] WATSON *(JOHN[2], ALONZO[1])* was born May 22, 1880, and died March 19, 1900. She married GEORGE VANDERGRIFE.

Notes for REBECCA WATSON:
page 43, 58
Died at the age of 20 years, 7 months

Child of REBECCA WATSON and GEORGE VANDERGRIFE is:
i. EDITH[4] VANDERGRIFE, b. Abt. 1900; m. ROBERT POST.

5. THOMAS S.[3] WATSON *(JOHN[2], ALONZO[1])*[1] was born August 06, 1882 in Gloucester County, NJ[1], and died May 03, 1964[1]. He married MARY EDNA CRAMER[1], daughter of GEORGE CRAMER and MARY CRAMER. She was born May 06, 1888[1], and died July 22, 1928[1].

Notes for THOMAS S. WATSON:
Thomas Watson Listed the names of Sara and John in the family bible. I believe that Sara may have died as a child as nothing else can be found on her. We have been searching for a Walker Watson and found out that John's middle name is Walker.
Daniel E. Iszard resident of Mays Landing, Atlantic County, NJ was made legal gaurdian of Thomas, Rebecca and Alonzo On October 25, 1892 by Surrogate John S. Risley. (Ella remarried in 1891 and may have had to give up her children because of her new husband)??
Thomas died at the age of 81 years 8 months and 27 days old.

More About THOMAS S. WATSON:
Burial: Hillside Cemetary[1]

Notes for MARY EDNA CRAMER:
Reference #2925
This should be a correction to the above reference.
Mary Edna Cramer had a daughter before she married Thomas Watson. Her daughter was named Maud Cramer born May 18, 1906, died June 6, 1923.
Maud Cramer is buried along side her mother Mary Edna Watson, at Hillside Cemetery, New Gretna, NJ.

More About MARY EDNA CRAMER:
Burial: Hillside Cemetary[1]

Children of THOMAS WATSON and MARY CRAMER are:
6. i. HILMA[4] WATSON, b. May 02, 1910.
7. ii. DORA WATSON, b. February 09, 1915; d. January 15, 1965.
iii. MARJORIE WATSON[1], b. 1921[1]; m. FRANK CUIFOLO[1].

Generation No. 4

6. HILMA[4] WATSON *(THOMAS S.[3], JOHN[2], ALONZO[1])*[1] was born May 02, 1910[1]. She married LINDLEY

Descendants of John Watson

Generation No. 1

1. JOHN[2] WATSON *(ALONZO[1])* was born Abt. 1839, and died September 13, 1889. He married ELLA PIERCE August 16, 1863, daughter of JOSIAH PIERCE and HANNAH NASH. She was born Abt. 1843.

Notes for JOHN WATSON:
Received from the National Archives are 83 Pages of facts about John Watson, they have been numbered 1 to 83 and the page number will be inserted as references for each person.
According to the Birth Certificate of Thomas Watson, his father John Watsons' occupation was called Colier,(as far as we can determine from what Tom Watson told his grandson Robert Sutton,) this could be the term used for the maker of Charcoal. The word Colier was used in mining Coal, etc.
John enlisted in the Army Sept. 2, 1862 at Beverly NJ. Company G 25th Regiment, discharged July 20, 1863 he served as a private.
John died of Chronic Diareah contracted in the Army. There is an affidavit signed by J. Gaunt Ewards or Edwards M.D, stating this fact.
John's children received minors pension #566424, filed 6/13/1895, Certificate #282983. Each child received $2.00 per month.

Pg 22, 23, 27, 54, 70,

Notes for ELLA PIERCE:
The name Pierce is also spelled Pearce on a few of the documents received.

Page 54, 46,82

Children of JOHN WATSON and ELLA PIERCE are:

i. SARAH[3] WATSON, b. Abt. 1869.

Notes for SARAH WATSON:

2. ii. JOHN WALKER WATSON, b. August 16, 1870; d. July 25, 1948.

iii. ALONZO WATSON, b. April 09, 1878; m. STELLA ?; d. December 09, 1903.

Notes for STELLA ?:
Page in family bible says: Etta watson, wife of A. H. Watson departed this life Dec. 9, 1903.

3. iv. REBECCA WATSON, b. May 22, 1880; d. March 19, 1900.

4. v. THOMAS S. WATSON, b. August 06, 1882, Gloucester County, NJ; d. May 03, 1964.

Generation No. 2

2. JOHN WALKER[3] WATSON *(JOHN[2], ALONZO[1])* was born August 16, 1870, and died July 25, 1948. He married ANNA ?. She was born 1873.

More About JOHN WALKER WATSON:
Burial: Piney Hollow Cemetary

Notes for ANNA ?:
Census of 1930 shows John and Anna with 2 children, Erwin and Emiline

Children of JOHN WATSON and ANNA ? are:

i. ERVIN[4] WATSON.
ii. EMILINE WATSON.

3. REBECCA[3] WATSON *(JOHN[2], ALONZO[1])* was born May 22, 1880, and died March 19, 1900. She married GEORGE VANDERGRIFE.

Notes for REBECCA WATSON:
page 43, 58
Died at the age of 20 years, 7 months

Child of REBECCA WATSON and GEORGE VANDERGRIFE is:
i. EDITH[4] VANDERGRIFE, b. Abt. 1900; m. ROBERT POST.

4. THOMAS S.[3] WATSON *(JOHN[2], ALONZO[1])*[1] was born August 06, 1882 in Gloucester County, NJ[1], and died May 03, 1964[1]. He married MARY EDNA CRAMER[1], daughter of GEORGE CRAMER and MARY CRAMER. She was born May 06, 1888[1], and died July 22, 1928[1].

Notes for THOMAS S. WATSON:
Thomas Watson Listed the names of Sara and John in the family bible. I believe that Sara may have died as a child as nothing else can be found on her. We have been searching for a Walker Watson and found out that John's middle name is Walker.
Daniel E. Iszard resident of Mays Landing, Atlantic County, NJ was made legal gaurdian of Thomas, Rebecca and Alonzo On October 25, 1892 by Surrogate John S. Risley. (Ella remarried in 1891 and may have had to give up her children because of her new husband)??
Thomas died at the age of 81 years 8 months and 27 days old.

More About THOMAS S. WATSON:
Burial: Hillside Cemetary[1]

Notes for MARY EDNA CRAMER:
Reference #2925
This should be a correction to the above reference.
Mary Edna Cramer had a daughter before she married Thomas Watson. Her daughter was named Maud Cramer born May 18, 1906, died June 6, 1923.
Maud Cramer is buried along side her mother Mary Edna Watson, at Hillside Cemetery, New Gretna, NJ.

More About MARY EDNA CRAMER:
Burial: Hillside Cemetary[1]

Children of THOMAS WATSON and MARY CRAMER are:
i. HILMA[4] WATSON[1], b. May 02, 1910[1]; m. LINDLEY LLEWELLYN NEWCOMER[1], September 1934, New York City, NY; b. March 08, 1906, Connellsville, PA; d. December 1992, Tampa, Fl.
ii. DORA WATSON[1], b. February 09, 1915[1]; d. January 15, 1965[1]; m. ROBERT O. SUTTON[1]; b. October 24, 1906[2,2,2,2,2,2,2,2,2,2,2,2,2,2,2,3,4]; d. August 1987[5,5,5,5,5,5,5,5,5,5,5,5,5,5,5,6,7].

Notes for DORA WATSON:
Reference #3180
The twins are buried behind Maud Cramer, there are two little stones sticking out of the ground to mark their graves.

More About DORA WATSON:
Burial: Hillside cemetery, New Gretna[8]

Notes for ROBERT O. SUTTON:
[Genealogy.com, Family Archive #110, Vol. 2 L-Z, Ed. 9, Social Security Death Index: U.S., Date of Import: Dec 30, 2000, Internal Ref. #1.112.9.111416.32]

Individual: Sutton, Robert

Social Security #: 148-07-6985
Issued in: New Jersey

Birth date: Oct 24, 1906
Death date: Aug 1987

Residence code: New Jersey

ZIP Code of last known residence: 08224
Location associated with this ZIP Code:

New Gretna, New Jersey

Robert Sutton told his childred that the O. in his name stood for Osborn but we have not been able to verify this. His grandfather's middle initial also was an O. (for some reason either lost in the mail, etc. his birth certificate has never been registered. I am going to try and register him through the family bible and other papers we have).

More About ROBERT O. SUTTON:
Burial: Hillside cemetery, New Gretna[8]
Social Security Number: Social Security #: 148-07-6985[9,10]

iii. MARJORIE WATSON[10], b. 1921[10]; m. FRANK CUIFOLO[10].

Endnotes

1. Mancuso.FTW, Date of Import: Sep 6, 2000.
2. Broderbund Family Archive #110, Vol. 2, Ed. 7, Social Security Death Index: U.S., Date of Import: May 20, 2000, Internal Ref. #1.112.7.115546.117
3. Mancuso.FTW, Date of Import: Sep 6, 2000.
4. Genealogy.com, Family Archive #110, Social Security Death Index: U.S. Ed. 9, Social Security Death Index, Release date: April 10, 2000, Internal Ref. #1.112.9.111416.32.
5. Broderbund Family Archive #110, Vol. 2, Ed. 7, Social Security Death Index: U.S., Date of Import: May 20, 2000, Internal Ref. #1.112.7.115546.117
6. Mancuso.FTW, Date of Import: Sep 6, 2000.
7. Genealogy.com, Family Archive #110, Social Security Death Index: U.S. Ed. 9, Social Security Death Index, Release date: April 10, 2000, Internal Ref. #1.112.9.111416.32.
8. Mancuso.FTW, Date of Import: Sep 6, 2000.
9. Broderbund Family Archive #110, Vol. 2, Ed. 7, Social Security Death Index: U.S., Date of Import: May 20, 2000, Internal Ref. #1.112.7.115546.117
10. Mancuso.FTW, Date of Import: Sep 6, 2000.

JOHN WATSON MARRIED ELLA PIERCE/WATSON
SON OF ALONZO WATSON AND ANN ?/WATSON

SERVED IN THE CIVIL WAR

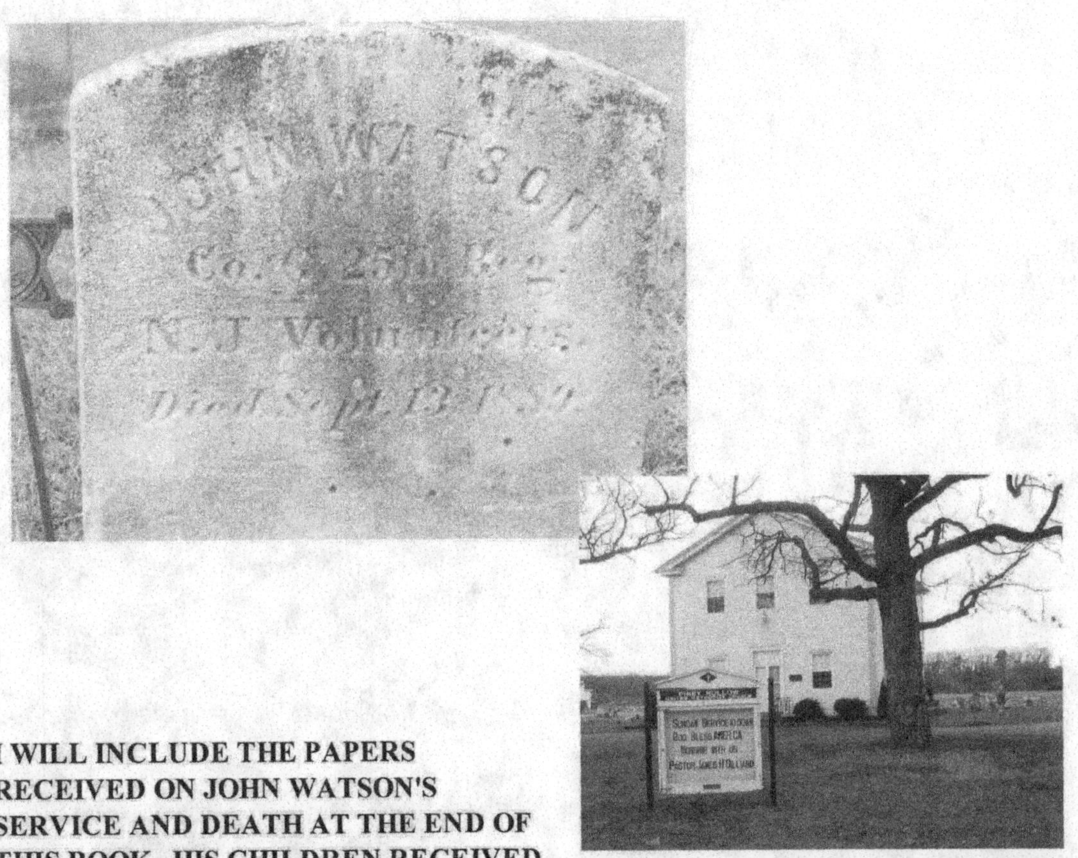

I WILL INCLUDE THE PAPERS RECEIVED ON JOHN WATSON'S SERVICE AND DEATH AT THE END OF THIS BOOK. HIS CHILDREN RECEIVED COMPENSATION FROM THE GOVERMENT. HIS DAUGHTER REBECCA DIED SOON AFTER GIVING CHILD BIRTH TO EDITH VANDERGRIEF. SO FAR I HAVE NOT BEEN ABLE TO FIND ANY RECORDS OF REBECCA'S HUSBAND. HER DAUGHTER EDITH MARRIED ROBERT POST FROM NEW GRETNA AND THEY LIVED IN FLORIDA UNTIL THEIR DEATH.

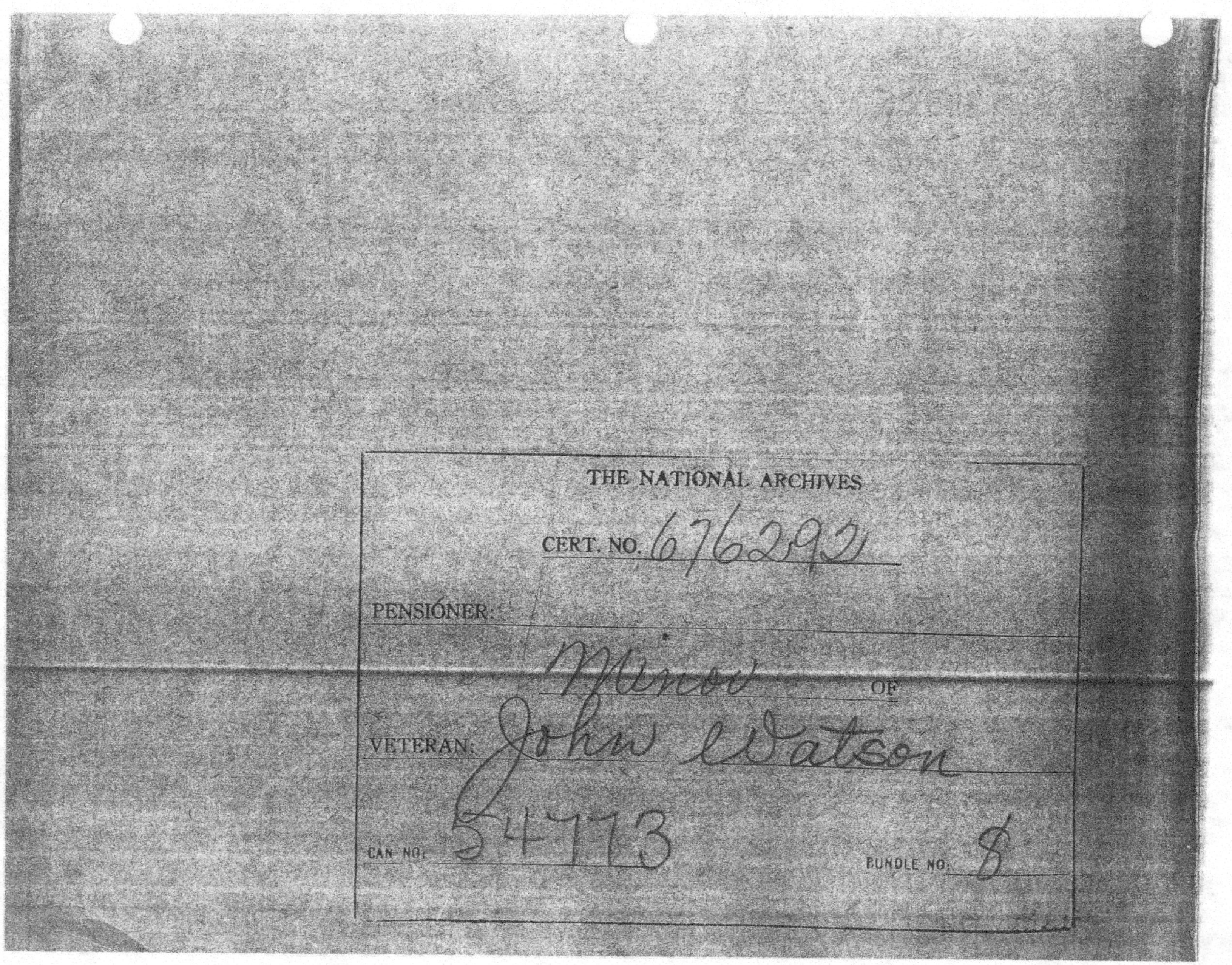
THE NATIONAL ARCHIVES

CERT. NO. 676292

PENSIONER: Minor OF

VETERAN: John Watson

CAN NO. 54773 BUNDLE NO. 8

Piney Hollow Cemetery, Franklin Twp

Howard Edward SUESS, Sr. Am.	Aug 12, 1919		Jun 18, 1959	U.S.N.R.
Linda Lee SUESS		1957		5 mo.
Ruth TRIMNELL	1915	1922		
Albert TICE	1894		Jan 3, 1973	
S. Roy TRIMNELL (hus)	1905	1973		
Jessie TRIMNELL (w)	1897	1973		
Alberta R. TICE	1907		Nov 30, 1969	
James A. VANDERSLICE			May 1, 1889	74y 4m 6
John J. WADE	1909	1974		
Mary WHITAKER (hus David)			Jul 18, 1868	71
Harriet WHITAKER (dau of Alex & Sarah)			Jul 25, 1872	2m 3d
X John WATSON (Co. C 25 Reg. N.J. Vol.)			Sep 13, 1889	
David WALKER (son)				
James L. WALKER (son)	Jan 6, 1873		Apr 28, 1875	
Charles P. WALKER (son)	May 6, 1871		Sep 21, 1872	
Anna R. WALKER (dau)	Aug 1, 1868		Jul 25, 1872	
Hannah R. WALKER (w)	Feb 5, 1835		Jul 1, 1883	
John F. WALKER (hus)	Sep 30, 1829		Jun 12, 1881	
Mary E. YAPP (hus Samuel YAPP)			Jan 26, 1863	24 yr.

GENERAL AFFIDAVIT.

State of New Jersey, County of Atlantic, ss:

In the matter of John Watson - Co I. 25. N.J.

ON THIS 18 day of December A. D. 1890; personally appeared before me a Surrogate in and for the aforesaid County duly authorized to administer oaths, Ella Watson aged 41 years, a resident of May's Landing in the County of Atlantic and State of N.J. whose Post Office address is Mays Landing N.J.

aged years, a resident of

in the County of and State of

whose Post Office address is

well known to me to be reputable and entitled to credit, and who, being duly sworn, declared in relation to aforesaid case as follows:

[NOTE.—Affiants should state how they gain a knowledge of the facts to which they testify.]

She is the claimant and that there is no record public or private of her marriage nor of the death of her husband, & That the minister who performed the marriage ceremony is now dead.

STATE OF New Jersey, COUNTY OF Atlantic, ss:

Sworn to and subscribed before me this day by the above-named affiant, and I certify that I read said affidavit to said affiant, including the words .... erased, and the words .... added and acquainted her with its contents before she executed the same. I further certify that I am in nowise interested in said case, nor am I concerned in its prosecution; and that said affiant is personally known to me and that she is a credible person.

J S Risley
(Official Signature.)

[L. S.]

Surrogate
(Official Character.)

I, ... Clerk of the County Court in and for aforesaid County and State, do certify that ...., Esq., who has signed his name to the foregoing declaration and affidavit was at the time of so doing .... in and for said County and State, duly commissioned and sworn; that all his official acts are entitled to full faith and credit, and that his signature thereunto is genuine.

Witness my hand and seal of office, this .... day of ...., 18 .....

[L. S.] Clerk of the ....

NOTE.—This should be sworn to before a CLERK OF COURT, NOTARY PUBLIC or JUSTICE OF THE PEACE. If before a JUSTICE or NOTARY, then CLERK OF COUNTY COURT must add his certificate of character hereon, and not on a separate slip of paper.

(3—143.)

Index Widow, Claim No. 408593

John Watson Co. G, 25th Reg't N. J. Vols.

ARRANGE PAPERS IN INVALID CLAIMS—1. Declaration; 2. Soldier's statements as to origin; 3. A. G.; 4. S. G.; 5. Cert. of Dis. Let history as to origin, continuance, &c., follow in regular order.

IN WIDOWS' AND DEPENDENT RELATIVES' CLAIMS—Let evidence of soldier's death, marriage, dependence, &c., follow evidence of origin and continuance of fatal disease.

o 6—113

NO.	NAME AND P. O. ADDRESS.	DATE OF FILING.	SUBJECT.
1	Claimant	July 28" 90	Declaration
2	Adjt. Genl's Rpt.	May 7" 90	
3	Claimant	Dec. 27" 90	As to marriage
4	Dr. J. G. Edwards Williamstown, N. J.	Sept. 18" 90	Date of death,
5	W. Graff, Shiloh, N. J.	Dec. 4" 90	Marriage, no prior, supp.
6	H. Brown Williamstown, N. J.	Dec. 4" 90	Marriage, no prior supp.
7	H. Brown Clementon, N. J.	—	Birth Alonzo
8	M. Clark — N. J.	—	Birth of Rebecca L.
9	Trans. from pet. rec	Jan 13" 90	Birth of Thomas

STATE OF NEW JERSEY.

ATLANTIC COUNTY, ss.

I, JOHN S. RISLEY, Surrogate of the County of Atlantic, do hereby certify that on the Twenty-fifth *day of* October *A. D. 189*2, *the Orphans' Court of said County of Atlantic,* not being in Session & *admitted* Daniel E. Isgara *of the County of* Atlantic *as Guardian of the person and property of* Alonzo Watson

being a minor above *the age of fourteen years.*

Witness my hand and seal of office the Twenty-fifth *day of* October *in the year of our Lord one thousand eight hundred and ninety* -two.

J S Risley *Surrogate.*

STATE OF NEW JERSEY.

ATLANTIC COUNTY, ss.

I, JOHN S. RISLEY, Surrogate of the County of Atlantic, do hereby certify that on the Twenty-fifth *day of* October *A. D. 1892, the Orphans' Court of said County of Atlantic,* not being in session I *admitted* Daniel E. Iszard *of the County of* Atlantic *as Guardian of the persons and property of* Rebecca L. Watson and Thomas S. Watson *being minors* under *the age of fourteen years.*

Witness my hand and seal of office the Twenty-fifth *day of* October *in the year of our Lord one thousand eight hundred and ninety-*two.

J. S. Risley *Surrogate.*

7

PENSION A NOV 27 189[illegible]

DANIEL E. ISZARD,
JUSTICE OF THE PEACE
AND
REAL ESTATE AGENT, CONVEYANCER
AND NOTARY PUBLIC,
Agent Cumberland Fire Insurance Co.
P. O. Box 242.

May's Landing, N. J. Nov 16th 1892

Jas F Rusling Esq

Dear Sir

Mrs Watson has not a family Bible. When they children were born they lived at Piney Hollow and I could only get evidence since they resided at Mays Landing or Atlantic county — I have given all the facts that I can obtain — She received her pension up to time of her marriage 2d time — and I cannot see why the children cannot get their just dues now

Yours Truly

D E Iszard

This Blank for use in Cases of JAMES F. RUSLING, only.

G C.

INSTRUCTIONS.—Execute before a NOTARY PUBLIC, JUSTICE OF THE PEACE, or other Officer authorized to take general affidavits, and return to JAMES F. RUSLING, Trenton, N. J.

STATE OF New Jersey } ss.
COUNTY OF Atlantic }

Co "G" 25 N.J.

In the matter of David E. Izzard Gdn. Chd. John Watson for Pension.

Personally came before me, a clerk of the circuit court in and for aforesaid County and State said Izzard who, being duly sworn, declares in relation to aforesaid case as follows: (See "Instructions" herewith. Comply with same, or explain why you cannot.)

that the contents of annexed letter to James F Rusling dated Nov. 16/93 are true & correct.

And as to whether the above testimony was all written, or prepared for type writing (as case may be) in my presence, and only from my oral statements then made, I say as follows; said letter was [Give fact.] written by me

and that said statements were ~~made by me to~~ [illegible] before [Give Notary or Magistrate's Name.], on the .... day of .... A. D. 18...., at .... in state of ....; that as to whether in making the same I used, or was aided or prompted by any written or printed statement or recital, prepared or dictated by any other person and not attached as an exhibit to this affidavit, I say as follows: I did not use any [Give facts.] statement whatever.

[OVER.]

If Deponent signs by *mark*, two witnesses here to *his* signature by *mark* opposite.

Residence and P. O. Address:

Residence and P. O. Address:

Daniel E. Ezard
[Deponent sign here.]

Residence and P. O. Address: Mays Landing N.J.

Sworn to and subscribed before me this day; and I further certify I read said affidavit to said deponent, or acquainted him with its contents fully, before he executed the same; I am in no wise interested in said case; and said deponent is known to me to be a credible person.

Witness my hand and official seal this 18th day of November A. D. 1893

SEAL

Sign here Lewis Evans
[Notary or Magistrate's Signature.]

(If any) P. O. Address [Notary or Magistrate's.] County Clerk [Official Character.]

☞ Note—The Officer should attach his Official Seal, or send Certificate of Official Character, unless already on file.

☞ Attention invited to this Trenton, N. J., Pension Claim Agency, with Army and Pension experience since 1861. Business with U. S. Gov't being *by letter*, and Trenton, N. J., only short distance from Washington, D. C., with *many mails there and return* daily, this N. J. Agency, of course, *not exceeded* by Washington, D. C., or other Agencies. *Experienced, prompt, successful.* None surer or quicker.

Many everywhere still entitled to **Pension**, or to **Increase of Pension**, under Old or New Law. **Now is** *good* time to apply. As a rule, increased age brings increased disability, and hence Increase of Pension now in order, if applied for properly, if worse or pensioned less than $12 a month.

☞ Remember this N. J. Agency not confined to New Jersey, but Pension Cases here from all United States Canada, Europe, &c., and prosecuted same as N. J. cases. Others in *your vicinity* or *knowledge* solicited. No charge, unless *successful*, and then fee, as fixed by U. S. Law.

☞ *Thousands of Pension, Bounty and other Claims, allowed through this Agency, and others being allowed here daily.*

G.C.

CASE OF

Ezard, Daniel E.

No. 356,424

FOR

PENSION.

GENERAL AFFIDAVIT

Claimant

FILED BY

JAMES F. RUSLING,

Counsellor at Law, U. S.

TRENTON, N. J.

(Brig. Gen'l, late U. S. Pension Agent, N. J.)

☞ Refers to Gov., Adj't Gen'l, U. S. Senators and M. C.'s of N. J.; Gen'ls Sewell, Price, Ward, Ramsey, Grubb, N. J.; Sickles, Sharpe, Carr, N. Y.; Wagner, Gregg, Pa.; Wood, O., and others.

This Blank for use in Cases of JAMES F. RUSLING, only.

GC.

INSTRUCTIONS.—Execute before a NOTARY PUBLIC, JUSTICE OF THE PEACE, or other Officer authorized to take general affidavits, and return to JAMES F. RUSLING, Trenton, N. J.

STATE OF New Jersey } ss.
COUNTY OF Atlantic }

In the matter of Daniel E Lizard Gd of child of John Watson "G" 25013 for Pension.

Personally came before me, a clerk of the said county of Atlantic in and for aforesaid County and State said claimant who, being duly sworn, declares in relation to aforesaid case as follows: (See "Instructions" herewith. Comply with same, or explain why you cannot.)

That he knows of no public or church record of the birth of said soldiers children Alonzo and Rebecca, that the physician present at their births is dead and the only other person who was present was the grand mother of said children and she is also dead in lieu thereof he herewith submits the affidavits of two persons who have known said children nearly ever since they were born and know that they were legitimate

And as to whether the above testimony was all written, or prepared for type-writing (as case may be) in my presence, and only from my oral statements then made, I say as follows; That I wrote the above facts myself [Give fact.]

and that said statements were made by me to .... [Give Notary or Magistrate's Name.] on the .... day of .... A. D. 18...., at .... in state of ....; that as to whether in making the same I used, or was aided or prompted by any written or printed statement or recital, prepared or dictated by any other person and not attached as an exhibit to this affidavit, I say as follows: I was not prompted or dictated to by any person [Give facts.]

[OVER.]

If Deponent signs by *mark*, two witnesses here to *his* signature by *mark* opposite.

....

Residence and P. O. Address: ....

....

Residence and P. O. Address: ....

Daniel E. Izard
[Deponent sign here.]

Residence and P. O. Address: Mays Landing N.J.

Sworn to and subscribed before me this day; and I further certify I read said affidavit to said deponent, or acquainted him with its contents fully, before he executed the same; I am in no wise interested in said case; and said deponent is known to me to be a credible person.

....

Witness my hand and official seal this 13th day of November A. D. 1893

(SEAL.) (If any.)

Sign here Lewis Evans
[Notary or Magistrate's Signature.]

P. O. Address .... [Notary or Magistrate's.]

County Clerk
[Official Character.]

☞ *Note.*—The Officer should attach his Official Seal, or send Certificate of Official Character, unless already on file.

G.C.

CASE OF

Izard Daniel E.
Gd. chd. John Staten,
dec'd. "G" 24 N.J.

No. 566,424

FOR

PENSION.

GENERAL AFFIDAVIT.

Daniel E. Izard

PENSION OFFICE NOV 20 1893

FILED BY

JAMES F. RUSLING,

Counsellor at Law, U. S.

TRENTON, N. J.

(Brig. Gen'l, late U.S. Pension Agent, N. J.)

☞ Refers to Gov., Adj't Gen'l, U.S. Senators and M. C.'s of N. J.; Gen'ls Sewell, Price, Ward, Ramsey, Grubb, N. J.; Sickles, Sharpe, Carr, N. Y.; Wagner, Gregg, Pa.; Wood, O., and others.

915.)

F F

Declaration for Pension of Children under Sixteen years of age.

STATE OF New Jersey, COUNTY OF Atlantic, ss:

On this Twelfth day of December, A. D. one thousand eight hundred and ~~eighty~~ ninety two personally appeared before me the same being a court of record within and for the county and State aforesaid, Daniel E Gazard a resident of Mays Landing, county of Atlantic, in the State of New Jersey aged 56 years, who, being duly sworn according to law, makes the following declaration in order to obtain the pension provided by Acts of Congress for children under sixteen years of age: That he is the only legal guardian of Alonzo Watson, Rebecca L Watson and Thomas S Watson three, legitimate children of John Watson enlisted under the name of John Watson at Beverly, on the second day of September, A. D. 1862 [2] in Company G 25th Regiment of N J vol in the war of Rebellion, who died [3] Sept 13th 1889 with Chronic diarrah supposed to have been contracted in army at Piney Holly, on the 13th day of September, A. D. 1889, and who bore at the time of his death the rank of Private citizen, in [4] that he left a widow surviving [5] Ella Watson now Ella Geiger - remarried November 17th 1891 that the above-named are the only surviving legitimate children of said John Watson who were under sixteen years of age at the time of his death, of whom [6]

that said children were the issue of said soldier as follows, the dates of their birth being as hereinafter stated:

[7] Alonzo Watson, of soldier by John & Ella Watson, born April 9th, 1878
Rebecca L Watson, of soldier by " " ", born May 22d, 1880
Thomas S Watson, of soldier by " " ", born Aug 6th, 1882
, of soldier by , born , 18
, of soldier by , born , 18
, of soldier by , born , 18
, of soldier by , born , 18
, of soldier by , born , 18
, of soldier by , born , 18
, of soldier by , born , 18
, of soldier by

That the father was married under the name of John Watson to [8] Ella Pierce, there being no legal barrier to such marriage; that the said children have not aided or abetted the rebellion; and that no prior application has been filed by Guardian - The widow Prior to her marriage to Geiger drew pension for children under certificate 283,8[illegible] but they have received nothing for over one year that declarant hereby appoints h attorney to prosecute the above claim; that my residence is ~~at No.~~ Mays Landing ~~street~~, in the of , county of Atlantic, State of New Jersey and that his post office address is Mays Landing, Atlantic county New Jersey

(Attest.)

[illegible] Daniel E Gazard [illegible]

M. V. B. Moore   Daniel E. Hazard, Guard

(Claimant's signature.)

Lewis W. Cramer

Also personally appeared Martin V. B. Moore, residing at No. .... in .... street, in Mays Landing NJ, and Lewis W. Cramer residing at No. ...., in .... street, in Mays Landing NJ, persons whom I certify to be respectable and entitled to credit, and who, being by me duly sworn, say that they were present and saw Daniel E. Hazard, the claimant, sign his name (make mark) to the foregoing declaration; that they have every reason to believe, from the appearance of said claimant and their acquaintance with him that he is the identical person he represents himself to be; and that they have no interest in the prosecution of this claim.

M. V. B. Moore

Lewis W. Cramer

(Signatures of witnesses.)

SWORN to and subscribed before me this Twelfth day of December, A. D. 1892 and I hereby certify that the contents of the above declaration, &c., were fully made known and explained to the applicant and witnesses before swearing, including the words .... erased, and the words .... added; and that I have no interest, direct or indirect, in the prosecution of this claim.

Lewis Cramer

(Signature.)

County Clerk

(Official character.)

1 "Was enlisted," "drafted," or otherwise, as the case may be.
2 State company and regiment, if in army; or vessel, &c., if in navy.
3 State nature of wounds and all circumstances attending them, or the disease and manner in which it was incurred, in either case showing soldier's death to have been the sequence.
4 "In the service aforesaid," or otherwise.
5 If widow survived so state, giving her name, and the date of her death or other facts divesting her title.
6 If any have died state date of death.
7 State names of children and of their mothers, and dates of birth.
8 If more than once married so state, giving names and dates and parties officiating.
9 If either soldier, widow, or guardian of children have previously applied, so state, giving date and number of application.

F No. 263593 F

MINOR CHILDREN.

CLAIM FOR PENSION.

ORIGINAL.

Guardian of minors of ...., Applicant.

Co., ... Regt. .... Vols.

PENSION U DEC 14 1892 S OFFICE.

FILED BY

STATE OF NEW JERSEY.

ATLANTIC COUNTY, *ss.*

I, JOHN S. RISLEY, Surrogate of the County of Atlantic, do hereby certify that on the Twenty-fifth *day of* October *A. D. Eighteen hundred and ninety-* two *, the Orphans' Court of said County of Atlantic,* not being in session I *admitted* Daniel E. Iszard *of the County of* Atlantic *as Guardian of the person and property of* Rebecca L Watson and Thomas S Watson *being minor*s under *the age of fourteen years.*

Witness my hand and seal of office the Ninth *day of* May *in the year of our Lord one thousand eight hundred and ninety-* five

J S Risley *Surrogate.*

STATE OF NEW JERSEY.

ATLANTIC COUNTY, ss.

I, JOHN S. RISLEY, Surrogate of the County of Atlantic, do hereby certify that

on the Twenty-fifth *day of* October

A. D. Eighteen hundred and ninety two, *the Orphans' Court of said County of*

Atlantic, not being in Session I *admitted* Daniel E. Isgard

of the County of Atlantic

as Guardian of the person and property of Alonzo Watson

being a minor above *the age of fourteen years.*

Witness my hand and seal of office the Ninth

day of May *in the year of our Lord one*

*thousand eight hundred and ninety-*five.

J S Risley *Surrogate.*

☞ Get good, *reliable persons*, male or female, who *can write*, if possible. This to prove *Existence* of disability at Discharge and its *Continuance* since. If they cannot cover whole period, alter Blank accordingly and send for another "S," for other persons other years.

S.

☞ NOTE.—Execute before a CLERK OF COURT with seal, NOTARY PUBLIC, MASTER IN CHANCERY or JUSTICE OF THE PEACE, and have *him fill up* Blank. NOT before Commissioner of Deeds. Return to **James F. Rusling**, Trenton, N. J.

STATE OF New Jersey }
COUNTY OF Atlantic }

In the matter of Ella widow John Watson pri "G" 25 NJ for Pension.

Personally came before me, a Surrogate (Notary or Magistrate's title.) in and for aforesaid County and State Joseph S Pearce and Charles Clark (Names of affiants, one or more, as per "Instructions" herewith.)

well known to be reputable and entitled to credit, and who, being duly sworn, declares in relation to aforesaid case each as follows: That affiants well knew said soldier, and had known him since 1863 (Give year.); that soon after his discharge and return home, on or about the month of June (First seen.) 1863, affiants saw and conversed with him familiarly, and he was then suffering from chronic diarrhoea and (Name injury or disease.)

& resultant *effects* thereof, which, he then said, he had incurred in said U. S. Service, in the line of duty; that said soldier then had the appearance or look of a man so suffering, and his *signs* or *symptoms* thereof were then as follows: + Pale and weak and not able to work to any (Give his *signs* or *symptoms* then fully—*how* he looked, *how* affected—as indicating said disability or disabilities, and effects thereof, or otherwise.) considerable extent — That he had Diarrhoea which gave him trouble both day and night. That he complained of Showing a great deal of pain while at stool — That he had no — but very little appetite — and could not eat strong food without its hurting him and he was consequently weak and feeble —

that he ~~has~~ continued to suffer from *same*, and *resulting effects* thereof, with like signs or symptoms, more or less, ~~ever since~~ until death, and by reason thereof, in each year, since discharge, has been incapacitated for manual labor to the extent of * Three fourths (Say *total*, *three-fourths*, *one-half*, or as fact may be. Important.) on an average, and is ~~so~~ now, ~~to the extent of~~ * deceased (Give same, as *fact* may be. Important.)

and that his means of knowledge as to *foregoing facts* are as follows: that they worked with him both before and after the war — and that they (State *how* you know—as employer, fellow laborer, old friends, etc., and explain accordingly. *Important.*) saw or had knowledge of him from his discharge until his death —

*Be sure to give *extent* or *degree* of disability. Very important.

[OVER.]

This Blank for use in cases of JAMES F. RUSLING, only.

that, in the opinion of affiant, the same was caused by his said U. S. service and has not been aggravated nor prolonged by intemperance or other bad habits.

He further declares each, that he has no interest in said case, and is not concerned in its prosecution, and is ~~not~~ related to said claimant.* both brothers in law — that no other can be obtained from the fact that those who know him many are away and they have not the means to procure their affidavits

If affiant signs by *mark*, two witnesses here to such signature.

L. B. Corson	Charles X Clark age 73 years (Affiant sign here.) his mark
Residence and P. O. Address: (Give always.) Mays Landing N.J.	Residence and P. O. Address: (Give always.) Mays Landing N.J. (Street No., if any.)
S. C. Sharp	Joseph X L. Pierce years (Affiant sign here.) his mark
Residence and P. O. Address: (Give always.) Mays Landing N.J.	Residence and P. O. Address: (Give always.) (Street No., if any.)

Sworn to and subscribed before me on the day aforesaid; and I further certify I read said affidavit to said affiant, or acquainted him with its contents fully, before he executed same each; I am in nowise interested in said case; and said affiant is known by me to be a credible person, each..........

Witness my hand and official seal this 24 day of January A. D. 1890

Sign here J. S. Risley [Notary or Magistrate's Signature.]

(SEAL.) [If any.] P. O. Address Mays Landing N.J. [Notary or Magistrate's.] Surrogate [Official Character.]

* *Relatives* will do, if no others *possible*. But if so, their *relationship* must be stated at above * and explanation given by Letter *why* "no others possible."

NOTE.—Attention invited to this **Trenton, N. J. Agency,** with Army and Pension experience of *over twenty-eight years.* Business with U. S. Gov't being *by letter*, and Trenton, N. J., only short distance from Washington, D. C., with *many mails* daily, this **N. J. Agency**, of course, *not exceeded* by Washington, D. C., or other Agencies. *Experienced, prompt, successful.*

Many everywhere, in all States and Territories, still entitled to **Pension,** or to **Increase of Pension. Now** is *good* time to *apply*. New policy in Pension Office now, and Increase cases regarded *more favorably* than formerly, especially *Disease* cases. As a rule, increased age brings increased disability, and hence Increase of Pension now in order, if applied for properly.

Remember this **N. J. Agency** not confined to New Jersey, but Pension Cases here from all United States, Canada, Europe, &c., and prosecuted same as N. J. cases. Others in *your vicinity* or *knowledge* solicited. No charge, unless *successful*, and then fee, by U. S. Law, payable by U. S. Pension Agent.

S.

CASE OF

No.

FOR

PENSION

Existence of Disability at Discharge

—AND—

Its Continuance.

FILED BY

JAMES F. RUSLING,

Counsellor at Law, U. S. and N. J.

TRENTON, N. J.

[Bvt. Brig. Gen'l, late U.S. Pension Agent, N.J.]

Refers to Gov., Adj't Gen'l, U.S. Senators and M. C.'s of N. J.; Gen'ls Sewell, McAllister, Karge, Price, Ward, Fisk, Grubb, &c., N. J.; Sickles, Graham, Carr, N. Y.; Hartranft, Wagner, Gregg, Pa.; Marston, N. H.; Wood, O.; Sherman, Mo., and others.

NOTE.—Execute before a CLERK OF COURT with seal, NOTARY PUBLIC, MASTER IN CHANCERY, or JUSTICE OF THE PEACE, and have *him fill up* Blank; NOT before Commissioner of Deeds. Return to JAMES F. RUSLING, Trenton, N. J.

STATE OF New Jersey } ss.
COUNTY OF Atlantic }

In the matter of Ella Watson wid. of John, Pvt. G. 25 N.J. for Pension.

Personally came before me, a Clerk of the County in and for aforesaid County and State said widow who, being duly sworn, declares in relation to aforesaid case as follows: [See "Instructions" herewith. Comply with same, or *explain* why you cannot.]

That the contents of the annexed letter dated Dec. 5" 1889 to James F. Rusling are correct and true.

[OVER.]

*

If Deponent signs by *mark*, two witnesses here to *his* signature by *mark* opposite

.... age........... years.

Residence and P. O. Address: ....

Lewis Evans .... age........... years.

Residence and P. O. Address: County Clerk Mays Landing

Ella Watson .... age 44 years.
[Deponent sign here.]

Residence and P. O. Address: Mays Landing

Sworn to and subscribed before me this day; and I further certify I read said affidavit to said deponent, or acquainted him with its contents fully, before he executed the same; I am in nowise interested in said case; and said deponent is known to me to be a credible person.

....

....

....

....

Witness my hand and official seal this........11th........day of........December........A.D. 1889

Sign here........Lewis Evans........
[Notary or Magistrate's Signature.]

SEAL.
[If any.]

P. O. Address........Mays Landing........ County Clerk
[Notary or Magistrate's.] [Official Character.]

* If executed by others than Claimant, add at end of Affidavit: "And I have no interest in said case."

☞ NOTE.—Attention invited to this Trenton, N. J., Pension and Claim Agency, with Army and Pension experience of *over twenty-five years.* Business with U. S. Gov't being *by letter,* and Trenton, N. J., only short distance from Washington, D. C., with *many mails* daily, this N. J. Agency, of course, *not exceeded* by Washington, D. C., or other Agencies. *Experienced prompt, successful.*

Many everywhere, in all States and Territories, still entitled to **Pension,** or to **Increase of Pension. Now** is *good* time to *apply.* Increase cases regarded *more favorably* now than formerly, especially *Disease* cases. As a rule, increased age brings increased disability, and hence Increase of Pension now in order, if applied for properly.

☞ Remember this N. J. Agency not confined to New Jersey, but Pension Cases here from all United States, Canada, Europe, &c., and prosecuted promptly and well as N. J. cases. Others in *your vicinity* or *knowledge* solicited. No charge, unless *successful,* and then fee, by U. S. Law, payable by U. S. Pension Agent.

CASE OF G.C.

No.........

FOR

PENSION.

AFFIDAVIT OF

FILED BY

JAMES F. RUSLING,

Counsellor at Law, U. S. and N. J.

TRENTON, N. J.

(Bvt. Brig. Gen'l, late U.S. Pension Agent, N. J.)

☞ Refers to Gov., Adj't Gen'l, U.S. Senators and M.C.'s of N. J.; Gen'ls Sewell, McAllister, Ward, N. J.; Sickles, Graham, Carr, N. Y.; Hartranft, Wagner, Gregg, Pa.; Marston, N. H.; Wood, O.; Logan, Ill.; Sherman, Mo., and others.

☞NOTE.—Execute before a CLERK OF COURT with seal, NOTARY PUBLIC, MASTER IN CHANCERY, or JUSTICE OF THE PEACE, and have *him fill up* Blank; NOT before Commissioner of Deeds. Return to JAMES F. RUSLING, Trenton, N. J.

STATE OF New Jersey } ss.
COUNTY OF Atlantic }

In the matter of Ella Watson wid. of John, Pri. "G" 25" N.J. for Pension.

Personally came before me, a Clerk of the County in and for aforesaid County and State said widow who, being duly sworn, declares in relation to aforesaid case as follows: [See "Instructions" herewith. Comply with same, or *explain* why you cannot.]

That the contents of the annexed letter dated Dec. 5" 1889 to James F. Rusling are correct and true.

Dec. 5/79

Mr Rusling-

I send you the only proof I can give you of marriage to my late husband. The justice is dead, and there is no public or church record of our marriage- and hope this will answer the purpose. As to the birth of children I could give proof by persons known at the time. Send blanks for that purpose. My address now is

Mays Landing N.J.

Truly &c

Ella Adrian

per D.

☞ This affidavit should be in *handwriting* of Physician. All the facts in his possession as to the *origin* and *continuance* of claimant's *disability* should be set forth, and the dates or years of treatment given, fully as possible. If prepared from books or memoranda in possession of Physician, *that fact* should be stated.

P

☞ NOTE.—Execute before a CLERK OF COURT with seal, NOTARY PUBLIC, MASTER IN CHANCERY or JUSTICE OF THE PEACE, and have *him fill up* Blank. NOT before Commissioner of Deeds. Return to **James F. Rusling**, Trenton, N. J.

PHYSICIAN'S AFFIDAVIT.

State of New Jersey, **County of** Gloucester **ss:**

In the matter of Ella widow of John Watson, G. 25 N.J. for Pension.

Personally appeared before me, a Notary Public in and for aforesaid County and State, J. Gaunt Edwards [Name of Physician] who, being duly sworn, declares, in relation to aforesaid case, as follows: That his residence and P. O. Address are as follows: Williamstown Gloucester County New Jersey that he is a practicing Physician, and has been for 11 years, and has been acquainted with said soldier for about —— years; that he has had knowledge of him and his disabilities as follows: On September 4th 1889 I was for the first time called to attend John Watson of Piney Hollow (Post Office Address being Cedar Lake Atlantic Co. N.J.) Found him very seriously ill of Bilious Remitting Fever and Dysentery. The Dysentery was a sub acute attack and was greatly aggravated by the Chronic Dysenetry or diarrhoea which he so stated to me that he was subject to ever since his discharge from the Army. Never knew said claimant before the day of my first visit above named (Sept. 4th 89.) His dysentery was incurable and I visited him daily and alternately till Sept. 13th 1889 when he died of Chronic dysenetry.

[Here state *all the facts* known or believed, in accordance with marginal instructions.]

READ. ...s Affidavit ...show t e ...ing facts: ...hether or ...onent knew ...dier prior to ...nent; the ...of time he ...im, whether ...amily physi... as a neigh... nd what his ...ition was ...he treated ...while in the ...either as ...imental sur... r while home ...rlough, that ...should be ... The sol... physical con...n at such ...should be ..., as well as ...ME AND NA... HIS DISABIL... d dates or ...f treatment, ...as practi... ...f he has ...d soldier ...discharge ...ould state *where* and *for*; the ...od during ...he treated ...and his ...ical condi...hen, and ap... before, ...lleged ...f; and ...d give *dates* ...rs of same ...y as prac... ...e extent or ...to which ...has been

This Blank for use in cases of JAMES F. RUSLING.

And he further declares that he has no interest, either direct or indirect, in the prosecution of this claim.

J. Gaunt Edwards M.D.
[*Physician's* Signature.]

Williamstown N.J.
[Residence and P. O. Address.]

Sworn to and subscribed before me this 14th day of November A.D. 1889

and I hereby certify that the deponent is a practicing physician in good professional standing; that the contents of the above affidavit, &c., were fully made known to him before he executed the same; and that I have no interest, direct or indirect, in the prosecution of this claim.

Joseph T. Wood
[Notary or Magistrate's Signature.]

Notary Public
[Official Character.]

Williamstown N.J.
[P. O. Address.]

CASE OF

P

No. ....

FOR

PENSION.

MEDICAL HISTORY

DISABILITY OR DISABILITIES.

FILED BY

JAMES F. RUSLING,

Counsellor at Law, U. S. and N. J.

TRENTON, N. J.

[Bvt. Brig. Gen'l, late U. S. Pension Agent, N. J.]

2.

May's Landing,
Sept 22d N.J.
1908

Mr. W. V. Sickel.

Dear Sir.
Reply to yours of the 17th
The pension you refer
to. was stoped for some
cause. Which we never
found out. When
my. mother. Wife of the
late John Watson.
in 1895
Was married. Then I
was about Eleven years
old. And we did not
receive our pension.

25

My fathers discharge pappers was given to Daniel Isgard of Mays Landing N.J. Esq.
These pappers must be in your office.

Please let me hear from you.

Yours very Resp.

Thos S Watson.
Mays Landing. N.J.
R.F.D.-1.

PENSION OFFICE JAN 27 1909

W. V. SICKEL,
PENSION ATTORNEY,
729 WALNUT ST.
PHILA., PENNA.

2

INQUIRY SLIP.

FROM

W. V. SICKEL
PENSION ATTORNEY,
PHILA., PENNA.

TO THE

PENSION BUREAU.

Thos. S. Watson, minor

RECORD DIVISION OCT 10 1908

LAW DIVISION OCT 9 1908 RECEIVED

Application No. 566424

Certificate No.

NAME OF SOLDIER:

John Watson

Co. G, 25" Reg't N. J. Vols.

INFORMATION DESIRED:

Hon Com of Pensions
Wash. D.C.

Sir:

This claim for minors pension has been pending for years — And the only survivor now files Power of Atty to complete his claim. Will you please make a call — and oblige

Yours truly

W. V. Sickel

OCT

No. 66,424

3-3

ACT OF JUNE 27, 1890.

ORIGINAL PENSION OF MINOR CHILDREN.

76292

Phila.

Child, Thomas S. Watson

Guardian,

P. O. Mays Landing - R.D. #1

County, Atlantic

State, New Jersey

Soldier, John Watson.

Rank, Private

Company, G,

Regiment, 25 N. J. Vol. Inf.

Rate, $8 per month, commencing June 13, 1895 and $2 a month additional for each child, as follows:

		Commencing
	Born , Sixteen ,	,
Thomas S. Watson	Born August 6, 1882 Sixteen August 5, 1898	" June 13, 1895
	Born , Sixteen ,	" ,
	Born , Sixteen ,	" ,
	Born , Sixteen ,	" ,
	Born , Sixteen ,	" ,
	Born , Sixteen ,	" ,
	Born , Sixteen ,	" ,
	Born , Sixteen ,	" ,

Pay child on individual voucher

EASTERN

RECOGNIZED ATTORNEY.

Name, N. V. Sickel,

Post-office, Philadelphia, Pa.

Fee, $10.–

Agent to pay.

APPROVALS.

Submitted for admin Feby 20, 1909, J. W. Reisner, Examiner.

Approved for Admission

Pay child on individual voucher.

February 24, 1909, J. E. Thompson, Legal Reviewer.

February 24, 1909, A. D. Albert, Re-Reviewer.

IMPORTANT DATES.

Enlistment, September 2, 1862	Minors' claim filed, June 13, 1895
Discharge, June 20, 1863	Guardian appointed, — , 1
Other service, none	Former marriage of soldier, none , 1
Death, September 13, 1889	Death or divorce of former wife, ✓ , 1
Invalid claim filed, none , 1	Last marriage of soldier, August 16, 1863 ✓
Invalid paid to ✓ , 1	~~Death or~~ remarriage of widow, Nov. 15, 1891 ✓
Widow's claim filed, July 23, 1890	Former marriage of — wife, — , 1
Widow paid to November 15, 1891.	Former husband ✓ , 1

Claimant does — write.

0-2

J J Gardner, M. C. —
C.C. — 9,1,2.

POWER OF ATTORNEY.

Know all men by these presents, That I, Thomas S. Watson - Minor child of John Watson Co. G. 25th N.J.V. of Mays Landing, State of New Jersey have made, constituted, and appointed, and by these presents do make, constitute and appoint W. V. SICKEL, of PHILA., PENNA. my true and lawful Attorney, irrevocable, for me and in my name, place and stead, hereby annulling and revoking all former Powers of Attorney authorizations whatever in the premises, to prosecute to final issue, my Claim for Minors pension #566424 filed June 13" 1895. and minors Alonzo - Rebecca L. and Thomas S. Watson claimed for -

and to, from time to time, furnish any further evidence necessary, or that may be demanded, giving and granting to my said attorney full power and authority to do and perform all and every act and thing whatsoever requisite and necessary to be done in and about the premises, as fully to all intents and purposes as I might or could do if personally present at the doing thereof, with full power of substitution and revocation, hereby ratifying and confirming all that my said Attorney or his substitute, may, or shall lawfully do or cause to be done by virtue hereof.

My Post Office address is Mays Landing New Jersey R.F.D. No 1

In Testimony Whereof, I have hereunto set my hand and seal, this Sixth day of October, nineteen hundred and eight

I. F. Issued

Thomas S. Watson

STATE OF New Jersey }
COUNTY OF Atlantic } ss.

BE IT KNOWN, That on this sixth day of October in the year nineteen hundred and Eight, before me, the undersigned, a Notary Public in and for the said County and State, personally appeared Thomas S. Watson to me well known to be the identical person who executed the foregoing Power of Attorney, and the same having been first fully read over to him and the contents thereof duly explained, acknowledged the same to be his act and deed, and that I have no interest, direct or indirect, in the claim to which this instrument is supplemental, and am not concerned in its prosecution.

IN TESTIMONY WHEREOF, I have hereunto set my hand and affixed my seal of office, the day and year last above written.

Daniel [illegible] (Official Signature.)

[L. S.]

Notary Public (Official Character.)

I, ______ Clerk of the County Court in and for aforesaid County and State, do certify that ______, Esq., who has signed his name to the foregoing Power of Attorney was, at the time of so doing, ______ in and for said County and State, duly commissioned and sworn; that all his official acts are entitled to full faith and credit, and that his signature thereunto is genuine.

Validity accepted
S. A. Cuddy,
Chief, Law Division,
per JTF. OC 9 08

Witness my hand and seal of office, this ______ day of ______, 190__

______
Clerk of the ______

[L. S.]

NOTE.—This should be acknowledged before a CLERK OF COURT, NOTARY PUBLIC, or JUSTICE OF THE PEACE, and his official seal should be attached. If he has no seal he should so state, and in that event the certificate of a CLERK OF COURT showing his official character should be attached, unless such certificate is already on file in the Pension Office, which fact should appear.

Eastern DIVISION.

Minors Pension.
Minor No. 566424

CLAIM OF
minors of
John Watson
Co. [illegible], 25" N. J. Inf

POWER OF ATTORNEY

RECORD DIVISION
OCT 10 1908
RECEIVED

LAW DIVISION
OCT 9 1908
RECEIVED

FILED BY
W. V. SICKEL,
ATTORNEY,
[illegible] Street, N.W.
WASHINGTON, D.C.

PHILA., PENNA.

M.L.

-8-

7-L

3—1865.

DEPARTMENT OF THE INTERIOR,

BUREAU OF PENSIONS,

WASHINGTON, D. C. January 29, 1909.

Eastern Div.
Min.566,424,
Thomas S. Watson,
John Watson,
G, 25 N.J.Inf.

EAST. DIV.
FEB 16 1909
RECEIVED

Mr. W. V. Sickel,

Philadelphia, Pa.

Sir:

Relative to the above entitled claim for pension under the act of June 27, 1890, you are informed that in your slip of October 8, 1908, you stated that Thomas S. is the only surviving child of the soldier.

The death of the child Rebecca L., who was under 16 years of age at the date of filing the declaration, should be shown by competent evidence.

Very respectfully,

Commissioner.

2

3—1865.

DEPARTMENT OF THE INTERIOR,

Eastern Div. BUREAU OF PENSIONS,

Min. No. 566424,
Thomas S. Watson
John Watson,
G, 25. N. J. Inf.

WASHINGTON, D. C., January 23, 1909.

JAN 27 190

Mr. W. V. Sickel,

Philadelphia, Pa.

Sir:

Relative to the above entitled claim for pension under the act of June 27, 1890, you are informed that the child Thomas S. should furnish his present post- office address over his own signature.

Very respectfully,

V. Warner

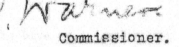

Commissioner.

Ex'r.

Minor No. Orig. 566,424

Act of June 27, 1890.

Daniel E. Iszard.
May's Landing N.J.
Gdn Min.
John Watson.
Pvt 'G' - 25 N.J. Inf

Died at

ABANDONED

No other claim

Wid. Ctf. 283,893
Min. O. 566,424

June 26, 1895

PENDING.

Clerk.

Numerical No.

Application filed: June 13, 189

Attorney: W. W. Sickel

P.O. Phila.

729 Walnut St. Pa

A.R. (5466—20,000.)

ME. To Atty any other minors. Dec 5/95 —

To P.M. cred of

N. H. Brown. To P.M. cred of McCurdy. ~~[illegible]~~

To Atty any other

VT. minors. Apr 24/96

MASS. ~~To Atty Sickle amounts above. Nov 24/1900 EMG.~~

R. I. ~~To P.M. cred of McCurdy Brown & [illegible]~~

CONN. To Atty Sickel. 7 clmt is only surviving child. Nov 18/1908 EMG

N. Y.

N. J. ~~Jan 23. 1909~~ ~~To Sickel [illegible]~~ 7C

DEL. Jan. 29. 1909 To ~~Sickel~~ [illegible] of Rebecca. 7C

No.

[3—218 a.]

Ex'r.

W. Org No. 408533

Act of June 27, 1890.

Ella Watson
Mays Landing N. J.
Wid. of
John Watson
G. 25. N. J. Inf.

Died at

Sept 13-1889.

No other claim.

Ns Ino

BOARD OF REVIEW
JAN 23 1891

Oct. 7, 1890. Brunson Clerk.
Nov. 1 "

Numerical No. 172,097, 3/29

Application filed: July 23, 1890

Attorney: Cadwell & Dorian

P. O. City

W. E.

Act of June 27, 1890.

No. 283,893.

Ella Watson

WIDOW OF

John Watson

Rank Pvt., Co. G

Regt. 25. N.J. Vol. Inf

Philadelphia Agency.

Rate per month, $ 8

Commencing July 23, 1890

Additional sum of $2 per month for each of the following children, until arriving at the age of 16 years, commencing July 23, 1890

Alonzo Apr. 8, 18[illegible]

Rebecca L. May 21, 18[illegible]

Thomas S. Aug 5, 18[illegible]

Certificate dated Feb. 20, 1891

Sent Mar. 7, 1891

Fee $10. Attorney.

Act 14th July, 1862.

Book ...., Vol ...., Page ....

Clerk.

3-732

No. 676292

Act of June 27, 1890.

Minor of

John Watson

Rank Pri

Company G

Regiment 25th N. J. Vol Inf

Inf

Rate per Month $8

Commencing June 13" 1895

Ending

Phila Agency.

Issued Feb 26, 1909.

Mailed FEB 26 1909, 190 .

Fee, $

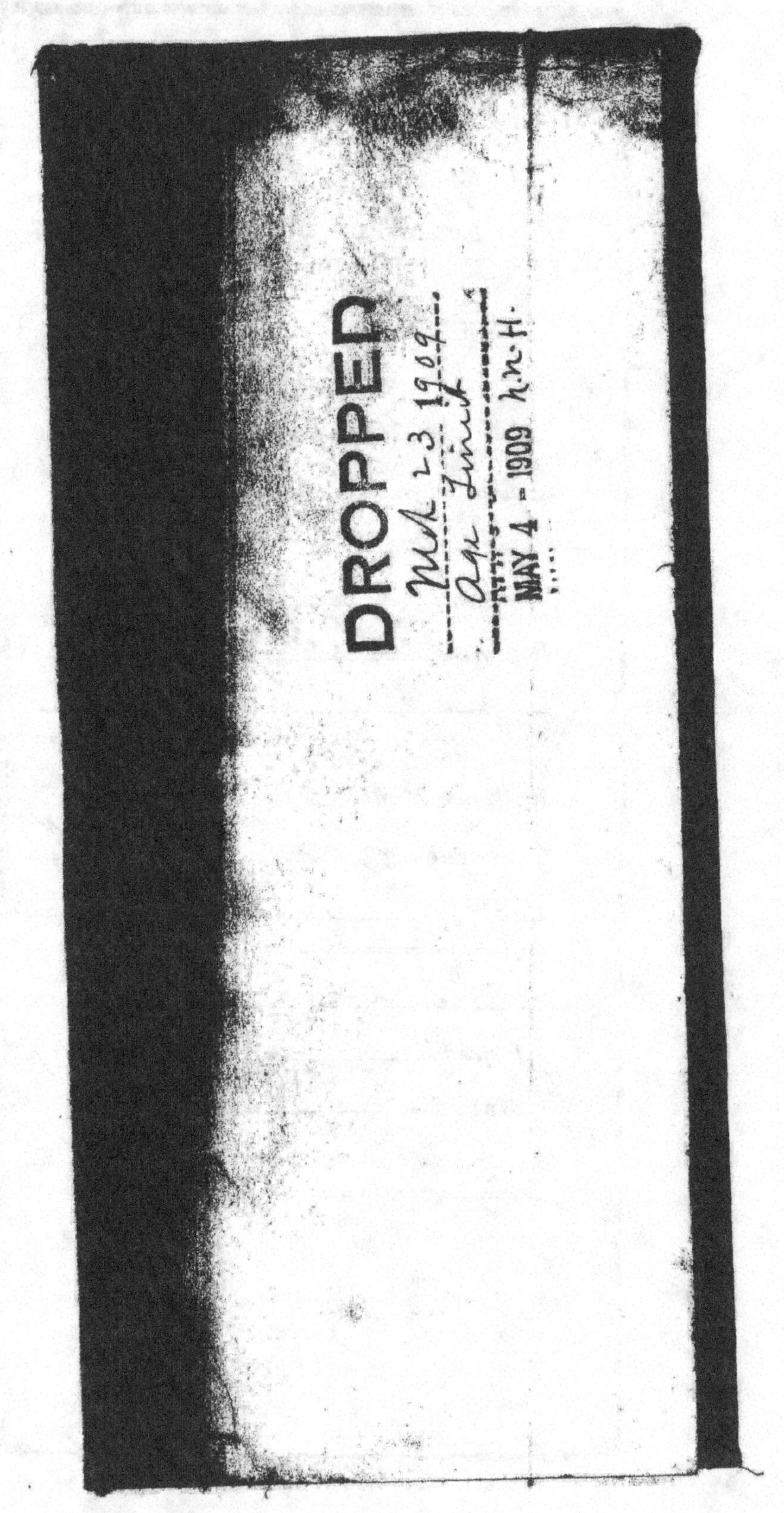
DROPPED
MAY 4 - 1909

GENERAL AFFIDAVIT.

State of New Jersey County of Atlantic ss.

In the matter of Claim 566.424 - minors of John Watson Co I 35th N. J. Vol. Infantry

ON THIS 15 day of July A. D. 1895; personally appeared before me a Surrogate in and for the aforesaid County, duly authorized to administer oaths, Herman Wottstein aged 29 years, a resident of Mays Landing in the County of Atlantic State of New Jersey whose Post Office address is Mays Landing N. J. and Joseph Leach aged 33 years, a resident of Mays Landing in the County of Atlantic State of New Jersey whose Post Office address is Same

and who, being duly sworn according to law, depose and say in relation to aforesaid case as follows:

[NOTE.—Affiants should state how they gain a knowledge of the facts to which they testify.]

We know that Alonzo Watson, Rebecca L Watson and Thomas S. Watson children of John Watson are still alive, We know this by seeing them nearly every day and living near them

The above was written in our presence by J. S. Risley at his office in Mays Landing N. J. on the 15th day of July AD 1895 and only from our Oral Statements then made and we was not added or prompted by by any written or printed Statement Not Attatched as an exhibit to this testimony

4

State of New Jersey *County of* Atlantic

Sworn to and subscribed before me this day by the within named affiants, and I certify that I read said affidavit to said affiants and acquainted them with its contents before they executed the same. I further certify that I am in no wise interested in said case, nor am I concerned in its prosecution.

J S Risley
[Signature.]

[L. S.]

Surrogate
[Official Character.]

I certify that .... Esq., who hath signed his name to the foregoing affidavit was at the time of so doing .... in and for said County and State, duly commissioned and sworn; that all his official acts are entitled to full faith and credit, and that his signature thereunto is genuine.

Witness my hand and seal of office, this .... day of 189

....

[L. S.] *Clerk of the* ....

NOTE.—This should be sworn to before a CLERK of COURT, NOTARY PUBLIC or JUSTICE OF THE PEACE. If before a JUSTICE or NOTARY, then CLERK OF COUNTY COURT must add his certificate of character hereon and not on a slip of paper.

FEB 16 1909
RECEIVE

State of New Jersey,

Bureau of Vital Statistics.

I, Bruce S. Keator, *Medical Superintendent of the Bureau of Vital Statistics of the State of New Jersey, do hereby Certify, that the foregoing and annexed is a true copy of a certain Certificate of Death, as taken from and compared with the original now remaining on file in my office.*

In Testimony Whereof, *I have hereunto set my hand and affixed the Official Seal of said Bureau, at Trenton, this* Thirteenth *day of* February *A.D.* 1909.

Bruce S. Keator, M.D.
Medical Superintendent.

ATTEST:
David S. Smith
Registrar.

DIVISION B
FEB 16 1909
U. S.
OFFICE.

E. B. DIV
FEB 16 1909
RECEIVED

STATE OF NEW JERSEY.

CERTIFICATE OF DEATH.

1. Full name of deceased Rebecca L. Vandergrift
(If an infant not named, so state and give sex.)

2. Age 20 years — 7 months — days — hours. Color White

3. ~~Single~~, married, ~~widow or widower~~. {Cross out all but the right one.} Occupation Housewife

4. Birthplace N. Jersey {State or county}

5. Last place of residence Clayton Gloucester Co. N.J. {If a city give name; if not, give county and township.}

6. How long resident in this State 20 Y. 7 Mo.

7. Place of death Clayton Gloucester Co. N.J.
(If in a city, give street and number; if in township, give name and county; if in an institution, so state.)

8. Father's name John Watson Country of birth U.S.

9. Mother's name Ella Griggs Country of birth U.S.

10. I hereby certify that I attended the deceased

during the last illness, and that she died on the 21st day of March,

1901, and that the cause of death was Chronic Inflamation of bowels

REQUESTED, BUT OPTIONAL.

a. Primary disease

b. Secondary disease (how long)

c. Remarks

Length of sickness 8 Months

A. Porch

Medical Attendant.

Residence Clayton, N.J.

Date

Name and residence of Undertaker Chas. W. Seeds Clayton, N.J.

Place of burial Pine hollow, N.J.

DIVISION B
FEB 16 1909
U. S. PENSION OFFICE.

4

CERTIFIED COPY OF

CERTIFICATE OF DEATH

OF

Rebecca L. Vandegrift

Cont Div.
Minors
#566424
John Watson
Co. 25 N.J. Inf

STATE OF NEW JERSEY.

LIBERTY AND PROSPERITY

BUREAU OF VITAL STATISTICS.

I, Ezra M. Hunt, Medical Superintendent of the Bureau of Vital Statistics of the State of New Jersey, do hereby Certify, *that the foregoing and annexed is a true copy of a certain Marriage Return, as taken from and compared with the original now remaining on file in my office.*

In Testimony Whereof, *I have hereunto set my hand and affixed the Official Seal of said Bureau, at Trenton, this* Thirtieth *day of* June *A. D.* 1893.

E M Hunt
Medical Superintendent.

Attest
Dallas Reeve
Reg.

46

STATE OF NEW JERSEY.

MARRIAGE RETURN.

SEE PENALTY FOR NON-REPORT.

☞Use ink, and *write plainly*, especially names.

1. Full name of husband Hiram Girie. White (If colored, so state.)

Place of residence Mayslanding, Atlantic Co, N.J. (If in city, give name, street and number; if not, give township and county.)

2. Age 42 ---- years --- months. Number of his marriage No. 2.

3. Occupation Baker ---- Country of birth Germany

4 Name of father Seeferd Garie Country of birth "

5. Maiden name of mother Roeada Dolth Country of birth "

1. Full maiden name of wife,

Ella Pearce. Country of birth N. Jersey White (If colored, so state.)

2. Place of residence Mayslanding, Atlantic County, N.J. (If in city, give name, street and number; if not, give township and county.)

3. Age, nearest birthday 42 --- {If in any trade or business, so state.} No trade

4. Last name if a widow Ella Watson Number of bride's marriage No 2.

5. Name of father Josiah Pearce Country of birth New Jersey

6. Maiden name of mother Hannah Nash Country of birth New Jersey

1. Date (in full) November 15 1891 Place Franklinville Gloucester Co N.J. (City or township and county.)

2. In presence of { John Girie & Mary Girie. (Be sure to have witnesses.)
Mayslanding, New Jersey (Add P. O. Addresses.)

3. Signature of minister, (what church pastor of) or person officiating. } Samuel McCurdy
Justice of the Peace

9-4

CERTIFIED COPY OF

MARRIAGE RETURN.

Hiram Giris &

Ella Pearce

Franklinville, N.J.

Nov. 15th 1891.

PENSION OFFICE JUL 12 1893

Case of

Izzard, Daniel E

Gd. Children of John Hat

"G" 25 N.J.

No. not yet given.
(O.L. No. 566,424)
Filed Apr. 29, 93

by

JAMES F. RUSLING,
COUNSELLOR AT LAW
22 E. STATE STREET,
TRENTON, N.J.

GENERAL AFFIDAVIT.

State of New Jersey, County of Cumberland ss:

In the matter of Ella Watson Wid of John Watson Co I. 25" N.J. Vol

ON THIS 20th day of November A. D. 1890, personally appeared before me a Justice of the Peace in and for the aforesaid County duly authorized to administer oaths, Hannah Groff aged 68 years, a resident of Stow Creek Tp in the County of Cumberland and State of N.J. whose Post Office address is Shiloh Cumberland Co N.J.

aged years, a resident of in the County of and State of whose Post Office address is

well known to me to be reputable and entitled to credit, and who, being duly sworn, declared in relation to aforesaid case as follows:

[NOTE.—Affiants should state how they gain a knowledge of the facts to which they testify.]

That she was present at the marriage of John Watson to Miss Clammont (Ella Watson) Aug 6" 1862 at Weymouth Tp Tuckaho Atlantic Co N.J. That neither of them had been previously married and that the said Ella has not remarried since his death. She further makes states that the said Ella has not sufficient income to support her without labor and is consequently dependent in part at least on her own labor for support

STATE OF New Jersey, COUNTY OF Salem, ss:

Sworn to and subscribed before me this day by the above-named affiant , and I certify that I read said affidavit to said affiant , including the words .... erased, and the words .... added and acquainted her with its contents before I executed the same. I further certify that I am in nowise interested in said case, nor am I concerned in its prosecution; and that said affiant is personally known to me and that she is a credible person.

Louis Schaible
(Official Signature.)

[L. S.]

Justice of the Peace
(Official Character.)

I, ... Clerk of the County Court in and for aforesaid County and State, do certify that ...., Esq., who has signed his name to the foregoing declaration and affidavit was at the time of so doing .... in and for said County and State, duly commissioned and sworn; that all his official acts are entitled to full faith and credit, and that his signature thereunto is genuine.

Witness my hand and seal of office, this .... day of ...., 18 ....

[L. S.]

Clerk of the ....

NOTE.—This should be sworn to before a CLERK OF COURT, NOTARY PUBLIC or JUSTICE OF THE PEACE. If before a JUSTICE or NOTARY, then CLERK OF COUNTY COURT must add his certificate of character hereon, and not on a separate slip of paper.

PENSION U S OFFICE D DEC 4 1890

Eye -
no pension
Support

GENERAL AFFIDAVIT.

State of New Jersey, County of Gloucester, ss:

In the matter of Ellen Watson Wid of John Watson Co. I. 25th N. J. Vol

ON THIS 22nd day of November A. D. 1890 personally appeared before me a Notary Public in and for the aforesaid County duly authorized to administer oaths, Hannah Brown aged 48 years, a resident of Williamstown in the County of Gloucester and State of N. J. whose Post Office address is as above

aged years, a resident of

in the County of and State of

whose Post Office address is

well known to me to be reputable and entitled to credit, and who, being duly sworn, declared in relation to aforesaid case as follows:

[NOTE.—Affiants should state how they gain a knowledge of the facts to which they testify.]

That she was present at the marriage of John Watson and Ellen Moffett at Weymouth Town Atlantic Co N. J. on the 6th day of August 1862. They were both single and free to marry and the said Ellen has not married since his death. I further state that the said Ellen is now dependent on her daily labor for her support, not having a sufficient income to enable her to live without work.

STATE OF New Jersey, COUNTY OF Gloucester, ss:

Sworn to and subscribed before me this day by the above-named affiant, and I certify that I read said affidavit to said affiant, including the words ________ erased, and the words ________ added and acquainted ________ with its contents before ________ executed the same. I further certify that I am in nowise interested in said case, nor am I concerned in its prosecution; and that said affiant is personally known to me and that she is credible person.

Joseph H. Wood
(Official Signature.)

Notary Public.
(Official Character.)

________ Clerk of the County Court in and for aforesaid County ... State, do certify that ________, Esq., who has signed his name to the foregoing declaration and affidavit was at the time of so doing ________ in and for said County and State, duly commissioned and sworn; that all his official acts are entitled to full faith and credit, and that his signature thereunto is genuine.

Witness my hand and seal of office, this ________ day of ________, 18 ____.

[L. S.] Clerk of the ________

NOTE.—This should be sworn to before a CLERK OF COURT, NOTARY PUBLIC or JUSTICE OF THE PEACE. If before a JUSTICE or NOTARY, then CLERK OF COUNTY COURT must add his certificate of character hereon, and not on a separate slip of paper.

Myrz - no pension - support - unknown

PENSION OFFICE U S DEC 4 1890

PHYSICIAN'S AFFIDAVIT.

TAKE NOTICE.—The affidavit should, if possible, be in the handwriting of the affiant; the marginal instructions must be carefully observed before writing out the statement All the facts in possession of affiant as to the origin and continuance of the disability should be fully set forth, and the dates of treatment should be specifically given. If the affidavit is prepared from memoranda in possession of the physician, that fact should be stated.

State of New Jersey, County of Gloucester, ss:

In the Pension Claim No. 408.533

of Ella Watson wid. of Jno. Watson late of Co. I. 25th N. Jersey.

(Company and regiment of service, if in the army; or vessel and rank if in the navy.)

Personally came before me, a Notary Public in and for the aforesaid County and State J Grant Edwards a citizen of Williamstown whose Post Office address is Williamstown well known to me to be reputable and entitled to credit, and who, being duly sworn, declares in relation to aforesaid case as follows:

That he is a Practicing Physician, and that he has been acquainted with said soldier for about during last illness years, and that Was summoned on Sept. 4th 1889 to see claimant who was then

(Here embody all the facts known to the affiant in accordance with the marginal instructions. No erasures or interlineations will be permitted unless the magistrate certifies in his jurat that they were made before executing the paper.)

very seriously ill of Billious Remitting Fever and Dysentery, this was my first acquaintance of said soldier. He had been treated formerly by a Dr. Smith of Malaga, Gloucester Co. N. J. Visited claimant on 5. 6. 7. 9. 13th of Sept. his Remitting fever was cured but his dysentery became chronic and he informed me that his bowels had always been weak from the army dysentery.
My stub of Death records shows that he died of Billious Fever and dysentery on the 13th day of September 1889 and was buried at Pineyhollow Gloucester Co. New Jersey by Wm P Buck of Williamstown Gloucester Co N. J.
Never knew or treated Claimant (John Watson) prior to above dates.

NOTES.—The Physician's Affidavit must show the following facts: 1st. Whether or not he knew the soldier prior to enlistment; the length of time he has known him how intimately and what opportunities he has had of observing his physical condition, whether as his family physician or as a neighbor; and how near he has lived to him. If he knew that the soldier was a sound man at enlistment, he should so state, adding, if true, that had he been unsound, he would have known it. 2d. If he treated claimant while in the service either as his regimental surgeon or while claimant was home on furlough, that fact should be stated. The claimant's physical condition at such times should be clearly shown, as well as the NATURE OF HIS DISABILITY and dates of treatment. 3d. If he has

He further declares that he has been a practitioner of medicine for (11) Eleven years, and that he has no interest, either direct or indirect, in the prosecution of this claim.

J. Gaunt Edwards M.D.
(Affiant's Signature. Give rank and service, if in the army)

Sworn to and subscribed before me this 10 day of September A. D. 1890

and I hereby certify that the affiant is a practicing physician in good professional standing; that the contents of the above declaration, &c., were fully made known to him before swearing, including the words .... erased, and the words .... added; and that I have no interest, direct or indirect, in the prosecution of this claim.

Joseph T. Wood
(Official Signature.)

Notary Public
(Official Character.)

.... Clerk of the County Court in and for aforesaid County and State, do certify that ...., Esq., who has signed his name to the foregoing declaration and affidavit was at the time of so doing .... in and for said County and State, duly commissioned and sworn; that all his official acts are entitled to full faith and credit, and that his signature thereunto is genuine.

Witness my hand and seal of office, this .... day of ...., 18 ....

[L. S.] Clerk of the ....

NOTE.—This should be sworn to before a CLERK OF COURT, NOTARY PUBLIC or JUSTICE OF THE PEACE. If before a JUSTICE or NOTARY, then CLERK OF COUNTY COURT must add his certificate of character hereon, and not on a separate slip of paper.

MEDICAL EVIDENCE.

AFFIDAVIT OF Dr. J. Frank Edwards

CLAIM OF Ella Watson, wid Jas. Watson, Co. D 25 N. J.

PENSION OFFICE SEP 18 1890

Filed by Crosby & Gorian, ATTORNEYS & SOLICITORS, WASHINGTON, D. C.

Printed and for sale by J. H. SOULE, Washington, D. C.

GET RECORD FROM CHURCH OR PUBLIC OFFICE, IF ANY. IF NONE, THEN FROM BIBLE OR OTHER PRIVATE RECORD.

M

NOTE.—Execute before a CLERK OF COURT with seal, NOTARY PUBLIC, MASTER IN CHANCERY, or JUSTICE OF THE PEACE; NOT before Commissioner of Deeds. And return to JAMES F. RUSLING, Trenton, N. J.

This Blank for use in cases of JAMES F. RUSLING, only.

STATE OF New Jersey
COUNTY OF Atlantic } ss.

In the matter of Ella Watson, wid. John, Co. G. 25 N.J. for Pension.

Personally came before me, a Clerk of the County in and for aforesaid County and State Hannah Brown who, being duly sworn according to law, declares that ~~deponent is the custodian of certain Marriage, Birth or Death Records, and the following is a true copy therefrom relating to said soldier:~~ she was present at the (Give his Marriages, Births of Children and Deaths of former Wives, Soldier and Children, so far as of Record.) marriage of John Watson late of Co. G 25th N.J. and Ella Pearce the applicant for pension in the above case. The marriage was performed by Elias Smith, Esq. on August 16th 1863 at his the said Elias Smith's residence in Weymouth Township, Atlantic County New Jersey.

that the same was entered therein apparently on or about the date of occurence thereof, or soon afterwards; and that said Records consist of the following: (Say Church Record, Board of Health, County, Township or other *Public* Record, if any—giving *name* and *place* of same. If *none*, say Bible Record, or other *Private* Record, as fact may be.)

And deponent knows of no other Record thereof.

[OVER.]

And deponent further declares deponent has no interest in this claim. (If executed by Widow, Children or Guardian, erase this.)

If Deponent signs by mark, two witnesses here to said signature by mark.

M. V. B. Moore

Residence and P. O. Address: Mays Landing NJ

Robt H. Risley

Residence and P. O. Address: Linwood NJ

Hannah her x mark Brown
[Deponent sign here.]

Residence and P. O. Address: Berlin NJ.

Sworn to and subscribed before me this day, and I further certify I read said affidavit to said deponent, or acquainted deponent with its contents fully, before deponent executed the same; I am in nowise interested in said case; and said deponent is known to me to be a credible person. ✱ ~~And I further certify that I have compared the foregoing with said Bible or Private Record and find same correct; that said Bible or Private Record appears to be not recent, but genuine and authentic; and that the date of said Bible or Private Record is as follows:~~ .... (Give same as printed on its *title-page* or otherwise, or explain why not. If there is a *Public* Record, let Notary or Magistrate erase all of above Jurat after the *Star*.)

Witness my hand and official seal this 3rd day of December A.D. 1889

SEAL. [If any.]

Sign here Lewis Evans
[Notary or Magistrate's Signature.]

P. O. Address .... [Notary or Magistrate's.]

County Clerk
Official Character.

☞ NOTE.—Attention invited to this Trenton, N. J., Pension and Claim Agency, with Army and Pension experience of *over twenty-five years*. Business with U. S. Gov't being *by letter*, and Trenton, N. J., only short distance from Washington, D. C., with *many mails* daily, this N. J. Agency, of course, *not exceeded* by Washington, D. C., or other Agencies. *Experienced, prompt, successful.*

Many everywhere, in all States and Territories, entitled to **Pension**, or to **Increase of Pension**. **Now is** *good* time to *apply*. New and more liberal policy now in Pension Bureau—especially as to *Disease* cases. As a rule, increased age brings increased disability, and hence Increase of Pension now in order, if applied for properly.

☞ Remember this **N. J. Agency** not confined to New Jersey, but Pension Cases here from all United States, Canada, Europe, &c. Others in *your vicinity* or *knowledge* solicited. No charge, unless *successful*, and then fee, by U. S. Law, payable by U. S. Pension Agent.

M

CASE OF

No.

FOR

PENSION.

RECORD PROOF OF MARRIAGES, BIRTHS OR DEATHS.

FILED BY

JAMES F. RUSLING,

Counsellor at Law, U. S. and N. J.

TRENTON, N. J.

[Bvt. Brig. Gen'l, late U.S. Pension Agent, N.J.]

☞ Refers to Gov., Adj't Gen'l, U.S. Senators and M.C.'s of N. J.; Gen'ls Sewell, McAllister, Ward, Fisk, Grubb, N. J.; Sickles, Graham, Carr, N. Y.; Hartranft, Wagner, Gregg, Pa.; Marston, N. H.; Wood, O.; Sherman, Mo., and others.

GET RECORD FROM CHURCH OR PUBLIC OFFICE, IF ANY. IF NONE, THEN FROM BIBLE OR OTHER PRIVATE RECORD.

M

NOTE.—Execute before a CLERK OF COURT with seal, NOTARY PUBLIC, MASTER IN CHANCERY, or JUSTICE OF THE PEACE; NOT before Commissioner of Deeds. And return to JAMES F. RUSLING, Trenton, N. J.

STATE OF New Jersey } ss.
COUNTY OF Camden

In the matter of Ella Watson wid. John. Co. G. "25" N. Jersey for Pension.

Personally came before me, a [illegible] Clerk of the County & Camden in and for aforesaid County and State Hannah Brown who, being duly sworn according to law, declares that deponent ~~is the custodian of certain Marriage, Birth or Death Records, and the following is a true copy therefrom relating to said soldier~~ was present at the birth (Give his Marriages, Births of Children and Deaths of former Wives, Soldier and Children, so far as of Record.) of Alonzo Watson son of the above named John and Ella Watson which took place on April 9th 1877 at Williamstown N. J.

that the same was entered therein apparently on or about the date of occurence thereof, or soon afterwards; and that said Records consist of the following: (Say Church Record, Board of Health, County, Township or other *Public* Record, if any—giving *name* and *place* of same. If *none*, say Bible Record, or other *Private* Record, as fact may be.

And deponent knows of no other Record thereof.

[OVER.]

This Blank for use in cases of JAMES F. RUSLING, only.

27

And deponent further declares deponent has no interest in this claim. (If executed by Widow, Children or Guardian, erase this.)

If Deponent signs by *mark*, two witnesses here to said signature by *mark*.

Willie B Brown

Residence and P. O. Address: Clementon N.J.

C Van Duyn

Residence and P. O. Address: Merchantville

her
Hannah X Brown
[Deponent sign here.]
mark

Residence and P. O. Address: Clementon N.J.

Sworn to and subscribed before me this day; and I further certify I read said affidavit to said deponent, or acquainted deponent with its contents fully, before deponent executed the same; ~~I am in nowise interested in said case;~~ and said deponent is [not] known to me [but I know] to be a credible person. ✱ ~~And I further certify that I have compared the foregoing with said Bible or Private Record and find same correct; that said Bible or Private Record appears to be not recent, but genuine and authentic; and that the *date* of said Bible or Private Record is as follows:~~ (Give same as printed on its *title-page* or otherwise, or explain why not. If there is a *Public* Record, let Notary or Magistrate erase all of above Jurat after the *Star*.)

The erasure "I am in nowise interested in said Case" is an error and should remain in full

Witness my hand and official seal this 3 day of January A.D. 1890

Sign here E Bennett
[Notary or Magistrate's Signature.]

[illegible] Address Camden N.J. [Notary or Magistrate's.] County Court Clerk Official Character.

[illegible]—Attention invited to this Trenton, N. J., Pension and Claim Agency, with Army and Pension ex[illegible] *over twenty-five years.* Business with U. S. Gov't being *by letter*, and Trenton, N. J., only short distance from Washington, D. C., with *many mails* daily, this N. J. Agency, of course, *not exceeded* by Washington, D. C., or other Agencies. *Experienced, prompt, successful.*

Many everywhere, in all States and Territories, entitled to **Pension**, or to **Increase of Pension. Now is** *good* time to *apply.* New and more liberal policy now in Pension Bureau—especially as to *Disease* cases. As a rule, increased age brings increased disability, and hence Increase of Pension now in order, if applied for properly.

☞ Remember this **N. J. Agency** not confined to New Jersey, but Pension Cases here from all United States, Canada, Europe, &c. Others in *your vicinity* or *knowledge* solicited. No charge, unless *successful*, and then fee, by U. S. Law, payable by U. S. Pension Agent.

Birth of Q[illegible]

CASE OF

M

No.

FOR

PENSION.

RECORD PROOF OF MARRIAGES, BIRTHS OR DEATHS.

FILED BY

JAMES F. RUSLING,

Counsellor at Law, U. S. and N. J.

TRENTON, N. J.

[Bvt. Brig. Gen'l, late U.S. Pension Agent, N. J.]

☞ Refers to Gov., Adj't Gen'l, U.S. Senators and M. C.'s of N. J.; Gen'ls Sewell, McAllister, Ward, Fisk, Grubb, N. J.; Sickles, Graham, Carr, N. Y.; Hartranft, Wagner, Gregg, Pa.; Marston, N. H.; Wood, O.; Sherman, Mo., and others.

State of New Jersey
County of Atlantic } SS-

In the matter of Ella Watson widow of John Late Private Co. G. 25th New Jersey Infty - Personally came before me a Clerk in and for the aforesaid County and State Mary Clark aged 46 yrs - who being by me duly sworn on her oath declares in relation to aforesaid case as follows - That she was present at the birth of Rebecca L. daughter of the aforesaid John and Ella Watson - that this birth took place on the 22nd day of May A.D. 1880 -

Witness
Lewis Evans
Frank R. Moore

her
Mary X Clark
mark

Sworn to and subscribed before me this day, and I further certify I read this affidavit to said deponent before she executed the same - I am in no wise interested in said case, and said deponent is known to me to be a credible person.

Witness my hand and official seal this 20 day of December A.D. 1889

Lewis Evans
County Clerk

BUREAU OF VITAL STATISTICS.

I, Ezra M. Hunt, Medical Superintendent of the Bureau of Vital Statistics of the State of New Jersey, do hereby Certify, *that the foregoing and annexed is a true copy of a certain Birth Return, as taken from and compared with the original now remaining on file in my office.*

In Testimony Whereof, *I have hereunto set my hand and affixed the Official Seal of said Bureau, at Trenton, this* Nineteenth *day of* December *A. D.* 1889.

Attest
Dallas Reeve
Regr.

E. M. Hunt
Medical Superintendent.

FORM 19 a.

One.

Treasury Department,

THIRD AUDITOR'S OFFICE,

April 5th, 1893.

Hon. Commissioner of Pensions.

Sir: In reply to your letter of April 1. 1893., *in case of*
Ella Watson <now Geiger> *Certificate* 283.893.
Philadelphia *Agency,* Oct June 27. 1890 <Widow> *Roll,*
the records of this Office show last *payment to have been made at* $14
per month in March 1892 to November 15
1891, date of remarriage.

Letter herewith returned.

Respectfully yours,

W H Hart

Auditor.

(Ed. 9-8-'92—1,000.) T. B.

283893

Phila

(3—128 a.)

ACT OF JUNE 27, 1890.

O. C. Pens

WIDOW'S PENSION.

Claimant Ella Watson

P. O. Mays Landing

County Atlantic, State N. J.

Soldier John Watson

Rank Private, Co. G.

Regiment 25" N. J. Vol Inft.

Rate, $8 per month, commencing July 23" 1890, and $2 per month additional for each child, as follows:

Name	Born / Sixteen	Commencing
Alonzo	Born, April 9", 1877 / Sixteen, " 8", 1893	July 23", 1890
Rebecca L.	Born, May 22", 1880 / Sixteen, " 21, 1896	July 23", 1890
Thomas S.	Born, August 6", 1882 / Sixteen, " 5", 1898	July 23", 1890
	Born, ..., 18 / Sixteen, ..., 18	........, 18
	Born, ..., 18 / Sixteen, ..., 18	........, 18
	Born, ..., 18 / Sixteen, ..., 18	........, 18
	Born, ..., 18 / Sixteen, ..., 18	........, 18
	Born, ..., 18 / Sixteen, ..., 18	........, 18

Payments on all former certificates covering any portion of same time to be deducted.

All pension to terminate ...., 189.., date of ....

RECOGNIZED ATTORNEY:

Name Crosby and Dorian

P. O. City

Fee $ 10. Agent to pay.

Articles Filed None, 189

APPROVALS.

Submitted for admission Jan 26" 1891, W. M. McKinley, Examiner.

Approved for admission

Jan 28, 1891 Zimbkins, Legal Reviewer.

The soldier was not pensioned at $ — per month for ....

6

[3—015 a.]

Act of June 27, 1890.

FF DECLARATION FOR CHILDREN UNDER SIXTEEN YEARS OF AGE. FF

[To be executed before any officer authorized to administer oaths for general purposes in the State, city, or county where said officer resides. If such officer has a seal and uses it upon such paper, no certificate of a county clerk or prothonotary or clerk of a court shall be necessary; but when no seal is used by the officer before whom the declaration is executed, then a clerk of a court of record or a county or city clerk shall affix his official seal thereto, and shall certify to the *signature* and *official character* of said officer.]

STATE OF New Jersey
COUNTY OF Atlantic } ss:

On this Eleventh day of June, A. D. one thousand eight hundred and ninety-five, personally appeared before me, a County Clerk & Clerk of the of the County Courts in and for the County and State aforesaid, Daniel E. Iszard, aged 58 years, who, being duly sworn according to law, makes the following declaration in order to obtain the pension provided by Act of Congress approved June 27, 1890: That he is the legal guardian of Alonzo; Rebecca E. and Thomas S. Wat legitimate children of John Watson, who enlisted under the name of John Watson, at New Jersey, on the 2 day of Sept, 1862, in Co 'G' 25th Regt New Jersey Vols.

[Here state rank, company, and regiment, if in the Military service, or vessel, if in Navy.]

and served at least ninety days in the War of the Rebellion, in the service of the United States; who was HONORABLY DISCHARGED June 20, 1863 and died ________. That he left a widow surviving him who was pension by Cert 283.893 – remarried Nov 15/1891

[Here state date of death or of remarriage.]

That the names and dates of birth of all the surviving children of the soldier under sixteen years of age are as follows:

Alonzo, born April 9th, 1878
Rebecca E., born May 22nd, 1880
Thomas S., born August 6th, 1882
________, born ________, 18__
________, born ________, 18__
________, born ________, 18__

That the father was married under the name of John Watson to

Also personally appeared M. V. B. Moore, residing at Mays Landing and L. W. Cramer, residing at Mays Landing persons whom I certify to be respectable and entitled to credit, and who, being duly sworn, say that they were present and saw Daniel E. Lozard, the claimant, sign his name (~~or make ... mark~~) to the foregoing declaration; that they have every reason to believe, from the appearance of said claimant and their acquaintance with him and the minors for ... years and ... years, respectively, that they are ~~is~~ the identical persons they represents themselves to be; and that they have no interest in the prosecution of this claim.

(1) M. V. B. Moore

(2) L. W. Cramer

[Signatures of witnesses.]

Sworn to and subscribed before me this 11 day of June A. D. 1895, and I hereby certify that the contents of the above declaration, etc., were fully made known and explained to the applicant and witnesses before swearing, including the words ... erased, and the words ... added; and that I have no interest, direct or indirect, in the prosecution of this claim.

Lewis Evans

[Signature.]

County Clerk

[Official character.]

The Act of June 27, 1890, requires that in minor children's cases:

1. That the soldier served at least ninety days in the War of the Rebellion and was HONORABLY DISCHARGED.

2. Proof of soldier's death [cause need not have been due to Army service], his marriage to mother, and proof of her death or divestment of title.

6

A.

Widow's Declaration for Pension.

☛ Execute before a Court of Record or some Officer thereof (usually County Clerk) having Custody of the Seal. ☚

☛ AND RETURN TO JAMES F. RUSLING, TRENTON, N. J. ☚

State of New Jersey, **County of** Atlantic, ss.

ON THIS 6 day of November A.D. one thousand eight hundred and eighty nine personally appeared before me, Clerk of the Court of the Orphans Court a Court of Record within and for the County and State aforesaid Ella Watson aged 48 years, who, being duly sworn according to law, makes the following Declaration in order to obtain the Pension provided by Acts of Congress granting Pension to widows: That she is the widow of John Watson, who enlisted under that name, at Beverly on the 2d day of September, A.D. 1864 in Company G of the 25" [Company and Regiment of service, if in the army; or vessel and rank if in the navy.] Regiment of N.J. Vols., in the war of 1861, and who died of disease [Wounds or disease] incurred in said service, in the line of duty, at Piney Holler [Place of death.] in the State of New Jersey on the 13th day of September, A.D. 1889

~~who bore at the time of his death the rank of ... in ...~~ ["In the service aforesaid," or otherwise.]

that she was married under the name of Ella Pierce to said soldier on the 16th day of August A.D. 1863 by Esq Elias Smith at Tuckahoe, N.J. there being no legal barrier to such marriage; that neither she nor her husband had been previously married [If either had been previously married so state, and give date of death or divorce of former spouse.]

that she has to present date remained his widow; that the following are the names and dates of birth of all his legitimate children yet surviving who were under sixteen years of age at the father's death, viz.:

HIS BY HERSELF.		HIS BY A FORMER MARRIAGE.	
Alonzo	born Apr. 9" 1877		born 18
Rebecca L.	born May 22 1880		born 18
Thomas S.	born Aug 6" 1882		born 18
	born 18		born 18
	born 18		born 18
	born 18		born 18

That she has not abandoned the support of any one of his children, but that they are still under her care or maintenance,

[For such children as are not under her care, claimant should account.]

Also personally appeared *Lucella Cain*, residing at *May's Landing N. J.*, and *Ella May Atkinson* residing at *May's Landing N. J.*, persons whom I certify to be respectable and entitled to credit, and who, being by me duly sworn, say that they were present and saw *Ella Watson*, the claimant, sign her name (or make her mark) to the foregoing declaration; that they have every reason to believe, from the appearance of said claimant and their acquaintance with her, that she is the identical person she represents herself to be; and that they have no interest in the prosecution of this claim.

Lusaty Cain

Ella May Atkinson

[If Affiants sign by mark, two persons who can write sign here.] [Signature of Affiants.]

Sworn to and subscribed before me this *6th* day of *November* A.D. 188*9*

and I hereby certify that the contents of the above declaration, &c., were fully made known and explained to the claimant and witnesses before swearing, including the words .... erased, and the words .... added; and that I have no interest, direct or indirect, in the prosecution of this claim.

[L. S.]

J. S. Risley [Official Signature.]

P. O. Address .... *Clerk of C. C.* [Official Character.]

(This Declaration must NOT be executed before a *Justice of the Peace, Notary Public, Master in Chancery, Commissioner of Deeds, or Alderman.* It MUST be executed only before some CLERK OF COURT, with SEAL—usually the COUNTY CLERK—with any two persons, who need not have been soldiers.)

A.

Declaration for Guardian or Children.

☞INSTRUCTIONS.—Execute before Clerk of any Court of Record with Seal, (County Clerk, Surrogate, Prothonotary, Register, &c.), *with any two acquaintances.* This Blank may also be executed before any Notary Public, Justice of the Peace, or Commissioner of Deeds, but he should have an *Official Seal*, and attach it always, or else send this Blank to County Clerk for Certificate of his Official Character. Return to JAMES F. RUSLING, TRENTON, N. J.☜

This Blank for use in cases of JAMES F. RUSLING, only.

State of New Jersey **County of** Atlantic, **ss:**

On this Twenty fifth day of April A. D. one thousand eight hundred and ninety-three personally appeared before me County Clerk (County Clerk or other Officer's Title.) in and for the County and State aforesaid, Daniel S. Ingol aged 57 years, who, being duly sworn according to law, makes the following declaration in order to obtain the Pension provided by Act of Congress, approved June 27, 1890: That he is the legal guardian of Alonzo, Rebecca L. & Thomas S. Watson legitimate children of John Watson dec'd who enlisted under the name of John Watson at .... on the 2 day of Sept. 1862 in Co. G. 25 N J Vols (Here state rank, company and regiment, if in the Army, or name of vessel, if in the Navy.) .... and served at least ninety days in the War of the Rebellion; who was HONORABLY DISCHARGED on the 20 day of June 1863 and died on the thirteenth day of September 1889 at Penny Holly in the State of New Jersey

That he left a widow surviving him who remarried on the 17th day of November A D 1891 (Here state date of death or of remarriage, if either.)

That the names and dates of birth of all the surviving children of the soldier under sixteen years of age are as follows:

x Alonzo Watson (Give name of child.) of soldier by John & Ella Watson (Give name of mother.) born April 9th (Date of birth.) 1878

x Rebecca L Watson of soldier by John & Ella Watson born May 22nd 1880

x Thomas S Watson of soldier by John & Ella Watson born Aug 6th 1882

.... of soldier by .... born .... 18....

.... of soldier by .... born .... 18....

.... of soldier by .... born .... 18....

.... of soldier by .... born .... 18....

That the mother was married under the name of ~~Ella Watson~~ Ella Pierce (Give her name at date of marriage.) to said father, there being no legal barrier to such marriage; that the said children have not aided or abetted the rebellion; and that ~~no~~ a prior application has been filed by ~~them or either of them~~ said guardian 566.421

PENSION MAY 4 1893 OFFICE

AFFIDAVIT OF IDENTITY.

(By any two acquaintances, male or female, soldiers or otherwise.)

Also personally appeared M. V. B. Moore residing at Mays Landing Atlantic county N.J. and Lewis W. Cramer residing at Mays Landing N.J. persons whom I certify to be respectable and entitled to credit, and who, being by me duly sworn according to law, say that they were present and saw Daniel V. Izard Guardian &c. the claimant sign his name (or make ...... mark) to the foregoing Declaration; that they have every reason to believe, from appearance of said claimant and their acquaintance with him, that he is the identical person he represent himself to be; and that they have no interest in this claim.

If affiant signs by mark, two witnesses here to SUCH signature.

....

P. O. Address..............................

....

P. O. Address..............................

M. V. B. Moore
(Affiant sign here.)

P. O. Address Mays Landing N.J.
(Give always.)

Lewis W. Cramer
(Affiant sign here.)

P. O. Address Mays Landing N.J.
(Give always.)

Sworn to and subscribed before me this Twenty fifth day of April A. D. 1893, and I hereby certify that the contents of the above Declaration, &c., were fully made known and explained to the applicant and witnesses before swearing, including the words Ella Watson erased, and the words Ella Pierce added; and that I have no interest, direct or indirect, in the prosecution of this claim.

[SEAL.]

Lewis Evans
(Signature of Notary or other Officer.)

County Clerk
(Official Character.)

P. O. Address..............................
(Notary or other Officer's.)

PENSION ~~AND~~ CLAIM AGENCY,
TRENTON, N. J.

PENSION MAY 4 1893 OFFICE

JAMES F. RUSLING,

Counsellor at Law, U. S. and N. J.

(Bvt. Brig. Gen'l, late U. S. Pension Agent, N. J.)

REFERS TO

HON. GOVERNOR OF NEW JERSEY,	Trenton, N. J.
HON. U. S. Senators and M. C.'s of N. J.,	Washington, D. C.
GEN. W. S. STRYKER, Adj't Gen'l of N. J.,	Trenton, N. J.
GEN. W. T. SHERMAN,	St. Louis, Mo.
GEN. W. S. ROSECRANS,	Washington, D. C.
GEN. D. E. SICKLES,	New York City.
GEN. J. B. CARR,	Troy, N. Y.
GEN. LOUIS WAGNER,	Phila., Pa.
GEN. JAMES STEWART,	Phila., Pa.
GEN. T. J. WOOD,	Ohio.
GEN. W. J. SEWELL,	Camden, N. J.
GEN. ROB'T MCALLISTER,	Belvidere, N. J.
GEN. E. B. GRUBB,	Edgewater Park, N. J.
GEN. JOHN RAMSEY,	Jersey City, N. J.
GEN. FRANCIS PRICE,	Oakland, N. J.
GEN. WM. WARD,	Newark, N. J.
HON. JAMES BUCHANAN, M. C.,	Trenton, N. J.
HON. J. A. BENTLEY, ex-Com. of Pensions,	Denver, Col.

And to Pensioners and Claimants through THIS AGENCY,

In every State and Territory.

Your attention invited to this **N. J. Agency.** Best place, of course, for all N. J. and other Soldiers. No Washington or other Agency or Attorney so advantageous. Experienced, prompt, *successful.* Not confined to N. J., but cases here from all U. S., Canada, Europe, &c.

1. **U. S. Pensions** due officers, soldiers, sailors, widows, children, mothers, fathers, according to facts. If *now disabled* by *wounds, injuries, disease* or *otherwise,* **Soldier,** *&c., entitled,* if not result of his own vicious habits. If soldier, &c., now deceased, **Widow** and **Children** (under 16 years,) *entitled,* if dependent on daily labor; or if Children insane, idiotic, or otherwise helpless, for life. If soldier, &c., now deceased (leaving no widow or child), **Mother** or **Father** entitled, if without adequate property or support *now.*

2. **Increase** of Pension due Invalid Pensioners, (*soldier, &c.*), if pensioned *too low,* or disability *worse,* or *other U. S. disabilities* exist. Many now *entitled* to Increase, especially if pensioned for *Disease,* or less than $12 a month.

(Widows, mothers, fathers *not entitled* to Increase.)

3. ☞ **Many everywhere entitled to Pension, or Increase, or Re-Rating,** under Old or New Laws. If in doubt, write here. No charge for advice. **No Fee,** *unless successful,* and then Fee as fixed by U. S. Law.

BUREAU OF VITAL STATISTICS.

I, Ezra M. Hunt, *Medical Superintendent of the Bureau of Vital Statistics of the State of New Jersey,* do hereby Certify, *that the foregoing and annexed is a true copy of a certain Certificate of Death, as taken from and compared with the original now remaining on file in my office.*

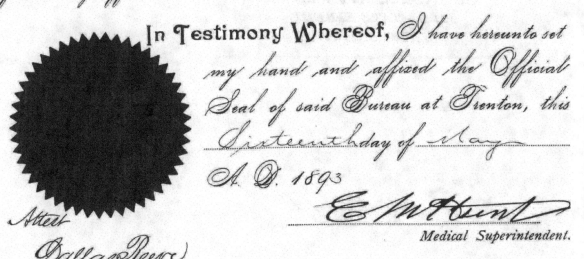

In Testimony Whereof, *I have hereunto set my hand and affixed the Official Seal of said Bureau at Trenton, this* Sixteenth *day of* May *A. D.* 1893

E M Hunt
Medical Superintendent.

Attest
Dallas Reeve
Registrar of Vital Statistics.

9-45

Case of X
Daniel E. Iszard
Gd. children of
John Watson, dec'd
"G" 25 N.J.

No. Not yet given.

CERTIFIED COPY OF

CERTIFICATE OF DEATH

—OF—

John Watson

PENSION OFFICE. MAY 22 1893

Filed by
JAMES F. RUSLING,
COUNSELLOR AT LAW,
224 E. STATE STREET,
TRENTON, N. J.

Ans. L.L.

STATE OF NEW JERSEY.

CERTIFICATE OF DEATH.

SEE PENALTY FOR NON-REPORT.

1. Full name of deceased John Watson (If an infant not named, so state, and give sex.)
2. Age 49 years —— months —— Color White
3. ~~Single~~, married, ~~widow or widower~~. {Cross out all but the right one.} Occupation Labore
4. Birthplace New Jersey U. S. A. {State or county. If of foreign birth give how long in United States.}
5. Last place of residence Franklin Tp. Gloucester Co. N.J. {If a city, give name; if not give county and township.}
6. How long resident in this State 49 yrs
7. Place of death Franklin Tp. Gloucester Co. N.J. (If in a city, give name, and street and number; if in township, give name and county; if in an institution, so state.)
8. Father's name Alonzo Watson Country of birth U. S.
9. Mother's name Ann Watson Country of birth U. S.
10. I hereby certify that I attended the deceased during the last illness, and that he died on the 13" day of Sept. 1889; and that the cause of death was Billious Dysentery and Inanition

Length of sickness 2 weeks

REQUESTED, BUT OPTIONAL.

a. Primary disease Billious Dysentery

b. Secondary disease (how long) Inanition

c. Remarks Asthenia

J. Gaunt Edwards
Medical Attendant.

Residence Williamstown N.J.

~~Date~~

Name and residence of Undertaker Wm. P. Buck Williamstown

Place of Burial Piney Hollow

7

BUREAU OF VITAL STATISTICS

PENSION OFFICE MAY 22 1893

Trenton, N. J. May 16" 1893.

To Whom it May Concern: This is to certify that we have searched, but can find no record in this office of the births of the children of John and Ellen Walton, viz:- Alonzo, born April 9" 1878, at Williamstown, Gloucester Co. N. J., Rebecca L. born at Downstown, Atlantic Co. N. J. May 22" 1880.

Dallas Reeve

Registrar.

Case of
Daniel E. Iszard
Gt. children of
John Watson, dec'd
"G" 25 N.J.
No. not yet given

CERTIFIED COPY OF

BIRTH RETURN

—OF—

Thomas Watson

PENSION OFFICE, U.S.
MAY 22 1893

Filed by
JAMES F. RUSLING,
COUNSELLOR AT LAW,
223 E. STATE STREET,
TRENTON, N. J.

BUREAU OF VITAL STATISTICS

I, Ezra M. Hunt, Medical Superintendent of the Bureau of Vital Statistics of the State of New Jersey, do hereby Certify, *that the foregoing and annexed is a true copy of a certain Birth Return, as taken from and compared with the original now remaining on file in my office.*

In Testimony Whereof, *I have hereunto set my hand and affixed the Official Seal of said Bureau, at Trenton, the* Sixteenth *day of* May *A.D.* 1893.

ATTEST:

Dallas Reeve
State Registrar of Vital Statistics.

E. M. Hunt
Medical Superintendent.

7

STATE OF NEW JERSEY.

BIRTH RETURN.

SEE PENALTY FOR NON-REPORT.

1. Full name of Child (if any) Thomas Watson. Color White
2. Date of Birth August 6" 1882. Sex Male
3. Place of Birth Downstown, Franklin Tp. Gloucester Co. N.J. (If city, give name, street and number; if not, give township and county.)
4. Name of Father John Watson. {If out of wedlock, write O. W.}
5. Maiden name of Mother Ellen Pierce
6. Country of Father's Birth America Age 43 Occupation Solier
7. Country of Mother's Birth America Age 39.
8. Number of Children in all by this Marriage 5 How many of them Living 5.
9. Name and P. O. address of Medical Attendant, in his own handwriting, with date, } Mrs E M Mull Midwife Landisville Mc Co. New Jer

Aug. 12" 1882.

7

BIRTH RETURN.

Name of Child's Parents,

John and Ellen
Watson.

City or Township and County,

Downstown Franklin Tp.
Gloucester Co. N.J.

Date of Birth,

Aug 6" 1882.

NOTE.—Birth Returns and all Blanks are to be procured of Clerks of Cities or of Township Assessors, as provided by the law for the Registry of Marriages, Births and Deaths; or in this form by postal to State Health Board, Trenton.

DECLARATION FOR WIDOW'S PENSION.

Act of June 27, 1890.

NOTE.—This can be executed before any officer authorized to administer oaths for general purposes. If such officer uses a seal, certificate of Clerk of Court is not necessary. If no seal is used, then such certificate must be attached.

State of New Jersey, **County of** Atlantic, **ss:**

ON THIS 22 day of July, A. D. one thousand eight hundred and ninety

personally appeared before me, a Surrogate

within and for the County and State aforesaid,

Ella Watson, aged 43 years, a resident of

the Town of Mays Landing, County of Atlantic, State of

New Jersey, who, being duly sworn according to law, declares that she is the widow of

John Watson who enlisted under the name of John Watson

at Beverly, on the second day of September

A. D. 1862, in Co. I. 25th N. J. Vols

(Here state rank, company, and regiment, if in the Military service; or vessel, if in Navy.)

and served at least ninety days in the late war of the Rebellion, who was HONORABLY DISCHARGED June 20th 1863, and died Sept 13th 1889

(The cause of death need not be stated.)

That she was married under the name of Ella Pierce name, to said John Watson, on the 16 day of August 1863, by Squire Elias Smith, at New Tuckahoe N. J.

there being no legal barrier to such marriage

(If there was a former marriage of claimant or her husband, state it here and how dissolved.)

That she has not remarried since the death of the said John Watson

(Name of soldier or sailor.)

That she is without other means of support than her daily labor. That names and dates of birth of all the children now living under sixteen years of age of the soldier are as follows:

Alonzo Watson, born April 9th, 1877

Rebecca L. " , born May 22d, 1880

Thomas S. " , born August 6th, 1882

, born , 18

, born , 18

, born , 18

#1,0526

Also personally appeared Hannah Carty, residing at Mays Landing N.J. and Mary Veal, residing at Mays Landing N.J., persons whom I certify to be respectable and entitled to credit, and who, being by me duly sworn, say they were present and saw Ella Watson claimant, sign her name (or make her mark) to the foregoing declaration; that they have every reason to believe from the appearance of said claimant and an acquaintance with her of 15 years and 1 years, respectively, that she is the identical person she represents herself to be; and that they have no interest in the prosecution of this claim.

Hannah Cartey
Mary Veal
(Signatures of witnesses.)

Sworn to and subscribed before me this 22d day of July, A. D. 1890

and I hereby certify that the contents of the above declaration, &c., were fully made known and explained to the applicant and witnesses before swearing, including the words ______ erased, and the words ______ added; and that I have no interest, direct or indirect, in the prosecution of this claim.

J. S. Risley
(Official Signature.)

[L. S.]

Surrogate
(Official Character.)

The Act of June 27, 1890, requires, in widow's case:

1. That the soldier served at least NINETY DAYS in the War of the Rebellion and was HONORABLY DISCHARGED.
2. Proof of soldier's death (death cause need not have been due to Army service).
3. That widow is "without other means of support than her daily labor.".
4. That widow was married to soldier prior to June 27, 1890, date of the Act.
5. That all pensions under this act commence from date of receipt of application (executed after the passage of act) in Pension Bureau.

6

Write nothing above this line.

(3—060.)

Adjutant Div.
[illegible] Ex'r.
No. 408,533
Widow

Department of the Interior,

BUREAU OF PENSIONS,

Washington, D. C., May 5th, 1896

SIR:

It is alleged that John Watson enlisted September 2nd 1862 and served as a private in Co. G, 25th Reg't N. J. Vols. also as a ________ in Co. ____, ____ Reg't ________

and was discharged at ________, ________, 18__

It is also alleged that while on duty at ________ on or about ________, 18__, he was disabled by disease

and was treated in hospitals of which the names, locations, and dates of treatment are as follows:

None alleged

In case of the above-named soldier the War Department is requested to furnish an official statement of the enrollment, discharge, and record of service so far as the same may be applicable to the foregoing allegation,

Write nothing to the left of this line.

(3—060.)

No. 408.533,

WAR DEPARTMENT,

RECORD AND PENSION DIVISION.

Respectfully returned to the Commissioner of Pensions.

John Watson

Co. G. 25, Reg't N. J. Vols,

was enrolled Sept. 2" , 1862

and Mus'd. out June 20, 1863.

with co.

From Sept 2", 1862, *to* June 20, 1863

he held the rank of Private

and during that period the rolls show him present, ~~*except as follows:*~~

Other records furnish nothing additional bearing upon this case.

The medical records show him treated as follows No record found.

By authority of the Secretary of War:

F. C. Ainsworth

Captain and Ass't Surgeon, U. S. Army.

Per R.

Date MAY 6 1890

G.

GENERAL AFFIDAVIT.

☞ *Instructions.*—Execute before a NOTARY PUBLIC, JUSTICE OF THE PEACE or other Officer authorized to take general affidavits (*not* Commissioner of Deeds) and return to **James F. Rusling, Trenton, N. J.**

State of New Jersey }
County of Atlantic } ss. Daziel E. Iszard Guardian of Children of John Watso

In the matter of "Alonzo Watson and Rebecca L Watson. for Pension.

Personally came before me, a Clerk of the County in and for aforesaid County and State John S. Risley and Martin V. B. Moore

citizens of the Town of Mays Landing, County of Atlantic, State of New Jersey, well known to me to be reputable and entitled to credit, and who, being duly sworn, declares each in relation to aforesaid case, as follows: Have known Alonzo Watson and Rebecca L. Watson for the past ten years, and know them to be the legitimate children of late John Watson, and our reasons for believing so is as follows: by their residing with their mother wife of said John Watson, and being recognized and acknowledged throughout the community as his children, and had the facts been otherwise we would have been likely to have known or heard of it, but never have.

Blank for use in Cases of JAMES F. RUSLING Only.

8

I further declare each that I ~~have no interest in said case, and~~ am not concerned in its prosecution, and am not related to said applicant.

Two Witnesses—when any affiant signs BY MARK.

....

....

Affiants sign here.

J. S. Risley
P. O. Address: Mays Landing
W. W. Moore
P. O. Address: Mays Landing

Sworn to and subscribed before me this day by the above named affiant each; and I certify that I read said affidavit to said affiant each, and acquainted him with its contents before he executed the same each. I further certify, that I am in nowise interested in said case, nor am I concerned in its prosecution; and that said affiant is personally known to me, each; that he is a creditable person, and so reputed in the community in which he resides, each.

....

....

Witness my hand and official seal this 13 day of November 1893

Sign here Lewis Evans
County Clerk

ADD SEAL HERE.

Note.—The Officer should attach his Official Seal, or send Certificate of Official Character, unless already on file.

No. 28, 6-'89.

RECORD PROOF OF MARRIAGES, ~~BIRTHS AND DEATHS.~~

State of New Jersey, County of Glouster, ss:

ON THIS 18 day of July A. D., one thousand eight hundred and ninety five personally appeared before me, a Notary Public within and for the County and State aforesaid, Samuel McCurdy, who, being duly sworn according to law, declares that he resides in Franklinville County of Gloucester State of New Jersey; and that he is was a Justice of the Peace in 1891 (Pastor, Rector, or Clerk, as the case may be.) of the County of Glouster (Church, Parish, or Board of Health.) located in Franklinville N. J. in the last-named County, and custodian of the records thereof; that the following is a true copy of an extract from the record of Marriage (Marriages, Births, or Deaths.) viz:

I Samuel McCurdy Doe Swear upon my oath that I was a Justice of the Peace at Franklinville County of Glouster for ten years time ending May the First 1894 I due swear that I married Ella Watson to Herman Geigies of May Landing County of Atlantic State New Jersey / on Sept the 17 1871

8

Sworn to and subscribed before me this 18 day of July, 1891, I have no interest in the prosecution of this claim for*

Wilson T. Jones
(Official Signature.)
Notary Public

I, ... Clerk of the County Court in and for aforesaid County and State, do certify that ...., Esq., who has signed his name to the foregoing declaration and affidavit, was at the time of so doing, ... in and for said County and State, duly commissioned and sworn; that all his official acts are entitled to full faith and credit, and that his signature thereunto is genuine.

Witness my hand and seal of office, this .... day of ...., 18....

[L. S.] Clerk of the ....

☞ To be executed before a Court of Record or some officer thereof having custody of its seal, a Notary Public, or Justice of the Peace, whose official signature shall be verified by his official seal, and in case he has none, his signature and official character shall be certified by a Clerk of a Court of Record, or a City or County Clerk.

STELLA WATSON
WIFE OF ALONZO

ALONZO WATSON IS SON OF JOHN WATSON

Form 15-6

DEPARTMENT OF COMMERCE—BUREAU OF THE CENSUS

FIFTEENTH CENSUS OF THE UNITED STATES: 1930

POPULATION SCHEDULE

State: New Jersey

County: Gloucester

Township or other division of county: Monroe Township

Unincorporated place: Williamstown

Enumeration District No. 8-71

Supervisor's District No. 12

Sheet No. 14

Enumerated by me on April 22, 1930, John W. Lord

John Watson +
Anna B
son Irving + daughter Emeline

Births

Watson Race.

Sarah Watson was Borned the year.

John Watson was Borned. the year. 1870.-
Aug. 16.-

Rebbeca Watson was Borned. the year. 1879.-

Alonzo Watson was Borned the year

Thos. S Watson. was Borned. the year. 1882.
Aug 26.-

Edith Vandegriffe Daughter of Rebbeca. & George was 1900
Borned. July-29.- 19

Mabel Cromer Doughter of. Edna Cromer. 1907.
was Borned. 1907.

Helena Virginia Watson Doughter of. Thos. & Edna. 1910
was Borned April-2-

Ervin Watson son of John Junior. & Anna
was Borned.

Etta Watson Wife of C. H. Watson Departed this life
Dec. 9. - 1903.
Rebbeca Watson. Vandegriffe. Departed this
life. March 19th 1900

Marjorie Watson daughter of Mary Edna and Thomas Watson. Née Cramner.

1922. Born

Marjorie Watson married to William Kent. 1941
[illegible] Church Wedding. All Kent family present. [illegible]
Watson Sutton. Née Cramner. D. McCall. [illegible] J. S. Watson.

Mary Edna Watson. Departed this life July 1928
Heart disease.

Dara Watson married Robert Sutton.
Daughter of the [illegible] Mary Watson.

Maud. Daughter of Mary E Watson. departed this life
1922. Kidney disease.

NEW JERSEY DEPARTMENT OF HEALTH AND SENIOR SERVICES
TRENTON, N.J.

January 9, 2002

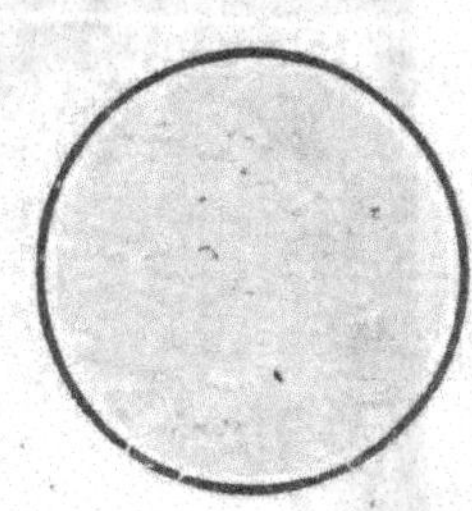

THIS IS TO CERTIFY THAT THE FOLLOWING IS A TRUE COPY OF A RECORD FILED IN THIS DEPARTMENT

Donald L. Lipira
Donald L. Lipira, State Registrar
Bureau of Vital Statistics

George T. DiFerdinando, Jr. MD MPH
George T. DiFerdinando, Jr., M.D., M.P.H., Acting Commissioner
Department of Health and Senior Services

REG-32
AUG 01

DO NOT accept this copy unless the RAISED GREAT SEAL of the State of New Jersey is affixed hereon.

%G807

W140

JULY '81. FORM B.

STATE OF NEW JERSEY.

BIRTH RETURN.

SEE PENALTY FOR NON-REPORT.

1. *Full name of Child (if any)* Thomas Watson *Color* White
2. *Date of Birth* August 6th 1882 *Sex* Male
3. *Place of Birth* Downstown Franklin Tp Gloucester Co. N.J. (If city, give name, street and number; if not, give township and county)
4. *Name of Father* John Watson {If out of wedlock, write O. W}
5. *Maiden name of Mother* Ellen Fullick
6. *Country of Father's Birth* America *Age* 42 (43) *Occupation* Cooper
7. *Country of Mother's Birth* America *Age* 39
8. *Number of Children in all by this Marriage* 6 *How many Living* 6
9. *Name and P. O. address of Medical Attendant in his own handwriting, with date,* Mrs. E. M[illegible] midwife Franklinville Glo. Co. New Jersey Aug 12 1882

No. [illegible]

INDIVIDUAL RECORD—CIVILIAN CONSERVATION CORPS

GENERAL INFORMATION*

No. CC2-311013.

(1) Name Thomas S. Watson (2) Address New Gretna, Burl. Co., N.J.

(3) Date of birth August 16, 1884 (4) Birthplace Downstown, N. J.

(5) Nearest relative Mrs. Lora Sutton (Name) (6) Unemployed since Sept. 1934

New Gretna, N. J. (Address)

(7) Citizenship ** Native born / Naturalized / Declarant (8) Color White

†(9) Were you previously a member of the Civilian Conservation Corps? Yes (Yes or no) If so, furnish the following informatio[n]

Company No. 225 Location Tuckerton, N.J. Date enrolled July 15, 1933

Date discharged September 30, 1934 Character of discharge Honorable (Honorable or dishonorable)

OATH OF ENROLLMENT

I, Thomas S. Watson do solemnly swear (or affirm) that [the] information given above as to my status is correct. I agree to remain in the Civilian Conservation Corps for the peri[od] terminating at the discretion of the United States between September 30 and October 15, 193[5], unless sooner released by prop[er] authority, and that I will obey those in authority and observe all the rules and regulations thereof to the best of my ability a[nd] will accept such allowances as may be provided pursuant to law and regulations promulgated pursuant thereto. I understa[nd] and agree that any injury received or disease contracted by me while a member of the Civilian Conservation Corps cannot [be] made the basis of any claim against the Government, except such as I may be entitled to under the act of September 7, 19[16] (39 Stat. 742) (an act to provide compensation for employees of the United States suffering injuries while in the performan[ce] of their duties and for other purposes), and that I shall not be entitled to any allowances upon release from camp, exce[pt] transportation in kind to the place at which I was accepted for enrollment. I understand further that any articles issued [to] me by the United States Government for use while a member of the Civilian Conservation Corps are, and remain, proper[ty] of the United States Government and that willful destruction, loss, sale, or disposal of such property renders me financial[ly] responsible for the cost thereof and liable to trial in the civil courts. I understand further that any infraction of the rules [or] regulations of the Civilian Conservation Corps renders me liable to expulsion therefrom. So help me God.

I HEREBY RE-ENROLL FOR THE SIXTH ENROLLMENT PERIOD OCTOBER 8 1935 TO MARCH 31, 1936, UNDER THE SAME CONDITIONS AS FOR PREVIOUS ENROLLMENT Thomas S Watson

(Signature) Thomas S Watson
Thomas S. Watson

(Place) Camp No. S-55, Tuckerton, N.J.

† Sworn to and subscribed before me this 16th day of July, nineteen hundred an[d] thirty Five.

I HEREBY RE-ENROLL FOR THE SIXTH ENROLLMENT PERIOD OCTOBER [illegible] 1935 TO MARCH 31 [illegible] UNDER THE SAME CONDITIONS AS FOR PREVIOUS ENROLLMENT.

Joel Shear
JOEL SHEAR, 1st. Lieut. Inf-Res. (Title)

* Print or type.
† Oath may be taken before any officer.

"I HEREBY RE-ENROLL FOR THE PERIOD APRIL 1 TO SEPTEMBER 30 TO OCTOBER 15, 1935 UNDER THE SAME CONDITIONS AS FOR MY PREVIOUS ENROLLMENT."
Thomas S Watson

† See paragraph 95, War Department Regulations—Relief of Unemployment, Civilian Conservation Corps.

C.C.C. Form No. 1
Feb. 15, 1934

3—10160 U. S. GOVERNMENT PRINTING OFFICE: 1934

DESCRIPTION

Height 5 feet 10 inches; Weight 140
Color of eyes BLUE; Color of hair BROWN; Complexion RUDDY
Previous occupation SAWYER

RECORD OF SERVICE IN CIVILIAN CONSERVATION CORPS

Served:*

a. From 7/15/33 to 9/30/34 under Forestry, Dept. at Camp 17-(NJ) Tuckerton, N.J.
Type of work Forest * Manner of performance Satisfactory
Last paid to incl. Sept. 30, 1934 on Vou. no. Sept (Month) 193?, accts. of T. D. Dabney, Maj (Name of disbursing officer)
Final Payment Roll.

b. From .... to .... under ...., Dept. at ....
Type of work .... * Manner of performance ....
Last paid to incl. ...., on Vou. no. .... (Month), 193..., accts. of .... (Name of disbursing officer)

c. From .... to .... under ...., Dept. at ....
Type of work .... * Manner of performance ....
Last paid to incl. ...., on Vou. no. .... (Month), 193..., accts. of .... (Name of disbursing officer)

d. From .... to .... under ...., Dept. at ....
Type of work .... * Manner of performance ....
Last paid to incl. ...., on Vou. no. .... (Month), 193..., accts. of .... (Name of disbursing officer)

e. From .... to .... under ...., Dept. at ....
Type of work .... * Manner of performance ....
Last paid to incl. ...., on Vou. no. .... (Month), 193..., accts. of .... (Name of disbursing officer)

Allotments:

No Allottee (Local Woodsman) (Name of allottee) (No. and street or rural route) (City and State) $........

.... (Name of allottee) (No. and street or rural route) (City and State) $........

.... (Name of allottee) (No. and street or rural route) (City and State) $........

Remarks [illegible]

No unauthorized absences.

** Discharged ~~[struck out]~~ Sept. 30, 1934, at Camp No. 7 (NJ) because of Honorable Discharge, end of enrollment period. Entitled to travel allowance in kind.

Transportation furnished from None to ——

W. N. Birkhart Capt. Engr-Res
W. N. BIRKHART, (Title)

* To be filled in and initialed by personnel officer whenever there is a change in employment. Use words "Excellent", "Satisfactory", or "Unsatisfactory".
** Line out the one inapplicable. Upon the permanent separation of this man from the Civilian Conservation Corps, the original of this form should be mailed to the Commanding Officer of the Army post or station at which the oath of enrollment was taken. See reverse side hereof.

DESCRIPTION

Height Five feet Eight inches; Weight 125

Color of eyes Gray; Color of hair Brown; Complexion Dark

Previous occupation Sawyer, experienced in woods & road work.

RECORD OF SERVICE IN CIVILIAN CONSERVATION CORPS

Served:*

a. From 7/16/35 to 9/30/37 under Forestry Dept. at Camp No. S-55, Tuckerton
Type of work Forest * Manner of performance Very satisfactory
Last paid to incl. 9/30/37, on Vou. no. F/P/R Sept. 1937, accts. of N. T. Legg (Name of disbursing officer)
awo 9/30/37 9/30/37

b. From ______ to ______ under ______, Dept. at ______
Type of work ______ * Manner of performance ______
Last paid to incl. ______, on Vou. no. ______ (Month) 193__, accts. of ______ (Name of disbursing officer)

c. From ______ to ______ under ______, Dept. at ______
Type of work ______ * Manner of performance ______
Last paid to incl. ______, on Vou. no. ______ (Month) 193__, accts. of ______ (Name of disbursing officer)

d. From ______ to ______ under ______, Dept. at ______
Type of work ______ * Manner of performance ______
Last paid to incl. ______, on Vou. no. ______ (Month) 193__, accts. of ______ (Name of disbursing officer)

e. From ______ to ______ under ______, Dept. at ______
Type of work ______ * Manner of performance ______
Last paid to incl. ______, on Vou. no. ______ (Month) 193__, accts. of ______ (Name of disbursing officer)

Allotments:

No Allotment (Local Woodsman) (Name of allottee) (No. and street or rural route) (City and State) $

______ (Name of allottee) (No. and street or rural route) (City and State)

______ (Name of allottee) (No. and street or rural route) (City and State)

Remarks A.W.P. 10/9 LWP 4/22/36 (1 day) per C.O. #11 dated 4/7/36
LWOP 5/1/36 (1 day) per C.O. #16 dated 5/4/36 LWP 11/3/36
LWP 12/17/36 to 12/27/36 (11 days) AWOL 2/17/37 (1 day);
AWP 4/9/37 to 4/14/37 (6 days);
LWOP 9/1 to 9/30/37 (30 days)
Local Experienced Man.

** Discharged Honorably ~~Transferred~~ from W.D. 9/30/37, at Camp S-55 Co 225 New Gretna, N.J., because of Expiration of term of enrollment.

Transportation furnished from None furnished

I accept transportation to ______ as a full and complete settlement of the Government's obligation to furnish transportation.

(Name)

* To be filled in and initialed by personnel officer whenever there is a change in employment ...

** Line out the one inapplicable. Upon the ... the Commanding Officer of the Army post or station at which the oath of enrollment was ...

I hereby [illegible] Emergency Conservation Work.

1. My name is Watson, Thomas S.

2. I am a citizen of the United States by birth (X) (check); or I secured final naturalization papers on ....

at ....

3. I was born at Downstown (Place) Atlantic (County) New Jersey (State)

On August (Month) 16 (Day) 1884 (Year)

4. My present marital condition is (check): Single ( ), Married ( ), Divorced ( ), Separated ( ) Widowed (X).

5. I have One (Number) total and No (Number) partial dependent members of my family group.

6. NOTE.—Allotment of pay is not required for local experienced men, but may be made. If so desired, in below name of dependent relative to receive allotment.

Name .... Relationship ....

Address .... Amount ....

7. I (have) (have not) previously been a member of the Civilian Conservation Corps. (If previously enrolled the following information.)

Company number 225 Location Burlington County, New Jer (County and State)

Serial number 222-12054 Status: (Check) Junior ( ) L. E. M. (X)

Date enrolled July 15, 1933 Date discharged September 30, 1934

Type of discharge Honorable discharge, end of enrollment period. (Honorable, administrative or dishonorable)

8. My education has been as follows: Third grade; 4 years night school

9. I have engaged in the following trades or occupations (indicate also number of years experience in each).

Sawyer - 25 years.

10. I have been unemployed since September 30, 1934 (Month) (Year)

11. My special abilities or skills, fitting me for work as a local experienced man, are: Sawyer, experienced in woods and road work.

I agree to abide faithfully by the rules and regulations governing the work and the camps in which I desire employed.

Signature Thomas S. Watson

The United States Department of Labor certifies that Thomas S. Watson (Name)

residing at New Gretna (Place) Burlington (County) New Jersey (State)

has been selected by the technical service subscribed below for enrollment as a local experienced man in Emer Conservation Work, and for the completion of his enrollment has been directed to report to United States authorities at Bass River State Forest, Camp S-55, New Gretna, N. J. (Name, number, and address of camp)

U. S DEPARTMENT OF AGRICUL
(Name of Technical Service)

F. A. SILCOX,
Departmental Representative for E. C.
(Name and title of chief officer)

By C. P. Wilber, Chief
(Name of Technical Agent)
Division of Forests & Parks - N
(Designation or title of Agent)

ROUTING OF COPIES.—Original (White) to Army, Duplicate (Blue) to Technical Agency and Triplicate (Yellow) to State Director of Selection.

Descendants of Thomas S. Watson

Generation No. 1

1. THOMAS S.[3] WATSON *(JOHN[2], ALONZO[1])[1]* was born August 06, 1882 in Gloucester County, NJ[1], and died May 03, 1964[1]. He married MARY EDNA CRAMER[1], daughter of GEORGE CRAMER and MARY CRAMER. She was born May 06, 1888[1], and died July 22, 1928[1].

Notes for THOMAS S. WATSON:
Thomas Watson Listed the names of Sara and John in the family bible. I believe that Sara may have died as a child as nothing else can be found on her. We have been searching for a Walker Watson and found out that John's middle name is Walker.
Daniel E. Iszard resident of Mays Landing, Atlantic County, NJ was made legal gaurdian of Thomas, Rebecca and Alonzo On October 25, 1892 by Surrogate John S. Risley. (Ella remarried in 1891 and may have had to give up her children because of her new husband)??
Thomas died at the age of 81 years 8 months and 27 days old.

More About THOMAS S. WATSON:
Burial: Hillside Cemetary[1]

Notes for MARY EDNA CRAMER:
Reference #2925
This should be a correction to the above reference.
Mary Edna Cramer had a daughter before she married Thomas Watson. Her daughter was named Maud Cramer born May 18, 1906, died June 6, 1923.
Maud Cramer is buried along side her mother Mary Edna Watson, at Hillside Cemetery, New Gretna, NJ.

More About MARY EDNA CRAMER:
Burial: Hillside Cemetary[1]

Children of THOMAS WATSON and MARY CRAMER are:

2. i. HILMA[4] WATSON, b. May 02, 1910.
3. ii. DORA WATSON, b. February 09, 1915; d. January 15, 1965.
   iii. MARJORIE WATSON[1], b. 1921[1]; m. FRANK CUIFOLO[1].

Generation No. 2

2. HILMA[4] WATSON *(THOMAS S.[3], JOHN[2], ALONZO[1])[1]* was born May 02, 1910[1]. She married LINDLEY LLEWELLYN NEWCOMER[1] September 1934 in New York City, NY, son of WILLIAM NEWCOMER and HELEN THOMAS. He was born March 08, 1906 in Connellsville, PA, and died December 1992 in Tampa, Fl.

Children of HILMA WATSON and LINDLEY NEWCOMER are:

i. JOHN[5] NEWCOMER[1], m. BARBARA LEE BOFFEMMYER, May 04, 1957, Media, PA.
ii. RONALD NEWCOMER[1], b. 1944, Westville, NJ; d. 1963, Wyoming.

   Notes for RONALD NEWCOMER:
   Died young in automobile accident.

3. DORA[4] WATSON *(THOMAS S.[3], JOHN[2], ALONZO[1])[1]* was born February 09, 1915[1], and died January 15, 1965[1]. She married ROBERT O. SUTTON[1], son of WILLIAM SUTTON and EMMA ROGERS. He was born October 24, 1906[2,2,2,2,2,2,2,2,2,2,2,2,2,2,3,4], and died August 1987[5,5,5,5,5,5,5,5,5,5,5,5,5,5,6,7].

Notes for DORA WATSON:

Reference #3180
The twins are buried behind Maud Cramer, there are two little stones sticking out of the ground to mark their graves.

More About DORA WATSON:
Burial: Hillside cemetery, New Gretna[8]

Notes for ROBERT O. SUTTON:
[Genealogy.com, Family Archive #110, Vol. 2 L-Z, Ed. 9, Social Security Death Index: U.S., Date of Import: Dec 30, 2000, Internal Ref. #1.112.9.111416.32]

Individual: Sutton, Robert
Social Security #: 148-07-6985
Issued in: New Jersey

Birth date: Oct 24, 1906
Death date: Aug 1987

Residence code: New Jersey

ZIP Code of last known residence: 08224
Location associated with this ZIP Code:

New Gretna, New Jersey

Robert Sutton told his childred that the O. in his name stood for Osborn but we have not been able to verify this. His grandfather's middle initial also was an O. (for some reason either lost in the mail, etc. his birth certificate has never been registered. I am going to try and register him through the family bible and other papers we have).

More About ROBERT O. SUTTON:
Burial: Hillside cemetery, New Gretna[8]
Social Security Number: Social Security #: 148-07-6985[9,10]

Children of DORA WATSON and ROBERT SUTTON are:

i. TWIN BABY[5] SUTTON, b. Abt. 1930; d. Abt. 1930.

More About TWIN BABY SUTTON:
Burial: Abt. 1930, Hillside cemetery, New Gretna

ii. TWIN BABY SUTTON, b. Abt. 1930; d. Abt. 1930.

More About TWIN BABY SUTTON:
Burial: Abt. 1930, Hillside cemetery, New Gretna

iii. ROBERT THOMAS SUTTON[10], b. December 07, 1932, Atlantic City, NJ[10]; m. JOYCE F.. MANCUSO, October 19, 1957, Pomona, NJ[10]; b. May 11, 1934, Bristol, PA.

Notes for ROBERT THOMAS SUTTON:
Bob was born on a Wednesday. His wife Joyce was born on a Friday two years later, each year their bithdays fall on the same day of the week.

Notes for JOYCE F.. MANCUSO:
DAR member number 831198, installed Oct. 16, 2004

iv. EDNA MAY SUTTON[10], b. November 20, 1937, Mt. Holly; m. GEORGE BORTON, December 22, 1984, St Pauls Medthodist Church, New Gretna, NJ; b. October 03, 1940; d. January 08, 2000, New Gretna.

v. MARJORIE LOUISE SUTTON[10], b. Abt. 1940; m. LAWRENCE ROSE.

Notes for MARJORIE LOUISE SUTTON:

THOMAS WATSON MARRIED MARY EDNA CRAMER/WATSON
SON OF JOHN AND ELLEN PIERCE/WATSON

THOMAS WATSON WITH GRANDSON ROBERT T. SUTTON

THOMAS S. WATSON WAS A SAWYER BY TRADE AND SIGNED UP TO WORK AT THE GOVERMENT CCC CAMPS AT BASS RIVER STATE FOREST. COPIES OF HIS RECORDS WILL BE ADDED AT THE END OF THIS BOOK.

Scrapbook of Thomas S. Watson

Tom Watson

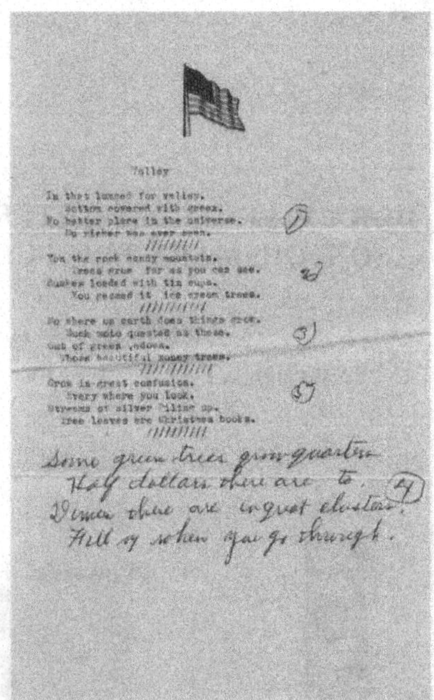

Valley

In that [illegible] for valley.
Bottom covered with green.
No better place in the universe.
[illegible]
//////////
Yes the rock candy mountain.
Trees grow far as you can see.
[illegible] loaded with tin cups.
You passed it ice cream trees.
///////////
No where on earth does things grow.
Such [illegible] as these.
Out of green [illegible].
Those beautiful money trees.
////////////
Grow in great confusion.
Every where you look.
Streams of silver [illegible] up.
Tree leaves are Christmas books.
//////////

Some green trees grow quarters
Half dollars there are to.
Dimes there are in great clusters.
Fill up when you go through.

Poem

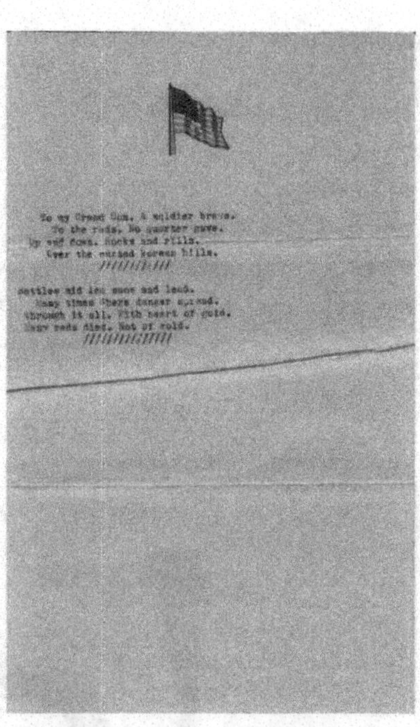

To my Grand Son. A soldier brave.
To the reds. No quarter gave.
Up and down. Rocks and rills.
Over the [illegible] Korean hills.
//////////////

Battles mid ice snow and lead.
Many times there danger spread.
Through it all. With heart of gold.
Many reds died. Not of cold.
////////////////

Tom Watson & Clara Sears

DORA WATSON DAUGHTER OF
THOMAS WATSON AND MARY EDNA CRAMER/WATSON

MARRIED
ROBERT O. SUTTON

Scrapbook of Dora Watson

Dora

daughter of Thomas Watson and Mary Edna Cramer

Descendants of Hilma Watson

Generation No. 1

1. HILMA[4] WATSON *(THOMAS S.[3], JOHN[2], ALONZO[1])[1]* was born May 02, 1910[1]. She married LINDLEY LLEWELLYN NEWCOMER[1] September 1934 in New York City, NY, son of WILLIAM NEWCOMER and HELEN THOMAS. He was born March 08, 1906 in Connellsville, PA, and died December 1992 in Tampa, Fl.

Children of HILMA WATSON and LINDLEY NEWCOMER are:

2. i. JOHN[5] NEWCOMER.

ii. RONALD NEWCOMER[1], b. 1944, Westville, NJ; d. 1963, Wyoming.

Notes for RONALD NEWCOMER:
Died young in automobile accident.

Generation No. 2

2. JOHN[5] NEWCOMER *(HILMA[4] WATSON, THOMAS S.[3], JOHN[2], ALONZO[1])[1]*. He married BARBARA LEE BOFFEMMYER May 04, 1957 in Media, PA.

Children of JOHN NEWCOMER and BARBARA BOFFEMMYER are:

i. JOHN WHITNEY[6] NEWCOMER, b. January 01, 1959; m. JOAN LIDA LUBY, June 21, 1981, Birmingham, Michigan.

ii. THOMAS ENGLAND NEWCOMER, b. February 23, 1966.

Endnotes

1. Mancuso.FTW, Date of Import: Sep 6, 2000.

HILMA WATSON DAUGHTER OF THOMAS AND MARY EDNA CRAMER/WATSON

MARRIED LINDLEY NEWCOMER

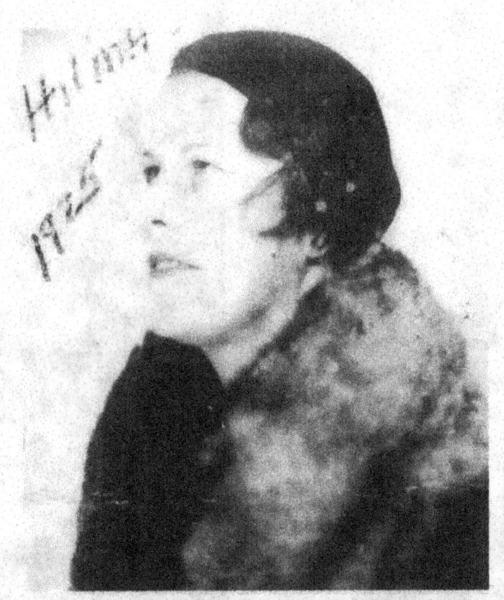

Top left
Grandma Nellie with
grandsons Ronnie & John

Top Right Hilma with son John

Bottom left Hilma

HILMA WATSON DAUGHTER OF THOMAS AND MARY EDNA CRAMER/WATSON

MARRIED LINDLEY NEWCOMER

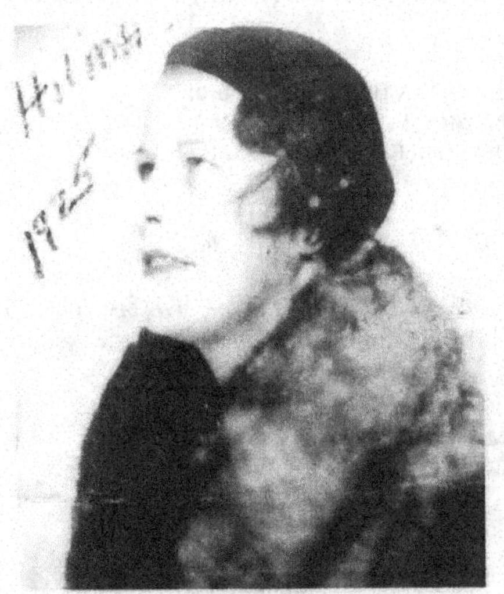

Descendants of John Newcomer

Generation No. 1

1. JOHN[3] NEWCOMER *(LINDLEY LLEWELLYN[2], WILLIAM HENRY[1])[1]*. He married BARBARA LEE BOFFEMMYER May 04, 1957 in Media, PA.

Children of JOHN NEWCOMER and BARBARA BOFFEMMYER are:

2. i. JOHN WHITNEY[4] NEWCOMER, b. January 01, 1959.
   ii. THOMAS ENGLAND NEWCOMER, b. February 23, 1966.

Generation No. 2

2. JOHN WHITNEY[4] NEWCOMER *(JOHN[3], LINDLEY LLEWELLYN[2], WILLIAM HENRY[1])* was born January 01, 1959. He married JOAN LIDA LUBY June 21, 1981 in Birmingham, Michigan.

Children of JOHN NEWCOMER and JOAN LUBY are:

i. LEAH ELIZA[5] NEWCOMER.
ii. ADAM SAMUEL NEWCOMER.

Endnotes

1. Mancuso.FTW, Date of Import: Sep 6, 2000.

JOHN NEWCOMER SON OF HILMAS WATSON/NEWCOMER AND LEN NEWCOMER

Descendants of Marjorie Watson

Generation No. 1

1. MARJORIE[4] WATSON *(THOMAS S.[3], JOHN[2], ALONZO[1])*[1] was born 1921[1]. She married FRANK CUIFOLO[1].

Endnotes

1. Mancuso.FTW, Date of Import: Sep 6, 2000.

MARJORIE WATSON
DAUGHTER OF THOMAS WATSON AND MARY EDNA CRAMER/WATSON

75 V. S.
81

Department of Health
State of New Jersey
Bureau of Vital Statistics

I, J. Lynn Mahaffey, M. D., *Director of the Department of Health of the State of New Jersey, do hereby Certify that the following is correctly copied from the records of Births in my office.*

Kent

NAME OF CHILD	SEX	PLACE OF BIRTH	DATE OF BIRTH
Marjorie Eliza Watson	Female	New Gretna, N. J.	Feb. 12, 1921

NAME OF FATHER	MAIDEN NAME OF MOTHER
Thomas Watson	Edna Cranmer

Note—An original certificate filed within one year after the date of birth does not bear the date of receipt by the State. No date will appear upon the "Date filed" line below unless the birth was reported later than one year after it occurred.

Date filed__________

In Testimony Whereof, *I have hereunto set my hand and affixed the official Seal of the Bureau of Vital Statistics, at Trenton, this* 13th *day of* May *A. D. 19*43

Attest Walter R. Scott
State Registrar

J. Lynn Mahaffey
Director

Scrapbook of Marjorie Watson

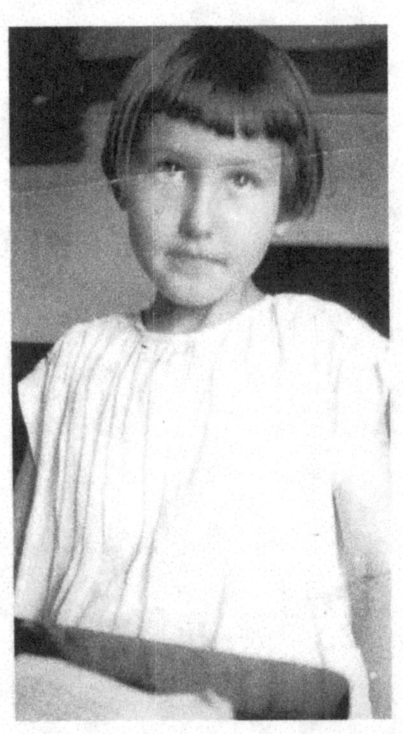

daughter of Thomas Watson and Mary Edna Cramer

HUSTED/LEVICK TO SUTTON

1700'S

1 David Husted 1737 - 1804
.. +Priscilla Diament 1739 -
...... 2 Henry Husted 1758 - 1849
.... +Ann Nancy Sheppard 1765 -
.... 3 Susannah Husted 1787 -
.... 3 Nancy Ann Husted 1788 -
.... 3 Elizabeth Husted 1789 -
.... 3 Henry Husted Jr. 1791 -
...... 2 David Husted 3rd 1762 - 1804
.... +Sarah ? 1771 -
.... 3 David Husted 4rd 1792 -
.... 3 Hannah Husted 1794 -
.... 3 Charlotte Husted 1796 -
.... 3 Mary Husted 1798 -
.... 3 George Husted 1800 -
...... 2 Daniel Husted 1767 - 1850
.... +Philah Bacon 1768 -
.... 3 Daniel Husted 1793 -
.... 3 Jane Bacon Husted 1796 -
.... 3 Clarissa Husted 1797 -
.... 3 Daniel Husted Jr. 1800 -
...... *2nd Wife of Daniel Husted:
.... +Hepzibah ? 1784 -
.... 3 Susannah Husted 1804 -
...... 2 John Husted 1770 - 1849
...... 2 Priscilla Husted 1778 - 1856
.... +Robert Levick
.... 3 Daniel Levick 1801 -
.... 3 Robert Levick 1807 - 1885
.... 3 Martha Levick 1814 - 1880
.... +Joseph Sutton 1800 - 1859
.... 4 Phebe Ann Sutton 1836 -
.... 4 Theophilus M. Sutton 1838 -
.... 4 Thomas Cerwin Sutton 1840 - 1871
.... +Margaret Husted 1840 -
.... 5 Daniel H. Sutton 1861 - 1911
.... +Emily F. Goff
.... 6 William G. Sutton 1887 -
.... 5 Theophilus Sutton 1865 -
.... 5 Gail Sutton 1866 -
.... 5 Joseph E. Sutton 1866 -
.... +Keziah Cheesman
.... 4 Samuel S. Sutton 1845 -
.... 4 Robert O. Sutton 1848 - 1914
.... +Christina Callahan 1843 - 1911
.... 5 William L. Sutton 1863 - 1950
.... +Josephine Nichols 1868 - 1904
.... 6 Frank R. Sutton 1888 -
.... 6 William L. Sutton Jr. 1890 - 1964
.... 6 Walter T. Sutton 1893 -
.... 6 Leon G. Sutton 1895 - 1940
.... 6 John R. G. Sutton 1898 - 1957
.... +Edith Lippencott Madden 1899 - 1985
.... 7 Margaret Sutton
.... 7 Marcella Sutton
.... 6 Alfred G. Sutton 1900 -
.... 6 George W. Sutton 1903 -
.... *2nd Wife of William L. Sutton:
.... +Emma Rogers 1870 -
.... 6 William Kerchoff Rogers 1902 -
.... 6 Robert O. Sutton 1906 - 1987
.... +Dora Watson 1915 - 1965
.... 7 Twin Baby Sutton 1930 - 1930
.... 7 Twin Baby Sutton 1930 - 1930
.... 7 Robert Thomas Sutton 1932 -
.... +Joyce F.. Mancuso 1934 -
.... 8 Dolores Lea Sutton 1958 -
.... 8 Susan Joyce Sutton 1964 -
.... +Christopher Keating
.... 9 Christopher Keating Jr.
.... 9 Benjamin Keating
.... 8 Bobbi Lynn Sutton 1968 -
.... +Karl Frank Chase
.... 9 Shawn Joseph Chase 1995 -
.... 9 Samantha Joyce Chase 1997 -

.... *Partner of Bobbi Lynn Sutton:
.... +Mr. McHenry
.... 9 Dani-Lynn McHenry 2006 -
.... 7 Edna May Sutton 1937 -
.... +George Borton 1940 - 2000
.... 7 Marjorie Louise Sutton 1940 -
.... +Lawrence Rose
.... 8 Lawrence Rose
.... 6 Reba Lyodd Sutton 1909 -
.... +Orion Doughty
.... 7 Dolores Doughty
.... 7 Orion Doughty, Jr
.... 6 Horace Woodruff Sutton 1911 - 1972
.... +Mildred Elizabeth Arnold 1911 -
.... 7 David Anthony Sutton 1939 - 1998
.... +Judith Williams
.... 8 David Anthony Sutton Jr. 1965 -
.... 8 Paula Marie Sutton 1968 -
.... +Jerry Leffers
.... 9 Zachary Chrisin Sutton- Leffers 1998 -
.... 8 Horace Sutton 1973 -
.... 7 Ann Katherine Sutton 1943 -
.... +Robert Edward Hellmig - 2007
.... 8 Debbie Leigh Hellmig 1967 -
.... +Edward Thomas Mount, Jr.
.... 9 Kelly Ann Mount 1992 -
.... 9 Melissa Leigh Mount 1995 -
.... 8 Robert Edward Hellmig, Jr. 1969 -
.... +Jeanine Parry Hargrove
.... 9 Tyler James Hellmig 1996 -
.... 9 Jacob Michael Hellmig 1998 -
.... 5 Susan Sutton
.... +Watkins
.... 5 Lydia Sutton
.... +Watkins
.... 4 Joseph W. Sutton 1850 - 1865
.... 4 Richard L. Sutton 1853 -
.... 4 Horace W. Sutton 1856 -
.... +Mary H. Spencer 1863 - 1942
.... 3 William Levick 1818 - 1870
.... +Pleasant Taylor 1821 -
.... 4 Emeline Levick 1840 -
.... 4 Hannah Levick 1843 -
.... 3 Priscilla Levick 1821 - 1884
.... +Horace Woodruff 1814 - 1894
.... 4 Hannah P. Woodruff 1819 -
.... +Casper Sheppard Sutton 1857 - 1929
.... 5 Nelson E. Sutton 1898 -
.... 5 Frank B Sutton 1895 - 1918

Descendants of Ozwell Sutton

1 Ozwell Sutton 1771 - 1802
.. +Rachel ?
.... 2 John Sutton 1791 - 1853
.... +Mary Woodroe 1793 - 1844
.... 3 Robert P. Sutton 1816 - 1890
.... +Edith Newcomb 1823 - 1907
.... 4 Chester Sutton 1855 - 1907
.... 4 Casper Sheppard Sutton 1857 - 1929
.... +Hannah P. Woodruff 1819 -
.... 5 Nelson E. Sutton 1898 -
.... 5 Frank B Sutton 1895 - 1918
.... 3 David Sutton 1819 - 1892
.... 3 Charles H. Sutton 1824 - 1898
.... +Hannah Kelsey Sheppard 1819 - 1905
.... 4 Charles Burley Sutton 1845 - 1924
.... +Lucy Jane Sutton 1855 - 1929
.... 5 Walter Charles Sutton 1890 - 1953
.... +Margaret Curry 1895 - 1937
.... 6 James Joseph Sutton 1923 - 1983
.... +Hazel Gatlin 1925 - 1991
.... 7 James Edward Sutton 1948 -
.... +Mary
.... 4 Larrissa Sutton 1857 - 1861
.... 4 John Sutton 1859 - 1861
.... 4 Franklin P. Sutton 1862 - 1903
.... +Emma P. ?
.... 5 Frank Sutton 1886 - 1905
.... 5 John Scott Sutton 1888 - 1955

Descendants of Josia Woodruff

Generation No. 1

1. JOSIA[1] WOODRUFF was born 1758. He married SARAH WOODRUFF. She was born 1762.

Child of JOSIA WOODRUFF and SARAH WOODRUFF is:
2. i. HORACE[2] WOODRUFF, b. August 09, 1814; d. December 24, 1894.

Generation No. 2

2. HORACE[2] WOODRUFF *(JOSIA[1])* was born August 09, 1814, and died December 24, 1894. He married PRISCILLA LEVICK, daughter of ROBERT LEVICK and PRISCILLA HUSTED. She was born 1821, and died December 27, 1884 in Cumberland Co..

More About HORACE WOODRUFF:
Burial: Fairton Methodist Cemetery, NJ

Notes for PRISCILLA LEVICK:
Priscilla Woodroff wife of Horace Woodruff, only children of late pensioner Priscilla Levik (widow of Robert Levick, former dragon in Rev..) who resided in Fairfield Twp. for 50 years, appoint Thomas J. Stryker Atty to collect arrears due from 4 Sept 1856 to Feb. 1857 the day of her death; sworn before William D. BarrettJ>P> witness James W. Trenchard, on 12 May 1857 County certification signed by Ephraim E. Sheppard, Clerk of CCP, who also certifies Barrett is J.P.
Trenton, 15 May 1857, Thos J. Stryker collected $.23: his oath heard same date by Phil. Dickinson Pension Agent.

Before I forget to do this...The ISAAC SUTTON LINE, Stowe Creek/Greenwich connect to your SUTTON LINE through the marriage of
Casper Sheppard Sutton and Hannah P. Woodruff November 15, 1843

Hannah P. Woodruff is the d/o Horace Woodruff and Priscilla Levick
Casper Sheppard Sutton is the s/o Robert P. Sutton & Edith Newcomb

Marriage Return
Casper S. Sutton
Place of Residence: Bowentown, Cumberland Co.
Age: 30
Occupation: Farmer
Name of Father: Robert P. Sutton
Maiden name of Mother: Edith Newcomb

Full Maiden name of wife: Hannah P. Woodruff
Place of Residence: Near Fairton
Age: 24
Name of Father: Horace Woodruff
Maiden name of Mother: Prescilla Levick
Date: July 4, 1888
Place: Fairton, Cumberland Co.
In Presence of: ? Kate Schaffer & Wm. K. Lippincott, Fairton
E. J. Lippincott, M. E. Church, Fairton

More About PRISCILLA LEVICK:
Burial: Fairton Methodist Cemetery, NJ

Child of HORACE WOODRUFF and PRISCILLA LEVICK is:

i. HANNAH P.[3] WOODRUFF, b. Abt. 1819; m. CASPER SHEPPARD SUTTON; b. August 23, 1857, Cumberland Co.; d. August 28, 1929.

Descendants of Isaac Sutton

Generation No. 1

1. ISAAC[1] SUTTON was born Bef. 1753, and died Abt. September 02, 1785 in Stowe Creek, Cumberland Co.. He married CHRISTIANNA. She died Abt. 1801.

Notes for ISAAC SUTTON:
Before I forget to do this...The ISAAC SUTTON LINE, Stowe Creek/Greenwich connect to your SUTTON LINE through the marriage of
Casper Sheppard Sutton and Hannah P. Woodruff November 15, 1843

Hannah P. Woodruff is the d/o Horace Woodruff and Priscilla Levick
Casper Sheppard Sutton is the s/o Robert P. Sutton & Edith Newcomb

Marriage Return
Casper S. Sutton
Place of Residence: Bowentown, Cumberland Co.
Age: 30
Occupation: Farmer
Name of Father: Robert P. Sutton
Maiden name of Mother: Edith Newcomb

Full Maiden name of wife: Hannah P. Woodruff
Place of Residence: Near Fairton
Age: 24
Name of Father: Horace Woodruff
Maiden name of Mother: Prescilla Levick
Date: July 4, 1888
Place: Fairton, Cumberland Co.
In Presence of: ? Kate Schaffer & Wm. K. Lippincott, Fairton
E. J. Lippincott, M. E. Church, Fairton

Will be sending more a bit later,
Mary

Mary S. Sutton

Child of ISAAC SUTTON and CHRISTIANNA is:
2. i. OZWELL[2] SUTTON, b. Bef. 1771; d. Aft. 1802.

Generation No. 2

2. OZWELL[2] SUTTON *(ISAAC[1])* was born Bef. 1771, and died Aft. 1802. He married RACHEL ?.

Child of OZWELL SUTTON and RACHEL ? is:
3. i. JOHN[3] SUTTON, b. Abt. 1791, Stowe Creek, Cumberland Co., NJ; d. July 25, 1853, Roadstown, NJ.

Generation No. 3

3. JOHN[3] SUTTON *(OZWELL[2], ISAAC[1])* was born Abt. 1791 in Stowe Creek, Cumberland Co., NJ, and died July 25, 1853 in Roadstown, NJ. He married MARY WOODROE. She was born Abt. 1793, and died May 1844.

More About JOHN SUTTON:
Burial: Cohansey Cemetery, Cumberland Co., NJ

More About MARY WOODROE:
Burial: Cohansey Cemetery, Cumberland Co., NJ

Children of JOHN SUTTON and MARY WOODROE are:

4. i. ROBERT P.[4] SUTTON, b. July 30, 1816, Roadstown, NJ; d. March 14, 1890, Bridgeton, NJ.

ii. DAVID SUTTON, b. Abt. 1819; d. August 14, 1892.

Notes for DAVID SUTTON:
A book titled Story of Greenwich Cumberland County, New Jersey The Tea Burning Town have mention of David Sutton. I sent the link to Mary Sutton who replied.....
This DAVID SUTTON is the s/o John SUTTON & Mary Woodroe (WOODS). Charles H. SUTTON & David were brother. All the SUTTON'S buried in the Greenwich Baptist cemetery are from the Isaac & Christianna SUTTON line. (from Mary Sutton)

copied from the page of above book.
Two women, one born in 1811 and another born in 1814 told the writer the same story. David Sutton was a shoemaker. The house in which he did his work stood right on the street on Market Lane. The house had a high and low art. Under the high part of the house was the cellar. This was close to the road. Mr. Sutton lived in a house near by. Both his home and the dwelling where he worked have been torn down. It is said a portion of the shop was moved and is now being used as a garage by Frank Craig. The garage is built of hand hewed logs and hand made nails are visible.

More About DAVID SUTTON:
Burial: Greenwich Baptist Cemetery, Cumberland Co. NJ

5. iii. CHARLES H. SUTTON, b. February 18, 1824; d. October 16, 1898, Alms House, Hopewell Township, NJ.

Generation No. 4

4. ROBERT P.[4] SUTTON *(JOHN[3], OZWELL[2], ISAAC[1])* was born July 30, 1816 in Roadstown, NJ, and died March 14, 1890 in Bridgeton, NJ. He married EDITH NEWCOMB November 08, 1843 in Cumberland Co.. She was born Abt. August 26, 1823 in Dividding Creek, Cumberland Co., and died 1907 in Greenwich, Cumberland Co..

More About ROBERT P. SUTTON:
Burial: Greenwich Baptist Cemetery, Cumberland Co. NJ

More About EDITH NEWCOMB:
Burial: Greenwich Baptist Cemetery, Cumberland Co. NJ

Children of ROBERT SUTTON and EDITH NEWCOMB are:

i. CHESTER[5] SUTTON, b. August 23, 1855; d. August 29, 1907.

More About CHESTER SUTTON:
Burial: Greenwich Baptist Cemetery, Cumberland Co. NJ

6. ii. CASPER SHEPPARD SUTTON, b. August 23, 1857, Cumberland Co.; d. August 28, 1929.

5. CHARLES H.[4] SUTTON *(JOHN[3], OZWELL[2], ISAAC[1])* was born February 18, 1824, and died October 16, 1898 in Alms House, Hopewell Township, NJ. He married HANNAH KELSEY SHEPPARD Bef. 1843, daughter of RICHARD SHEPPARD and PRUDENCE ?. She was born April 05, 1819 in NJ, and died March 18, 1905 in Dividing Creek, Downe Twp. Cumberland Co..

More About CHARLES H. SUTTON:
Burial: Greenwich Baptist Cemetery, Cumberland Co. NJ

Children of CHARLES SUTTON and HANNAH SHEPPARD are:

7. i. CHARLES BURLEY[5] SUTTON, b. October 01, 1845, Bayside, NJ; d. July 25, 1924, Millville, NJ.

ii. LARRISSA SUTTON, b. May 11, 1857; d. October 02, 1861.

More About LARRISSA SUTTON:
Burial: Greenwich Baptist Cemetery, Cumberland Co. NJ

iii. JOHN SUTTON, b. July 05, 1859; d. October 15, 1861.

More About JOHN SUTTON:
Burial: Greenwich Baptist Cemetery, Cumberland Co. NJ

8. iv. FRANKLIN P. SUTTON, b. February 10, 1862; d. February 13, 1903.

Generation No. 5

6. CASPER SHEPPARD[5] SUTTON *(ROBERT P.[4], JOHN[3], OZWELL[2], ISAAC[1])* was born August 23, 1857 in Cumberland Co., and died August 28, 1929. He married HANNAH P. WOODRUFF, daughter of HORACE WOODRUFF and PRISCILLA LEVICK. She was born Abt. 1819.

Children of CASPER SUTTON and HANNAH WOODRUFF are:

i. NELSON E.[6] SUTTON, b. Abt. 1898.

Notes for NELSON E. SUTTON:
Sutton E. Nelson Pvt Co G 1st Inf P.R.M.
Place of enlistment Chester
Residence Eddystone
Age 20 years
Phys. Des. 6 ft. dark comp D Brown Eyes Black Hair
Occupation Belt Fixer
Promotions None
Discharged November 1, 1921 M. O. of company
Federal Service None

ii. FRANK B SUTTON, b. Abt. 1895; d. October 17, 1918.

Notes for FRANK B SUTTON:
Sutton B Frank Pvt Co G 1st Inf P.R.M.
Enlisted April 10, 1918
Place of Enlistment not given
Residence Eddystone
Age 25 years
Phy. Des. 6 ft Dark comp Dark eyes Dark hair
Occupation Machine operator
Promotions None
Discharged See remarks
Federal Service none

Remarks Deceased October 7, 1918

7. CHARLES BURLEY[5] SUTTON *(CHARLES H.[4], JOHN[3], OZWELL[2], ISAAC[1])* was born October 01, 1845 in Bayside, NJ, and died July 25, 1924 in Millville, NJ. He married LUCY JANE SUTTON August 16, 1876 in Cohansey Bpt Church, Roadstown, NJ. She was born February 07, 1855 in NJ, and died September 29, 1929 in Fairfield Township, Cumberland Co..

Child of CHARLES SUTTON and LUCY SUTTON is:

9. i. WALTER CHARLES[6] SUTTON, b. July 08, 1890, Roadstown, NJ; d. July 14, 1953, Millville, NJ.

8. FRANKLIN P.[5] SUTTON *(CHARLES H.[4], JOHN[3], OZWELL[2], ISAAC[1])* was born February 10, 1862, and died February 13, 1903. He married EMMA P. ?.

More About FRANKLIN P. SUTTON:
Burial: Greenwich Baptist Cemetery, Cumberland Co. NJ

Children of FRANKLIN SUTTON and EMMA ? are:

i. FRANK[6] SUTTON, b. Abt. 1886; d. August 29, 1905.

More About FRANK SUTTON:
Burial: Greenwich Baptist Cemetery, Cumberland Co. NJ

ii. JOHN SCOTT SUTTON, b. Abt. 1888; d. 1955.

More About JOHN SCOTT SUTTON:
Burial: Greenwich Baptist Cemetery, Cumberland Co. NJ

Generation No. 6

9. WALTER CHARLES[6] SUTTON *(CHARLES BURLEY[5], CHARLES H.[4], JOHN[3], OZWELL[2], ISAAC[1])* was born July 08, 1890 in Roadstown, NJ, and died July 14, 1953 in Millville, NJ. He married MARGARET CURRY November 30, 1912. She was born July 07, 1895 in Bridgeton, NJ, and died April 24, 1937 in Bridgeton, Cumberland Co. NJ.

Child of WALTER SUTTON and MARGARET CURRY is:

10. i. JAMES JOSEPH[7] SUTTON, b. March 06, 1923, Millville, NJ; d. January 03, 1983, Millville, NJ.

Generation No. 7

10. JAMES JOSEPH[7] SUTTON *(WALTER CHARLES[6], CHARLES BURLEY[5], CHARLES H.[4], JOHN[3], OZWELL[2], ISAAC[1])* was born March 06, 1923 in Millville, NJ, and died January 03, 1983 in Millville, NJ. He married HAZEL GATLIN February 12, 1944 in Winona, MS. She was born August 13, 1925 in Eupora, Webster Co., MS, and died June 27, 1991 in Millville, NJ.

Child of JAMES SUTTON and HAZEL GATLIN is:

i. JAMES EDWARD[8] SUTTON, b. February 17, 1948, Millville, Cumberland Co., NJ; m. MARY.

Descendants of Robert Alan Levick

Generation No. 1

1. ROBERT ALAN[1] LEVICK He married ? PETERSON, daughter of HAROLD PETERSON and EMMA PETZKE.

Notes for ROBERT ALAN LEVICK:
Sources from Cumberland County Marriages Author: H. Stanley Craig
Census 1900 Hopewell Twp, Cumberland Co., NJ
Census 1910 Stowe Creek, Cumberland Co., NJ
Richard Husted Hustedrw02 - Charles KnightHawk7@ispwest.com
Barbara McCormick Geneslady@ec.rr.com - Rootsweb.com

Child of ROBERT LEVICK and ? PETERSON is:
2. i. ROBERT[2] LEVICK, b. Maryland.

Generation No. 2

2. ROBERT[2] LEVICK *(ROBERT ALAN[1])* was born in Maryland. He married PRISCILLA HUSTED November 15, 1797, daughter of DAVID HUSTED and PRISCILLA DIAMENT. She was born Abt. 1778 in NJ, and died February 06, 1856 in Cumberland Co..

More About ROBERT LEVICK:
Burial: Swing Cemetery

More About PRISCILLA HUSTED:
Burial: Swing Cemetery Cumberland Co.

Children of ROBERT LEVICK and PRISCILLA HUSTED are:
i. DANIEL[3] LEVICK, b. Abt. 1801.
ii. ROBERT LEVICK, b. Abt. 1807; d. 1885.

Notes for ROBERT LEVICK:
On his headstone:
Private in Battery B.1st N.? Artillery
(could say N.J.)

More About ROBERT LEVICK:
Burial: Swing Cemetery

3. iii. MARTHA LEVICK, b. Abt. 1814; d. 1880.
4. iv. WILLIAM LEVICK, b. Abt. 1818; d. 1870.
5. v. PRISCILLA LEVICK, b. 1821; d. December 27, 1884, Cumberland Co..

Generation No. 3

3. MARTHA[3] LEVICK *(ROBERT[2], ROBERT ALAN[1])* was born Abt. 1814, and died 1880. She married JOSEPH SUTTON September 27, 1835 in Cumberland Co.. He was born Abt. 1800 in Fairfield Township, Cumberland Co., and died June 25, 1859 in Hering Roe, NJ.

More About MARTHA LEVICK:
Burial: Swing Cemetery

Notes for JOSEPH SUTTON:
Return of Death
Vol. H

Descendants of Josia Woodruff

Generation No. 1

1. JOSIA[1] WOODRUFF was born 1758. He married SARAH WOODRUFF. She was born 1762.

Child of JOSIA WOODRUFF and SARAH WOODRUFF is:
2. i. HORACE[2] WOODRUFF, b. August 09, 1814; d. December 24, 1894.

Generation No. 2

2. HORACE[2] WOODRUFF *(JOSIA[1])* was born August 09, 1814, and died December 24, 1894. He married PRISCILLA LEVICK, daughter of ROBERT LEVICK and PRISCILLA HUSTED. She was born 1821, and died December 27, 1884 in Cumberland Co..

More About HORACE WOODRUFF:
Burial: Swing Cemetery

Notes for PRISCILLA LEVICK:
Priscilla Woodroff wife of Horace Woodruff, only children of late pensioner Priscilla Levik (widow of Robert Levick, former dragon in Rev..) who resided in Fairfield Twp. for 50 years, appoint Thomas J. Stryker Atty to collect arrears due from 4 Sept 1856 to Feb. 1857 the day of her death; sworn before William D. BarrettJ>P> witness James W. Trenchard, on 12 May 1857 County certification signed by Ephraim E. Sheppard, Clerk of CCP, who also certifies Barrett is J.P.
Trenton, 15 May 1857, Thos J. Stryker collected $.23: his oath heard same date by Phil. Dickinson Pension Agent.

Before I forget to do this...The ISAAC SUTTON LINE, Stowe Creek/Greenwich connect to your SUTTON LINE through the marriage of
Casper Sheppard Sutton and Hannah P. Woodruff November 15, 1843

Hannah P. Woodruff is the d/o Horace Woodruff and Priscilla Levick
Casper Sheppard Sutton is the s/o Robert P. Sutton & Edith Newcomb

Marriage Return
Casper S. Sutton
Place of Residence: Bowentown, Cumberland Co.
Age: 30
Occupation: Farmer
Name of Father: Robert P. Sutton
Maiden name of Mother: Edith Newcomb

Full Maiden name of wife: Hannah P. Woodruff
Place of Residence: Near Fairton
Age: 24
Name of Father: Horace Woodruff
Maiden name of Mother: Prescilla Levick
Date: July 4, 1888
Place: Fairton, Cumberland Co.
In Presence of: ? Kate Schaffer & Wm. K. Lippincott, Fairton
E. J. Lippincott, M. E. Church, Fairton

More About PRISCILLA LEVICK:

Burial: Swing Cemetery

Child of HORACE WOODRUFF and PRISCILLA LEVICK is:
3. i. HANNAH P.[3] WOODRUFF, b. Abt. 1819.

Generation No. 3

3. HANNAH P.[3] WOODRUFF *(HORACE[2], JOSIA[1])* was born Abt. 1819. She married CASPER SHEPPARD SUTTON, son of ROBERT SUTTON and EDITH NEWCOMB. He was born August 23, 1857 in Cumberland Co., and died August 28, 1929.

Children of HANNAH WOODRUFF and CASPER SUTTON are:

i. NELSON E.[4] SUTTON, b. Abt. 1898.

Notes for NELSON E. SUTTON:
Sutton E. Nelson Pvt Co G 1st Inf P.R.M.
Place of enlistment Chester
Residence Eddystone
Age 20 years
Phys. Des. 6 ft. dark comp D Brown Eyes Black Hair
Occupation Belt Fixer
Promotions None
Discharged November 1, 1921 M. O. of company
Federal Service None

ii. FRANK B SUTTON, b. Abt. 1895; d. October 17, 1918.

Notes for FRANK B SUTTON:
Sutton B Frank Pvt Co G 1st Inf P.R.M.
Enlisted April 10, 1918
Place of Enlistment not given
Residence Eddystone
Age 25 years
Phy. Des. 6 ft Dark comp Dark eyes Dark hair
Occupation Machine operator
Promotions None
Discharged See remarks
Federal Service none

Remarks Deceased October 7, 1918

Descendants of Martha Levick

Generation No. 1

1. MARTHA[3] LEVICK *(ROBERT[2], ROBERT ALAN[1])* was born Abt. 1814, and died 1880. She married JOSEPH SUTTON September 27, 1835 in Cumberland Co.. He was born Abt. 1800 in Fairfield Township, Cumberland Co., and died June 25, 1859 in Hering Roe, NJ.

More About MARTHA LEVICK:
Burial: Swing Cemetery

Notes for JOSEPH SUTTON:
Return of Death
Vol. H
Page No. 650
Town/Township: Fairfield
County: Cumberland
Death Date: June 25, 1959
Deceased Name; Joseph Sutton
Sex: Male
Marital Status: Married
Age: 59
Deceased's Occupation: Laborer
Death Place: Hering Roe
Birth Place: Cumberland Co.
Parent's Names:________________
Death Cause:__________________
Time Record Made: 1861

this family was compiled from the 1850 census - Stowe Creek
Joseph Sutton, 50 M. Farmer
Martha 36 F.
Phebe A. 14 F.
Theophilus 12 M.
Thomas Cerwin 10 M.
Samuel S. 5 M.
Joseph W. 4/12 M.

More About JOSEPH SUTTON:
Burial: Swing Cemetery

Marriage Notes for MARTHA LEVICK and JOSEPH SUTTON:
Marriage information taken from:
S. Craig's Cumberland County Marriages

Children of MARTHA LEVICK and JOSEPH SUTTON are:

i. PHEBE ANN[4] SUTTON, b. Abt. 1836.
ii. THEOPHILUS M. SUTTON, b. Abt. 1838.

Notes for THEOPHILUS M. SUTTON:
Militay Records - Civil War

Surprise, GETTYSBURG AND ANDERSONVILLE PRISON

Theophilus M. Sutton (Reminder the s/o Joseph Sutton & Martha Levick)
b. c 1838
d. October 28, 1864, Andersonville Prison

Read attachment first..and you will understand why I only listed 4

Cumberland County and South Jersey During the Civil War
Page 65 & 66
The following members of this Company died on the field and in hospital:
AARON TERRY, at Andersonville, Ga. prison, March 24, 1864, of disease and hunger, buried at National Cemetery, Andersonville, grave 133
THOMAS C. GALLOWAY, died of scurvy at Andersonville prison, Ga., august 28th, 1864, buried in National Cemetery, Andersonville, Grave 7,039
Theophilus sutton, died of scurvy, at Andersonville prison, Ga., October 28, 1864, buried at National Cemetery, Andersonville, grave 11, 615.
*Samuel S. Sutton, died at Field Hospital, white House, Va., June 8th, 1864, of wounds received in action at Cold Harbor, VA (son of Joseph Sutton & Martha Levick-will give you information on Samuel after I'm finished with Theophilus)

I started researching this in 1998 and is really the highlight of my research. After calling Andersonville to see if it was possible for a prisoner taken at Gettysburg to end up in Andersonville, they thought it was highly unlikely because of the distance. Well, look what I found.

Civil War Record
Theophilus Sutton
Pvt. Co. K, 12 Reg't New Jersey Infantry
Age 24 years
Company Must-in-Roll
Of the organization named above. Roll dated
Woodbury, N.J., Sept. 4, 1862
Muster-in-date, Sept. 4, 1862
Joined for duty and enrolled:
When Aug 11, 1862
Where Bridgeton N.J.
Period 3 years.
Remarks, Bounty $25.00
Present$2.00

Theophilus Sutton
Pvt. Co. K, 12 Reg't New Jersey Infantry
Appears on
Company Muster Roll
For Sept 4 to Oct 31, 1862
Present or Absent-Present

Theophilus Sutton
Pvt. Co. K, 12 Reg't New Jersey Infantry
Appears on
Company Muster Roll
For Nov & Dec, 1862
Present or Absent-Present

Theophilus Sutton
Pvt. Co. K, 12 Reg't New Jersey Infantry
Appears on
Company Muster Roll
For Jan & Feb, 1863
Present or Absent-Present

Theophilus Sutton
Pvt. Co. K, 12 Reg't New Jersey Infantry
Appears on
Special Muster Roll
For Apr 10, 1863
Present or Absent-Present

Theophilus Sutton
Pvt. Co. K, 12 Reg't New Jersey Infantry
Appears on

Company Muster Roll
For Mar & Apr, 1863
Present or Absent-Present

Theophilus Sutton
Pvt. Co. K, 12 Reg't New Jersey Infantry
Appears on
Company Muster Roll
For May & June, 1863
Present or Absent-Present

Theophilus Sutton
Pvt. Co. K, 12 Reg't New Jersey Infantry
Appears on
Company Muster Roll
For July & Aug, 1863
Present or Absent-Absent
Remarks: Missing in Action July 2, 1863

Theophilus Sutton
Pvt. Co. K, 12 Reg't New Jersey Infantry
Appears on
Company Muster Roll
For Sept & Oct, 1863
Present or Absent-Absent
Remarks: Missing in Action July 3, 1863, at Gettysburg, Pa.

Theophilus Sutton
Pvt. Co. K, 12 Reg't New Jersey Infantry
Appears on
Company Muster Roll
For Nov & Dec, 1863
Present or Absent-Absent
Remarks: Missing July 3, 1863

Theophilus Sutton
Pvt. Co. K, 12 Reg't New Jersey Infantry
Appears on
Company Muster Roll
For Jan & Feb, 1864
Present or Absent-Absent
Remarks: Missing July 3, 1863 at Gettysburg

Theophilus Sutton
Pvt. Co. K, 12 Reg't New Jersey Infantry
Appears on
Company Muster Roll
For Mar & Apr, 1864
Present or Absent-Absent
Remarks: PRISONER IN RICHMOND SINCE JULY 3, 1863

Theophilus Sutton
Pvt. Co. K, 12 Reg't New Jersey Infantry
Age: 25 years
Appears on Company Muster-out Roll, dated
Nr Washington D.C. July 15, 1865
Last paid to: Feb. 28, 1863
Remarks: Died Oct. 28, 1864 Andersonville Ga., of disease

Joyce, I sent a copy of the records to Andersonville and they sent me a lovely letter. THE FILE ON THEOPHILUS SUTTON HAS BEEN OPENED FOR RESEARCH IN ANDERSONVILLE.

James E. and Mary S. Sutton
107 Union Street
Mount Holly, NJ 08060

609-261-7215

Monday, November 17, 1997

Eastern National
Andersonville NHS
Mr. Alan Marsh
Route 1, Box 800
Andersonville, Georgia 31711

Dear Alan,

A very special THANK YOU for your note and enclosed information of Theophilus Sutton. I did send for pension and military records and would be more than happy to send copies of any and all information I receive.

My interest peaked when I noticed the date and place of capture where left blank. The book, ***Cumberland County and South Jersey during the Civil War***, a reprint of ****Historic Days in Cumberland County, New Jersey, 1855-1865*** by Isaac T. Nichols and ***To Gettysburg & Beyond, the 12th New Jersey Volunteer Infantry, II Corps. Army of the Potomac, 1862-1865.*** "the casualties in Company K…at Gettysburg - …missing"

12th New Jersey Infantry Volunteers, **Company "K"**

Missing

1. Aaron Terry – Grave #133 (Sergeant)
2. Thomas C. Galloway – Grave #7039
3. Theophilus Sutton – Grave #11615

All three died at Andersonville (see enclosed packet). ***Prisoners who died at Andersonville Prison Atwater List***, has Aaron Terry listed under New York. *A picture of Aaron Terry, taken from the above mentioned book, and the response from the National Archives regarding pension records on Theophilus Sutton is also enclosed. I will send any military records I receive.

Sincerely,

Mary S. Sutton

Mary S. Sutton

C: POW division

Cumberland County
And
South Jersey
During the
Civil War

DEDICATION

This reprint is dedicated to the brave Union soldiers of southern New Jersey, who heroically served so that our nation would remain whole and free

"Cumberland County and South Jersey during the Civil War" (originally entitled Historic Days, Cumberland County, New Jersey: 1855-1865) is the work of Isaac T. Nichols. Through his many hours of diligent labor, Mr. Nichols has immortalized the courage and sacrifice of southern New Jersey Union troops.

First published in 1908, this book has been reprinted from the original work by Robert R. lacovara and Thomas W. Lacovara.

Page 106

The afternoon of July 2d, 1863, at Gettysburg, brought still greater honors to the Twelfth Regiment. The five centre companies were ordered to charge the Bliss barn, which stood in the open field, some distance from the stone wall. The barn was occupied by Confederate sharpshooters, who were picking off the Union soldiers wherever a head appeared. In this charge, Captain Frank M. riley, of Bridgeton, then in command of Company F, took and important part, bravely leading his men to the attack. The assault was successful, the barn captured, and a large number of prisoners taken. The companies were soon obliged to abandon the barn, and fall back with their prisoners to the stone wall again, owing to a heavy Confederate fire. On the morning of July 3d, a second charge of the remaining five companies of the regiment was ordered. The charge was gallantly led by Captain richard S. Thompson, of Company K, Bridgeton. The barn was again captured, and a few more prisoners taken. The Confederates rallied and began to surround the barn, when the companies fell back to the stone wall. When the order to retire rang out, Sergeant Aaron Terry, of Company K, a native of Downe Township, Cumberland County, a noble fellow, and Private John J. Boone, of Company A, were engaged in firing from the main floor above the basement, in which they had got comfortably fixed. They immediately returned to the basement of the barn to rejoin their comrades, when they found themselves alone. Their fellow-soldiers were nearly back to their old position on the Emmettsburg Road. A line of Confederates perhaps seventy-five yards long could be seen behind a fence on each side of the field through which Terry and Boone must pass to reach safety in the Union lines. A glance disclosed the fact that they must run for their lives or submit to capture. Accordingly, they started for the Union position on a double-quick. The attention of the Confederates being on the main body of Federals which had just escaped them, they did not discover the two Jerseymen until they were about two-thirds of the way through their line. Then suddenly came the challenge, sharp and short: "Halt, you Yankees!" But the command was not obeyed. It only added fleetness to the sprinters. Bullets flew like hail 'round and about the runners, whistling about their ears, striking the ground in every direction, but neither Terry nor Boone were hit. Fortune had favored them, and they arrived safely at the position occupied by their comrades at the stone wall, very happy over their close escape from death. That night, however, Sergeant Terry was captured on the picket line, and his heroic soul departed this life of disease and starvation at the Confederate prison, Andersonville, Georgia. The casualties in Company K. during the two sanguinary days at Gettysburg were: Killed-Simon W. Creamer, Henry S. sockwell; wounded-Daniel H. Carman (who afterwards died at Field Hospital), william H. dickson, Charles H. Simpkins, Bollmfield spencer, Samuel tomlinson; missing-Aaron Terry, thomas C. Gallloway, THEOPHILUS SUTTON.

9594

Sutton Theophilus

Co. K, 12 New Jersey In

Private | Private

CARD NUMBERS.

1	18041011	26	
2	18041112	27	
3	18041212	28	
4	18041309	29	
5	18041405	30	
6	18041501	31	
7	18041592	32	
8	18041681	33	
9	18041768	34	
10	18041860	35	
11	18041931	36	
12	18042012	37	
13	18042752	38	
14		39	
15		40	
16		41	
17		42	
18		43	
19		44	
20		45	
21		46	
22		47	
23		48	
24		49	
25		50	

Number of personal papers herein 0

Book Mark:

See also

ANDERSONVILLE NHS
Civil War Resource File
Information Sheet

Instructions: Complete the appropriate sections, recording all requested information available. Place additional information in the "Remarks" section.

Personal Information
Last Name Sutton First/Middle Name Theophilus
Regiment/Ship 12 NJ Infantry Company K Rank Private
Date of Enlistment ______ Age at Enlistment ______
Alternate Name 1 ______ Alternate Name 2 ______
****

Union Personnel
Known Camp Sumter Prisoner ✓ Reported Camp Sumter Prisoner ______
Capture Date ______ Place of Capture ______
Parole Date ______ Parole Location ______
Died at Camp Sumter ✓ Reported to Have Died at Camp Sumter ______
Death Date 29 Oct 1864 Cause of Death Scorbutus Grave # 11615
Others Prisons Held ______
****

Confederate Personnel
Stationed at Camp Sumter ______ Reported Stationed at Camp Sumter ______
Dates of Duty at Camp Sumter ______
Prisoner of War? ______ Prisons Held ______
Capture Date ______ Place of Capture ______
Parole Date ______ Parole Location ______
Death Date ______ Cause of Death ______
Grave Location ______ Grave # ______
****

Information Contained in File (Place a Check Mark for all that apply)
Compiled Military Service Record ______
Memorandum from Prisoner of War Records only ______
Pension Files ____ Application Only? ____
Additional Information? ✓ Type of Info Historic Narrative of Regiment
****

Remarks ______

Date records entered into Resource File 12/12/97 **Entered by** J W Stiltz
Database Code Number 21615

2593 Samuel.

Sutton Samuel S.

Co. K, 12 New Jersey Inf.

Private. | Private.

CARD NUMBERS.

1	18041010	26	
2	18041111	27	
3	18041211	28	
4	18041308	29	
5	18041404	30	
6	18041500	31	
7	18041591	32	
8	18041680	33	
9	18041767	34	
10	18041849	35	
11	18041930	36	
12	18042011	37	
13	18042091	38	
14	18042744	39	
15		40	
16		41	
17		42	
18		43	
19		44	
20		45	
21		46	
22		47	
23		48	
24		49	
25		50	

Number of personal papers herein 3

Book Mark:

See also

THEOPHILUS SUTTON
SON OF JOSEPH AND MARTHA LEVICK/SUTTON

CIVIL WAR SOLDIER
CAPTURED AT GETTYSBURG,PA
DIED AT ANDERSONVILLE PRISON, GA

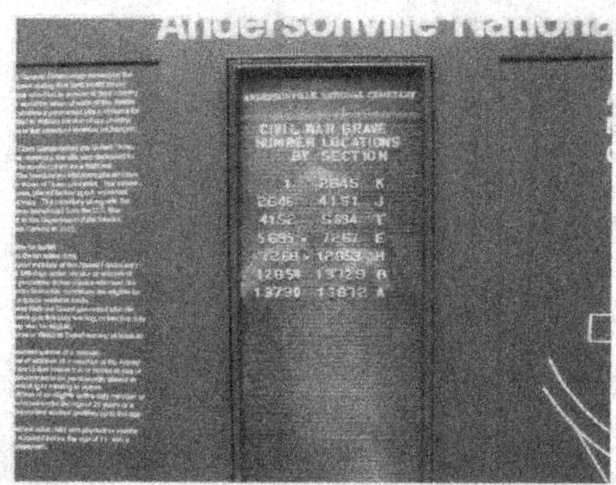

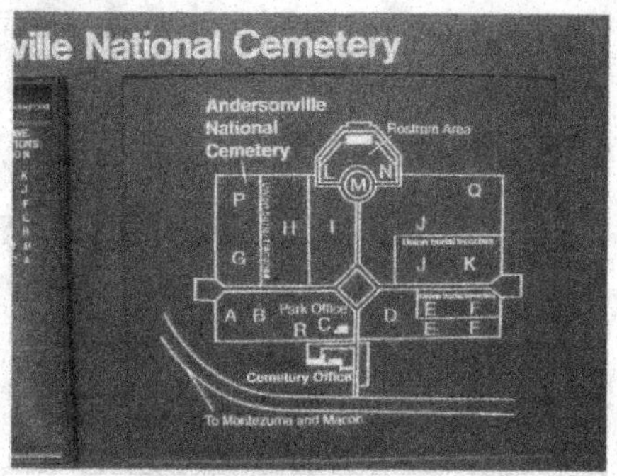

United States Department of the Interior

NATIONAL PARK SERVICE

K14(ANDE)

January 13, 1998

Mary S. Sutton
107 Union Street
Mount Holly, NJ 08060

Dear Mrs. Sutton:

Thank you for providing us information about **Theophilus Sutton.** The information you sent has been used to establish an individual file on him which is available for researchers and park staff.

We appreciate your interest in the park. Individuals like yourself make our job of telling the Andersonville story much easier. Thank you again.

Sincerely,

Joan P. Stibitz
Park Ranger

Letter from Andersonville

WE DEDICATE THIS PAGE TO ALL THE BOYS THAT SERVED AND DIED FOR THEIR COUNTRY. FOLLOWING ARE THE HEAD STONES FOR THE OTHER BOYS THAT WERE CAPTURED AT GETTYSBURG ALONG WITH THEOPHILUS.

who died at white House Va June 8, 1864 of wounds received in action at Coal Harbor Va June 3rd 1864
1. Advance Bounty received-$25.00
2. Last paid by Maj U. K.? Hutchins to include Feb 29th 1864
3. Pay due to date of death (3 months & 8 days)
Two the Sutler-$3.00
Amount of Clothing drawn since last settlement aug 2nd 1863-$30.90
Allowance for same period (10 Mon & 8 days)-$35.93

DECLARATION OF RECRUIT.
I, Samuel S. Sutton desiring to VOLUNTEER as a Soldier in the ARMY of the UNITED STATES, for the term of THREE YEARS, Do declare, that I am seventeen years and------------months of age; that I have never been discharged from the United States service on acccount of disability or by sentence of a court-martial, or by order before the expiration of a term of enlistment; and I know of no impediment to my serving honestly and faithfully as a soldier for three years.
Given at Bridgeton
The fourth day of July
Witness: Charles? O. L? Riley
No. 63
Samuel S. Sutton
Volunteered at Bridgeton
Second August 1862,
By Lieut. Dan'l Dare
12 Regiment of the NJ Vol. K

CONSENT IN CASE OF MINOR.
I Martha sutton, Do CERTIFY, That I am the Mother of Samuel S. Sutton; that the said Samuel S. Sutton is Seventeen years of age; and I do hereby freely give my CONSENT to his volunteering as a SOLDIER in the ARMY OF THE UNITED STATES for the period of THREE YEARS
Given at Bridgeton
The fourth? day of August 1862
Witnes: Isaac F. ????
Copy: Martha Sutton

Samuel S. Sutton
Pvt. Co. K, 12 Reg't New Jersey Inf.
Age 17 years
Appears on
Company Must-in-Roll
Of the organization named above. Roll dated
Woodbury, N.J., Sept. 4, 1862
Muster-in-date, Sept. 4, 1862
Joined for duty and enrolled:
When Aug 21, 1862
Where Bridgeton N.J.
Period 3 years.
Remarks, Bounty $25.00
Present? $2.00
Present$2.00

Samuel S. Sutton
Pvt. Co. K, 12 Reg't New Jersey Infantry
Appears on
Company Muster Roll
For Sept 4 to Oct 31, 1862
Present or Absent-Present

Samuel S. Sutton
Pvt. Co. K, 12 Reg't New Jersey Infantry
Appears on
Company Muster Roll
For Nov & Dec, 1862
Present or Absent-Present

Samuel S. Sutton

Pvt. Co. K, 12 Reg't New Jersey Infantry
Appears on
Company Muster Roll
For Jan & Feb, 1863
Present or Absent-Present

Samuel S. Sutton
Pvt. Co. K, 12 Reg't New Jersey Infantry
Appears on
Special Muster Roll
For Apr 10, 1863
Present or Absent-Present

Samuel S. Sutton
Pvt. Co. K, 12 Reg't New Jersey Infantry
Appears on
Company Muster Roll
For Mar & Apr, 1863
Present or Absent-Present

Samuel S. Sutton
Pvt. Co. K, 12 Reg't New Jersey Infantry
Appears on
Company Muster Roll
For May & June, 1863
Present or Absent-Present

Samuel S. Sutton
Pvt. Co. K, 12 Reg't New Jersey Infantry
Appears on
Company Muster Roll
For July & Aug, 1863
Present or Absent-Present

Samuel S. Sutton
Pvt. Co. K, 12 Reg't New Jersey Infantry
Appears on
Company Muster Roll
For Sept & Oct, 1863
Present or Absent-Present

Samuel S. Sutton
Pvt. Co. K, 12 Reg't New Jersey Infantry
Appears on
Company Muster Roll
For Nov & Dec, 1863
Present or Absent-Present
Remarks: Shopped? for 1 knapsack $2.14

Samuel S. Sutton
Pvt. Co. K, 12 Reg't New Jersey Infantry
Appears on
Company Muster Roll
For Jan & Feb, 1864
Present or Absent-Present

Samuel S. Sutton
Pvt. Co. K, 12 Reg't New Jersey Infantry
Appears on
Company Muster Roll
For Mar & Apr, 1864
Present or Absent-Present

Samuel S. Sutton

SCHEDULE I.—Free Inhabitants in Stoe Creek Township **in the County of** Cumberland **State of** New Jersey **enumerated by me, on the** 5th **day of** Aug **1850.** J. Coweng **Ass't Marshal.** 232

563

Dwelling-houses numbered in the order of visitation.	Families numbered in the order of visitation.	The Name of every Person whose usual place of abode on the first day of June, 1850, was in this family.	Age.	Sex.	Color, White, black, or mulatto.	Profession, Occupation, or Trade of each Male Person over 15 years of age.	Value of Real Estate owned.	Place of Birth. Naming the State, Territory, or Country.	Married within the year.	Attended School within the year.	Persons over 20 y'rs of age who cannot read & write.	Whether deaf and dumb, blind, insane, idiotic, pauper, or convict.
1	2	3	4	5	6	7	8	9	10	11	12	13
72	78	John S. Wood	61	M		Farmer	4000	N. J.				
"	"	Sarah A. "	50	F				"				
"	"	Warren B. "	15	M				"		1		
"	"	Lucy J. "	8	F				"		1		
"	"	Mary Pierce	20	F	M			"				
"	"	Rachel Fox	14	F				"				
"	"	Joseph Brinkley	11	M	B	Laborer		"				
"	"	Isaiah Hicks	19	M	B	do		"				
73	79	William S. Wood	43	M		Shoemaker	600	"				
"	"	Hannah A. "	36	F				"				
"	"	Sarah S. "	12	F				"		1		
"	"	Cornelia S. "	4	F				"		1		
"	"	William H. "	1	M				"				
74	80	Edward Denham	33	M		Waterman	300	"				
"	"	Nancy "	34	F				"				
"	"	Clemenza "	13	F				"		1		
"	"	Susan "	8	F				"		1		
"	"	Richard "	6	M				"		1		
"	"	Amy L. "	4	F				"	1			
"	"	Isaac E. "	1	M				"				
75	81	Joseph Sutton	57	M		Farmer		"				
"	"	Martha "	35	F				"				
"	"	Phebe A. "	16	F				"		1		
"	"	Theophilus "	12	M				"		1		
"	"	Thomas Corwin "	10	M				"		1		
"	"	Robert A. "	7	M				"		1		
"	"	Samuel S. "	5	M				"				
"	"	Joseph W. "	4/12	M				"				
76	82	David Elwell	54	M		Sawyer	5000	"				
"	"	Rhoda "	50	F				"				
77	83	Daniel Fisler	35	M				"				
"	"	Elizabeth "	26	F				"				
"	"	John W. "	13	M				"		1		
"	"	Catharine "	4	F				"				
"	"	Margaret "	2	F				"				
78	84	George Demans	40	M		Laborer		"				
"	"	Hannah "	45	F				"				
"	"	William "	12	M				"		1		
79	85	William E. Garrison	26	M		Shoemaker		"				
"	"	Margaret "	27	F				"				
"	"	Lewis "	2	M				"				
"	"	John "	17	M		Laborer		"				

Wm. Sutton Martha's Brother

Page No. 78

SCHEDULE 1.—Free Inhabitants in Fairfield Township in the County of Cumberland State of New Jersey enumerated by me, on the 14th day of July 1860. Benj. F. Lee Ass't Marshal.

Post Office Port Elizabeth N.J.

Dwelling-houses—numbered in the order of visitation.	Families numbered in the order of visitation.	The name of every person whose usual place of abode on the first day of June, 1860, was in this family.	Age.	Sex.	Color, White, black, or mulatto.	Profession, Occupation, or Trade of each person, male and female, over 15 years of age.	Value of Real Estate.	Value of Personal Estate.	Place of Birth, Naming the State, Territory, or Country.	Married within the year.	Attended School within the year.	Persons over 20 y'rs of age who cannot read & write.	Whether deaf and dumb, blind, insane, idiotic, pauper, or convict.
1	2	3	4	5	6	7	8	9	10	11	12	13	14
		Chas Hoffman	11	M					Pa		1		
		Roy F. "	6	M					NJ		1		
		Alma B. "	2	F					"				
606	601	Clarissa Mitchell	57	F			300	100	"				
		John B "	30	M		Laborer 1			Ohio				
607	602	Wm Storck	42	M		Oysterman (m...)	1000	1000	NJ				
		Amanda Storck	33	F					"				
		Hannah "	7	F					"				
		David "	6	M					Pa		1		
		Priscilla	4	F					NJ				
		William "	2	M					"				
608	603	Martha Sutton	44	F				50	"				
		Theoph. "	21	M		Oysterman 1			"				
		Thomas "	19	M		do do 1			"				
		Robt "	17	M					"				
		Samuel "	14	M					"				
		Joseph	11	M					"		1		
		Richard	6	M					"		1		
		Horace	4	M					"				
609	604	Henry Husted	55	M		Farmer 1	4000	1000	"				
		Hannah Husted	55	F					"				
		Henry B "	22	M					"				
		William B. "	13	M					Pa		1		
610	605	Robt J Mears	29	M		Master Seaman 1	425	800	Va				
		Mary A "	27	F					Va				
		Henry	6	M					Pa		1		
		Anna E.	4	F					"				
		Mary V.	4/12	F					"				
	606	Orpha Only	53	F					"				
611	607	Matitta Bishop	71	M		Laborer 1	300	150	NJ				
		Mary Bishop	56	F					"				
612	608	Horace Bishop	32	M		Farmer 1	2000	600	"				
		Phebe D "	26	F					"				
		Anna M	7	F					"		1		
		Laura K.	3/12	F					"				
613	609	Samuel N Williams	30	M		Merchant 1		300	Pa				
		Abigail B "	27	F		X			NJ				
		Mary A "	6	F					"		1		
		Henry L	5	M					"		1		
		Marcus B "	2	M					"				
		No. white males, 21 23 No. colored males, — No. white females, 19 17 No. colored females, —				No. foreign born, — No. deaf and dumb, — No. blind, — No. insane, —	8025	4000	No. idiotic, — No. paupers, —		10		No. convicts, —

110

MY SOLDIER HAS FOUND HIS FAMILY!!!

I will send you a copy of the Civil War records.

2. iii. THOMAS CERWIN SUTTON, b. Abt. 1840, Fairfield, Cumberland Co., NJ; d. May 18, 1871, Fairfield Township, Cumberland Co..

iv. SAMUEL S. SUTTON, b. Abt. 1845.

Notes for SAMUEL S. SUTTON:
Military Records - Civil War

Cumberland County and South Jersey During the Civil War
Page 65 & 66
The following members of this Company died on the field and in hospital:
AARON TERRY, at Andersonville, Ga. prison, March 24, 1864, of disease and hunger, buried at National Cemetery, Andersonville, grave 133
THOMAS C. GALLOWAY, died of scurvy at Andersonville prison, Ga., august 28th, 1864, buried in National Cemetery, Andersonville, Grave 7,039
Theophilus sutton, died of scurvy, at Andersonville prison, Ga., October 28, 1864, buried at National Cemetery, Andersonville, grave 11, 615.
*Samuel S. Sutton, died at Field Hospital, white House, Va., June 8th, 1864, of wounds received in action at Cold Harbor, VA (son of Joseph Sutton & Martha Levick-will give you information on Samuel after I'm finished with Theophilus)

I started researching this in 1998 and is really the highlight of my research. After calling Andersonville to see if it was possible for a prisoner taken at Gettysburg to end up in Andersonville, they thought it was highly unlikely because of the distance. Well, look what I found.

You will notice that some of these entries have Coal Harbor it really should be Cold Harbor. These records have CONSENT IN CASE OF MINOR form stating very clearly that Martha Sutton was Samuel S. Sutton's mother.

Samuel S. Sutton
b. c Abt. 1845, Fairfield, Cumb. Co., NJ
d. June 8, 1864, White House, VA

Inventory of the Effects
Of
Samuel S. Sutton
Late of Company K
12th Reg't of New Jersey Volunteers, who died at White House VA
On the 8th day of June 1864
Final Statement enclosed

Inventory of the effects of Samuel Sutton late a private at Bridgeton in the State of New Jersey on the 2nd day of August 1862, and mustered into the service of the United States as a private on the 4th day of Sept. 1862, at Woodbury, NJ in Company K, 12th Regiment of New Jersey Volunteers, to serve 3 years or during the war; he was born in Fairfield in the State of New Jersey; he was 17 years of age, 5 feet 6 1/2 inches high, light complexion, Grey eyes, light hair, and by occupation, when enrolled, an oysterman; he died in Field Hospital, at white House Va on the 8th day of June 1864, by reason of wounds rec in action at Coal Harbor Va June 3, 1864.

Inventory-No Effects

Final Statement of Samuel S. Sutton late of Co. K. 12th N. J. V.
Died June 8.1864
Final Statement of Samuel S. Sutton late a private of Co. K. 12th Regiment of New Jersey Volunteer Infantry, who died at white House Va June 8, 1864 of wounds received in action at Coal Harbor Va June 3rd 1864
1. Advance Bounty received-$25.00
2. Last paid by Maj U. K.? Hutchins to include Feb 29th 1864
3. Pay due to date of death (3 months & 8 days)
Two the Sutler-$3.00

Amount of Clothing drawn since last settlement aug 2nd 1863-$30.90
Allowance for same period (10 Mon & 8 days)-$35.93

DECLARATION OF RECRUIT.
I, Samuel S. Sutton desiring to VOLUNTEER as a Soldier in the ARMY of the UNITED STATES, for the term of THREE YEARS, Do declare, that I am seventeen years and------------months of age; that I have never been discharged from the United States service on acccount of disability or by sentence of a court-martial, or by order before the expiration of a term of enlistment; and I know of no impediment to my serving honestly and faithfully as a soldier for three years.
Given at Bridgeton
The fourth day of July
Witness: Charles? O. L? Riley
No. 63
Samuel S. Sutton
Volunteered at Bridgeton
Second August 1862,
By Lieut. Dan'l Dare
12 Regiment of the NJ Vol. K

CONSENT IN CASE OF MINOR.
I Martha sutton, Do CERTIFY, That I am the Mother of Samuel S. Sutton; that the said Samuel S. Sutton is Seventeen years of age; and I do hereby freely give my CONSENT to his volunteering as a SOLDIER in the ARMY OF THE UNITED STATES for the period of THREE YEARS
Given at Bridgeton
The fourth? day of August 1862
Witnes: Isaac F. ????
Copy: Martha Sutton

Samuel S. Sutton
Pvt. Co. K, 12 Reg't New Jersey Inf.
Age 17 years
Appears on
Company Must-in-Roll
Of the organization named above. Roll dated
Woodbury, N.J., Sept. 4, 1862
Muster-in-date, Sept. 4, 1862
Joined for duty and enrolled:
When Aug 21, 1862
Where Bridgeton N.J.
Period 3 years.
Remarks, Bounty $25.00
Present? $2.00
Present$2.00

Samuel S. Sutton
Pvt. Co. K, 12 Reg't New Jersey Infantry
Appears on
Company Muster Roll
For Sept 4 to Oct 31, 1862
Present or Absent-Present

Samuel S. Sutton
Pvt. Co. K, 12 Reg't New Jersey Infantry
Appears on
Company Muster Roll
For Nov & Dec, 1862
Present or Absent-Present

Samuel S. Sutton
Pvt. Co. K, 12 Reg't New Jersey Infantry
Appears on
Company Muster Roll
For Jan & Feb, 1863
Present or Absent-Present

Samuel S. Sutton

Pvt. Co. K, 12 Reg't New Jersey Infantry
Appears on
Special Muster Roll
For Apr 10, 1863
Present or Absent-Present

Samuel S. Sutton
Pvt. Co. K, 12 Reg't New Jersey Infantry
Appears on
Company Muster Roll
For Mar & Apr, 1863
Present or Absent-Present

Samuel S. Sutton
Pvt. Co. K, 12 Reg't New Jersey Infantry
Appears on
Company Muster Roll
For May & June, 1863
Present or Absent-Present

Samuel S. Sutton
Pvt. Co. K, 12 Reg't New Jersey Infantry
Appears on
Company Muster Roll
For July & Aug, 1863
Present or Absent-Present

Samuel S. Sutton
Pvt. Co. K, 12 Reg't New Jersey Infantry
Appears on
Company Muster Roll
For Sept & Oct, 1863
Present or Absent-Present

Samuel S. Sutton
Pvt. Co. K, 12 Reg't New Jersey Infantry
Appears on
Company Muster Roll
For Nov & Dec, 1863
Present or Absent-Present
Remarks: Shopped? for 1 knapsack $2.14

Samuel S. Sutton
Pvt. Co. K, 12 Reg't New Jersey Infantry
Appears on
Company Muster Roll
For Jan & Feb, 1864
Present or Absent-Present

Samuel S. Sutton
Pvt. Co. K, 12 Reg't New Jersey Infantry
Appears on
Company Muster Roll
For Mar & Apr, 1864
Present or Absent-Present

Samuel S. Sutton
Pvt. Co. K, 12 Reg't New Jersey Infantry
Appears on
Company Muster Roll
For May & June, 1864
Present or Absent-Blank
Remarks: Died June 8, 1864 at White House Va from wounds received in action at Coal Harbor Va June 3, 1864

Samuel S. Sutton

Priv. Co. K, 12 Reg't New Jersey Infantry
Age: 17 years
Appears on Company Muster-out Roll, dated
Nr Washington D.C. July 15, 1865
Last paid to: Feb. 29, 1864
Remarks: Died June 8, 1864 at White House Va of wounds
Final statement unto-rendered

3. v. ROBERT O. SUTTON, b. August 25, 1848; d. October 11, 1914.
vi. JOSEPH W. SUTTON, b. May 16, 1850; d. May 30, 1865.

Notes for JOSEPH W. SUTTON:
Cause of Death; Drowning. in Record of Deaths in the Township of Fairfield May1, 1864 to May 1, 1865
Date of Death; Cannot read (see headstone information)
Name of Deceased; Joseph Sutton
Sex of Deceased; Male
Married or Single; Single
Age; 17
Occupation; Waterman
Birth; Fairfield
Name of Parents: Joseph Sutton
Cause of Death; Drowning
Time making Record: Cannot Read

More About JOSEPH W. SUTTON:
Burial: Swing Cemetery

vii. RICHARD L. SUTTON, b. November 24, 1853.
viii. HORACE W. SUTTON, b. November 02, 1856, Fairfield Township, Cumberland Co.; m. MARY H. SPENCER; b. February 17, 1863; d. September 16, 1942.

Notes for HORACE W. SUTTON:
NJ State Archives
Certificate and Record of Death
County; Cumberland
Township; Downe
Full Name of Deceased; Horace Sutton
Sex; Male
Coror; White
Married
Date of Birth; Nov. 2, 1856
Age; 57 yrs. 13 days
Occupation; Farmer
Place of Birth; NJ
Name of Father; Joseph Sutton
Place of birth; NJ
Maiden name of Mother; Martha Levick
Place of birth; NJ
Informant; Mr. Horace Sutton, Newport, NJ
Date of Death; Nov. 15, 1913
I hereby certify that I attended deceased from Nov. 9, 1913 to Nov. 14, 1913. That I last saw him alive on Nov. 14, 1913.
Cause of Death; Septic infection folowing a large absess of lower jaw
Place of Burial; Cedarville Cedar Hill
Date of Burial; Nov. 19, 1913
Undertaker; David J? Johnson, Bridgeton

Married: Mary H. Spencer
b. Feb. 17, 1863
d. Sept. 16, 1942 (Headstone - Cemetery Records.)
Buried; Cedar Hill Demetery, Cedarville, NJ

1880 Densus - Downe, Cumberland, NJ
Source; FHL Film 1254775 National Archives Film T9-0775 Page 238A

Relation - Sex - Marr - Race - Age - Birthplace

Hiran Spencear Self M M W 52 Acc; Farmer Fa; NJ Mo; NJ
Rachel Spencer Wife FMW 44 NJ Occ; Keeping House Fa; NJ Mo; NJ
Samuel Spencer Son MSW 24 NJ Occ; Fish Huckster Fa; NJ Mo; NJ
Charles Spencer Son MSW 21 NJ Occ; Oysterman Fa; NJ Mo; NJ
Mary Sutton Dau FMW 18 NJ Occ. At Home Fa; NJ Mo; NJ
Amelia Spencer Dau FSW 12 NJ Occ; At School Fa; NJ Mo; NJ
Horrace Sutton SonL MMW 23 NJ Occ; Oysterman Fa; NJ Mo; NJ
Mary Ann Hutton Mother-in-Law FW 87 DE, Fa; DE Mo. DE

More About HORACE W. SUTTON:
Burial: November 19, 1913, Cedar Hill Cemetery, Dedarville, NJ

More About MARY H. SPENCER:
Burial: Cedar Hill Cemetery, Dedarville, NJ

Generation No. 2

2. THOMAS CERWIN[4] SUTTON *(MARTHA[3] LEVICK, ROBERT[2], ROBERT ALAN[1])* was born Abt. 1840 in Fairfield, Cumberland Co., NJ, and died May 18, 1871 in Fairfield Township, Cumberland Co.. He married MARGARET HUSTED. She was born Abt. 1840.

Notes for THOMAS CERWIN SUTTON:
Military Records - Civil War.

Thomas Cerwin Sutton
b. Abt. 1840 Fairfield, Cumb. Co., NJ
d. May 18, 1870 Fairfield, Cumb. Co., NJ
Married Margaret Husted, b. c Abt. 1840
Issue:
Daniel H. Sutton, b. November 12, 1861 (Record of Birth, NJ State Archives, H2, 217.)
Theophilus Sutton, b. c May 1865
Gail Sutton, b. c 1866
Joseph E. Sutton, b. November 7, 1866 (Record of Birth, NJ State Archives, H2, 300.)

Joyce you may have information on this family...I just found it in my notes section of FTW
I believe Margaret Husted Sutton married a Mr. Miller after the death of Thomas Sutton
1900 Federal Census-Bridgeton, Sheet 84 A & B
190, 141, 142
Miller, Maggie, Head, w, f, Sept. 1840, 59, wd, 6-4, RH
Cramer, Bertha, Dau. (this may be stepdau.), w, f, Oct 1877, married 2 yrs. 0-0
Cramer, George C., Son-In-Law, w, m, May 1877, 23, married 2 yrs.
Sutton, Daniel H., son, w, m, Nov. 1861, 38, S (he was actually divorced)
Thom?Theo?, son, w, m, May 1865, 35, S.(This is Theophilus Sutton)
Watson, Emma, boarder, w, f, May 1857, 49, S,

Civil War Record
Thomas Sutton
Pvt. Co. D, 25 Reg't New Jersey Mil. Inf,
Age 21 years
Appears on
Company Must-in-Roll
Of the organization named above. Roll dated
Beverly, N.J., Sept. 26, 1862

Muster-in-date, Sept. 26, 1862
Joined for duty and enrolled:
When Sep. 1, 1862
Where Beverly, N.J.
Period 9 Months.

Thomas Sutton
Pvt. Co. D, 25 Reg't New Jersey Inf,
Appears on
Company Muster Roll
for Sep. 1 to Oct 31, 1962
Joined for duty and enrolled:
When Sep. 1, 1862
Where Beverly, N.J.
Period 9 Months
Present or Absent-Present

Thomas Sutton
Pvt. Co. D, 25 Reg't New Jersey Inf,
Appears on
Company Muster Roll
for Nov & Dec, 1962
Joined for duty and enrolled:
When Sep. 1, 1862
Where Beverly, N.J.
Period 9 Months
Present or Absent-Present

Thomas Sutton
Pvt. Co. D, 25 Reg't New Jersey Inf,
Appears on
Company Muster Roll
for Jan & Feb, 1963
Joined for duty and enrolled:
When Sep. 1, 1862
Where Beverly, N.J.
Period 9 Months
Present or Absent-Present

Thomas Sutton
Pvt. Co. D, 25 Reg't New Jersey Inf,
Appears on
Company Muster Roll
for Mar & April, 1963
Joined for duty and enrolled:
When Sep. 1, 1862
Where Beverly, N.J.
Period 9 Months
Present or Absent-Present

Thomas Sutton
Pvt. Co. D, 25 Reg't New Jersey Inf,
Appears on
Special Muster Roll
for April 10, 1963
Present or Absent-Present

Thomas Sutton
Pvt. Co. D, 25 Reg't New Jersey Mil. Inf,

CALLAHAN and SUSIE ?. She was born February 14, 1843 in Bridgeton, NJ Cumberland Co., and died May 17, 1911 in Bridgeton, NJ Cumberland Co..

Notes for ROBERT O. SUTTON:
Record of Death, NJ State Archives
Certificate and Record of Death
County: Cumberland
City: Bridgeton
401 Spruce St., 2nd Ward
Full Name of Deceased: Robert O. Sutton
Sex: Male
Color: White
Widowed
Date of Birth: Aug. 25, 1848
Age: 71 yrs
Occupation: Farmer
Place of Birth: US
Name of Father: Joseph Sutton
Place of Birth: US
Maiden name of Mother: Martha Levick
Place of Birth: US
E.L. Diament MD Bridgeton, NJ
Date of Death: Oct. 11, 1914
I hereby certify that I attended deceased from Sept. 25, 1913 to Oct. 11, 1914. That I last saw him alive on Oct. 11, 1914
Cause of Death: Brights Disease
Place of Burial: Broad St. Cemetery
Date of Burial: Oct 13, 1914
Undertaker: Harry J. Garrison, Bridgeton

Sutton, Robert O. Callahan, Christiana P. Bridgeton 5 May 1863 Cumberland County : Bridgeton Bk. H : Pg. 465

More About ROBERT O. SUTTON:
Burial: October 13, 1914, Broad St. Cemetery, Bridgeton, NJ

More About CHRISTINA CALLAHAN:
Burial: May 20, 1911, Broad St. Cemetery, Bridgeton, NJ

Children of ROBERT SUTTON and CHRISTINA CALLAHAN are:

5. i. WILLIAM L.[5] SUTTON, b. January 17, 1863, Fairton, NJ; d. March 04, 1950, New Gretna, NJ.
ii. SUSAN SUTTON[1], m. WATKINS[1], Coatsville, PA[1].
iii. LYDIA SUTTON[1], m. WATKINS[1], Bridgeton, NJ[1].

Generation No. 3

4. DANIEL H.[5] SUTTON *(THOMAS CERWIN[4], MARTHA[3] LEVICK, ROBERT[2], ROBERT ALAN[1])* was born November 12, 1861, and died July 11, 1911 in Hopewell Township, Cumberland Co.. He married EMILY F. GOFF June 11, 1887 in Shiloh, Hopewell, Cumberland Co., daughter of WILLIAM GOFF and SARA MUGLICH.

Notes for DANIEL H. SUTTON:
Died in Hospital for the insane

Notes for DANIEL H. SUTTON:
Marriage Return:
Daniel H. Sutton
Place of Residence: No: 9 Academy St. Bridgeton, NJ
Age: 24

Occupation:
Name of Father: Thomas Sutton
Maiden Name of Mother: Margaret Husted
Full Maiden Name of Wife: Emily F. Goff
Place of Residence: No: 11 Burlington Avenue
Age: 19
Name of Father: William Goff
Maiden Name of Mother: Sara Muliash?
Date: June 11, 1887
Place: Shiloh, Hopewell
In presence of: Emily ? Gardner & E O Gardner
Tho. L. Gardiner, Pastor S.E.B. Church Shiloh

Headstone: Daniel H, son of Thomas and Margaret Sutton, died July 11, 1911, aged 49 years. Bridgeton First Baptist Church Cemetery/Pearl Street

Daniel was divorced from Emily Goff

More About DANIEL H. SUTTON:
Burial: July 14, 1911, Pearl St. Cemetery, Bridgeton, NJ
Cause of Death: General Paresis, Contributing Cause-Syphilas
Occupation: Laborer

Child of DANIEL SUTTON and EMILY GOFF is:
i. WILLIAM G.4 SUTTON, b. August 30, 1887, Bridgeton, Cumberland Co. , NJ.

Child of DANIEL SUTTON and EMILY GOFF is:
i. WILLIAM G.^{6} SUTTON, b. August 30, 1887, Bridgeton, Cumberland Co. NJ.

5. WILLIAM L.^{5} SUTTON *(ROBERT O.^{4}, MARTHA^{3} LEVICK, ROBERT^{2}, ROBERT ALAN^{1})*[1] was born January 17, 1863 in Fairton, NJ[1], and died March 04, 1950 in New Gretna, NJ[1]. He married (1) JOSEPHINE NICHOLS[1] July 17, 1886 in Bridgeton, Cumberland Co., NJ, daughter of MR. NICHOLS and ? LOWE. She was born March 12, 1868 in Fairton,NJ[1], and died March 07, 1904[1]. He married (2) EMMA ROGERS[1] Abt. 1905. She was born May 11, 1870[1].

Notes for WILLIAM L. SUTTON:
obit
William Sutton, Sr., 85 Expires Early Today
3/4/1950
Word was received here this morning of the death of William Sutton Sr. 85, of New Gretna. Mr. Sutton expired at six O'clock this morning. The deceased had been taken ill three weeks ago with pneumonia and was apparently fully recovered when he suffered a stroke three days ago. He is a former sesident of Bridgeton, but has been residing with a son, Robert, in New Gretna, for quite a while.
Surviving are one daughter and eight sons, Mrs. Reba Doughty of Leeds Point, William Rogers of Washington, D.C., Robert of New Gretna, Alfred of Atlantic City, Horace of Masonville, Frank, George and William Jr. of Bridgeton and John C. Sutton of Millville. Two sisters, Lida Westcott of Bridgeton and Susie Watkins of Coatesville, Pa., also survive. In addition there are several grandchildren and great grandchildren.
Funeral arrangements have not been completed as yet although interment will be held in Bridgeton.

More About WILLIAM L. SUTTON:
Burial: March 08, 1950, Broad St. Cemetery, Bridgeton, NJ

More About JOSEPHINE NICHOLS:
Burial: Broad St. Cemetery, Bridgeton, NJ

Marriage Notes for WILLIAM SUTTON and JOSEPHINE NICHOLS:
Marriage Record, Certificate
S4, 359-26
b. c 1868
d. unknown

Children of WILLIAM SUTTON and JOSEPHINE NICHOLS are:

i. FRANK R.[6] SUTTON[1], b. April 15, 1888[1].

ii. WILLIAM L. SUTTON JR.[1], b. May 30, 1890[1]; d. May 14, 1964.

Notes for WILLIAM L. SUTTON JR.:
On William L. Sutton Jr.
b. May 30, 1890, NJ
d. May have died 5/9/1964 with burial 5/14/1964...This needs documentation
Married
Mary Ann Bedwell
b. c 1884

Certificate and Record of Marriage
Full Name of Husband: William L. Sutton Jr.
Maiden Name of Wife: Mary Anna Bedwell, (Daretty)
Place of Marriage:72 S. Pine Street, Bridgeton
Date of Marriage: April 30, 1912, 8:15 p.m.
Residence of Groom: 72 South Pine, Bridgeton
Color: White
Age of Groom: 22
# of Marriage: First
Occupation of Groom: Glassworker
Birthplace of Groom: New Jersey
Father's Name: William L. Sutton, Sr.
Mother's Maiden Name: Josephine Nichols

Residence of Bride: 72 South Pine Street, Bridgeton
Age of Bridge: 28
Color: White
# of Marriage: Second
Name if Widowed: Mrs. Mary Anna Daretty
Birth place of Bride: New Jersey
Father's Name: John Bedwell
Mother's Maiden Name: Hannah Wallace
Witnesses: Walter T. Sutton & Herbert Surran, Bridgeton
Person Officiating: A. S. Allyn, Pastor, Berean Baptist Church, Bridgeton, NJ

iii. WALTER T. SUTTON[1], b. March 18, 1893[1].

Notes for WALTER T. SUTTON:
Obit-Millville Historical Society
Brother of Local Man Dies Today
11/5/38
The death of Walter T. Sutton, 46 of Glassboro, occurred suddenly today of hemorrhage. The deceased is a brother of John Sutton, Main Street, this city.
A glassworker, the deceased is survived by his wife, Bertha; his father,William of Absecon; eight other brothers and a sister. Frank and William Sutton, Bridgeton; Leon, George, Robert and Reba Sutton, Absecon; Alfred Sutton, Atlantic City, Horace Sutton, Hightstown; and William Rogers of Washington, D.C.
Funeral services will be conducted from the Christy Funeral Home this city. Tuesday afternoon with interment in Mount Pleasant Cemetery.

iv. LEON G. SUTTON[1], b. May 06, 1895[1]; d. Abt. 1940.

Notes for LEON G. SUTTON:
Leon was pouring a footing for a zinc factory in Chatsworth, NJ when he and two other men were buried alive in a cave in. The other two were rescued but Leon lost his life.

6. v. JOHN R. G. SUTTON, b. February 27, 1898; d. October 16, 1957.

vi. ALFRED G. SUTTON[1], b. November 20, 1900[1].

Notes for ALFRED G. SUTTON:
Record of Birth, NJ State Archives.

Return of Birth
Full name of Child; Alfred C. Sutton
Sex; Male
Color; White
DOB; Nov. 20, 1900
Place of Birth; Morris Ave. Bridgeton, NJ
Name of Father; Wm L. Sutton
Maiden name of Mother; Josephine Nichols
Country of Father's Birth; US
Age; 37
Accupation; Laborer
Country of Mother's Birth; US
Age; 34
# of Children in all by this Marriage; 6
How many living; 6

vii. GEORGE W. SUTTON[1], b. February 22, 1903[1].

Children of WILLIAM SUTTON and EMMA ROGERS are:

viii. WILLIAM KERCHOFF[6] ROGERS[1], b. December 03, 1902[1].
7. ix. ROBERT O. SUTTON, b. October 24, 1906; d. August 1987.
8. x. REBA LYODD SUTTON, b. May 12, 1909.
9. xi. HORACE WOODRUFF SUTTON, b. December 11, 1911, Bridgeton, NJ; d. February 06, 1972, Mt. Laurel, NJ.

Generation No. 4

6. JOHN R. G.[6] SUTTON *(WILLIAM L.[5], ROBERT O.[4], MARTHA[3] LEVICK, ROBERT[2], ROBERT ALAN[1])*[1] was born February 27, 1898[1], and died October 16, 1957. He married EDITH LIPPENCOTT MADDEN. She was born 1899, and died 1985.

Notes for JOHN R. G. SUTTON:
Obit
John C. Sutton, 59 Bus Driver, Dies 10/17/1957
Death of John C. Sutton, 59 of 429 Pine St. occurred yesterday.
The deceased a member of West Side Methodist Church, formerly operated a trolley between Millville and Bridgeton for the past 25 years and has been a driver for the Public Service Transportation Co.
Surviving are his wife, Edith L. Sutton; two daughters, Mrs. Margaret Yough, Wilmington, and Mrs. Marcella Barker, Philadelphia; a sister Mrs. Reba Doughty, Leeds Point and seven brothers, Frank and William Sutton, Bridgeton, Alfred Sutton, Atlantic City; George Sutton, Gandy's Beach; Robert Sutton, New Gretna, Horace Sutton, Masonville and William Rogers, Washington, D.C. Eight Grandchildren also service.
Funeral services will be condusted from the Christy Funeral Home Saturday at 2 p.m. with interment in Mt. Pleasant Cemetery.

John Callahan Sutton
b. Abt. 1898
d. October 16, 1957, Millville NJ (Obit-Millville Historical Society.)
married
Edith Lippincott Madden
b. 1899
d. 1985 (Headstone - Cemetery Records) have to see where I put the headstone information

Issue:
Margaret Sutton married Unknown Young
Marcella Sutton married Unknown Barker
Martha Madden Sutton

b. March 18, 1919
d. March 18, 1919

Martha Madden Sutton
b. March 18, 1919
d. March 18, 1919
Buried March 19, 1919 Mount Pleasant Cemetery, (Record of Death, NJ State Archives.)
Katherine Hinson Sutton, b. 1920 married Vernon Montgomery Abt. 1936
Issue of Katherine:
John Gilbert Montgomery
Information on Vernon Montgomery & family was provided by Nancy and as you can see really needs more documentation on this line.

Children of JOHN SUTTON and EDITH MADDEN are:

i. MARGARET[7] SUTTON.
ii. MARCELLA SUTTON.

7. ROBERT O.[6] SUTTON *(WILLIAM L.[5], ROBERT O.[4], MARTHA[3] LEVICK, ROBERT[2], ROBERT ALAN[1])[1]* was born October 24, 1906[2,2,2,2,2,2,2,2,2,2,2,2,2,2,2,3,4], and died August 1987[5,5,5,5,5,5,5,5,5,5,5,5,5,5,5,6,7]. He married DORA WATSON[8], daughter of THOMAS WATSON and MARY CRAMER. She was born February 09, 1915[8], and died January 15, 1965[8].

Notes for ROBERT O. SUTTON:
[Genealogy.com, Family Archive #110, Vol. 2 L-Z, Ed. 9, Social Security Death Index: U.S., Date of Import: Dec 30, 2000, Internal Ref. #1.112.9.111416.32]

Individual: Sutton, Robert
Social Security #: 148-07-6985
Issued in: New Jersey

Birth date: Oct 24, 1906
Death date: Aug 1987

Residence code: New Jersey

ZIP Code of last known residence: 08224
Location associated with this ZIP Code:

New Gretna, New Jersey

Robert Sutton told his childred that the O. in his name stood for Osborn but we have not been able to verify this. His grandfather's middle initial also was an O. (for some reason either lost in the mail, etc. his birth certificate has never been registered. I am going to try and register him through the family bible and other papers we have).

More About ROBERT O. SUTTON:
Burial: Hillside cemetery, New Gretna[8]
Social Security Number: Social Security #: 148-07-6985[9,10]

Notes for DORA WATSON:
Reference #3180
The twins are buried behind Maud Cramer, there are two little stones sticking out of the ground to mark their graves.

More About DORA WATSON:
Burial: Hillside cemetery, New Gretna[10]

Children of ROBERT SUTTON and DORA WATSON are:

i. TWIN BABY[7] SUTTON, b. Abt. 1930; d. Abt. 1930.

More About TWIN BABY SUTTON:
Burial: Abt. 1930, Hillside cemetery, New Gretna

ii. TWIN BABY SUTTON, b. Abt. 1930; d. Abt. 1930.

More About TWIN BABY SUTTON:
Burial: Abt. 1930, Hillside cemetery, New Gretna

10. iii. ROBERT THOMAS SUTTON, b. December 07, 1932, Atlantic City, NJ.

iv. EDNA MAY SUTTON[10], b. November 20, 1937, Mt. Holly; m. GEORGE BORTON, December 22, 1984, St Pauls Medthodist Church, New Gretna, NJ; b. October 03, 1940; d. January 08, 2000, New Gretna.

11. v. MARJORIE LOUISE SUTTON, b. Abt. 1940.

8. REBA LYODD[6] SUTTON *(WILLIAM L.[5], ROBERT O.[4], MARTHA[3] LEVICK, ROBERT[2], ROBERT ALAN[1])*[10] was born May 12, 1909[10]. She married ORION DOUGHTY.

Notes for ORION DOUGHTY:
Regarding the Baby and Anna May grave stones. This is Dolores' baby that died from the cord being wrapped around her neck during birth. She was buried on the grandparents cemetery site.

Children of REBA SUTTON and ORION DOUGHTY are:

i. DOLORES[7] DOUGHTY.

ii. ORION DOUGHTY, JR.

9. HORACE WOODRUFF[6] SUTTON *(WILLIAM L.[5], ROBERT O.[4], MARTHA[3] LEVICK, ROBERT[2], ROBERT ALAN[1])*[10] was born December 11, 1911 in Bridgeton, NJ[10], and died February 06, 1972 in Mt. Laurel, NJ. He married MILDRED ELIZABETH ARNOLD, daughter of HERMAN ARNOLD and MARIE ARNOLD. She was born October 24, 1911 in New Milford, NJ.

Notes for HORACE WOODRUFF SUTTON:
Died of a Heart Attck while out on a Tow call on Texas Ave. in Mt. Laurel, NJ

Record of Birth, NJState Archives
Certificate and Record of Birth
Name of this Child; Horace Sutton
Sex; Male
Color: White
DOB; De. 11, 1912
Place of Birth; 700 S. East Ave. Bridgeton, Cumberland Co., NJ
Name of Father: William Sutton
Birthplace of Father; US
Maiden name of Mother: Emma Rogers
Mother's place of birth; US
Age of Father: 49
Occupation: Laborer
Age of Mother: 44
Occupation: Housewife
# of Children in all by this marriage: 3
# of children now living: 3

Children of HORACE SUTTON and MILDRED ARNOLD are:

12. i. DAVID ANTHONY[7] SUTTON, b. November 16, 1939, Mt. Holly, NJ; d. September 26, 1998, Englishtown, NJ.

13. ii. ANN KATHERINE SUTTON, b. August 21, 1943, Mt. Holly, NJ.

Generation No. 5

10. ROBERT THOMAS[7] SUTTON *(ROBERT O.[6], WILLIAM L.[5], ROBERT O.[4], MARTHA[3] LEVICK, ROBERT[2], ROBERT ALAN[1])*[10] was born December 07, 1932 in Atlantic City, NJ[10]. He married JOYCE F.. MANCUSO October 19, 1957 in Pomona, NJ[10], daughter of THOMAS MANCUSO and LOIS HOVATTER. She was born May 11, 1934 in Bristol, PA.

Notes for ROBERT THOMAS SUTTON:
Bob was born on a Wednesday. His wife Joyce was born on a Friday two years later, each year their bithdays fall on the same day of the week.

Notes for JOYCE F.. MANCUSO:
DAR member number 831198, installed Oct. 16, 2004

Children of ROBERT SUTTON and JOYCE MANCUSO are:

i. DOLORES LEA[8] SUTTON[10], b. September 24, 1958[10].
14. ii. SUSAN JOYCE SUTTON, b. December 01, 1964.
15. iii. BOBBI LYNN SUTTON, b. November 09, 1968.

11. MARJORIE LOUISE[7] SUTTON *(ROBERT O.[6], WILLIAM L.[5], ROBERT O.[4], MARTHA[3] LEVICK, ROBERT[2], ROBERT ALAN[1])*[10] was born Abt. 1940. She married LAWRENCE ROSE.

Notes for MARJORIE LOUISE SUTTON:

Kenneth's father is Austin Gibbons.

Child of MARJORIE SUTTON and LAWRENCE ROSE is:

i. LAWRENCE[8] ROSE.

12. DAVID ANTHONY[7] SUTTON *(HORACE WOODRUFF[6], WILLIAM L.[5], ROBERT O.[4], MARTHA[3] LEVICK, ROBERT[2], ROBERT ALAN[1])* was born November 16, 1939 in Mt. Holly, NJ, and died September 26, 1998 in Englishtown, NJ. He married JUDITH WILLIAMS June 24, 1964 in Hainesport, NJ.

Children of DAVID SUTTON and JUDITH WILLIAMS are:

i. DAVID ANTHONY SUTTON[8] JR., b. December 20, 1965.
16. ii. PAULA MARIE SUTTON, b. September 03, 1968.
iii. HORACE SUTTON, b. November 12, 1973.

13. ANN KATHERINE[7] SUTTON *(HORACE WOODRUFF[6], WILLIAM L.[5], ROBERT O.[4], MARTHA[3] LEVICK, ROBERT[2], ROBERT ALAN[1])* was born August 21, 1943 in Mt. Holly, NJ. She married ROBERT EDWARD HELLMIG August 07, 1965 in Masonville, NJ. He was born in Mt. Laurel, NJ, and died July 20, 2007.

Notes for ROBERT EDWARD HELLMIG:
Hi!

I have some bad news, Bob passed away this evening at home, he has been suffering for some time and I thank God he is at peace.
I'Il write again soon. Love, Ann

(received 7/20/2007)

Marriage Notes for ANN SUTTON and ROBERT HELLMIG:
Married at the Bible Calvary Church in Masonville, NJ by Rev. William A. Raymond
Debbie was Christened at the Bible Calvary Church on De. 31, 1967 by Rev. William Raymond.

Children of ANN SUTTON and ROBERT HELLMIG are:

17. i. DEBBIE LEIGH[8] HELLMIG, b. March 05, 1967.
18. ii. ROBERT EDWARD HELLMIG, JR., b. May 10, 1969.

Generation No. 6

14. SUSAN JOYCE[8] SUTTON *(ROBERT THOMAS[7], ROBERT O.[6], WILLIAM L.[5], ROBERT O.[4], MARTHA[3] LEVICK, ROBERT[2], ROBERT ALAN[1])[10]* was born December 01, 1964*[10]*. She married CHRISTOPHER KEATING*[10]*, son of WILTON KEATING and MARGUERITE TOTH.

Notes for SUSAN JOYCE SUTTON:
DAR member number 831199

Children of SUSAN SUTTON and CHRISTOPHER KEATING are:

i. CHRISTOPHER KEATING[9] JR.*[10]*.
ii. BENJAMIN KEATING*[10]*.

15. BOBBI LYNN[8] SUTTON *(ROBERT THOMAS[7], ROBERT O.[6], WILLIAM L.[5], ROBERT O.[4], MARTHA[3] LEVICK, ROBERT[2], ROBERT ALAN[1])[10]* was born November 09, 1968*[10]*. She married (1) KARL FRANK CHASE*[10]*, son of KARL SR. and CATHY. She met (2) MR. MCHENRY.

Notes for BOBBI LYNN SUTTON:
DAR member number 831200, installed Oct. 16, 2004

Children of BOBBI SUTTON and KARL CHASE are:

i. SHAWN JOSEPH[9] CHASE*[10]*, b. March 14, 1995*[10]*.
ii. SAMANTHA JOYCE CHASE*[10]*, b. April 06, 1997*[10]*.

Child of BOBBI SUTTON and MR. MCHENRY is:

iii. DANI-LYNN[9] MCHENRY, b. June 08, 2006.

16. PAULA MARIE[8] SUTTON *(DAVID ANTHONY[7], HORACE WOODRUFF[6], WILLIAM L.[5], ROBERT O.[4], MARTHA[3] LEVICK, ROBERT[2], ROBERT ALAN[1])* was born September 03, 1968. She married JERRY LEFFERS April 10, 1999.

Marriage Notes for PAULA SUTTON and JERRY LEFFERS:
They had an Outdoor Wedding, Brothers David and Horace stood up for her giving their consent of marriage.

Child of PAULA SUTTON and JERRY LEFFERS is:

i. ZACHARY CHRISIN SUTTON-[9] LEFFERS, b. March 11, 1998.

Notes for ZACHARY CHRISIN SUTTON- LEFFERS:
Zachary was born on a Wednesday at 3:59 PM. Weighed 7lbs. 12oz. at birth.

17. DEBBIE LEIGH[8] HELLMIG *(ANN KATHERINE[7] SUTTON, HORACE WOODRUFF[6], WILLIAM L.[5], ROBERT O.[4], MARTHA[3] LEVICK, ROBERT[2], ROBERT ALAN[1])* was born March 05, 1967. She married EDWARD THOMAS MOUNT, JR. April 25, 1992 in Medford Lakes, NJ.

Notes for DEBBIE LEIGH HELLMIG:
Born on A Sunday at 7:10PM, Weighed 6lbs. 10ozs. and was 21" long. Attending Physician was Dr. John C. Mutch of Moorestown, NJ

Marriage Notes for DEBBIE HELLMIG and EDWARD MOUNT:
Married at the Catheral of Woods Church in Medford Lakes, NJ.

Children of DEBBIE HELLMIG and EDWARD MOUNT are:

i. KELLY ANN[9] MOUNT, b. September 20, 1992, Mt. Holly, NJ.

Notes for KELLY ANN MOUNT:
Born Sunday at 9:48A.M. Weighed 6 lbs. 13 oz. 20" long

ii. MELISSA LEIGH MOUNT, b. October 17, 1995.

Notes for MELISSA LEIGH MOUNT:
Milissa was born at 8:03 P.M. on Tuesday weighed 8 lbs. 1 oz and was 20 1/2" long

18. ROBERT EDWARD[8] HELLMIG, JR. *(ANN KATHERINE[7] SUTTON, HORACE WOODRUFF[6], WILLIAM L.[5], ROBERT O.[4], MARTHA[3] LEVICK, ROBERT[2], ROBERT ALAN[1])* was born May 10, 1969. He married JEANINE PARRY HARGROVE October 04, 1992 in Medford Lakes, NJ.

Notes for ROBERT EDWARD HELLMIG, JR.:
Robert was born on A Saturday at 12:27P.M. , weighed 5lbs. 15oz, and was 181/2" long, delivered by attended physician Dr. John S. Mutch, of Moorestown, NJ.

Marriage Notes for ROBERT HELLMIG and JEANINE HARGROVE:
Married at the Catheral of Woods, Church in Medford Lakes, NJ.

Children of ROBERT HELLMIG and JEANINE HARGROVE are:

i. TYLER JAMES[9] HELLMIG, b. February 10, 1996.

Notes for TYLER JAMES HELLMIG:
Born at 2:46 P.M. Saturday at West Jersey Hopital. Weighed 10 lbs. 11 oz.

ii. JACOB MICHAEL HELLMIG, b. June 10, 1998.

Notes for JACOB MICHAEL HELLMIG:
Borned Wednesday at 8:05 A.M. in West Jersey Hospital. Weighed 9lbs. 6 oz

Endnotes

1. Mancuso.FTW, Date of Import: Sep 6, 2000.
2. Broderbund Family Archive #110, Vol. 2, Ed. 7, Social Security Death Index: U.S., Date of Import: May 20, 2000, Internal Ref. #1.112.7.115546.117
3. Mancuso.FTW, Date of Import: Sep 6, 2000.
4. Genealogy.com, Family Archive #110, Social Security Death Index: U.S. Ed. 9, Social Security Death Index, Release date: April 10, 2000, Internal Ref. #1.112.9.111416.32.
5. Broderbund Family Archive #110, Vol. 2, Ed. 7, Social Security Death Index: U.S., Date of Import: May 20, 2000, Internal Ref. #1.112.7.115546.117
6. Mancuso.FTW, Date of Import: Sep 6, 2000.
7. Genealogy.com, Family Archive #110, Social Security Death Index: U.S. Ed. 9, Social Security Death Index, Release date: April 10, 2000, Internal Ref. #1.112.9.111416.32.
8. Mancuso.FTW, Date of Import: Sep 6, 2000.
9. Broderbund Family Archive #110, Vol. 2, Ed. 7, Social Security Death Index: U.S., Date of Import: May 20, 2000, Internal Ref. #1.112.7.115546.117
10. Mancuso.FTW, Date of Import: Sep 6, 2000.

Leonard, Samuel [envelope] [N.J.] [1818]

Morris Co., N.J., 10 Sep 1821, Samuel Leonard [s] (former private in Rev. in Capt. Patterson's Co., Col. Dayton's Regt., when disabled at battle of Monmouth by musket ball through the ankle on 28 Jun 1778), resident of Morristown for 50 years and is now in 65th year, appoints Silas L. Condict atty to collect pension due from 4 Mar 1820 to 4 Sep 1821; sworn before Lewis Condict [s], a Judge of ICCP, who also hears oath of atty; witness Sophia W. Condict [s]. On 15 Sep 1825, Lewis Condict M.D. [s] and John B. Johnes, M.D. [s] certify Leonard's disability continues undiminished; sworn before Edward Condict J.P. [s].

Trenton, 18 Sep 1821, Silas L. Condict [s] collected $72.00.

Lesuer, William N.J. 1818

Middlesex Co., N.J., 4 Nov 1826, Nathaniel Hillyer [s] and John Burlew [s] make oaths William Lesuer was a pensioner (former private in Rev.) who resided at South Amboy and died on 19 Sep 1826; sworn before William Herbert J.P. [s]. On 22 Sep 1826, Charles Carson [s], Surrogate, grants administration of William *Lesure*'s estate to Stephen Hall of this county.

Trenton, 2 Apr 1827, Stephen Hall [s] collected $52.00 arrears due from 4 Mar 1826 to 19 Sep 1826; his oath of identity heard same date by David Johnston J.P. [s] of Hunterdon Co.

Letson, John N.J. 1832

Middlesex Co., N.J., 13 Mar 1851, Nicholas Booraem [s], Clerk of CCP, certifies court satisfied John Letson was a pensioner (former private in Rev.) who resided and died here on 6 Jan 1851 leaving no widow but five children only: Etty (wife of John Terhune), Elizabeth (wife of James Campbell), Mary (wife of Jacob Wall), Robert Letson, and Joseph C. Letson. On 29 Apr 1851, Etty Terhune [s], Elizabeth W. Campbell [s], Mary L. Wall [s], Robert Letson [s], and Joseph C. Letson [s], children, make oaths John resided in this county for at least 40 years, and appoint Nicholas Wyckoff atty to collect arrears due from 4 Sep 1850 to 6 Jan 1851; sworn before Peter P. Runyon J.P. [s] who on 29 May hears oath of atty; witness John Terhune [s].

Trenton, 29 May 1851, N. Wyckoff [s] collected $24.84.

Letts, Francis N.J. 1832

Middlesex Co., N.J., 11 Mar 1847, Nicholas Booraem [s], Clerk of CCP, certifies court satisfied Francis Letts was a pensioner (former private in Rev.) who resided and died here on 2 Dec 1846 leaving no widow but one child only: Isaac Letts. On 17 Mar 1847, Isaac Letts [s], son of the pensioner, makes oath Francis resided in this county at least 50 years, and appoints David F. Randolph atty to collect pension due from 4 Sep 1846 to 2 Dec 1846; sworn before Frederick Stults J.P. [s]; *witness Wm. F. Smith [s]*.

Trenton, 3 Apr 1847, D. FitzRandolph [s] collected $19.55; his oath heard on 2 Apr 1847 by Peter P. Runyon J.P. [s] of Middlesex Co.

Levick, Priscilla (Robert) N.J. 1848

Cumberland Co., N.J., 4 Mar 1857, Daniel Levick [s], Robert Levick [s], William Levick [s], Martha Sutton [s] (wife of Joseph Sutton [s]), Priscilla Woodruff [s] (wife of Horace Woodruff [s]), only children of late pensioner Priscilla Levick (widow of Robert Levick, former dragoon in Rev.) who resided in Fairfield Twp. for 50 years, appoint Thomas J. Stryker atty to collect arrears due from 4 Sep 1856 to 6 Feb 1857, the day of her death; sworn before William D. Barrett J.P. [s]; witness James W. Trenchard [s]. On 12 May 1857, county certification signed by Ephraim E. Sheppard [s], Clerk of CCP, who also certifies Barrett is a J.P.

Trenton, 15 May 1857, Thos. J. Stryker [s] collected $42.23; his oath heard same date by Phil. Dickinson [s], Pension Agent.

Lewis, Daniel N.J. 1818

Monmouth Co., N.J., 3 Sep 1830, Richard Britton [x] and David Karr [signs "Carr"] of this county make oaths they well knew Daniel Lewis to be a pensioner (former private in Rev.) who died on 14 May 1830 both being present when he died; sworn before William J. Emley J.P. [s]. On 31 Aug 1830, Peter C. Vanderhoef [s], Surrogate, certifies that administration of Daniel Lewis's estate granted to Isaac N. Woodward Esq. On 7 Sep 1830, Richard Britton [x] and Isaac N. Woodward [s], both of Upper Freehold Twp., make oaths Daniel died in this township leaving no widow or lawful children, and that Woodward is his

Descendants of Joseph Sutton

Generation No. 1

1. JOSEPH[1] SUTTON was born Abt. 1800 in Fairfield Township, Cumberland Co., and died June 25, 1859 in Hering Roe, NJ. He married MARTHA LEVICK September 27, 1835 in Cumberland Co., daughter of ROBERT LEVICK and PRISCILLA HUSTED. She was born Abt. 1814, and died 1880.

Notes for JOSEPH SUTTON:
Return of Death
Vol. H
Page No. 650
Town/Township: Fairfield
County: Cumberland
Death Date: June 25, 1959
Deceased Name; Joseph Sutton
Sex: Male
Marital Status: Married
Age: 59
Deceased's Occupation: Laborer
Death Place: Hering Roe
Birth Place: Cumberland Co.
Parent's Names:________________
Death Cause:__________________
Time Record Made: 1861

this family was compiled from the 1850 census - Stowe Creek
Joseph Sutton, 50 M. Farmer
Martha 36 F.
Phebe A. 14 F.
Theophilus 12 M.
Thomas Cerwin 10 M.
Samuel S. 5 M.
Joseph W. 4/12 M.

More About JOSEPH SUTTON:
Burial: Swing Cemetery

Marriage Notes for JOSEPH SUTTON and MARTHA LEVICK:
Marriage information taken from:
S. Craig's Cumberland County Marriages

Children of JOSEPH SUTTON and MARTHA LEVICK are:

i. PHEBE ANN[2] SUTTON, b. Abt. 1836.

ii. THEOPHILUS M. SUTTON, b. Abt. 1838.

Notes for THEOPHILUS M. SUTTON:
Militay Records - Civil War

Surprise, GETTYSBURG AND ANDERSONVILLE PRISON

Theophilus M. Sutton (Reminder the s/o Joseph Sutton & Martha Levick)
b. c 1838
d. October 28, 1864, Andersonville Prison

ROW 1
1. Unknown
2. Unknown
3. Unknown
4. Ireland,William 1808-1880
5. Unknown
6. Unknown
7. Ireland, Zechariah
8. Unknown
9. Unknown

ROW 2
1. Levick, Robert 1732-1816
2. Levick, Priscilla 1828-1857
3. Woodruff, George 1/1854-7/1854
4. Woodruff, Priscilla 1821-1883
5. Woodruff, Horace 1814-1894
6. Davis, Daniel F. 1830-1865
7. Davis, Maranda 1832-1875
8. Unknown
9. Unknown
10. Unknown
11. Unknown
12. Davis, Mary 1864-1902

ROW 3
1. Levick, Robert 1807-1885
2. Sutton, Joseph 1800-1859
3. Sutton, Joseph W. 1850-1865
4. Lieutenant Sheppard (Co. C)

ROW 4
1. Levick, Carrie 1818- ?
2. Levick, Hanna ?- 1863
3. Levick, Priscilla Ethel 1856-1881
4. Wescott, Daniel T. 1828-1897
5. Wescott, Abigail B. 1828-1901
6. Unknown
7. Unknown
8. Unknown
9. Picken, Rebecca 1843-1847
10. Burr, Lillie 1856-1858
11. Unknown
12. Veteran
13. Dutch, Nueal 1849-1896
14. Unknown
15. Dutch, Charles 1876-1878

ROW 5
1. Lawrence,William 1789-1832
2. Lawrence, Pamelia 1790-1869
3. Danzenbaker, Bower J.
4. Danzenbaker, Martha K. 1835-1857
5. Unknown
6. Lawrence, John
7. Shimp, Anna ?-1858
8. Everingham, Abijah
9. Jerrel, Issac 1801-183?
10. Unknown
11. Unknown
12. Unknown
13. Hepner, Martha Ellen 1833-1865
14. Bowe, Isabella 1848-1905
15. Harris, Alexander 1847-1880
16. Dean, Victoria 1873-1940 /
   Enoch Sr. 1869-1951
17. Unknown

ROW 6
1. Unknown
2. M.L.
3. Unknown

ROW 7
1. Shaw, Judith 1780-1847
2. Jerrel, Zachariah Fitz 1770-1837
3. Unknown
4. Jerrel, Hannah 1817-1845
5. B.S.J.
6. H.O.J.
7. Unknown
8. E.J.
9. Jerrel, Abigail 1817-1853
10. Garretson, Captain E.T.
11. Garretson
12. Garretson,Ernest 1863-1929
13. Jarrel, Martha E. ?-1885
14. Jarrel, Emma F. 1868-1878
15. Jarrel, Martha E. ?-1861
16. Jarrel Wilmina 1835-1855
17. Jarrel, John F. 11/1851-02/1852
18. Jarrel, Elizabeth 1833-1857
19. Jarrel, Zachareal 1832-1894
20. Wescott, Gilbert ?-1871
21. Wescot, Hannah 1795-1865
22. G.H.N.
23. Shumen, Daniel 1720-1890
24. Shumen, Harriet 1832-1881
25. M.E.S.
26. Unknown
27. Shumen, Joseph 1848-1897
28. Dean, Enoch Sr. 1827-1914/
   Dean, Angeline 1842-1917

ROW 8
1. Cliff, Martha 1812-1830
2. Keen, Sallie ? -1859
3. Everingham, Martha
4. Everingham, James
5. Davis, Hannah W.
6. Everingham, Alfred ? /1846
7. Everingham, Alfred 1816-1856
8. Davis, Mary 1786-1814
9. Davis, William ? / 1844
10. J.E.D
11. J.E.D.
12. Taylor, Mary B. 1825-1877
13. Taylor, Benjamin 1824-1850
14. Taylor, Harriet ? /1840
15. Wescott, Nathaniel ? /1890
16. Wescott, Ellen 1836-1863
17. Wescott, Florence P. 1859-1880
18. J.P.P. / M.S.
19. Loder, Joseph (Veteran)

ROW 9
1. Marts, Susan 1810-1897
2. Marts, Elijah ? /1872
3. Rebecca
4. Ogden, Jane ? /1810 /
   Barret, Lydia ? /1840
5. Senton, John ? /1854
6. Riley, Elizabeth 1816-1857
7. Riley, Rebecca 1902-1865
8. Riley, Daniel 1798-1843
9. Dallas, Rebecca Jane 1853-1855
10. Camm, Simon 1820-1906
11. Ward, Caroline 1828-19_0
12. Camm, Elmer
13. Camm, Howard B.
14. Camm, Phoebe 1828-1931
15. Nugent, Charles 1848-1866
16. Nugent, Sarah ? /1884
17. Churon, Anna Lewis 1855-1863
18. Loder, Sallie 1831-1889 w/our children
   K.L. , L.L. , L.J.L. , L.J.L. , W.P.L.

This map depicts the layout of The Church of Christ burying ground and the Methodist cemetery as surveyed on September 26, 1900 by F.B. Sheppard

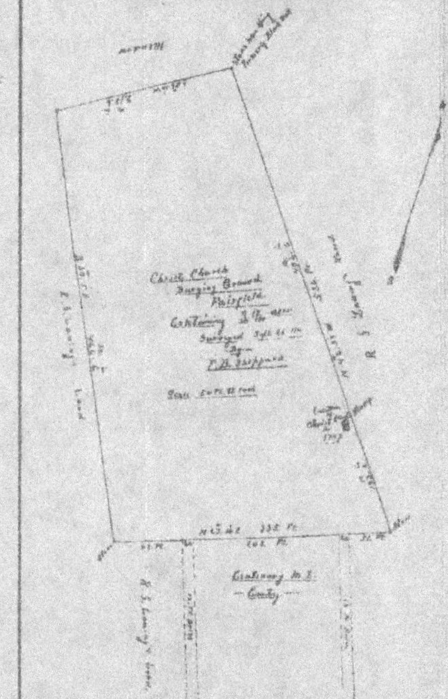

Farmer's Field

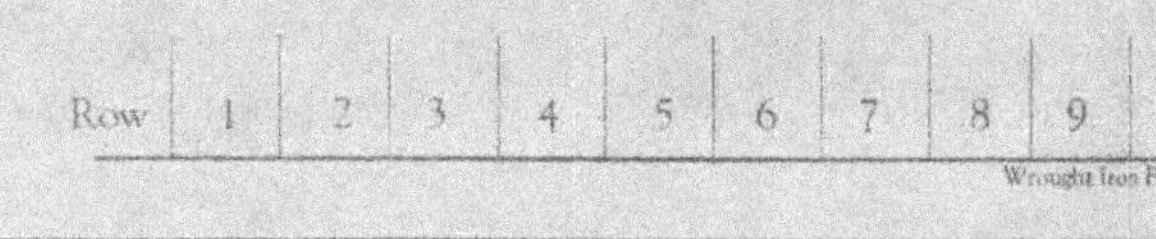

← Sea Breeze   Rt. 601   Back Neck

Michael Swin

ROW 10
1. Marts, William 1886-1895
2. Marts, William W. 1838-1886 /
   Marts, Anna B. 1844-1915
3. Fowler, James ? /1882
4. Fowler, Mary ? /18_2
5. Bamford, Sophia 1776-1853
6. Parvin, Anna E. 1816-1894
7. Parvin, Horace ? /1847
8. Parvin, Amy 1823-1851
9. Parvin, Jonathan ? /1816
10. Ogden, John 1788-1875
11. Ogden, Lydia 1807-1863
12. Ogden, Ellen
13. Ogden, Richard 1838-1878
14. Ogden, Carrie F. 1845-1894
15. Ogden, Susan 1840-1920
16. Johnson, Lydia Mara 1851-1907 /
   Johnson, Edmund 1849-1911
17. Mills, LeRoy 1878 - ?
18. Unknown
19. Unknown

ROW 11
1. Unknown
2. Riley, Sammiee 1857-1860
3. Riley, Millie 1865-1868 /
   Riley, Chester 1868-1873
4. Riley, Anna 1835-1912
5. Dallas, George 1831-1886
6. Mills, David 1826-1888
7. Mills, Amy A.
8. Mills, Ida ? /1867
9. Mills, Leonard R. ? /1869
10. Mills, Simon 1853-1923
11. Sink, Hannah 1822-1905
12. Sink, Thomas P. 1816-1871
13. Miller, Joseph
14. Miller, Catherine
15. Miller, Caroline
16. Ware, Jane M. ? /1835
17. Moore, Albert 2/1882 - 8/1882
18. Moore, Phyllis 8/1924 - 12/1924
19. W.B.
20. H.S.

JOSEPH W.
Sutton
Drowned
30 1865

ROBERT LEVIC.
ARTILLERY.
1807 — 1885.

Pusilla w/o Horace

Born
1856
Died
1884

BORN AUG. 1814
DIED DEC. 24 1894
AT REST

JOSEPH SUTTON,
who died
June 25, 1859.

Births in [illegible] from the first day of May 1853 to the first day of May 1854

DATE OF BIRTH	PLACE OF BIRTH	NAME OF CHILD	SEX OF CHILD	NAMES OF PARENTS	OCCUPATION OF FATHER	RESIDENCE OF PARENTS	TIME OF MAKING RECORD
Jan 31st 1854	Fairfield	Ann Rebecca Gould	Female	Jonathan & Harriet Gould	Laborer	Fairfield	May 6th 1854
Oct 4th 1853	Do	Charles Hall	Male	Robert & Emily Hall	Farmer	Do	" 6th "
March 24th 1854	Do	No Name (B)	Female	James H. & Ann Brown	Laborer	Do	" 6th "
April 20th 1854	Do	Addison H. Whiticar	Male	George S. & Emily Whiticar	Shoe-Maker	Do	" 6th "
Aug 23 1853	Do	Alonzo Marker Roray	Male	David H. & Jane B. Roray	Waterman	Do	" 6th "
Feb 13th 1853	Do	Nathan Foster Colvin	Male	Lewis & Ruth Colvin	Shoe-Maker	Do	" 6th "
Aug 5th 1853	Do	Lyman Camm Mills	Male	David H. & Amy Mills	Waterman	Do	" 6th "
April 4th 1854	Do	Henry Franklin Camm	Male	Eli & Ruth Camm	Waterman	Do	" 6th "
Aug 15th 1853	Do	John B. Husted	Male	John & Harriet V. Husted	Waterman	Do	" 6th "
May 10th 1853	Do	James P. Davis	Male	David & Eunice Davis	Farmer	Do	May 10: 1854
Sept 4th 1853	Do	Emma A. Hitchner	Female	Levi & Mary Ann Hitchner	Farmer	Do	" 11th 1854
March 8th 1854	Do	No Name	Female	Ethan W. & Mary E Henry	Waterman	Do	" 11th 1854
Jan 21st 1854	Do	Ellen Louisa Sheppard	Female	Robt. H. & Amanda Sheppard	Farmer	Do	" 13th "
Nov 24th 1853	Do	George M. Howell	Male	Edmund & Hannah Howell	Farmer	Do	" 13th "
Jan 21st 1854	Do	Joseph C. Morrison	Male	Jos. C. & Sarah Morrison	Waterman	Do	" 13th "
March 21st 1854	Do	Jane Westcott Ware	Female	Reuben & Abigail Ware	Chair-Maker	Do	" 13th "
June 8th 1853	Do	Jane Louisa Bow	Female	Timothy & Catharine Bow	Laborer	Do	" 13th "
Aug 1853	Do	Edo Mounce	Male	John & Theresa Mounce	Laborer	Do	" 13th "
Oct 19th 1853	Do	Elizabeth W. Marts	Female	Elijah B. & Susanth. Marts	Farmer	Do	" 13th "
July 17th 1853	Do	Coates Ewing	Male	Stimon S. & Judith L. Ewing	Farmer	Do	" 13th "
June 22 1853	Do	Eli Bateman Tarlton	Male	Daniel & Caroline Tarlton	Farmer	Do	" 13th "
Dec 16th 1853	Do	George Woodruff	Male	Horace & Priscilla Woodruff	Waterman	Do	" 13 "
July 4th 1853	Do	Hannah Maria Bishop	Female	Horace & Phebe D Bishop	Farmer	Do	" 13th "
Sept 3d 1853	Do	Mary Adaline Williams	Female	Saml. H. & Abigail B. Williams	Farmer	Do	" 13th "
April 28th 1854	Do	No Name	Male	Smith & Fanny N. Davis	Farmer	Do	" 13th "
April 26 1854	Do	No Name (B)	Male	Charles & Elizabeth Williams	Laborer	Do	" 13th "
Aug 8th 1853	Do	Henrietta Harmer (B)	Female	Levi & Nancy Harmer	Farmer	Do	" 13th "
Aug 20 1853	Do	Ephraim Mulford	Male	David & Hannah B. Mulford	Farmer	Do	" 13th "
Aug 26th 1853	Do	George Martin (B)	Male	William & Sarah F. Martin	Laborer	Do	" 13th "
Jan 1854	Salem Co. N. J.	Anna Frances Willet (B)	Female	Andrew & Ann Maria Willet	Laborer	Unknown	" 13th "
Dec 27th 1853	Fairfield N. J.	Ebenezer Whitaker Laning	Male	Richard & Violetta W. Laning	Farmer	Fairfield	" 13th "
June 4th 1853	Do "	Hannah S. Westcott	Female	Ephraim & Elizabeth Westcott	Farmer	Do	" 13th "
Nov 24 1853	Do	Richard S. Sutton	Male	Joseph & Martha Sutton	Laborer	Do	" 13th "
January 1854	Do	Benj Franklin Hoffman	Male	Michael & Harriet Hoffman	Farmer	Do	" 13th "
Oct 11th 1854	Do	Thomas Scull Willis	Male	Isaac & Sarah S. Willis	Waterman	Do	" 13th "

Fairfield
George Woodruff
Dec 16, 1853
Horace & Priscilla
Woodruff

Richard (Lord)
Sutton
Nov 24, 1853
Joseph & Martha
Sutton

NEW JERSEY STATE ARCHIVES

DEPARTMENT OF STATE 185 West State Street,
CN 307 Trenton, New Jersey 08625 Telephone: (609) 292-62

e following was copied retaining any errors, misspellings, and omissions from RETURNS OF BIRTH

LUME	PAGE NO.	TOWN / TOWNSHIP	COUNTY
, H-2	145	Fairfield	Cumberland

H DATE	BIRTH PLACE	CHILD'S NAME	SEX
November 1856	Fairfield	Horace W.	Male

NTS' NAMES	PARENTS' OCCUPATIONS
Joseph & Martha Sutton	Laborer

NTS' RESIDENCE	TIME RECORD MADE
Fairfield	May 1857

R INFORMATION OR RECORD / EXPLANATORY NOTES

REBY CERTIFY THAT THE FOREGOING IS AN URATE TRANSCRIPT OF AN ORIGINAL RECORD FILE AT THE NEW JERSEY STATE ARCHIVES.	CHIEF OF ARCHIVES (Signature)	DATE
	[signature]	27 Feb. 98

Return of Births in the Township of Fairfield County of Cumberland State of New Jersey, from the first day of May 1868 to the first day of [illegible]

No.	Date of Birth.	Name of Child.	Place of Birth.	Sex of Child.	Names of Parents.	Occupation of Parents.	Residence of Parents.	Time of
	1868							
1	June 29	Pamela	Fairfield	Female	Wallace & Francis Pierce	Farmer	Fairfield	Sept
2	Nov	Violette	"	"	Richard & Hannah Pierce	"	"	
3	April 27	Persilia	"	"	Isaiah & Louisa Pierce	[illegible]	"	
4	"	Mary E	"	"	Jacob & Clara Combs	"	"	
5	July 27	Mary J	"	"	Jeptha & Susan Taylor	"	"	
6	1869 March 7	Arcurius	"	male	Jacob & Anna Wright	"	"	
7	March 17 '68	Amy	"	Female	Silas Mary & Sophia Sayre?	"	"	
8	" "	Almina	"	"	Nathan & Sarah Gould	"	"	
9	" "	Jonathan	"	male	Lewis & Hannah Shaw	"	"	
10	Dec 12	Hannah	"	Female	John Tompkins & Eliza Shaw	"	"	
11	July 19	Elbonia?	"	"	Daniel & Abby Earle	Farmer	"	
12	May 2	Rachel G	"	"	Daniel & Rachel Hausler?	"	"	
13	April 1/69	Samuel	"	male	Robert & Christina Sutton	"	"	
14	March 6/7	Smith	"	"	Smith & Francis Davis	"	"	
15	[illegible]	Milton	"	"	Bedford B & Lucy Russell	[illegible]	"	
16	[illegible]	Herbert	"	"	John & Anna Pincer?	Farmer	"	
17	April 27	Harrison	"	"	William & Hannah Taylor	waterman	"	
18	Dec 1 1868	Leonard	"	"	David & Amy Hitts?	carpenter	"	
19	March 1 /69	Christopher	"	"	Moses & Matilda Kinnear?	Laborer	"	
20	Nov 13/68	Samuel	"	"	Mark & Jane Westcott	Farmer	"	
21	[illegible]	[illegible]		Female	Isaiah & Mariah Westcott	"	"	

Samuel April 1, 1869 Fairfield Robert O. & Christiana Sutton

Don't have him in the family tree

Notes for ROBERT O. SUTTON:
Record of Death, NJ State Archives
Certificate and Record of Death
County: Cumberland
City: Bridgeton
401 Spruce St., 2nd Ward
Full Name of Deceased: Robert O. Sutton
Sex: Male
Color: White
Widowed
Date of Birth: Aug. 25, 1848
Age: 71 yrs
Occupation: Farmer
Place of Birth: US
Name of Father: Joseph Sutton
Place of Birth: US
Maiden name of Mother: Martha Levick
Place of Birth: US
E.L. Diament MD Bridgeton, NJ
Date of Death: Oct. 11, 1914
I hereby certify that I attended deceased from Sept. 25, 1913 to Oct. 11, 1914. That I last saw him alive on Oct. 11, 1914
Cause of Death: Brights Disease
Place of Burial: Broad St. Cemetery
Date of Burial: Oct 13, 1914
Undertaker: Harry J. Garrison, Bridgeton

Sutton, Robert O. Callahan, Christiana P. Bridgeton 5 May 1863 Cumberland County : Bridgeton Bk. H : Pg. 465

More About ROBERT O. SUTTON:
Burial: October 13, 1914, Broad St. Cemetery, Bridgeton, NJ

More About CHRISTINA CALLAHAN:
Burial: May 20, 1911, Broad St. Cemetery, Bridgeton, NJ

Children of ROBERT SUTTON and CHRISTINA CALLAHAN are:

i. WILLIAM L.[3] SUTTON[1], b. January 17, 1863, Fairton, NJ[1]; d. March 04, 1950, New Gretna, NJ[1]; m. (1) JOSEPHINE NICHOLS[1], July 17, 1886, Bridgeton, Cumberland Co., NJ; b. March 12, 1868, Fairton,NJ[1]; d. March 07, 1904[1]; m. (2) EMMA ROGERS[1], Abt. 1905; b. May 11, 1870[1].

Notes for WILLIAM L. SUTTON:
obit
William Sutton, Sr., 85 Expires Early Today
3/4/1950
Word was received here this morning of the death of William Sutton Sr. 85, of New Gretna. Mr. Sutton expired at six O'clock this morning. The deceased had been taken ill three weeks ago with pneumonia and was apparently fully recovered when he suffered a stroke three days ago. He is a former sesident of Bridgeton, but has been residing with a son, Robert, in New Gretna, for quite a while.
Surviving are one daughter and eight sons, Mrs. Reba Doughty of Leeds Point, William Rogers of Washington, D.C., Robert of New Gretna, Alfred of Atlantic City, Horace of Masonville, Frank, George and William Jr. of Bridgeton and John C. Sutton of Millville. Two sisters, Lida Westcott of Bridgeton and Susie Watkins of Coatesville, Pa., also survive. In addition there are several grandchildren and great grandchildren. Funeral arrangements have not been completed as yet although interment will be held in Bridgeton.

More About WILLIAM L. SUTTON:
Burial: March 08, 1950, Broad St. Cemetery, Bridgeton, NJ

2nd Gen.

Christina Callahan
Wife of Robert O.

Wife of Robert O. ...

State of New Jersey—Bureau of Vital Statistics.

CERTIFICATE AND RECORD OF DEATH.

Place of Death: Cumberland

Registered No.

South Ave. St. 2d Ward

Name of Deceased: Christina Sutton

Personal and Statistical Particulars

White — Married

Feb. 14, 1849

... 2 ...

Housewife

New Jersey

... Callahan

New Jersey

... Callahan

New Jersey

... Diament M.D.

Bridgeton N.J.

Medical Certificate of Death

Date of Death: May 17, 1916

I HEREBY CERTIFY, That I attended deceased from May 1 — , 1907, to May 17 — , 1916, that I last saw h... alive on May 17 — , 1916, and that death occurred, on the date stated above, at 6:10 ...

The CAUSE OF DEATH was as follows:

Bright's disease

(Signed) E. L. Diament

May 18, 1916 (Address) Bridgeton N.J.

Place of Burial or Removal: Broad St. Cemetery

Date of Burial: May 20, 1916

Undertaker: Harry J. Garrison — Bridgeton

2nd Generation
Robert O. Son of
Joseph

State of New Jersey Bureau of Vital Statistics.

CERTIFICATE AND RECORD OF DEATH.

Cumberland

Registered No.

Bridgeton ... 411 Spruce St. ... 2nd Ward

1. Name of Deceased: Robert O. Sutton

Personal and Statistical Particulars

White — Widowed

Aug. 25, 1898

71 ... 1 ... 16 ...

Farmer

U.S.

Joseph Sutton

U.S.

Martha Leach

U.S.

E. L. Diament M.D.

Bridgeton N.J.

Medical Certificate of Death

Date of Death: Oct. 11, 1914

I HEREBY CERTIFY, That I attended deceased from Sept 25, 1913, to Oct 11 — , 1914, that I last saw him alive on Oct 11 — , 1914, and that death occurred, on the date stated above, at ...

The CAUSE OF DEATH was as follows:

Bright's disease

(Signed) E. L. Diament M.D.

Oct 11, 1914 (Address) Bridgeton N.J.

Place of Burial or Removal: Broad St. Cemetery

Date of Burial: Oct 13, 1914

Undertaker: Harry J. Garrison — Bridgeton

not a direct line a 2nd generation – daughter of Robert O + Christina Callahan

STATE OF NEW JERSEY.

MARRIAGE RETURN.

SEE PENALTY FOR NON-REPORT WITHIN 30 DAYS.

Use ink and write plainly, especially names.

Full Name of Husband George W. Watkins (If Col., so state.)

Place of Residence 226 South Avenue Bridgeton N.J. (If in city, give name, street and number; if not, give township and county.)

Age 25 years 2 months. Number of his Marriage First

Occupation Glassblower Country of Birth U. S. A.

Name of Father William Watkins Country of Birth "

Maiden Name of Mother Hannah Vinaman Country of Birth "

Full Maiden Name of Wife,

Susie Sutton Country of Birth U. S. A. (If Col., so state.)

Place of Residence Spruce St Bridgeton (If in city, give name, street and number; if not, give township and county.)

Age, nearest birthday 19 yrs (If in any trade or business, so state.)

Maiden name, if a Widow — Number of Bride's Marriage 1st

Name of Father Robert Sutton Country of Birth U. S. A.

Maiden Name of Mother Christina Callahan Country of Birth U. S. A.

Date (in full) Sept 1 189 Place Bridgeton N.J. (City or township and county.)

Witnesses of { T. W. Smith (No one to have witnesses.)

Signature of Minister, or Church Pastor of person officiating. } W. T. Smith President of the [illegible] Bridgeton.

NOTE.—All the items called for in this Blank are important, and should be accurately given.

Marriage Notes for WILLIAM SUTTON and JOSEPHINE NICHOLS:
Marriage Record, Certificate
S4, 359-26
b. c 1868
d. unknown

ii. SUSAN SUTTON[1], m. WATKINS[1], Coatsville, PA[1].
iii. LYDIA SUTTON[1], m. WATKINS[1], Bridgeton, NJ[1].

Endnotes

1. Mancuso.FTW, Date of Import: Sep 6, 2000.

Descendants of Robert O. Sutton

Generation No. 1

1. ROBERT O.[2] SUTTON *(JOSEPH[1])* was born August 25, 1848, and died October 11, 1914. He married CHRISTINA CALLAHAN May 05, 1863 in Cumberland Co., daughter of JOHN CALLAHAN and SUSIE ?. She was born February 14, 1843 in Bridgeton, NJ Cumberland Co., and died May 17, 1911 in Bridgeton, NJ Cumberland Co..

Notes for ROBERT O. SUTTON:
Record of Death, NJ State Archives
Certificate and Record of Death
County: Cumberland
City: Bridgeton
401 Spruce St., 2nd Ward
Full Name of Deceased: Robert O. Sutton
Sex: Male
Color: White
Widowed
Date of Birth: Aug. 25, 1848
Age: 71 yrs
Occupation: Farmer
Place of Birth: US
Name of Father: Joseph Sutton
Place of Birth: US
Maiden name of Mother: Martha Levick
Place of Birth: US
E.L. Diament MD Bridgeton, NJ
Date of Death: Oct. 11, 1914
I hereby certify that I attended deceased from Sept. 25, 1913 to Oct. 11, 1914. That I last saw him alive on Oct. 11, 1914
Cause of Death: Brights Disease
Place of Burial: Broad St. Cemetery
Date of Burial: Oct 13, 1914
Undertaker: Harry J. Garrison, Bridgeton

Sutton, Robert O. Callahan, Christiana P. Bridgeton 5 May 1863 Cumberland County : Bridgeton Bk. H : Pg. 465

More About ROBERT O. SUTTON:
Burial: October 13, 1914, Broad St. Cemetery, Bridgeton, NJ

More About CHRISTINA CALLAHAN:
Burial: May 20, 1911, Broad St. Cemetery, Bridgeton, NJ

Children of ROBERT SUTTON and CHRISTINA CALLAHAN are:
2. i. WILLIAM L.[3] SUTTON, b. January 17, 1863, Fairton, NJ; d. March 04, 1950, New Gretna, NJ.
ii. SUSAN SUTTON[1], m. WATKINS[1], Coatsville, PA[1].
iii. LYDIA SUTTON[1], m. WATKINS[1], Bridgeton, NJ[1].

Generation No. 2

2. WILLIAM L.[3] SUTTON *(ROBERT O.[2], JOSEPH[1])[1]* was born January 17, 1863 in Fairton, NJ[1], and died March 04,

1950 in New Gretna, NJ[1]. He married (1) JOSEPHINE NICHOLS[1] July 17, 1886 in Bridgeton, Cumberland Co., NJ. She was born March 12, 1868 in Fairton,NJ[1], and died March 07, 1904[1]. He married (2) EMMA ROGERS[1] Abt. 1905. She was born May 11, 1870[1].

Notes for WILLIAM L. SUTTON:
obit
William Sutton, Sr., 85 Expires Early Today
3/4/1950
Word was received here this morning of the death of William Sutton Sr. 85, of New Gretna. Mr. Sutton expired at six O'clock this morning. The deceased had been taken ill three weeks ago with pneumonia and was apparently fully recovered when he suffered a stroke three days ago. He is a former sesident of Bridgeton, but has been residing with a son, Robert, in New Gretna, for quite a while.
Surviving are one daughter and eight sons, Mrs. Reba Doughty of Leeds Point, William Rogers of Washington, D.C., Robert of New Gretna, Alfred of Atlantic City, Horace of Masonville, Frank, George and William Jr. of Bridgeton and John C. Sutton of Millville. Two sisters, Lida Westcott of Bridgeton and Susie Watkins of Coatesville, Pa., also survive. In addition there are several grandchildren and great grandchildren.
Funeral arrangements have not been completed as yet although interment will be held in Bridgeton.

More About WILLIAM L. SUTTON:
Burial: March 08, 1950, Broad St. Cemetery, Bridgeton, NJ

Marriage Notes for WILLIAM SUTTON and JOSEPHINE NICHOLS:
Marriage Record, Certificate
S4, 359-26
b. c 1868
d. unknown

Children of WILLIAM SUTTON and JOSEPHINE NICHOLS are:

i. FRANK R.[4] SUTTON[1], b. April 15, 1888[1].
ii. WILLIAM L. SUTTON JR.[1], b. May 30, 1890[1]; d. May 14, 1964.

Notes for WILLIAM L. SUTTON JR.:
On William L. Sutton Jr.
b. May 30, 1890, NJ
d. May have died 5/9/1964 with burial 5/14/1964...This needs documentation
Married
Mary Ann Bedwell
b. c 1884

Certificate and Record of Marriage
Full Name of Husband: William L. Sutton Jr.
Maiden Name of Wife: Mary Anna Bedwell, (Daretty)
Place of Marriage:72 S. Pine Street, Bridgeton
Date of Marriage: April 30, 1912, 8:15 p.m.
Residence of Groom: 72 South Pine, Bridgeton
Color: White
Age of Groom: 22
# of Marriage: First
Occupation of Groom: Glassworker
Birthplace of Groom: New Jersey
Father's Name: William L. Sutton, Sr.
Mother's Maiden Name: Josephine Nichols

Residence of Bride: 72 South Pine Street, Bridgeton
Age of Bridge: 28
Color: White
# of Marriage: Second
Name if Widowed: Mrs. Mary Anna Daretty
Birth place of Bride: New Jersey
Father's Name: John Bedwell

Mother's Maiden Name: Hannah Wallace
Witnesses: Walter T. Sutton & Herbert Surran, Bridgeton
Person Officiating: A. S. Allyn, Pastor, Berean Baptist Church, Bridgeton, NJ

iii. WALTER T. SUTTON[1], b. March 18, 1893[1].

Notes for WALTER T. SUTTON:
Obit-Millville Historical Society
Brother of Local Man Dies Today
11/5/38
The death of Walter T. Sutton, 46 of Glassboro, occurred suddenly today of hemorrhage. The deceased is a brother of John Sutton, Main Street, this city.
A glassworker, the deceased is survived by his wife, Bertha; his father, William of Absecon; eight other brothers and a sister. Frank and William Sutton, Bridgeton; Leon, George, Robert and Reba Sutton, Absecon; Alfred Sutton, Atlantic City, Horace Sutton, Hightstown; and William Rogers of Washington, D.C.
Funeral services will be conducted from the Christy Funeral Home this city. Tuesday afternoon with interment in Mount Pleasant Cemetery.

iv. LEON G. SUTTON[1], b. May 06, 1895[1]; d. Abt. 1940.

Notes for LEON G. SUTTON:
Leon was pouring a footing for a zinc factory in Chatsworth, NJ when he and two other men were buried alive in a cave in. The other two were rescued but Leon lost his life.

v. JOHN R. G. SUTTON[1], b. February 27, 1898[1]; d. October 16, 1957; m. EDITH LIPPENCOTT MADDEN; b. 1899; d. 1985.

Notes for JOHN R. G. SUTTON:
Obit
John C. Sutton, 59 Bus Driver, Dies 10/17/1957
Death of John C. Sutton, 59 of 429 Pine St. occurred yesterday.
The deceased a member of West Side Methodist Church, formerly operated a trolley between Millville and Bridgeton for the past 25 years and has been a driver for the Public Service Transportation Co.
Surviving are his wife, Edith L. Sutton; two daughters, Mrs. Margaret Yough, Wilmington, and Mrs. Marcella Barker, Philadelphia; a sister Mrs. Reba Doughty, Leeds Point and seven brothers, Frank and William Sutton, Bridgeton, Alfred Sutton, Atlantic City; George Sutton, Gandy's Beach; Robert Sutton, New Gretna, Horace Sutton, Masonville and William Rogers, Washington, D.C. Eight Grandchildren also service.
Funeral services will be condusted from the Christy Funeral Home Saturday at 2 p.m. with interment in Mt. Pleasant Cemetery.

John Callahan Sutton
b. Abt. 1898
d. October 16, 1957, Millville NJ (Obit-Millville Historical Society.)
married
Edith Lippincott Madden
b. 1899
d. 1985 (Headstone - Cemetery Records) have to see where I put the headstone information

Issue:
Margaret Sutton married Unknown Young
Marcella Sutton married Unknown Barker
Martha Madden Sutton
b. March 18, 1919
d. March 18, 1919

Martha Madden Sutton
b. March 18, 1919
d. March 18, 1919
Buried March 19, 1919 Mount Pleasant Cemetery, (Record of Death, NJ State Archives.)
Katherine Hinson Sutton, b. 1920 married Vernon Montgomery Abt. 1936
Issue of Katherine:
John Gilbert Montgomery
Information on Vernon Montgomery & family was provided by Nancy and as you can see really needs more

documentation on this line.

vi. ALFRED G. SUTTON[1], b. November 20, 1900[1].

Notes for ALFRED G. SUTTON:
Record of Birth, NJ State Archives.

Return of Birth
Full name of Child; Alfred C. Sutton
Sex; Male
Color; White
DOB; Nov. 20, 1900
Place of Birth; Morris Ave. Bridgeton, NJ
Name of Father; Wm L. Sutton
Maiden name of Mother; Josephine Nichols
Country of Father's Birth; US
Age; 37
Accupation; Laborer
Country of Mother's Birth; US
Age; 34
# of Children in all by this Marriage; 6
How many living; 6

vii. GEORGE W. SUTTON[1], b. February 22, 1903[1].

Children of WILLIAM SUTTON and EMMA ROGERS are:

viii. WILLIAM KERCHOFF[4] ROGERS[1], b. December 03, 1902[1].

ix. ROBERT O. SUTTON[1], b. October 24, 1906[2,2,2,2,2,2,2,2,2,2,2,2,2,3,4]; d. August 1987[5,5,5,5,5,5,5,5,5,5,5,5,5,6,7]; m. DORA WATSON[8]; b. February 09, 1915[8]; d. January 15, 1965[8].

Notes for ROBERT O. SUTTON:
[Genealogy.com, Family Archive #110, Vol. 2 L-Z, Ed. 9, Social Security Death Index: U.S., Date of Import: Dec 30, 2000, Internal Ref. #1.112.9.111416.32]

Individual: Sutton, Robert
Social Security #: 148-07-6985
Issued in: New Jersey

Birth date: Oct 24, 1906
Death date: Aug 1987

Residence code: New Jersey

ZIP Code of last known residence: 08224
Location associated with this ZIP Code:

New Gretna, New Jersey

Robert Sutton told his childred that the O. in his name stood for Osborn but we have not been able to verify this. His grandfather's middle initial also was an O. (for some reason either lost in the mail, etc. his birth certificate has never been registered. I am going to try and register him through the family bible and other papers we have).

More About ROBERT O. SUTTON:
Burial: Hillside cemetery, New Gretna[8]
Social Security Number: Social Security #: 148-07-6985[9,10]

Notes for DORA WATSON:
Reference #3180
The twins are buried behind Maud Cramer, there are two little stones sticking out of the ground to mark their

graves.

More About DORA WATSON:
Burial: Hillside cemetery, New Gretna[10]

x. REBA LYODD SUTTON[10], b. May 12, 1909[10]; m. ORION DOUGHTY.

Notes for ORION DOUGHTY:
Regarding the Baby and Anna May grave stones. This is Dolores' baby that died from the cord being wrapped around her neck during birth. She was buried on the grandparents cemetery site.

xi. HORACE WOODRUFF SUTTON[10], b. December 11, 1911, Bridgeton, NJ[10]; d. February 06, 1972, Mt. Laurel, NJ; m. MILDRED ELIZABETH ARNOLD; b. October 24, 1911, New Milford, NJ.

Notes for HORACE WOODRUFF SUTTON:
Died of a Heart Attck while out on a Tow call on Texas Ave. in Mt. Laurel, NJ

Record of Birth, NJState Archives
Certificate and Record of Birth
Name of this Child; Horace Sutton
Sex; Male
Color: White
DOB; De. 11, 1912
Place of Birth; 700 S. East Ave. Bridgeton, Cumberland Co., NJ
Name of Father: William Sutton
Birthplace of Father; US
Maiden name of Mother: Emma Rogers
Mother's place of birth; US
Age of Father: 49
Occupation: Laborer
Age of Mother: 44
Occupation: Housewife
# of Children in all by this marriage: 3
# of children now living: 3

Endnotes

1. Mancuso.FTW, Date of Import: Sep 6, 2000.
2. Broderbund Family Archive #110, Vol. 2, Ed. 7, Social Security Death Index: U.S., Date of Import: May 20, 2000, Internal Ref. #1.112.7.115546.117
3. Mancuso.FTW, Date of Import: Sep 6, 2000.
4. Genealogy.com, Family Archive #110, Social Security Death Index: U.S. Ed. 9, Social Security Death Index, Release date: April 10, 2000, Internal Ref. #1.112.9.111416.32.
5. Broderbund Family Archive #110, Vol. 2, Ed. 7, Social Security Death Index: U.S., Date of Import: May 20, 2000, Internal Ref. #1.112.7.115546.117
6. Mancuso.FTW, Date of Import: Sep 6, 2000.
7. Genealogy.com, Family Archive #110, Social Security Death Index: U.S. Ed. 9, Social Security Death Index, Release date: April 10, 2000, Internal Ref. #1.112.9.111416.32.
8. Mancuso.FTW, Date of Import: Sep 6, 2000.
9. Broderbund Family Archive #110, Vol. 2, Ed. 7, Social Security Death Index: U.S., Date of Import: May 20, 2000, Internal Ref. #1.112.7.115546.117
10. Mancuso.FTW, Date of Import: Sep 6, 2000.

STATE OF NEW JERSEY.

MARRIAGE RETURN.

[illegible] PENALTY FOR NON-REPORT WITHIN 30 DAYS.

[illegible], and write plainly, especially names.

1. Full Name of Husband William [illegible] Sutton (If old, so state.)

[illegible] 19 Washington St Bridgeton New Jersey
(If in city, give name, street and number; if not, give township and county.)

[illegible] years [illegible] months. Number of his Marriage First

[illegible] Day laborer Country of Birth America

[illegible] Albert [illegible] Sutton Country of Birth America

[illegible] [illegible] Country of Birth [illegible]

[illegible] Name of Wife.

Josephine Nichols Country of Birth [illegible] (If Col., so state.)

[illegible] [illegible] [illegible] Cumberland [illegible] New Jersey
(If in city, give street and number; if not, give township and county.)

[illegible] 18 (If in any trade or business, so state.)

[illegible] Number of Bride's Marriage First

[illegible] Name of Father Country of Birth [illegible]

[illegible] Maiden name of Mother Lawe Country of Birth America

[illegible] Date (in full) July 17 [illegible] Place Bridgeton [illegible] (City or township and county.)

[illegible] [illegible] Mrs [illegible] (Two or more witnesses.)
And Mrs Rev [illegible] Sykes

[illegible] } Rev Geo [illegible] Sykes Past of Central M.E. Church Bridgeton N.J.

Bridgeton, N. J. Mar 10th 1906

Mr William L Sutton Dr. to

W. F. GARRISON

UNDERTAKER

319 North Laurel Street

Inter-State 'Phone, 175-B. Bell 'Phone 301X

To the funeral Expences of
Josephine Sutton Dec

Black Cloth Casket Outside
Case 6 Silver Handles Silver
Engraved Plate White Satten
Lining and Pillow Black Cashmeer
Burial Robe cut flowers notices
taking Care of the remains and
Herse and Service for the agreed
sum of $60.00

Two Cabs at 2.50 each 5.00

Total $65.00

Mar 10th 1906 Received on Account 50.00

Balance 15.00

WILLIAM L. SUTTON		LOT 443
JOSEPHINE SUTTON NEE NICHOLS	1ST WIFE	LOT 443
EMMA SUTTON NEE ROGERS	2ND WIFE	LOT 443

LEON SUTTON SON OF WILLIAM AND JOSEPHINE	LOT 263
WILLIAM L. SUTTON JR. SON OF WILLIAM AND JOSEPHINE	LOT 263
GEORGE SUTTON SON OF WILLIAM AND JOSEPHINE	LOT 263

Bridgeton, N. J.

S. W. SECTION

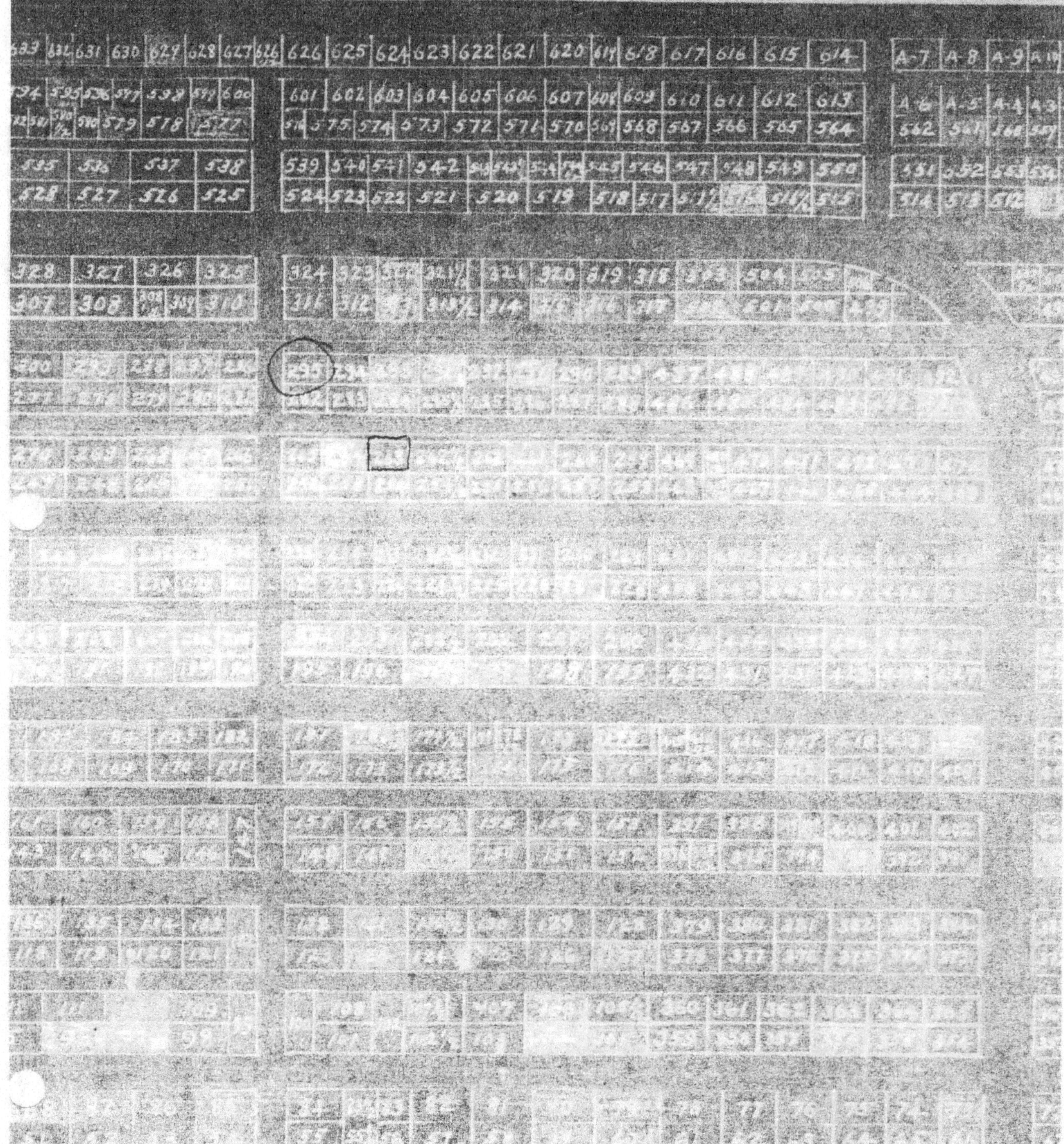

LEON C. SUTTON
SUTTON JR.

LEON C. SUTTON
1895 — 1941

GEORGE SUTTON
NEW JERSEY
PVT US ARMY
WORLD WAR II

JOSEPHINE R.
WIFE OF
WILLIAM L. SUTTON,
MARCH 12, 1868,
MARCH 7, 1904.
PEACEFUL SLEEP.

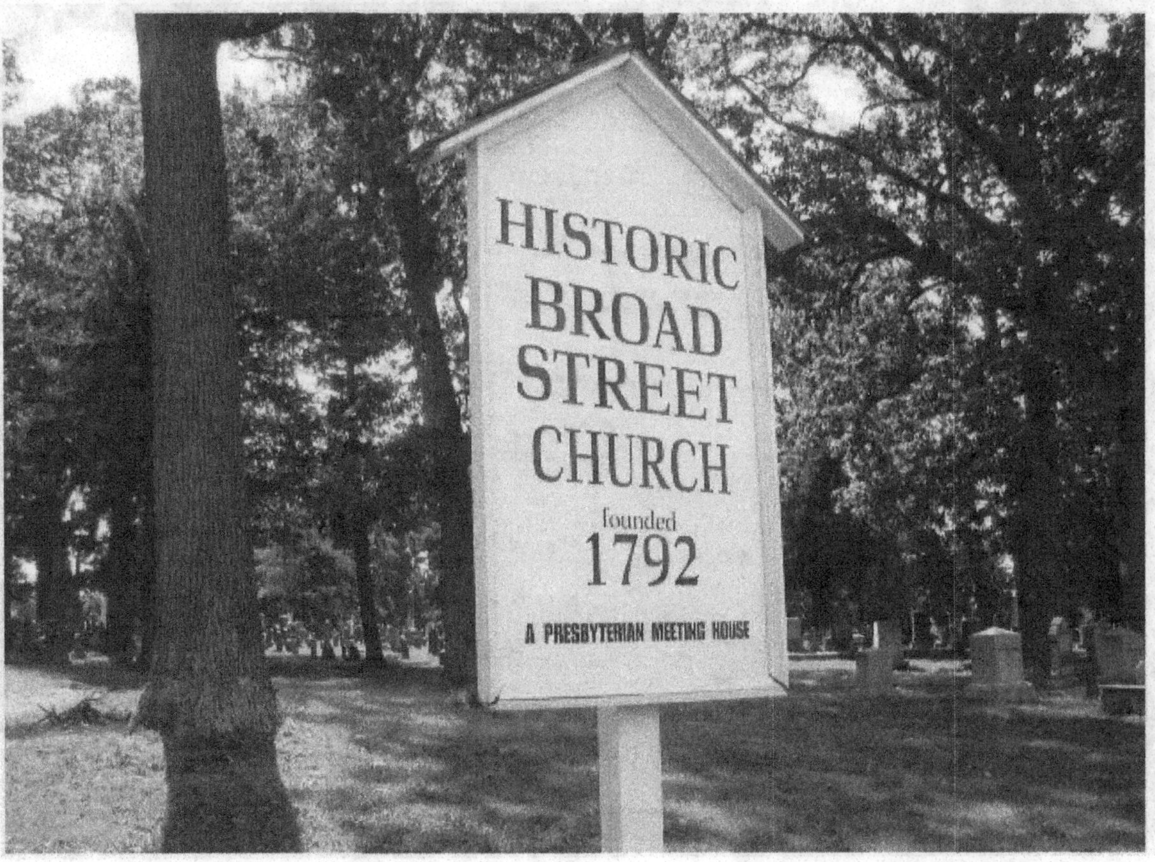
HISTORIC
BROAD
STREET
CHURCH
founded
1792
A PRESBYTERIAN MEETING HOUSE

REGISTRATION CARD—(Men born on or after April 28, 1877 and on or before February 16, 1897)

ORDER NUMBER

SERIAL NUMBER U 542

1. NAME (Print) Frank (First) Ray (Middle) Sutton (Last)

2. PLACE OF RESIDENCE (Print) 90 West Ave (Number and street) Bridgeton (Town, township, village, or city) Cumb (County) NJ (State)

[THE PLACE OF RESIDENCE GIVEN ON THE LINE ABOVE WILL DETERMINE LOCAL BOARD JURISDICTION; LINE 2 OF REGISTRATION CERTIFICATE WILL BE IDENTICAL]

3. MAILING ADDRESS same

[Mailing address if other than place indicated on line 2. If same insert word same]

4. TELEPHONE Br. Gandy (Exchange) 2294 W (Number)

5. AGE IN YEARS 54

DATE OF BIRTH April (Mo.) 15 (Day) 1888 (Yr.)

6. PLACE OF BIRTH Bridgeton (Town or county) NJ (State or country)

7. NAME AND ADDRESS OF PERSON WHO WILL ALWAYS KNOW YOUR ADDRESS Mrs. Sara Sutton - same

8. EMPLOYER'S NAME AND ADDRESS Bridgeton Gas Light Co

9. PLACE OF EMPLOYMENT OR BUSINESS Water St. (Number and street or R. F. D. number) Bridgeton (Town) Cumb (County) NJ (State)

I AFFIRM THAT I HAVE VERIFIED ABOVE ANSWERS AND THAT THEY ARE TRUE.

16—21630-2 Frank R. Sutton (Registrant's signature)

D. S. S. Form 1 (Revised 4-1-42) (over)

REGISTRATION CARD—(Men born on or after April 28, 1877 and on or before February 16, 1897)

ORDER NUMBER

SERIAL NUMBER U 2707

1. NAME (Print) WILLIAM (First) LEVICK (Middle) SUTTON, JR. (Last)

2. PLACE OF RESIDENCE (Print) 90 WEST AVE (Number and street) BRIDGETON, (Town, township, village, or city) CUMBERLAND (County) N.J. (State)

[THE PLACE OF RESIDENCE GIVEN ON THE LINE ABOVE WILL DETERMINE LOCAL BOARD JURISDICTION; LINE 2 OF REGISTRATION CERTIFICATE WILL BE IDENTICAL]

3. MAILING ADDRESS SAME

[Mailing address if other than place indicated on line 2. If same insert word same]

4. TELEPHONE (Exchange) (Number)

5. AGE IN YEARS 52

DATE OF BIRTH MAY (Mo.) 30 (Day) 1890 (Yr.)

6. PLACE OF BIRTH BRIDGETON, (Town or county) N.J. (State or country)

7. NAME AND ADDRESS OF PERSON WHO WILL ALWAYS KNOW YOUR ADDRESS FRANK SUTTON – 90 WEST AVE BRIDGETON, N.J.

8. EMPLOYER'S NAME AND ADDRESS J.P. RITTER – LAUREL ST.

9. PLACE OF EMPLOYMENT OR BUSINESS S. LAUREL ST. (Number and street or R. F. D. number) BRIDGETON, (Town) CUMBERLAND, (County) N.J. (State)

I AFFIRM THAT I HAVE VERIFIED ABOVE ANSWERS AND THAT THEY ARE TRUE.

16—21630-2 William L. Sutton Jr (Registrant's signature)

D. S. S. Form 1 (Revised 4-1-42) (over)

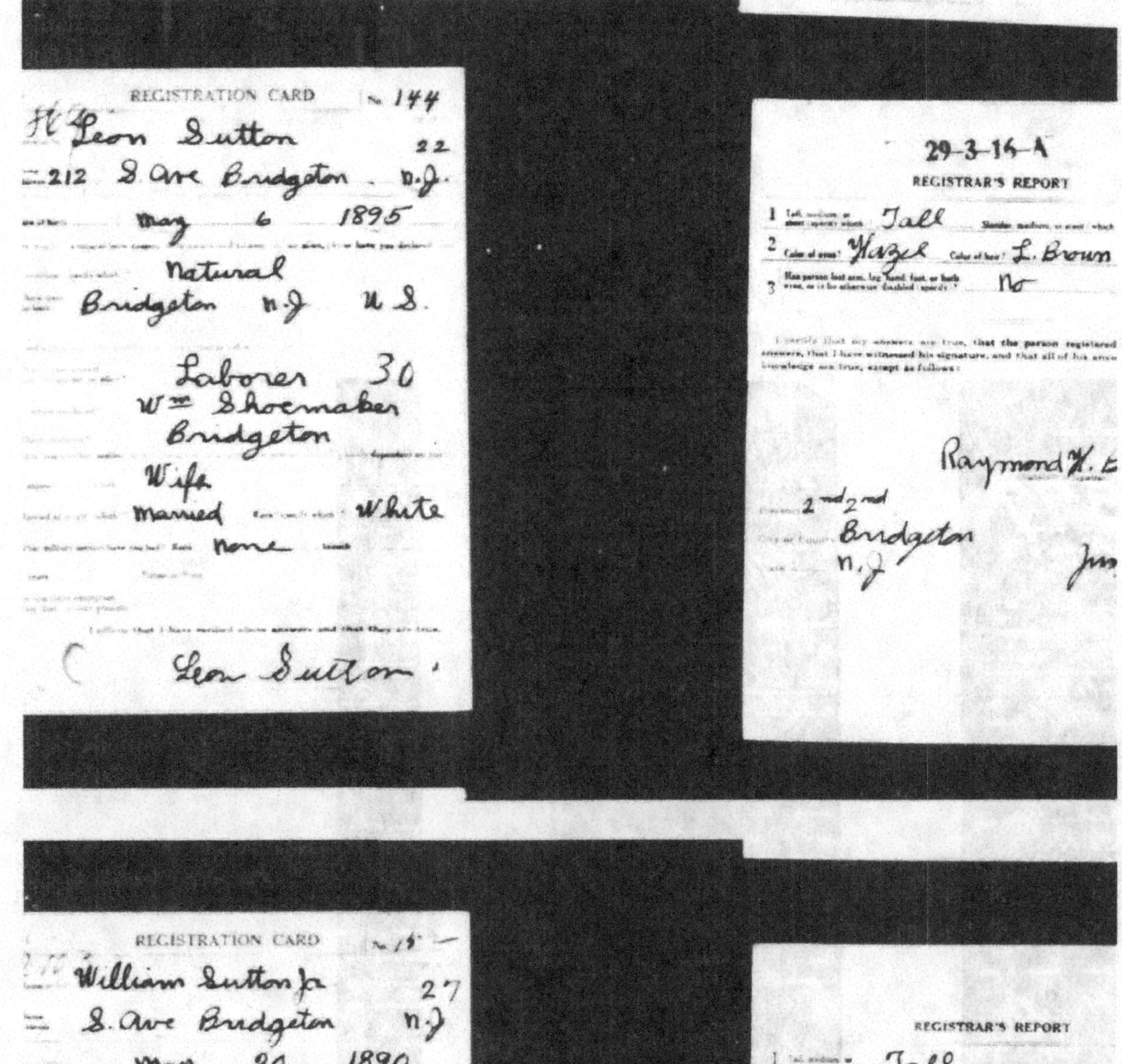

REGISTRATION CARD No. 144

Leon Sutton 22

212 S. Ave Bridgeton N.J.

May 6 1895

Natural

Bridgeton N.J. U.S.

Laborer 30

Wm Shoemaker

Bridgeton

Wife

Married White

None

I affirm that I have verified above answers and that they are true.

Leon Sutton

29-3-16-A

REGISTRAR'S REPORT

1 Tall

2 Color of eyes? Hazel Color of hair? L. Brown

3 Has person lost arm, leg, hand, foot, or both eyes, or is he otherwise disabled (specify)? No

I certify that my answers are true, that the person registered has read or has had read to him his own answers, that I have witnessed his signature, and that all of his answers of which I have knowledge are true, except as follows:

Raymond W. [illegible]

2nd 2nd

Bridgeton

N.J.

REGISTRATION CARD No. 15[illegible]

William Sutton Jr 27

S. Ave Bridgeton N.J.

May 30 1890

Natural

Bowentown N.J. U.S.

Glass worker

Cumberland Glass Co

Bridgeton

Wife and 2 Children

Married White

None

I affirm that I have verified above answers and that they are true.

William Sutton Jr

REGISTRAR'S REPORT

1 Tall

2 Color of eyes? Blue Color of hair? Brown

3 Has person lost arm, leg, hand, foot, or both eyes, or is he otherwise disabled (specify)? No

I certify that my answers are true, that the person registered has read or has had read to him his own answers, that I have witnessed his signature, and that all of his answers of which I have knowledge are true, except as follows:

Raymond [illegible]

2nd 2nd

Bridgeton

N.J.

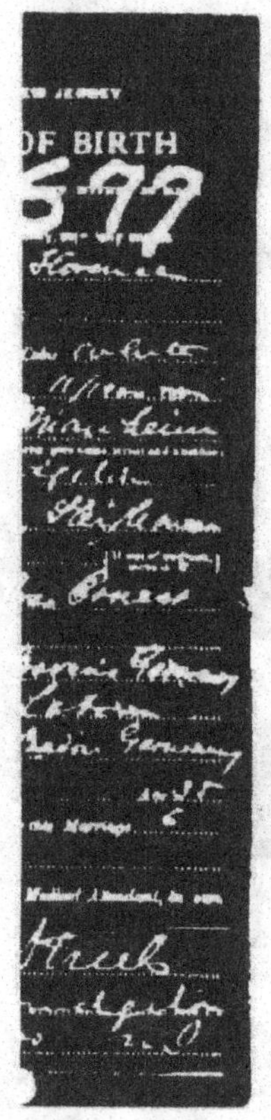

OF BIRTH

577

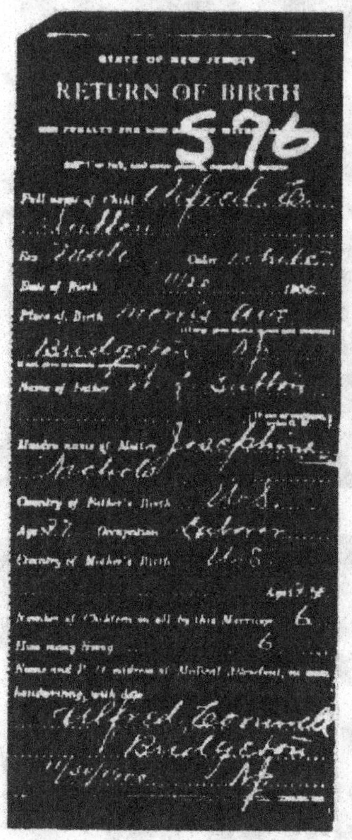

STATE OF NEW JERSEY

RETURN OF BIRTH

596

Full name of Child Alfred B. Sutton

Sex Male Color White

Date of Birth [illegible] 1900

Place of Birth Morris Ave. Bridgeton N.J.

Name of Father W. J. Sutton

Maiden name of Mother Josephine Nichols

Country of Father's Birth U.S.

Age 37 Occupation Laborer

Country of Mother's Birth U.S.

Age 34

Number of Children in all by this Marriage 6

How many living 6

Name and P. O. address of Medical Attendant, in own handwriting, with date

Alfred Cornwell
Bridgeton
11/30/1900 N.J.

RETU

Alfred Sutton
Son of Wm + Josephine

BIRTHS

BIRTHS in the township of Fairfield county of Cumberland State of New Jersey, from the first day of May 186[illegible] to the first day of May

DATE OF BIRTH.	PLACE OF BIRTH.	NAME OF CHILD.	SEX OF CHILD.	NAMES OF PARENTS.	OCCUPATION OF FATHER.	RESIDENCE OF PARENTS.
March 18th 1864	~~[illegible]~~ Gouldtown B	Catharine Pierce B	Female	Richard & Hannah S Pierce	Labourer	Gouldtown
July 22d 1863	Gouldtown	Louisa D. Jones B	do	Joseph E Davis and Christiana Jones	do	do
[illegible] 20th 1864	Gouldtown	Albert Loyde B	Male	Isaac Cook & Amanda Loyde	do	do
March 20th 1864	do	Smith Gould B	do	Jeremiah & Ruth Gould	do	do
Feb 22d do	" "	William H Pierce B	"	Horace & Sarah J Pierce	" "	"
March 30 [illegible]	" "	Sarah J Gould B	Female	Elmer & Martha Gould	do	"
July 20th 1863	" "	Jeszabell Gould B	"	Mahlon and Ann Elizabeth Gould	"	"
January 19 1864	Fairfield	Albert J Willis	Male	John " Sarah Willis	Farmer	Fairfield
December 22 1863	" "	Daniel Pierce B	"	William " Rebecca Pierce		"
January 17 1864	"	William L Sutton	"	Robert " Christiana Sutton	Labourer	"
November 3 1863	"	Laura S Ewing	Female	Simeon S " Juttah Ewing	Farmer	"
[illegible] 6 1864	"	Sarah A Lummis	"	George " Harriet S Lummis	Miller	"
March 29 "	"	Julia M Banks	"	Edd " Rhoda Banks	Farmer	"
January 22 "	"	Philip L Husted	Male	Seth P " Mary J Husted	Merchant	"
September 27 1863	"	Margaret Daily	Female	Simon " Caroline Daily	Farmer	"
February 22 1864	"	Jenny Elvis Garton	"	John E " Eliza Garton	Farmer	"
March 6 "	"	Elizabeth F Cory	"	James C " Elizabeth Cory	Farmer	"
March 22 "	"	William S Davis	Male	Daniel " Maranda Davis	Waterman	"
April 19 "	"	Daniel H Husted	"	Thomas " Sarah Sutton	"	"
[illegible] "	"	Henry L Gandy	Male	Henry L Mary H Gandy	Farmer	"
April 8 "	"	Fanny A Demeritt	Female	Firman Eunice Demeritt	Oysterman	"
August 14 1863	"	Hannah L Reany	"	Charles L Rachael Reany	[illegible]	"
December 17 "	"	Margaret E Demeritt	"	George Rebecca Demeritt	Oysterman	"
September 25 "	"	Ephraim S Bateman	Male	Albert F Mary J Bateman	Carpenter	"
[illegible] 20 "	"	Joseph T Bateman	"	Samuel Lydia Bateman	Oysterman	"
March 6th 1864	"	Laura E Parvin	Female	Robert E Caroline Parvin	Blacksmith	"
[illegible] 15 "	"	William R Bennet	Male	Rufus Mary E Bennet	Oysterman	"
~~[illegible]~~ 1863	"	Alden E Burk	"	Jeremiah Harriet Burk	"	"
" "	"	William E Burk	"			"
March 14 "	"	Mary E Henry	Female	Elijah Mary Henry	Carpenter	"
July 31 1863	"	Susanna Blizzard	"	Hiram Elizabeth Blizzard	Oysterman	"
April 1 1864	"	John Blizzard	Male	John Susanna J Blizzard	Soldier	"
July 24 1863	"	Harriet W Ford	Female	Charles Anna Maria Ford	Carpenter	"
August 7 "	"	Harriet R Bateman	"	Benjamin J Elizabeth Bateman	Oysterman	"
March 11 1864	"	Alice H Nixon	"	William Ella L Nixon	"	"
December 19 1863	"	Enoch B Sitts	Male	Job Hannah Sitts	Soldier	"
January 24 1864	"	Mary F Foster	Female	Charles Unice Foster	Labourer	"

DEPARTMENT OF COMMERCE AND LABOR—BUREAU OF THE CENSUS

THIRTEENTH CENSUS OF THE UNITED STATES: 1910 POPULATION

Wm. L. Sutton with second wife Emma + children from first + second wife

DEPARTMENT OF COMMERCE—BUREAU OF THE CENSUS

FOURTEENTH CENSUS OF THE UNITED STATES: 1920—POPULATION

STATE New Jersey

COUNTY Cumberland

TOWNSHIP OR OTHER DIVISION OF COUNTY Fairfield Township

NAME OF INCORPORATED PLACE

NAME OF INSTITUTION

ENUMERATED BY ME ON THE 13 DAY OF January, 1920. Robert S. Schmitzer, ENUMERATOR

SUPERVISOR'S DISTRICT NO. 2-07 ENUMERATION DISTRICT NO. 14 SHEET NO. 8 B

Name	Relation	Sex	Color	Age	Marital	Place of birth	Occupation	Industry
Sutton William [illegible]	Head	M	W	55	M	New Jersey	Farmer	Truck Farm
Emma	Wife	F	W	48	M	New Jersey	none	
Alfred	Son	M	W	16	S	New Jersey	none	
George	Son	M	W	15	S	New Jersey	none	
Robert G	Son	M	W	13	S	New Jersey	none	
Reba	Daughter	F	W	10	S	New Jersey	none	
[illegible]	Son	M	W	7	S	New Jersey	none	
Rogers William	Son	M	W	18	S	New Jersey	none	
Johnson Samuel	Head	M	W	57	M	New Jersey	Farmer	General Farm
[illegible]	Wife	F	W	46	M	New Jersey	None	
Sonder Jennie R	Granddaughter	F	W	10	S	New Jersey	None	
[illegible]	Head	M	W	52	M	Virginia	Farm	
[illegible]	Wife	F	W	49	M	Virginia	None	
Annie L	Daughter	F	W	25	S	Virginia	none	
Elbert M	Son	M	W	23	S	Virginia	[illegible]	[illegible]
Mary	Daughter	F	W	20	S	Virginia	[illegible]	[illegible]
Edward F	Son	M	W	19	S	Virginia	[illegible]	[illegible]
Benjamin N	Son	M	W	15	S	Virginia	[illegible]	[illegible]
Eva L	Daughter	F	W	16	S	Virginia	none	
Sabrina B	Daughter	F	W	14	S	Virginia	none	
Carrie	Daughter	F	W	12	S	Virginia	None	
Emma A	Daughter	F	W	10	S	Virginia	None	
[illegible]	Son	M	W	6	S	Virginia	none	
Murray John	Head	M	Mu	61	M	New Jersey	Farmer	General Farm
[illegible]	Wife	F	Mu	53	M	New Jersey	None	
John A	Son	M	Mu	16	S	New Jersey	none	
Simpkins Edward	Head	M	W	28	M	New Jersey	Farmer	General Farm
Ethel	Wife	F	W	26	M	New Jersey	none	
Earl C	Son	M	W	4	S	New Jersey	none	
Simpkins Harry	Head	M	W	26	M	New Jersey	Farmer	Truck Farm
[illegible]	Wife	F	W	23	M	New Jersey	none	
[illegible]	Son	M	W	[illegible]	S	New Jersey	none	
Dorothy	Daughter	F	W	1	S	New Jersey	none	
Elmer [illegible]	Head	M	W	64	S	New Jersey	Farmer	General Farm
Eva R	Sister	F	W	47	S	New Jersey	none	
Sayers Daniel	Head	M	W	53	M	New Jersey	Farmer	Truck Farm
Ida	Wife	F	W	46	M	New Jersey	none	
Hugh	Son	M	W	27	S	New Jersey	[illegible]	Machine Shop
Verna	Daughter	F	W	[illegible]	S	New Jersey	None	
Mattie	Daughter	F	W	19	S	New Jersey	Sewing	Waist Factory
Lillie	Daughter	F	W	9	S	New Jersey	none	
Pearl	Daughter	F	W	[illegible]	S	New Jersey	none	
Schmitzer Henry W	Head	M	W	61	M	New Jersey	Farmer	General Farm
[illegible]	Wife	F	W	63	M	New Jersey	None	
[illegible] Wesley	Head	M	B	41	M	Delaware	Farm Laborer	General Farm
[illegible]	Wife	F	B	31	M	Delaware	none	
George	Son	M	B	[illegible]	S	New Jersey	none	
[illegible]	Daughter	F	B	[illegible]	S	New Jersey	none	
Husted [illegible]	Head	M	W	[illegible]	M	New Jersey	None	
Louisa	Wife	F	W	69	M	[illegible]	[illegible]	

Emma R. Rogers. Sutton was born
... 1873,
... Wife of Wm. L. Sutton

FAMILY RECORD.

DEATHS.

William Kerchoff Rogers 130 ...
was born Dec 3. - 1902
Son of Mrs Wm. L. Sutton nee Emma Rogers

Mrs Josephine Sutton
Died March 7th 1904
Wife of Wm. L. Sutton

THE

NEW TESTAMENT

OF OUR

LORD AND SAVIOUR JESUS CHRIST:

TRANSLATED OUT OF

THE ORIGINAL GREEK;

AND WITH

THE FORMER TRANSLATIONS DILIGENTLY COMPARED AND REVISED.

NEW YORK:
AMERICAN BIBLE SOCIETY,
INSTITUTED IN THE YEAR MDCCCXVI.

[Nonpareil, 12mo.] 1872.

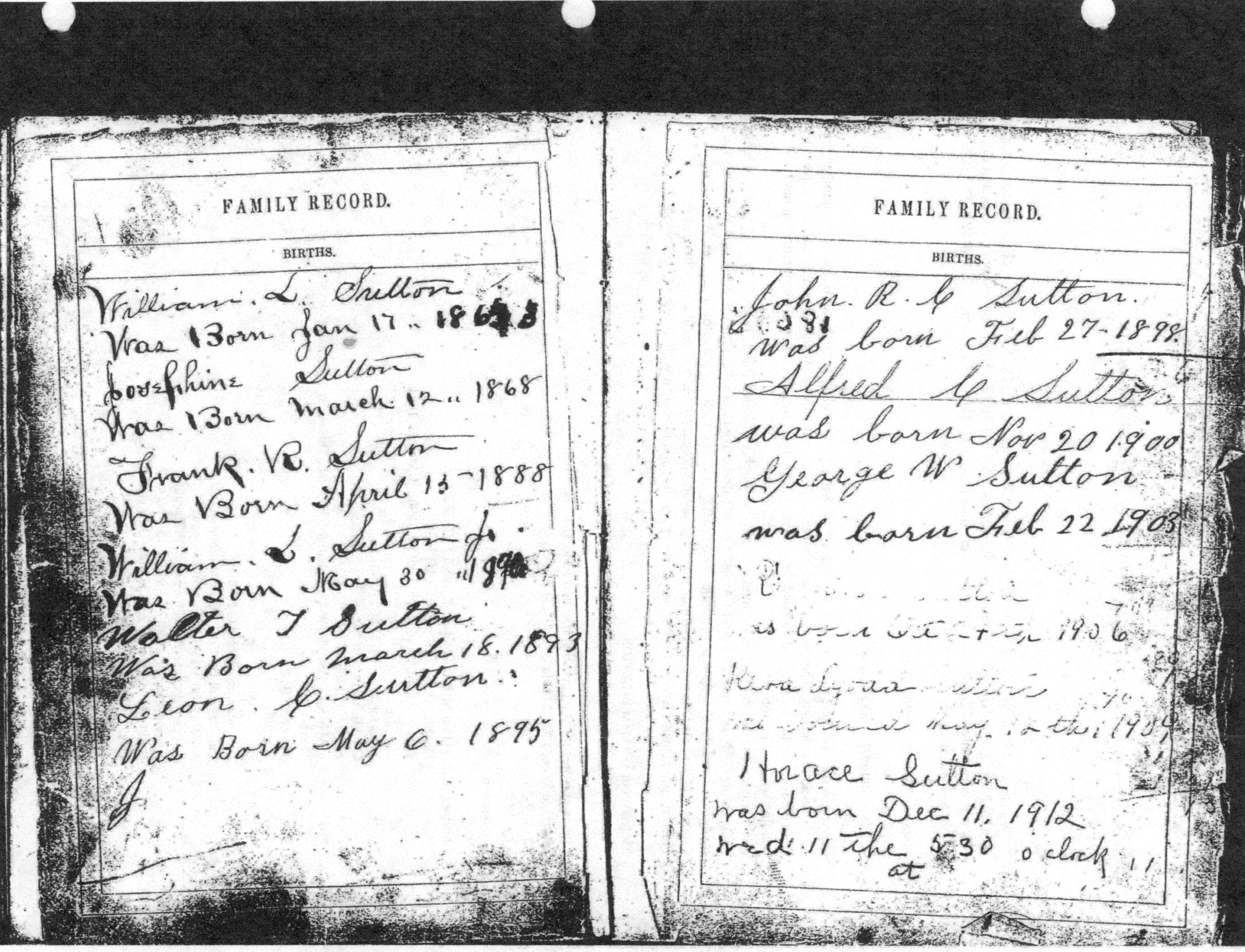

FAMILY RECORD.

BIRTHS.

William L. Sutton
Was Born Jan 17 " 1863
Josephine Sutton
Was Born March 12 " 1868
Frank R. Sutton
Was Born April 13 1888
William L. Sutton Jr.
Was Born May 30 " 1890
Walter T Sutton
Was Born March 18. 1893
Leon C. Sutton
Was Born May 6. 1895

FAMILY RECORD.

BIRTHS.

John R. C Sutton.
was born Feb 27-1898.
Alfred C Sutton
was born Nov 20 1900
George W. Sutton
was born Feb 22 1903
[illegible]
was born [illegible] 1906
Reva Lydia [illegible]
was born May [illegible] 1909
Horace Sutton
was born Dec 11, 1912
Wed. 11 the at 5:30 o clock

Descendants of William L. Sutton

Generation No. 1

1. WILLIAM L.[3] SUTTON *(ROBERT O.[2], JOSEPH[1])*[1] was born January 17, 1863 in Fairton, NJ[1], and died March 04, 1950 in New Gretna, NJ[1]. He married (1) JOSEPHINE NICHOLS[1] July 17, 1886 in Bridgeton, Cumberland Co., NJ. She was born March 12, 1868 in Fairton,NJ[1], and died March 07, 1904[1]. He married (2) EMMA ROGERS[1] Abt. 1905. She was born May 11, 1870[1].

Notes for WILLIAM L. SUTTON:
obit
William Sutton, Sr., 85 Expires Early Today
3/4/1950
Word was received here this morning of the death of William Sutton Sr. 85, of New Gretna. Mr. Sutton expired at six O'clock this morning. The deceased had been taken ill three weeks ago with pneumonia and was apparently fully recovered when he suffered a stroke three days ago. He is a former sesident of Bridgeton, but has been residing with a son, Robert, in New Gretna, for quite a while.
Surviving are one daughter and eight sons, Mrs. Reba Doughty of Leeds Point, William Rogers of Washington, D.C., Robert of New Gretna, Alfred of Atlantic City, Horace of Masonville, Frank, George and William Jr. of Bridgeton and John C. Sutton of Millville. Two sisters, Lida Westcott of Bridgeton and Susie Watkins of Coatesville, Pa., also survive. In addition there are several grandchildren and great grandchildren.
Funeral arrangements have not been completed as yet although interment will be held in Bridgeton.

More About WILLIAM L. SUTTON:
Burial: March 08, 1950, Broad St. Cemetery, Bridgeton, NJ

Marriage Notes for WILLIAM SUTTON and JOSEPHINE NICHOLS:
Marriage Record, Certificate
S4, 359-26
b. c 1868
d. unknown

Children of WILLIAM SUTTON and JOSEPHINE NICHOLS are:

i. FRANK R.[4] SUTTON[1], b. April 15, 1888[1].

ii. WILLIAM L. SUTTON JR.[1], b. May 30, 1890[1]; d. May 14, 1964.

Notes for WILLIAM L. SUTTON JR.:
On William L. Sutton Jr.
b. May 30, 1890, NJ
d. May have died 5/9/1964 with burial 5/14/1964...This needs documentation
Married
Mary Ann Bedwell
b. c 1884

Certificate and Record of Marriage
Full Name of Husband: William L. Sutton Jr.
Maiden Name of Wife: Mary Anna Bedwell, (Daretty)
Place of Marriage:72 S. Pine Street, Bridgeton
Date of Marriage: April 30, 1912, 8:15 p.m.
Residence of Groom: 72 South Pine, Bridgeton
Color: White
Age of Groom: 22
# of Marriage: First
Occupation of Groom: Glassworker
Birthplace of Groom: New Jersey
Father's Name: William L. Sutton, Sr.

Mother's Maiden Name: Josephine Nichols

Residence of Bride: 72 South Pine Street, Bridgeton
Age of Bridge: 28
Color: White
# of Marriage: Second
Name if Widowed: Mrs. Mary Anna Daretty
Birth place of Bride: New Jersey
Father's Name: John Bedwell
Mother's Maiden Name: Hannah Wallace
Witnesses: Walter T. Sutton & Herbert Surran, Bridgeton
Person Officiating: A. S. Allyn, Pastor, Berean Baptist Church, Bridgeton, NJ

iii. WALTER T. SUTTON[1], b. March 18, 1893[1].

Notes for WALTER T. SUTTON:
Obit-Millville Historical Society
Brother of Local Man Dies Today
11/5/38
The death of Walter T. Sutton, 46 of Glassboro, occurred suddenly today of hemorrhage. The deceased is a brother of John Sutton, Main Street, this city.
A glassworker, the deceased is survived by his wife, Bertha; his father,William of Absecon; eight other brothers and a sister. Frank and William Sutton, Bridgeton; Leon, George, Robert and Reba Sutton, Absecon; Alfred Sutton, Atlantic City, Horace Sutton, Hightstown; and William Rogers of Washington, D.C.
Funeral services will be conducted from the Christy Funeral Home this city. Tuesday afternoon with interment in Mount Pleasant Cemetery.

iv. LEON G. SUTTON[1], b. May 06, 1895[1]; d. Abt. 1940.

Notes for LEON G. SUTTON:
Leon was pouring a footing for a zinc factory in Chatsworth, NJ when he and two other men were buried alive in a cave in. The other two were rescued but Leon lost his life.

2. v. JOHN R. G. SUTTON, b. February 27, 1898; d. October 16, 1957.
vi. ALFRED G. SUTTON[1], b. November 20, 1900[1].

Notes for ALFRED G. SUTTON:
Record of Birth, NJ State Archives.

Return of Birth
Full name of Child; Alfred C. Sutton
Sex; Male
Color; White
DOB; Nov. 20, 1900
Place of Birth; Morris Ave. Bridgeton, NJ
Name of Father; Wm L. Sutton
Maiden name of Mother; Josephine Nichols
Country of Father's Birth; US
Age; 37
Accupation; Laborer
Country of Mother's Birth; US
Age; 34
# of Children in all by this Marriage; 6
How many living; 6

vii. GEORGE W. SUTTON[1], b. February 22, 1903[1].

Children of WILLIAM SUTTON and EMMA ROGERS are:
viii. WILLIAM KERCHOFF[4] ROGERS[1], b. December 03, 1902[1].
3. ix. ROBERT O. SUTTON, b. October 24, 1906; d. August 1987.
4. x. REBA LYODD SUTTON, b. May 12, 1909.

5. xi. HORACE WOODRUFF SUTTON, b. December 11, 1911, Bridgeton, NJ; d. February 06, 1972, Mt. Laurel, NJ.

Generation No. 2

2. JOHN R. G.[4] SUTTON *(WILLIAM L.[3], ROBERT O.[2], JOSEPH[1])[1]* was born February 27, 1898[1], and died October 16, 1957. He married EDITH LIPPENCOTT MADDEN. She was born 1899, and died 1985.

Notes for JOHN R. G. SUTTON:
Obit
John C. Sutton, 59 Bus Driver, Dies 10/17/1957
Death of John C. Sutton, 59 of 429 Pine St. occurred yesterday.
The deceased a member of West Side Methodist Church, formerly operated a trolley between Millville and Bridgeton for the past 25 years and has been a driver for the Public Service Transportation Co.
Surviving are his wife, Edith L. Sutton; two daughters, Mrs. Margaret Yough, Wilmington, and Mrs. Marcella Barker, Philadelphia; a sister Mrs. Reba Doughty, Leeds Point and seven brothers, Frank and William Sutton, Bridgeton, Alfred Sutton, Atlantic City; George Sutton, Gandy's Beach; Robert Sutton, New Gretna, Horace Sutton, Masonville and William Rogers, Washington, D.C. Eight Grandchildren also service.
Funeral services will be condusted from the Christy Funeral Home Saturday at 2 p.m. with interment in Mt. Pleasant Cemetery.

John Callahan Sutton
b. Abt. 1898
d. October 16, 1957, Millville NJ (Obit-Millville Historical Society.)
married
Edith Lippincott Madden
b. 1899
d. 1985 (Headstone - Cemetery Records) have to see where I put the headstone information

Issue:
Margaret Sutton married Unknown Young
Marcella Sutton married Unknown Barker
Martha Madden Sutton
b. March 18, 1919
d. March 18, 1919

Martha Madden Sutton
b. March 18, 1919
d. March 18, 1919
Buried March 19, 1919 Mount Pleasant Cemetery, (Record of Death, NJ State Archives.)
Katherine Hinson Sutton, b. 1920 married Vernon Montgomery Abt. 1936
Issue of Katherine:
John Gilbert Montgomery
Information on Vernon Montgomery & family was provided by Nancy and as you can see really needs more documentation on this line.

Children of JOHN SUTTON and EDITH MADDEN are:

i. MARGARET[5] SUTTON.
ii. MARCELLA SUTTON.

3. ROBERT O.[4] SUTTON *(WILLIAM L.[3], ROBERT O.[2], JOSEPH[1])[1]* was born October 24, 1906[2,2,2,2,2,2,2,2,2,2,2,2,2,2,3,4], and died August 1987[5,5,5,5,5,5,5,5,5,5,5,5,5,5,5,6,7]. He married DORA WATSON[8], daughter of THOMAS WATSON and MARY CRAMER. She was born February 09, 1915[8], and died January 15, 1965[8].

Notes for ROBERT O. SUTTON:
[Genealogy.com, Family Archive #110, Vol. 2 L-Z, Ed. 9, Social Security Death Index: U.S., Date of Import:

Dec 30, 2000, Internal Ref. #1.112.9.111416.32]

Individual: Sutton, Robert
Social Security #: 148-07-6985
Issued in: New Jersey

Birth date: Oct 24, 1906
Death date: Aug 1987

Residence code: New Jersey

ZIP Code of last known residence: 08224
Location associated with this ZIP Code:

New Gretna, New Jersey

Robert Sutton told his childred that the O. in his name stood for Osborn but we have not been able to verify this. His grandfather's middle initial also was an O. (for some reason either lost in the mail, etc. his birth certificate has never been registered. I am going to try and register him through the family bible and other papers we have).

More About ROBERT O. SUTTON:
Burial: Hillside cemetery, New Gretna[8]
Social Security Number: Social Security #: 148-07-6985[9,10]

Notes for DORA WATSON:
Reference #3180
The twins are buried behind Maud Cramer, there are two little stones sticking out of the ground to mark their graves.

More About DORA WATSON:
Burial: Hillside cemetery, New Gretna[10]

Children of ROBERT SUTTON and DORA WATSON are:

i. TWIN BABY[5] SUTTON, b. Abt. 1930; d. Abt. 1930.

More About TWIN BABY SUTTON:
Burial: Abt. 1930, Hillside cemetery, New Gretna

ii. TWIN BABY SUTTON, b. Abt. 1930; d. Abt. 1930.

More About TWIN BABY SUTTON:
Burial: Abt. 1930, Hillside cemetery, New Gretna

iii. ROBERT THOMAS SUTTON[10], b. December 07, 1932, Atlantic City, NJ[10]; m. JOYCE F.. MANCUSO, October 19, 1957, Pomona, NJ[10]; b. May 11, 1934, Bristol, PA.

Notes for ROBERT THOMAS SUTTON:
Bob was born on a Wednesday. His wife Joyce was born on a Friday two years later, each year their bithdays fall on the same day of the week.

Notes for JOYCE F.. MANCUSO:
DAR member number 831198, installed Oct. 16, 2004

iv. EDNA MAY SUTTON[10], b. November 20, 1937, Mt. Holly; m. GEORGE BORTON, December 22, 1984, St Pauls Medthodist Church, New Gretna, NJ; b. October 03, 1940; d. January 08, 2000, New Gretna.

v. MARJORIE LOUISE SUTTON[10], b. Abt. 1940; m. LAWRENCE ROSE.

Notes for MARJORIE LOUISE SUTTON:

Kenneth's father is Austin Gibbons.

4. REBA LYODD[4] SUTTON *(WILLIAM L.[3], ROBERT O.[2], JOSEPH[1])[10]* was born May 12, 1909[10]. She married ORION DOUGHTY.

Notes for ORION DOUGHTY:
Regarding the Baby and Anna May grave stones. This is Dolores' baby that died from the cord being wrapped around her neck during birth. She was buried on the grandparents cemetery site.

Children of REBA SUTTON and ORION DOUGHTY are:

i. DOLORES[5] DOUGHTY.
ii. ORION DOUGHTY, JR.

5. HORACE WOODRUFF[4] SUTTON *(WILLIAM L.[3], ROBERT O.[2], JOSEPH[1])[10]* was born December 11, 1911 in Bridgeton, NJ[10], and died February 06, 1972 in Mt. Laurel, NJ. He married MILDRED ELIZABETH ARNOLD, daughter of HERMAN ARNOLD and MARIE ARNOLD. She was born October 24, 1911 in New Milford, NJ.

Notes for HORACE WOODRUFF SUTTON:
Died of a Heart Attck while out on a Tow call on Texas Ave. in Mt. Laurel, NJ

Record of Birth, NJState Archives
Certificate and Record of Birth
Name of this Child; Horace Sutton
Sex; Male
Color: White
DOB; De. 11, 1912
Place of Birth; 700 S. East Ave. Bridgeton, Cumberland Co., NJ
Name of Father: William Sutton
Birthplace of Father; US
Maiden name of Mother: Emma Rogers
Mother's place of birth; US
Age of Father: 49
Occupation: Laborer
Age of Mother: 44
Occupation: Housewife
# of Children in all by this marriage: 3
# of children now living: 3

Children of HORACE SUTTON and MILDRED ARNOLD are:

i. DAVID ANTHONY[5] SUTTON, b. November 16, 1939, Mt. Holly, NJ; d. September 26, 1998, Englishtown, NJ; m. JUDITH WILLIAMS, June 24, 1964, Hainesport, NJ.
ii. ANN KATHERINE SUTTON, b. August 21, 1943, Mt. Holly, NJ; m. ROBERT EDWARD HELLMIG, August 07, 1965, Masonville, NJ; b. Mt. Laurel, NJ.

Marriage Notes for ANN SUTTON and ROBERT HELLMIG:
Married at the Bible Calvary Church in Masonville, NJ by Rev. William A. Raymond
Debbie was Christened at the Bible Calvary Church on De. 31, 1967 by Rev. William Raymond.

Endnotes

1. Mancuso.FTW, Date of Import: Sep 6, 2000.
2. Broderbund Family Archive #110, Vol. 2, Ed. 7, Social Security Death Index: U.S., Date of Import: May 20, 2000, Internal Ref. #1.112.7.115546.117
3. Mancuso.FTW, Date of Import: Sep 6, 2000.

THE CHILDREN OF WILLIAM AND JOSEPHINE NICHOLS SUTTON

FRANK SUTTON
WILLIAM L. SUTTON JR.
WALTER T. SUTTON
LEON SUTTON
JOHN SUTTON
ALFRED SUTTON
GEORGE SUTTON

GEORGE SUTTON

GEORGE, STANDING ON FIRST STEP IS AS TALL AS THOSE STANDING ON SECOND STEP.

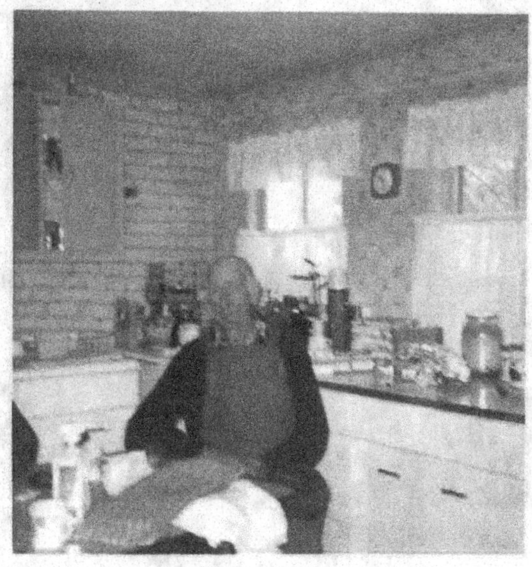

WILLIAM L. SUTTON
SON OF ROBERT O. AND CHRISTINA CALLAHAN/SUTTON

MARRIED JOSEPHINE NICHOLS AFTER HER DEATH HE MARRIED EMMA ROGERS

Emma Rogers

Descendants of Reba Lyodd Sutton

Generation No. 1

1. REBA LYODD[4] SUTTON *(WILLIAM L.[3], ROBERT O.[2], JOSEPH[1])[1]* was born May 12, 1909[1]. She married ORION DOUGHTY.

Notes for ORION DOUGHTY:
Regarding the Baby and Anna May grave stones. This is Dolores' baby that died from the cord being wrapped around her neck during birth. She was buried on the grandparents cemetery site.

Children of REBA SUTTON and ORION DOUGHTY are:
- i. DOLORES[5] DOUGHTY.
- ii. ORION DOUGHTY, JR.

Endnotes

1. Mancuso.FTW, Date of Import: Sep 6, 2000.

USE INK AND WRITE PLAINLY.

STATE OF NEW JERSEY. BUREAU OF VITAL STATISTICS

CERTIFICATE AND RECORD OF BIRTH.

WRITE PLAINLY WITH UNFADING INK—THIS IS A PERMANENT RECORD. No incomplete or mutilated certificate will be received.

Name of Child: Reba L. Sutton 610

Sex: female Color: white Date of Birth: May 12 1909

Place of Birth: South East Avenue, Bridgeton N. J.

Name of Father: Wm Sutton Father's Birthplace: N. J.

Maiden Name of Mother: Emma Rogers Mother's Birthplace: N. J.

Age of Father: 45 Occupation of Father: Farmer

Age of Mother: 40 Occupation of Mother: Housewife

Number of Children in all by this marriage: 2 Number of Children now living: 2

Name and P. O. Address of Professional Attendant in own handwriting.

Reba Hope (Signature of Professional Attendant.)

Date of this Report: June 4, 1909 Reba H.

Daughter of Wm L. Sutton – Rogers, Emma (2nd wife)

DEPARTMENT OF COMMERCE—BUREAU OF THE CENSUS

FIFTEENTH CENSUS OF THE UNITED STATES: 1930

POPULATION SCHEDULE

State: New Jersey | County: Atlantic | Township or other division of county: [illegible] | Enumeration District No. 1-48 | Supervisor's District No. 13 | Sheet No. 7 B

[illegible]

Reba Sutton married O. Doughty and 2 children

REBA LOYDD SUTTON MARRIED ORION DOUGHTY DAUGHTER OF WILLIAM AND EMMA ROGERS/SUTTON

Reba

Bob & Reba August (1965)

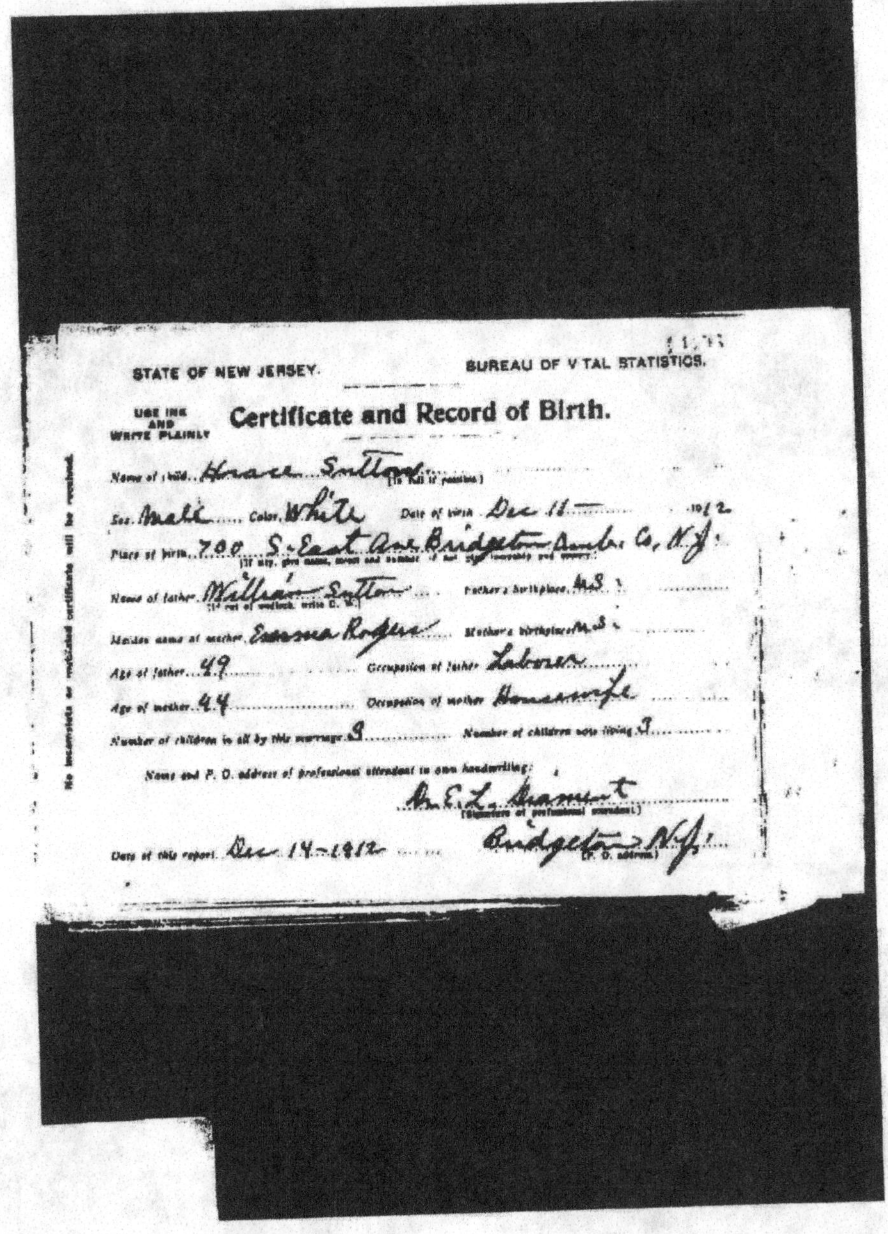

STATE OF NEW JERSEY. BUREAU OF VITAL STATISTICS.

USE INK AND WRITE PLAINLY

Certificate and Record of Birth.

No incomplete or mutilated certificate will be received.

Name of child Horace Sutton (In full if possible)

Sex Male Color White Date of birth Dec 11 1912

Place of birth 700 S. East Ave Bridgeton Cumb. Co, N.J. (If city, give name, street and number; if not, give township and county)

Name of father William Sutton (If out of wedlock, write O. W.) Father's birthplace U.S.

Maiden name of mother Emma Rogers Mother's birthplace U.S.

Age of father 49 Occupation of father Laborer

Age of mother 44 Occupation of mother Housewife

Number of children in all by this marriage 3 Number of children now living 3

Name and P. O. address of professional attendant in own handwriting:

Dr. E. L. Diament (Signature of professional attendant.)

Bridgeton N.J. (P. O. address)

Date of this report Dec 14-1912

Descendants of Horace Woodruff Sutton

Generation No. 1

1. HORACE WOODRUFF[4] SUTTON *(WILLIAM L.[3], ROBERT O.[2], JOSEPH[1])[1]* was born December 11, 1911 in Bridgeton, NJ[1], and died February 06, 1972 in Mt. Laurel, NJ. He married MILDRED ELIZABETH ARNOLD, daughter of HERMAN ARNOLD and MARIE ARNOLD. She was born October 24, 1911 in New Milford, NJ.

Notes for HORACE WOODRUFF SUTTON:
Died of a Heart Attck while out on a Tow call on Texas Ave. in Mt. Laurel, NJ

Record of Birth, NJState Archives
Certificate and Record of Birth
Name of this Child; Horace Sutton
Sex; Male
Color: White
DOB; De. 11, 1912
Place of Birth; 700 S. East Ave. Bridgeton, Cumberland Co., NJ
Name of Father: William Sutton
Birthplace of Father; US
Maiden name of Mother: Emma Rogers
Mother's place of birth; US
Age of Father: 49
Occupation: Laborer
Age of Mother: 44
Occupation: Housewife
# of Children in all by this marriage: 3
# of children now living: 3

Children of HORACE SUTTON and MILDRED ARNOLD are:
2. i. DAVID ANTHONY[5] SUTTON, b. November 16, 1939, Mt. Holly, NJ; d. September 26, 1998, Englishtown, NJ.
3. ii. ANN KATHERINE SUTTON, b. August 21, 1943, Mt. Holly, NJ.

Generation No. 2

2. DAVID ANTHONY[5] SUTTON *(HORACE WOODRUFF[4], WILLIAM L.[3], ROBERT O.[2], JOSEPH[1])* was born November 16, 1939 in Mt. Holly, NJ, and died September 26, 1998 in Englishtown, NJ. He married JUDITH WILLIAMS June 24, 1964 in Hainesport, NJ.

Children of DAVID SUTTON and JUDITH WILLIAMS are:
i. DAVID ANTHONY SUTTON[6] JR., b. December 20, 1965.
ii. PAULA MARIE SUTTON, b. September 03, 1968; m. JERRY LEFFERS, April 10, 1999.

Marriage Notes for PAULA SUTTON and JERRY LEFFERS:
They had an Outdoor Wedding, Brothers David and Horace stood up for her giving their consent of marriage.

iii. HORACE SUTTON, b. November 12, 1973.

3. ANN KATHERINE[5] SUTTON *(HORACE WOODRUFF[4], WILLIAM L.[3], ROBERT O.[2], JOSEPH[1])* was born August 21, 1943 in Mt. Holly, NJ. She married ROBERT EDWARD HELLMIG August 07, 1965 in Masonville, NJ. He was born in Mt. Laurel, NJ.

Subj: **Bob**
Date: 7/20/2007 10:22:44 PM Eastern Daylight Time
From: ann.hellmig1@comcast.net
To: JSutton639@aol.com
CC: JSutton639@aol.com

Hi!

I have some bad news, Bob passed away this evening at home, he has been suffering for some time and I thank God he is at peace.
I'II write again soon. Love, Ann

FREE Animations for your email - by IncrediMail! Click Here!

Marriage Notes for ANN SUTTON and ROBERT HELLMIG:
Married at the Bible Calvary Church in Masonville, NJ by Rev. William A. Raymond
Debbie was Christened at the Bible Calvary Church on De. 31, 1967 by Rev. William Raymond.

Children of ANN SUTTON and ROBERT HELLMIG are:

i. DEBBIE LEIGH[6] HELLMIG, b. March 05, 1967; m. EDWARD THOMAS MOUNT, JR., April 25, 1992, Medford Lakes, NJ.

Notes for DEBBIE LEIGH HELLMIG:
Born on A Sunday at 7:10PM, Weighed 6lbs. 10ozs. and was 21" long. Attending Physician was Dr. John C. Mutch of Moorestown, NJ

Marriage Notes for DEBBIE HELLMIG and EDWARD MOUNT:
Married at the Catheral of Woods Church in Medford Lakes, NJ.

ii. ROBERT EDWARD HELLMIG, JR., b. May 10, 1969; m. JEANINE PARRY HARGROVE, October 04, 1992, Medford Lakes, NJ.

Notes for ROBERT EDWARD HELLMIG, JR.:
Robert was born on A Saturday at 12:27P.M. , weighed 5lbs. 15oz, and was 181/2" long, delivered by attended physician Dr. John S. Mutch, of Moorestown, NJ.

Marriage Notes for ROBERT HELLMIG and JEANINE HARGROVE:
Married at the Catheral of Woods, Church in Medford Lakes, NJ.

Endnotes

1. Mancuso.FTW, Date of Import: Sep 6, 2000.

HORACE SUTTON MARRIED MILDRED ARNOLD

SON OF WILLIAM AND EMMA ROGERS/SUTTON

Horace in front of Garage on Rt. 38 in the Forties

Mildred and Marie

Horace

Marie , Herman and Mildred

State of New Jersey

DEPARTMENT OF HEALTH AND SENIOR SERVICES

VITAL STATISTICS REGISTRATION
PO BOX 370
TRENTON, N.J. 08625-0370

JAMES E. MCGREEVEY
Governor

www.state.nj.us/health

CLIFTON R. LACY, M.D.
Commissioner

Re: Robert O. Sutton
DOB: 10/24/1906

Dear Mr. Sutton:

We regret that we can be of no immediate help to you in your present situation. It is unfortunate that a record of birth was never filed for Robert O. Sutton who was born on 10/24/1906. It is the State's position that it serves no legal purpose to establish a record of birth for an individual who have since passed away. Additionally, our requirements would have to be met regarding the completion of the delayed report.

Sincerely Yours,

Melinda Garay
Record Modification Unit
(609) 292-4087 X507

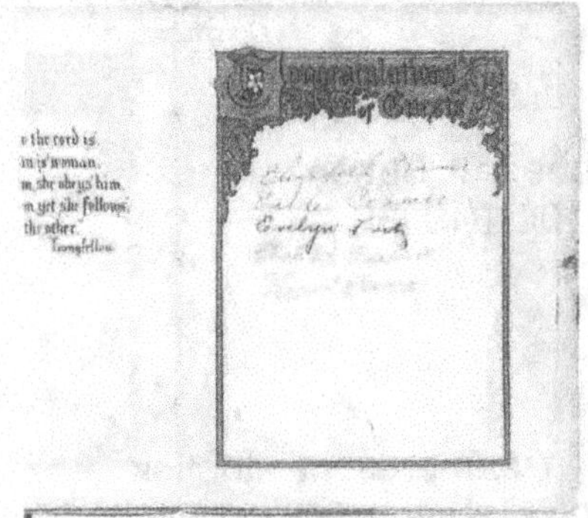

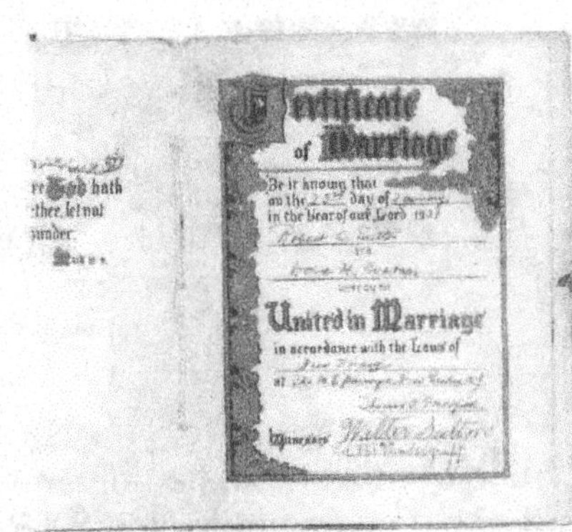

Wedding Certificate

Wedding Guest

Descendants of Robert O. Sutton

Generation No. 1

1. ROBERT O.[4] SUTTON *(WILLIAM L.[3], ROBERT O.[2], JOSEPH[1])[1]* was born October 24, 1906[2,2,2,2,2,2,2,2,2,2,2,2,2,2,2,3,4], and died August 1987[5,5,5,5,5,5,5,5,5,5,5,5,5,5,5,6,7]. He married DORA WATSON[8], daughter of THOMAS WATSON and MARY CRAMER. She was born February 09, 1915[8], and died January 15, 1965[8].

Notes for ROBERT O. SUTTON:
[Genealogy.com, Family Archive #110, Vol. 2 L-Z, Ed. 9, Social Security Death Index: U.S., Date of Import: Dec 30, 2000, Internal Ref. #1.112.9.111416.32]

Individual: Sutton, Robert
Social Security #: 148-07-6985
Issued in: New Jersey

Birth date: Oct 24, 1906
Death date: Aug 1987

Residence code: New Jersey

ZIP Code of last known residence: 08224
Location associated with this ZIP Code:

New Gretna, New Jersey

Robert Sutton told his childred that the O. in his name stood for Osborn but we have not been able to verify this. His grandfather's middle initial also was an O. (for some reason either lost in the mail, etc. his birth certificate has never been registered. I am going to try and register him through the family bible and other papers we have).

More About ROBERT O. SUTTON:
Burial: Hillside cemetery, New Gretna[8]
Social Security Number: Social Security #: 148-07-6985[9,10]

Notes for DORA WATSON:
Reference #3180
The twins are buried behind Maud Cramer, there are two little stones sticking out of the ground to mark their graves.

More About DORA WATSON:
Burial: Hillside cemetery, New Gretna[10]

Children of ROBERT SUTTON and DORA WATSON are:

i. TWIN BABY[5] SUTTON, b. Abt. 1930; d. Abt. 1930.

More About TWIN BABY SUTTON:
Burial: Abt. 1930, Hillside cemetery, New Gretna

ii. TWIN BABY SUTTON, b. Abt. 1930; d. Abt. 1930.

More About TWIN BABY SUTTON:
Burial: Abt. 1930, Hillside cemetery, New Gretna

2. iii. ROBERT THOMAS SUTTON, b. December 07, 1932, Atlantic City, NJ.

Subj: **Re: (no subject)**
Date: 9/20/2007 7:16:51 PM Eastern Daylight Time
From: je.sutton2@verizon.net
To: JSutton639@aol.com

Feel free to use any and all information, it's all in the family. I know there is a Sutton/Sutton connection here we just need to figure it out. (ha, ha). You've also filled in missing information for me.
Mary S. Sutton
107 Union Street
Mount Holly, New Jersey 08060

#7009

je.sutton2@verizon.net

> ----- Original Message -----
> **From:** JSutton639@aol.com
> **To:** je.sutton2@verizon.net
> **Sent:** Thursday, September 20, 2007 6:37 PM
> **Subject:** Re: (no subject)
>
> No, I don't have the draft cards. I sure hope someone in the family cares enough to carry on all the work that has gone into the family tree.
> I am going to put all the info into a research book, do you mind if I put all the info that you sent me in it? What ever you sent will be credited to you.
>
> ---
>
>

THESE ARE SUTTONS THAT I HAVEN'T FOUND WHERE THEY CONNECT TO OUR FAMILY LINE BUT THEY MAY BE OF SOME VALUE TO OTHER RESEARCHERS ....

COHANSEY CEMETERY RECORDS, BRIDGETON, NJ

CEMETERY HEADSTONE FROM THE HISTORIC BROAD STREET CHURCH IN BRIDGETON, NJ PLUS WAR RECORDS.

CORRESPONDENCE FROM OTHER SUTTONS

Cohansey Cemetery Record of Suttons

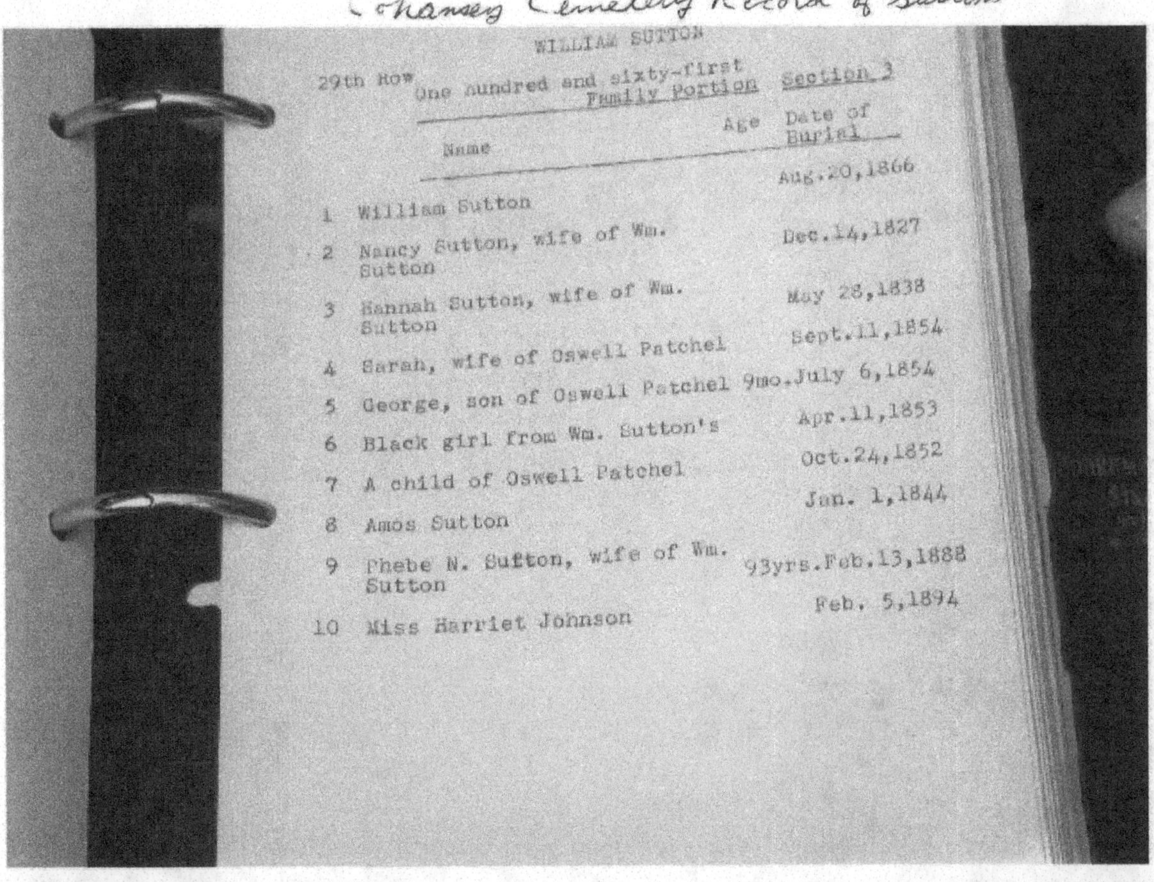

WILLIAM SUTTON

29th Row One hundred and sixty-first Family Portion Section 3

	Name	Age	Date of Burial
1	William Sutton		Aug.20,1866
2	Nancy Sutton, wife of Wm. Sutton		Dec.14,1827
3	Hannah Sutton, wife of Wm. Sutton		May 28,1838
4	Sarah, wife of Oswell Patchel		Sept.11,1854
5	George, son of Oswell Patchel	9mo.	July 6,1854
6	Black girl from Wm. Sutton's		Apr.11,1853
7	A child of Oswell Patchel		Oct.24,1852
8	Amos Sutton		Jan. 1,1844
9	Phebe N. Sutton, wife of Wm. Sutton	93yrs.	Feb.13,1888
10	Miss Harriet Johnson		Feb. 5,1894

HENRY SUTTON

2nd Row Section 4

	Name	Age	Date of Burial
1	Henry Sutton	36yrs. 27days	June 3,1861
2	Leslie B. Sutton, son of Henry Sutton	11mo. 1ds.	Feb.21,1861
3	A child of Henry Sutton	6mo.	Apr. 2,1854
4	Wife of Henry Sutton		Nov. 8,1853
5	Emily Sutton (wife of Richard Sutton)	75	Jan.28,1876
6	Richard S. Sutton	79	Jan.25,1881

BORN
JANUARY 7TH, 1787.
DIED

BORN
JANUARY 7TH, 1787.
DIED

TWELFTH CENSUS OF THE UNITED STATES. **B**

SCHEDULE No. 1.—POPULATION.

State: New Jersey
County: Cumberland

Supervisor's District No. 6
Enumeration District No. 127
Sheet No. 4

Township or other division of county: Deerfield Township 1st Precinct
Name of Institution:

Name of incorporated city, town, or village, within the above-named division:
Ward of city:

Enumerated by me on the 7th day of June, 1900, Thomas M Barracliff, Enumerator.

House number	Dwelling number	Family number	Name	Relation	Color	Sex	Month of birth	Year of birth	Age	Marital status	Years married	Mother of how many children	Children living	Birthplace of person	Birthplace of father	Birthplace of mother	Year of immigration	Years in U.S.	Naturalization	Occupation	Months not employed	Attended school (months)	Can read	Can write	Can speak English	Owned or rented	Free or mortgaged	Farm or house	Number of farm schedule
			Richards Leon E	Son	W	M	Dec	1892	7	S				New Jersey	New Jersey	New Jersey				At School		9	yes	yes	yes				
			Marshall Henrietta	Housekeeper	W	F	Sep	1858	41	S				Pennsylvania	England	Pennsylvania				Housekeeper			yes	yes	yes				
			Hamilton Clarence	Laborer	W	M	Mar	1877	23	S				New Jersey	New Jersey	New Jersey				Farm Laborer			yes	yes	yes				
	87	91	Ware D Henry	Head	W	M	Aug	1844	55	M	31			New Jersey	New Jersey	New Jersey				Farmer			yes	yes	yes	O	M	F	40
			— Anna	Wife	W	F	Dec	1847	52	M	31	3	3	New Jersey	New Jersey	New Jersey							yes	yes	yes				
			— Harry H	Son	W	M	July	1877	22	M				New Jersey	New Jersey	New Jersey							yes	yes	yes				
	88	92	Padgett John	Head	W	M	Mar	1847	53	M	25			New Jersey	New Jersey	New Jersey				Farmer			yes	yes	yes	O	M	F	41
			— Anna M	Wife	W	F	Feb	1849	51	M	25	1	1	New Jersey	New Jersey	New Jersey							yes	yes	yes				
			— Leander S	Son	W	M	May	1876	24	S				New Jersey	New Jersey	New Jersey				Farm Laborer			yes	yes	yes				
			Courtney James R	Taken for	W	M	Mar	1887	13	S				Scotland	Scotland	Scotland				at school		5	yes	yes	yes				
	89	93	Woodruff Enoch	Head	W	M	June	1835	64	Wd				New Jersey	New Jersey	New Jersey				Farmer			yes	yes	yes	O	M	F	42
			— Susannah S	Daughter	W	F	May	1882	18	S				New Jersey	New Jersey	New Jersey							yes	yes	yes				
			— Norton	Son	W	M	May	1884	16	S				New Jersey	New Jersey	New Jersey				Farm Labor			yes	yes	yes				
	90	94	Halter Alfred	Head	W	M	July	1831	68	M	31			New Jersey	New Jersey	New Jersey				Farmer			yes	yes	yes	O	M	F	43
			— Elizabeth	Wife	W	F	Oct	1846	53	M	31	0	0	New Jersey	New Jersey	New Jersey							yes	yes	yes				
	91	95	Davis James	Head	W	M	Ap	1851	49	M	21			New Jersey	New Jersey	New Jersey				Farmer			yes	yes	yes	O	F	F	44
			— Matilda E	Wife	W	F	Ap	1856	44	M	21	2	1	New Jersey	New Jersey	New Jersey							yes	yes	yes				
			— Robert H	Son	W	M	Dec	1882	17	S				New Jersey	New Jersey	New Jersey				at school		9	yes	yes	yes				
	92	96	Davis Ephraim	Head	W	M	Oct	1861	38	M	17			New Jersey	New Jersey	New Jersey				Farmer			yes	yes	yes	O	M	F	45
			— Anna E	Wife	W	F	Sep	1862	37	M	17	5	4	New Jersey	New Jersey	New Jersey							yes	yes	yes				
			— Margaret E	Daughter	W	F	July	1885	14	S				New Jersey	New Jersey	New Jersey				at School			yes	yes	yes				
			— Lillian	Daughter	W	F	Oct	1890	9	S				New Jersey	New Jersey	New Jersey				at school			yes	yes	yes				
			— John N	Son	W	M	July	1895	4	S				New Jersey	New Jersey	New Jersey													
			— Nelson	Son	W	M	Aug	1897	2	S				New Jersey	New Jersey	New Jersey													
	93	97	Barker Charles	Head	W	M	Nov	1834	65	M	31			New Jersey	New Jersey	New Jersey				Farmer			yes	yes	yes	O	M	F	46
			— Mary	Wife	W	F	Sep	1846	53	M	31	1	1	New Jersey	New Jersey	New Jersey							yes	yes	yes				
			— Alma L	Daughter	W	F	Nov	1870	29	S				New Jersey	New Jersey	New Jersey							yes	yes	yes				
			— Elizabeth	Sister	W	F	May	1817	83	S				New Jersey	New Jersey	New Jersey							yes	yes	yes				
			Richards William	Laborer	W	M	Nov	1862	37	S				New Jersey	New Jersey	New Jersey				Farm Laborer			yes	yes	yes				
	94	98	Hand James	Head	W	M	July	1860	39	M	9			New Jersey	New Jersey	New Jersey				Sawyer & Lumber Dealer			yes	yes	yes	O	M	H	
			— Susan A	Wife	W	F	May	1867	33	M	9	3	3	New Jersey	New Jersey	New Jersey							yes	yes	yes				
			— Walter L	Son	W	M	Ap	1894	6	S				New Jersey	New Jersey	New Jersey							yes	yes	yes				
			— Ethel M	Daughter	W	F	Mar	1896	4	S				New Jersey	New Jersey	New Jersey							yes	yes	yes				
			— Laura	Daughter	W	F	Sep	1897	2	S				New Jersey	New Jersey	New Jersey													
		99	Hand Abijah	Head	W	M	Mar	1833	67	M				New Jersey	New Jersey	New Jersey				Wheelwright			yes	yes	yes	R	M	H	
			— Martha	Wife	W	F	Aug	1839	60	M		5	4	New Jersey	New Jersey	New Jersey							yes	yes	yes				
	95	100	Garton Lorenzo	Head	W	M	Nov	1848	51	M				Pennsylvania	New Jersey	New Jersey				Grocer			yes	yes	yes	O	F	H	
			— Atlanta H	Wife	W	F	Mar	1850	50	M		3	3	New Jersey	New Jersey	New Jersey							yes	yes	yes				
			Parker Ruth D	Daughter	W	F	Nov	1874	25	Wd		1	1	New Jersey	Pennsylvania	New Jersey							yes	yes	yes				
			— Frank	G-Daughter	W	F	Nov	1897	2	S				New Jersey	New Jersey	New Jersey													
	96	101	Vanmeter Edward	Head	W	M	Dec	1861	38	M	14			New Jersey	New Jersey	New Jersey				Carpenter			yes	yes	yes	O	M	H	
			— Anna	Wife	W	F	Feb	1865	35	M	14	2	1	New Jersey	New Jersey	New Jersey							yes	yes	yes				
			— Verna L	Daughter	W	F	Feb	1890	10	S				New Jersey	New Jersey	New Jersey				at School		9	yes	yes	yes				
	97	102	Sutton William	Head	W	M	Feb	1839	61	M	38			New Jersey	New Jersey	New Jersey				Carpenter			yes	yes	yes	R	M	H	
			— Alice M	Wife	W	F	Nov	1841	58	M	38	8	3	New Jersey	New Jersey	New Jersey							yes	yes	yes				
			— Mary	Daughter	W	F	Nov	1864	35	S				New Jersey	New Jersey	New Jersey							[illegible]	yes	yes				
			— Alice	Daughter	W	F	Aug	1867	32	S				New Jersey	New Jersey	New Jersey							yes	yes	yes				
			— Adelia	Daughter	W	F	Mar	1876	24	S				New Jersey	New Jersey	New Jersey							yes	yes	yes				
	98	103	Weaver Reuben	Head	W	M	Sep	1870	[illegible]	M	[illegible]			Pennsylvania	Pennsylvania	Pennsylvania				Miller			yes	yes	yes	R	M	H	
			[illegible]	Wife	W	F	[illegible]	1875	[illegible]	M	[illegible]	[illegible]	[illegible]	Pennsylvania	Pennsylvania	Pennsylvania							yes	yes	yes				

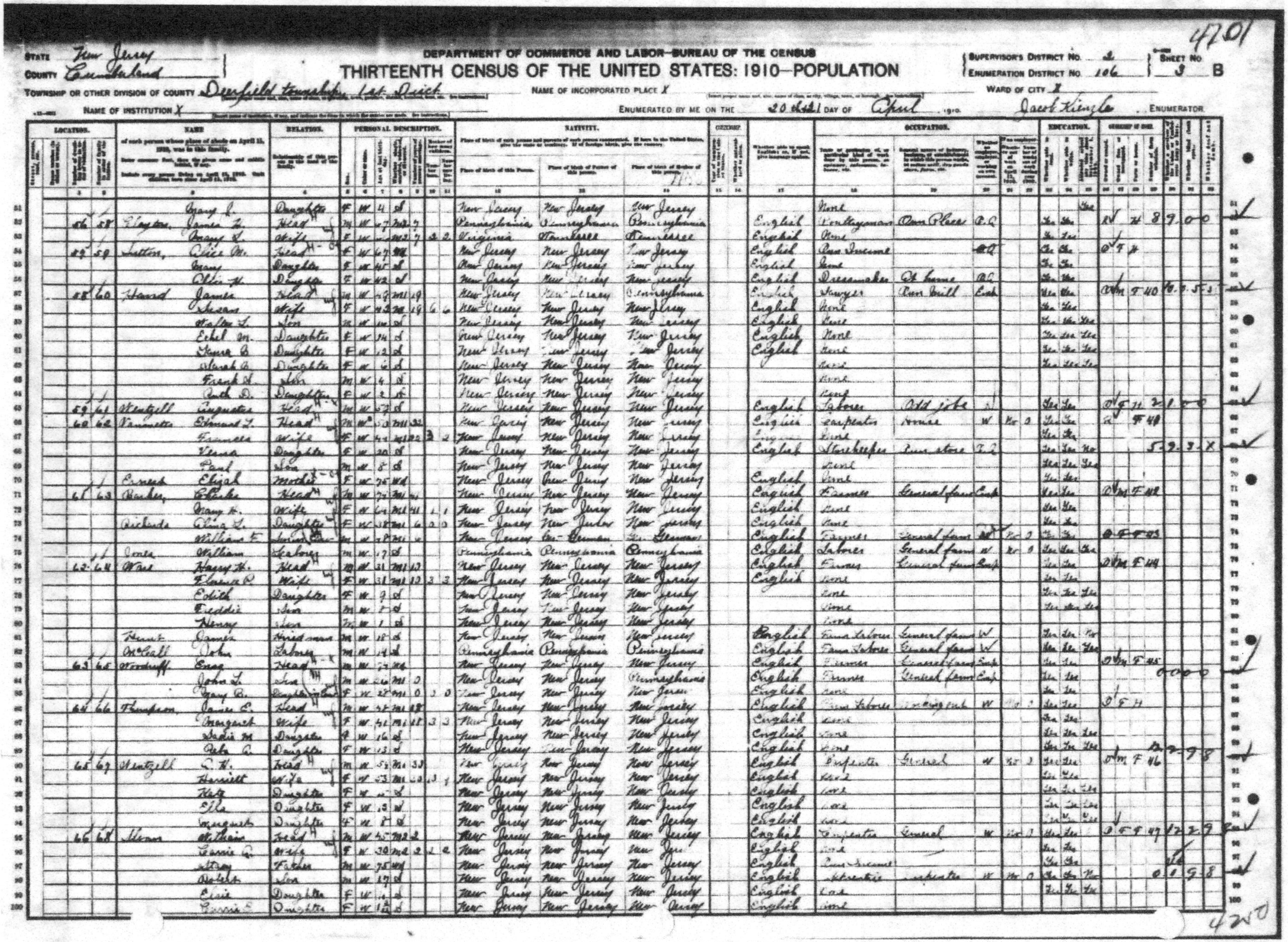

DEPARTMENT OF COMMERCE AND LABOR—BUREAU OF THE CENSUS

THIRTEENTH CENSUS OF THE UNITED STATES: 1910—POPULATION

State: New Jersey
County: Cumberland
Township or other division of county: Deerfield township, 1st Dist.
Name of incorporated place: X
Name of institution: X
Ward of city: X
Supervisor's District No. 2
Enumeration District No. 106
Sheet No. 3 B
Enumerated by me on the 20th–21st day of April, 1910. Jacob Kienzle, Enumerator

4701

Line	Dwelling	Family	Name	Relation	Sex	Color	Age	Marital	Yrs married	Children born	Living	Birthplace	Father's birthplace	Mother's birthplace	Language	Occupation	Industry	Emp./W/OA	Read	Write	School	Home
51			Mary J.	Daughter	F	W	4	S				New Jersey	New Jersey	New Jersey		None					Yes	
52	56	58	Clayton, James L.	Head	M	W	47	M2	7			Pennsylvania	Pennsylvania	Pennsylvania	English	Poultryman	Own Place	OA	Yes	Yes		R H 8 9.0 0
53			Mary L.	Wife	F	W		M2	7	2	2	Virginia	Tennessee	Tennessee	English	None			Yes	Yes		
54	57	59	Sutton, Alice M.	Head	F	W	67	Wd				New Jersey	New Jersey	New Jersey	English	Own Income		OA	Yes	Yes		O F H
55			Mary	Daughter	F	W	45	S				New Jersey	New Jersey	New Jersey	English	None			Yes	Yes		
56			Allie H.	Daughter	F	W	42	S				New Jersey	New Jersey	New Jersey	English	Dressmaker	At home	OA	Yes	Yes		
57	58	60	Hand, James	Head	M	W	49	M1	19			New Jersey	New Jersey	Pennsylvania	English	Sawyer	Saw mill	Emp	Yes	Yes		O M F 40
58			Susan	Wife	F	W	43	M1	19	6	6	New Jersey	New Jersey	New Jersey	English	None			Yes	Yes		
59			Walter L.	Son	M	W	16	S				New Jersey	New Jersey	New Jersey	English	None			Yes	Yes	Yes	
60			Ethel M.	Daughter	F	W	14	S				New Jersey	New Jersey	New Jersey	English	None			Yes	Yes	Yes	
61			Laura B.	Daughter	F	W	12	S				New Jersey	New Jersey	New Jersey	English	None			Yes	Yes	Yes	
62			Sarah A.	Daughter	F	W	6	S				New Jersey	New Jersey	New Jersey		None			Yes	Yes	Yes	
63			Frank A.	Son	M	W	4	S				New Jersey	New Jersey	New Jersey		None						
64			Ruth D.	Daughter	F	W	2	S				New Jersey	New Jersey	New Jersey		None						
65	59	61	Wentzell, Augustus	Head	M	W	57	S				New Jersey	New Jersey	New Jersey	English	Laborer	Odd jobs	OA	Yes	Yes		O F H
66	60	62	Vannetta, Edmund L.	Head	M	W	50	M1	32			New Jersey	New Jersey	New Jersey	English	Carpenter	House	W	Yes	Yes		R F 40
67			Frances	Wife	F	W	44	M1	32	3	2	New Jersey	New Jersey	New Jersey	English	None			Yes	Yes		
68			Verna	Daughter	F	W	20	S				New Jersey	New Jersey	New Jersey	English	Storekeeper	Own store	OA	Yes	Yes	No	
69			Paul	Son	M	W	8	S				New Jersey	New Jersey	New Jersey		None			Yes	Yes	Yes	
70			Ernest, Elijah	Mother	F	W	75	Wd				New Jersey	New Jersey	New Jersey	English	None			Yes	Yes		
71	61	63	Barker, Charles	Head	M	W	72	M1	41			New Jersey	New Jersey	New Jersey	English	Farmer	General farm	Emp	Yes	Yes		O M F 42
72			Mary H.	Wife	F	W	64	M1	41	1	1	New Jersey	New Jersey	New Jersey	English	None			Yes	Yes		
73			Richards, Eliza L.	Daughter	F	W	38	M1	6	0	0	New Jersey	New Jersey	New Jersey	English	None			Yes	Yes		
74			William E.	Son-in-law	M	W	28	M1	6			New Jersey	Germany	Germany	English	Farmer	General farm	W	Yes	Yes		O F F 43
75			Jones, William	Laborer	M	W	17	S				Pennsylvania	Pennsylvania	Pennsylvania	English	Laborer	General farm	W	Yes	Yes	Yes	
76	62	64	Ware, Harry H.	Head	M	W	31	M1	13			New Jersey	New Jersey	New Jersey	English	Farmer	General farm	Emp	Yes	Yes		O M F 44
77			Florence R.	Wife	F	W	31	M1	13	3	3	New Jersey	New Jersey	New Jersey	English	None			Yes	Yes		
78			Edith	Daughter	F	W	9	S				New Jersey	New Jersey	New Jersey		None			Yes	Yes	Yes	
79			Freddie	Son	M	W	5	S				New Jersey	New Jersey	New Jersey		None			Yes	Yes	Yes	
80			Henry	Son	M	W	1	S				New Jersey	New Jersey	New Jersey		None						
81			Hunt, James	Hired man	M	W	18	S				New Jersey	New Jersey	New Jersey	English	Farm Laborer	General farm	W	Yes	Yes	No	
82			McCall, John	Laborer	M	W	14	S				Pennsylvania	Pennsylvania	Pennsylvania	English	Farm Laborer	General farm	W	Yes	Yes	Yes	
83	63	65	Woodruff, Enos	Head	M	W	74	Wd				New Jersey	New Jersey	New Jersey	English	Farmer	General farm	Emp	Yes	Yes		O M F 45
84			John L.	Son	M	W	26	M1	0			New Jersey	New Jersey	Pennsylvania	English	Farmer	General farm	Emp	Yes	Yes		
85			Mary B.	Daughter-in-law	F	W	28	M1	0	0	0	New Jersey	New Jersey	New Jersey	English	None			Yes	Yes		
86	64	66	Thompson, James E.	Head	M	W	47	M1	18			New Jersey	New Jersey	New Jersey	English	Farm Laborer	Working out	W	Yes	Yes		O F H
87			Margaret	Wife	F	W	41	M1	18	3	3	New Jersey	New Jersey	New Jersey	English	None			Yes	Yes		
88			Sadie M.	Daughter	F	W	16	S				New Jersey	New Jersey	New Jersey	English	None			Yes	Yes	Yes	
89			Reba A.	Daughter	F	W	13	S				New Jersey	New Jersey	New Jersey	English	None			Yes	Yes	Yes	
90	65	67	Wentzell, C. H.	Head	M	W	54	M1	33			New Jersey	New Jersey	New Jersey	English	Carpenter	General	W	Yes	Yes		O M F 46
91			Harriett	Wife	F	W	53	M1	33			New Jersey	New Jersey	New Jersey	English	None			Yes	Yes		
92			Kate	Daughter	F	W		S				New Jersey	New Jersey	New Jersey	English	None			Yes	Yes	Yes	
93			Ella	Daughter	F	W	13	S				New Jersey	New Jersey	New Jersey	English	None			Yes	Yes	Yes	
94			Margaret	Daughter	F	W	8	S				New Jersey	New Jersey	New Jersey	English	None			Yes	Yes	Yes	
95	66	68	Moore, William	Head	M	W	45	M2	2			New Jersey	New Jersey	New Jersey	English	Carpenter	General	W	Yes	Yes		O F F 47
96			Carrie A.	Wife	F	W	30	M2	2	2	2	New Jersey	New Jersey	New Jersey	English	None			Yes	Yes		
97			Henry	Father	M	W	75	Wd				New Jersey	New Jersey	New Jersey	English	Own Income			Yes	Yes		
98			Robert	Son	M	W	17	S				New Jersey	New Jersey	New Jersey	English	Apprentice	Carpenter	W	Yes	Yes	No	
99			Elsie	Daughter	F	W	10	S				New Jersey	New Jersey	New Jersey	English	None			Yes	Yes	Yes	
100			Bessie E.	Daughter	F	W	1 1/12	S				New Jersey	New Jersey	New Jersey	English	None						

4270

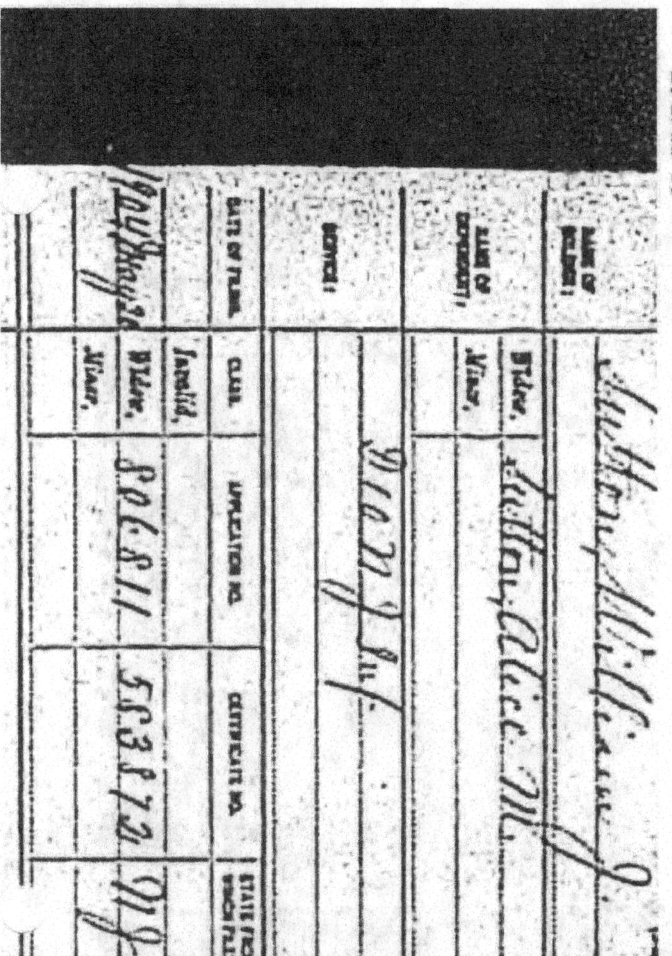

NAME OF SOLDIER: Sutton, William J.

NAME OF DEPENDENT: Widow, Sutton, Alice M.; Minor

SERVICE: D 12 N.J. Inf.

DATE OF FILING	CLASS	APPLICATION NO.	CERTIFICATE NO.	STATE FROM WHICH FILED
	Invalid,			
1904 May 23	Widow,	806811	563872	N.J.
"	Minor,			

Mary Sutton

From: Bill McLean <wmcl@eticomm.net>
To: <StowCreek@aol.com>
Sent: Thursday, May 10, 2001 10:17 PM
Subject: Re: SUTTON/Fairton

I know a number of the Fairton group. Jim died a few years ago but his widow, Irma, still lives on Main Street. He died while deer hunting, unfortunately, alone. Another Sutton committed suicide several years ago. Bill

----- Original Message -----
From: StowCreek@aol.com
To: wmcl@eticomm.net
Sent: Thursday, May 10, 2001 8:30 PM
Subject: Re: SUTTON/HAND Census

In a message dated 5/10/01 5:07:51 PM Pacific Daylight Time, wmcl@eticomm.net writes:

Rosenhayn

Bill you did it again, "Rosenhayn"-James C. Sutton married Elizabeth M. Maul. James died from measles during the Civil War & is buried in the Shiloh Baptist Cemetery. Margaret Alice Sutton (Hand) has an affidavit in James' pension file. In this file it states that Elizabeth lived in Rosenhayn. James & Elizabeth had no children & she later married into the Ayres family, however, Elizabeth has an affidavit (sp) in William J. Sutton's file. I think William & James may have been brothers. If Seeley is close to Rosenhayn would you think this highly possible.

About 3 years ago I purchased the book **Cumberland County and South Jersey during the Civil War** on page 185 is a picture of William J. Sutton, he is a very nice looking man, and then when you read his pension record, you find how the war affected him, it's so sad. I sent for pension records on all the Sutton's in the book and sent copies to the Lummis Library in Greenwich. All of them came back with problems.

On a lighter note-I don't know if this "Sutton Family" is related to my husbands, but I seem to find 3 different groups, the Stow Creek/Greenwich group, Fairfield/Fairton, & the Downe/Maurice group. I'm not sure if my township lines are correct, but this would be about 1850.

Your help is greatly appreciated,
Mary

TWELFTH CENSUS OF THE UNITED STATES.

SCHEDULE No. 1.—POPULATION.

SUTTON

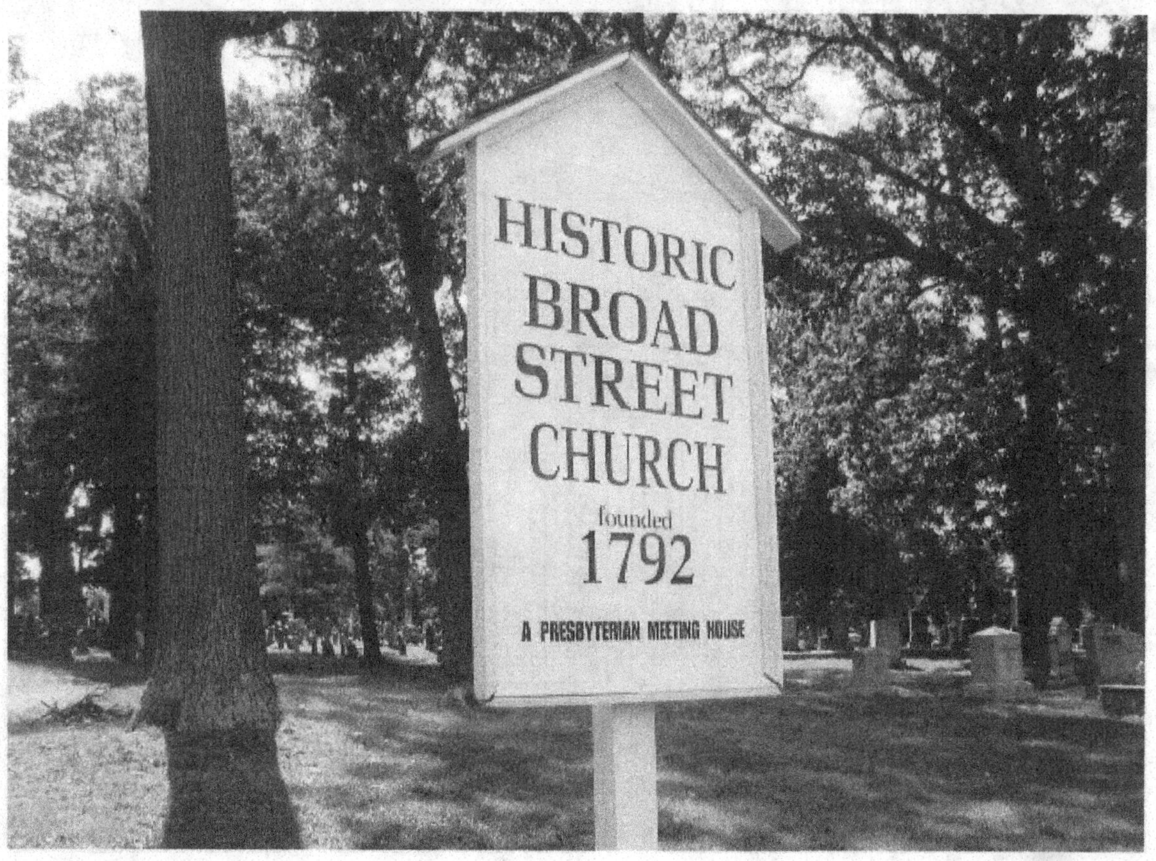
HISTORIC
BROAD
STREET
CHURCH
founded
1792
A PRESBYTERIAN MEETING HOUSE

1904 ROLL # 239 NJA

State of New Jersey—Bureau of Vital Statistics.
CERTIFICATE AND RECORD OF DEATH.

Full Name of Deceased William J. Sutton
[If an infant not named, so state, and give sex.]

Years.	Months.	Days.	Hours.

William J. Sutton

2. Age 65 years 2 months .... days .... hours.

3. Color White Occupation Carpenter

4. Single, married, widow or widower { Cross out all but the right one.

5. Birthplace Cumberland Co. N.J.
(State or country.)

6. Last place of residence Seeley - Deerfield
(If in a city, give name, street and number; if in township, give name
Township - Cumberland Co
and county; if in an institution, so state.)

7. How long resident in this state

8. Place of death Seeley - Deerfield
(If in a city, give name, street and number; if in township, give name
Township - Cumberland Co
and county; if in an institution, so state.)

9. Father's name Ozwell Sutton

Country of Birth U.S.

10. Mother's name [illegible] Sutton

Country of Birth U.S.

11. I hereby certify that I attended the deceased during the last illness, and that he died on the 3rd day of April 1904, and that the cause of death was Pulmonary Abscess

Length of sickness 3 months { See over and particulars.

S. M. Wilson

Medical Attendant.

Residence Bridgeton

Name of Undertaker Harry J. Garrison

Residence of Undertaker Bridgeton

Place of Burial Broad St. Bridgeton

PART I

THE NATIONAL ARCHIVES

CERT. NO.

PENSIONER

OF

VETERAN

BUNDLE NO.

No other claimant

3–1081

PENSIONER DROPPED.

United States Pension Agency,

PHILADELPHIA, PA.

MAY 12 1904 190

Certificate No. 173624. OK

Class Inv. C.W.

Pensioner William J. Sutton

Soldier

Service D. 10" N.J.

The Commissioner of Pensions.

SIR: I have the honor to report that the above-named pensioner who was last paid at $ 40 to Feb 4 1904, has been dropped because of

Death, reported by the Hon. Commissioner of Pensions.

Very respectfully,

C.A. Mulholland

United States Pension Agent.

NOTE.—Every name dropped to be thus reported at once, and where cause of dropping is death, state date of death when known.

GROUP 2 3-888
3—1081

PENSIONER DROPPED April.

DEPARTMENT OF THE INTERIOR

BUREAU OF PENSIONS

30 8/4/20

AUG 6 1920, 19

Certificate No. 583,872

Class ACT OF MAY 1, 1920

Pensioner Alice M. Sutton

Soldier William J. Sutton

Service 1st Sgt. & 2d Lt. D 10th N.J. Inf.

The Commissioner of Pensions.

Sir:

I have the honor to report that the name of the above-described pensioner who was last paid at $25, to MAY 4 1920 has this day been dropped from the roll because of death, June 5, 1920

ALICE M SUTTON
BRIDGETON N J
583872 ACT APR
R R BOX 36

Very respectfully,

[signature]

Chief, Finance Division.

NOTE.—Every name dropped to be thus reported at once, and when cause of dropping is death, state date of death when known.

8—2249

M.W.

Check No. 710742 date AUG 4 1920 cancelled

War Department,

ADJUTANT GENERAL'S OFFICE,

Washington, D. C. August 24, 1880.

Sir:

I have the honor to acknowledge the receipt from your Office of application for Pension No. 278918, and to return it herewith, with such information as is furnished by the files of this Office.

It appears from the Rolls on file in this Office that William J. Sutton was enrolled on the 8th day of October, 1861, at Philadelphia Pa., in Co. "D" 10th Regiment of New Jersey Infantry Volunteers, to serve three years or during the war, and mustered into service as a Sergeant on the 30th day of October, 1861, at Beverly N.J., in Co. "D", 10th Regiment of New Jersey Infantry Volunteers, to serve three years, or during the war. On the Muster Roll of Co. "D" of that Regiment, ~~for the months of~~ to December 31st, 1861, he is reported present. January and February 1862 absent sick in Hospital at Washington. March & April 1862 present. Same to December 31. 1862. January & February 1863 name borne without remark. March & April 1863 present. Same to December 31. 1863. Re-enlisted as a Veteran Volunteer January 3 1864. January & February 1864 present. March and April 1864 same. May & June 1864 absent wounded and in Hospital since May 6 1864 (when the Company was in action at the Wilderness Va.) Similar report to October 31. 1864 (in Hospital at Newark) November & December 1864, 1st Sergeant present. January & February 1865 same. March & April 1865 Promoted from 1st Sergeant to 2nd Lieutenant same Company March 27. 1865.

This man was "Wounded in the hand in action at the Wilderness Va. May 6 1864, Discharged to date March 27. 1865 for promotion to 2nd Lieut. same Co. and Regt. S.O. No. 74. 6th Corps March 27. 1865."

I am, sir, very respectfully,

Your obedient servant,

[signature]

Assistant Adjutant General.

To The Commissioner of Pensions

Washington D.C.

9387 A AGO (E13) 1880

GENERAL AFFIDAVIT.

State of New Jersey, County of Cumberland ss.

In the matter of William J Sutton Late Soldier Co D 10th N J Vols

ON THIS 18th day of May A. D. 1895 personally appeared before me Notary Publicct in and for the aforesaid County, duly authorized to administer oaths, Isaac H Neugent aged 48 years, a resident of Cedarville in the County of Cumberland and State of New Jersey well known to me to be reputable and entitled to credit, and who, being duly sworn, declared in relation to aforesaid case as follows:

[NOTE.—Affiants should state how they gain a knowledge of the facts to which they testify.]

I was a comrade of William J Sutton late Soldier Co D 10th N J Vols we were on the march from Suffolk Va to Bowers Hill Va William J Sutton was Sunstruck July 3rd 1863 while on this march and was completely disabled from duty. was sent to Douglas Hospital Washington D C Since that time Mr Sutton has been left a Physical wreck from the result of that Sunstrucke

H Post Office address is Cedarville Cumberland Co N J

I further declare that I have no interest in said case and I am not concerned in its prosecution.

Jeannette H. Claypoole | Isaac H Neugent

[If Affiants sign by mark, two persons who can write sign here.] [Signature of Affiants.]

52

Eastern Div:
William J. Sutton.
Co. "D" 10th Regt. N.J. Vols.
Certificate, 173,624.

[illegible]ich N.J. May 8. 1893.

To whom it may concern—

I testify that Wm J Sutton came to consult me in regard to himself. On May 4th 1893 with the following history. Having been in Army during Late Civil War. during which time had Measles. during the Eruptive period of same was exposed to cold. Had relapse. laid unconscious for two weeks. and ever since has been deaf in right ear. ~~Has~~ been more or less aggravated with headache. Want of acute perception of surrounding events. Has periods of heart weakness pain in Chest & back. Has difficulty in walking. During an engagement he lost a thumb of right hand. When I made an Examination May 5 1893 I found him suffering from pain over kidneys. roaring in head. tenderness over umbilical region Heart murmurs & somewhat labored breathing. Also found his right lung somewhat diseased. and tenderness over middle portion of spine, and great lassitude. with general Malaise. tired feeling slowness in moving limbs. dragging of feet. All of which symptoms together with sugar in urine & slight traces of Albumen would in my mind indicate general breaking down of vitality totally unfitting said W. J. Sutton for performing any manual labor. and as he is a man of good repute having the respect of his neighbors & is considered by his former family physician (J. G. Swinney M.D.) as an honest & trustworthy man. I certainly think that

over

His present debility and diseased condition can be no less than the result of exposure of his army life, That He is entitled to be considered worthy an Examination by any Physician to this end.

I would further state that there are signs indicative of slow or non inflammatory softening of Brain tissue (there is also tenderness at base of Brain)

I am Very Truly

A.W. Sullivan M.D. [illegible]

State of New Jersey }
Cumberland County } SS

Personally appeared before me a Justice of the Peace in said County, A. W. Sullivan M.D. who upon oath declares that the above statement is just and true to the best of his knowledge and belief and that the two interlineations were made before signing A. W. Sullivan MD [illegible]

Sworn & subscribed before me this 8th Day of May A.D. 1893 Theo F. Davis J.P.

Div. 17 1898 COMMISSIONER.

Affidavit.

State of New Jersey County of Cumberland ss:

In the Pension Claim of Wm J Sutton

D, 10th N.J. Vls.

Company and Regiment of Service, if in the Army; or Vessel and Rank, if in the Navy.

Personally came before me, a Notary Public, in and for the County and State foresaid Elizabeth M Ayars whose Residence and Post Office address is: Shiloh N.J. well known to me to be reputable and entitled to credit, and who being duly sworn, declares in relation to aforesaid case as follows:

Affiant should here state all the known facts pertaining to the case, and how a knowledge of them has been obtained.

I was at the residence of Mr Sutton seven days during his present sickness I consider his case very crittecle he complained of pains in the regeon of the kidneys and through the bowels and throug the left breast and frequent discharge of blood and mucus from the bowels he was completely prostrated he also had severe cough his pension is his only income

I further declare that I have no interest, either direct or indirect, in the prosecution of said claim.

Witness present

Theo F. Davis

Elizabeth M Ayars

Affiant sign here.

74

If affiant signs by mark, two persons who can write must sign here.

State of New Jersey }
Cumberland County } ss.

In the matter of the application for pension of William J. Sutton.

This is to certify that I am personally acquainted with William J. Sutton, late 2nd Lieut. Co. "D" 10th Regt N. J. Vols. Became acquainted with him shortly after his discharge in July, 1865; knew that his hearing was defective at that time, and has increased continually up to the present time so that he is entirely deaf in the right ear, and the hearing of the left ear is very defective.

P.O. address is Bridgeton. Isaac W Elwell

Sworn to and subscribed before me this 28th day of April A.D. 1888 and I hereby certify that the contents of the above declaration were fully made known + explained to the affiant before swearing, and that I have no interest in the prosecution of this claim.

Jas. S. Ware
Master in Chancery
of N.J.

3–173.

Eastern Div.

Ctf No. 173624

William J. Sutton

Co. D, 10th Reg't N.J. Vol. Inf.

Ex'r

EAST. DIV. MAR 17 1898 RECEIVED

Department of the Interior,

BUREAU OF PENSIONS,

Washington, D. C., March 12, 1898

SIR:

Will you kindly answer, at your earliest convenience, the questions enumerated below? The information is requested for future use, and it may be of great value to your family.

Very respectfully,

Mr. Wm J. Sutton,
Seeley, N.J.

H. Clay Evans
Commissioner.

No. 1. Are you a married man? If so, please state your wife's full name, and her maiden name.
Answer: I am. Alice Margaret Sutton, maiden name Hand.

No. 2. When, where, and by whom were you married? Answer: 3rd of October, 1861
M.E. Parsonage Commerce St, Bridgeton N.J. J. R. Dobbins.

No. 3. What record of marriage exists? Answer: Marriage Certificate

No. 4. Were you previously married? If so, please state the name of your former wife and the date and place of her death or divorce. Answer: I was not.

No. 5. Have you any children living? If so, please state their names and the dates of their birth. Answer: Yes, three.
Mary Cake Sutton, Born November 2nd 1864
Alice Hand Sutton Born August 11th 1867
Adelia James Sutton, Born March 10th 1876

Date of reply, March 14th, 1898.

William J. Sutton
(Signature.)

0–2

16

3—044

APPLICATION FOR REIMBURSEMENT.

(This application, when properly executed before some officer having authority to administer oaths for general purposes, should be forwarded, together with the pension certificate and itemized bills of all expenses, to the Commissioner of Pensions, Washington, D. C.)

STATE OF New Jersey } ss:
COUNTY OF Cumberland }

On this 31 day of July, A. D. one thousand nine hundred and Twenty personally appeared before me, a Notary Public within and for the County and State aforesaid, Alice H. Sutton, aged 52 years, a resident of Deerfield Township, County of Cumberland, State of New Jersey, who, being duly sworn according to law, makes the following declaration in order to obtain reimbursement from the accrued pension for expenses paid (or obligation incurred) in the last sickness and burial of Alice M Sutton, who was a pensioner of the United States by certificate No. 583872, on account of the service of William J Sutton (Name of soldier or sailor.) in 10 Regt N J Vol Inf - 1st Serg 2nd Lieutenant (Describe service by company and regiment, etc., if in the Army, or by the words U. S. Navy, if in the Navy.)
That pension was last paid to May 4, 1920

That the answers to questions propounded below are full, complete, and truthful to the best of my knowledge, information, and belief, and that no evidence necessary to a proper adjustment of all claims against the accrued pension is suppressed or withheld.

1. What was the full name of the deceased pensioner? Alice Margaret Sutton

2. In what capacity was decedent pensioned? (As invalid soldier or sailor, or as a widow, minor child, dependent relative, etc.) Widow

3. If decedent was pensioned as an invalid soldier or sailor—
   (a) Was he ever married? (Answer yes or no.) to widow abov mentioned
   (b) How many times, and to whom? 1
   (c) If married, did his wife survive him? (Answer yes or no.) Yes
   (d) If so, is she still living? (Answer yes or no.) No
   (e) If not living, give full names and dates of death of all wives
   (f) Was he ever divorced? (Answer yes or no.) No
   (g) If so, is the divorced wife still living? (Answer yes or no.) .... (If living, a copy of the decree of divorce must be filed.)
   (h) If not living, give her full name and the date of her death

4. Did pensioner leave a child under 16 years of age? (Answer yes or no.) No ✓
5. Is any such child still living? (Answer yes or no.)
6. Were any sick or death benefits paid on pensioner's account? If so, give name of society and amount paid No ✓
7. Was there insurance (life, accident, or health) in force on life of pensioner at time of death? (Answer yes or no.) yes
8. If so, give the name of each company in which a policy was carried and the amount in which each policy was written The Prudential Ins. Co. $128.15 ✓
9. Who was the beneficiary named in each policy? none
10. What was the relation of each beneficiary to the pensioner? Daughters
11. Were the premiums paid by the deceased pensioner? Self & daughter
12. If not paid by the deceased pensioner, state the amount of premiums paid by each person who made payment on that account No account kept

6—1572

13. Is there an executor or administrator, or will application be made for appointment of any person as administrator? No

14. Did the deceased pensioner leave any money, real estate, or personal property? No

15. If so, state the character and value of all such property —

16. What was the assessed value (last assessment) of the real estate? —

17. How was the pensioner's property disposed of? —

18. Did pensioner leave an unindorsed pension check? (Answer yes or no.) No

19. What was your relation to the deceased pensioner? Daughter

20. Are you married? (Answer yes or no.) No

21. What was the cause of pensioner's death? Cerebral Hemorrhage

22. When did the pensioner's last sickness begin? Day of Death

23. From what date did the pensioner become so ill as to require the regular and daily attendance of another person constantly until death? Day of Death

24. Give the name and post-office address of each physician who attended the pensioner during last sickness Not at all Died suddenly

25. State the names of the persons by whom the pensioner was nursed during the last sickness Daughter

26. Where did the pensioner live during last sickness? (Seeley) Bridgeton N. J. R. F. D. #8

27. Where did the pensioner die? Home " " "

28. When did the pensioner die? Saturday, June 5th 1920

29. Where was the pensioner buried? Broad St. Bridgeton, N. J.

30. Has there been paid, or will application be made for payment to you or any other person, any part of the expenses of the pensioner's last sickness and burial by any State, County, or municipal corporation? (Answer yes or no.) No

31. State below the expenses of the pensioner's last sickness and burial. Write the word *none* where no charge is made in case of any item of expense noted.

(Each charge entered below should be supported by an itemized bill of the person who rendered the service or furnished any supplies for which reimbursement is demanded, and should show, over his signature, by whom paid, or who is held responsible for payment, and contain the name of the pensioner for whom the expense was incurred or service rendered.)

Names.	Nature of Expenses.	State Whether Paid or Unpaid.	Amount.
Dr. H. H. Wilson	Physician	Paid	2 50
	Medicine	none	
	Nursing and care	None	
Harry J. Harrison & Son	Undertaker	Paid	161 75
	Livery		
	Cemetery		
	Other expenses and their nature:		
	Total		$164 25

32. **Is the above a complete list of *all* the expenses of the last sickness and burial of the deceased pensioner?** (Answer yes or no.) Yes

That my post-office address is No. Bridgeton, on New Jersey—R. F. D. 8 Box 36 street, town or city of ——, County of Cumberland State of New Jersey

(When the claimant for reimbursement is a married woman, she is required to sign the application with her own full name, not using the Christian name or the initials of her husband, and all bills should be receipted to her in her own name.)

Miss Alice Hand Sutton
(Claimant's signature in full.)

6—1572

DECLARAT... A CLAIM... MARG...

3

Also appeared Robert Peacock and F. Boyd Woodruff who, being duly sworn, say that they saw Alice Hand Dutton, the claimant, sign her name (or make .... mark) to this application; that they know the claimant herein and that their answers to the following questions are true:

1. Did pensioner (if a soldier or sailor) leave a widow or a minor child under age of sixteen years surviving?

2. When did the pensioner die? June 5 1920

3. Did pensioner leave any property? If so, state its character and value No

4. We knew pensioner 20 years. We believe above statements to be true because

Name Robert Peacock Name F. Boyd Woodruff
P. O. Address Deerfield N.J. P. O. Address Bridgeton N.J.

Subscribed and sworn to before me, this 30 day of July A. D. 1920; and I certify that the contents of the foregoing application were fully made known and explained to the claimant and witnesses before swearing, that I have no interest, direct or indirect, in the prosecution of this claim, and I further certify that the reputation for credibility of the witnesses whose signatures appear above is true

Commission Expires July 14 1920

Opeites Cook (Signature.)
Notary Public of New Jersey (Official character.)

STATEMENT OF ATTENDING PHYSICIANS.

Give date of the pensioner's death June 5. 1920

Give date of commencement of pensioner's last sickness June 5. 1920

From what date did the pensioner require the regular and daily attendance of another person constantly until death? not at all

During what period did you attend the pensioner? not at all except day of death

State nature of disease from which pensioner died Cerebral Haemorrhage

Give name of each person who rendered service as nurse, and who has made or will make a charge for such service none

Give name of any other physician who attended the pensioner in last sickness none

Does your bill include a charge for all medicine furnished the pensioner during last sickness? Yes

Has your bill been paid; if so, by whom? Yes
[illegible] Miss Alice Sutton

Mention any other facts within your knowledge which in your opinion would be helpful in adjusting this claim for reimbursement: none

I certify that the foregoing statement is correct.

July 24, 1920 [illegible] Attending Physician.

........, 191 .... Attending Physician.

5—1572

ar

Widow's Application for Pension.

~~This must be Executed before a Court of Record, or some Officer thereof having Custody of its Seal, as the Law requires.~~

State of New Jersey, **County of** Cumberland ss:

ON THIS 19th day of May A. D. 1904, before me, Notary Public ~~a Court of Record~~ within and [Here state title of the officer] for the County and State aforesaid, personally appeared Alice M. Sutton (Claimant) aged about 62 years, who being duly sworn according to law, makes the following declaration in order to obtain the pension provided for by Acts of Congress granting pension to widows:

That I am the widow of William J. Sutton, late Lieut. Co. D., 10th Reg. N. J. Vols. Inf., who died at ~~Seeley, Deerfield Township, Cumberland Co. New Jersey~~, on the 3d day of April A. D. 1904 of disease (Here state the cause of his death)

which I believe to have originated while he belonged to Company D, 10th Regiment of N. J. Vols. Vols., about January or February, 1862.

That I was married under the name of Alice M. Hand to my said husband on or about 3d day of October 1861 by Rev. Jos. B. Dobbins, pastor M. E. Church at Bridgeton, New Jersey, there being no legal barrier to such marriage;

That neither William J. Sutton or claimant had ever been previously married (Here state whether you or he, or both had been previously married; and, if so, give the name and date of death or divorce of the former spouse)

That I have remained his widow to the present date. (If re-married, state when and to whom)

That the following are the names and dates of birth of all his children, under 16 years of age when he died;

, born 18
, born 18
, born 18
, born 18
, born 18
, born 18

That I have not abandoned the support of any of said children, they being under my care and maintenance;

(If any of said children are not under your care, they should be accounted for. If dead, the name and date of death of each should be stated)

Margaret Sutton, died Nov. 9th, 1870.

That I did not engage in, or aid or abet the late rebellion against the authority of the United States.

That William J. Sutton was a pensioner under certificate No. 173624 (Here state whether a prior application has been filed by yourself or deceased husband; and if so, give the number of the claim if possible) That claimant has not made application heretofore.

That I hereby appoint **J. W. MORRIS**, of **Washington, D. C.**, as my true and lawful attorney to prosecute said claim, with full power of substitution and revocation.

That my residence is Seeley, Cumberland County, New Jersey and my post-office address is Seeley, New Jersey.

Jesse R. Davis
N. P. Cannon
[Two witnesses who can write sign here]

Alice M Sutton
[Signature of Claimant]

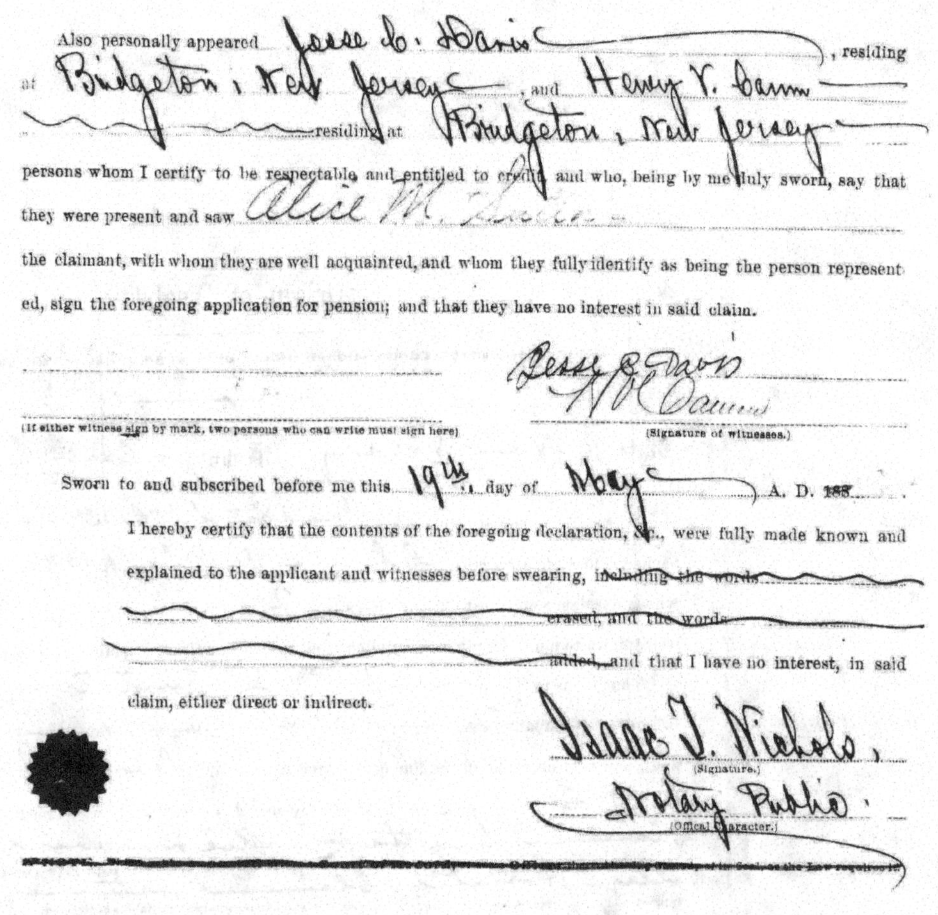

Also personally appeared Jesse C. Davis, residing at Bridgeton, New Jersey, and Henry V. Camm residing at Bridgeton, New Jersey

persons whom I certify to be respectable and entitled to credit, and who, being by me duly sworn, say that they were present and saw Alice M. Sutton

the claimant, with whom they are well acquainted, and whom they fully identify as being the person represented, sign the foregoing application for pension; and that they have no interest in said claim.

(If either witness sign by mark, two persons who can write must sign here)

Jesse C. Davis
H. V. Camm
(Signature of witnesses.)

Sworn to and subscribed before me this 19th day of May A. D. ~~188~~

I hereby certify that the contents of the foregoing declaration, &c., were fully made known and explained to the applicant and witnesses before swearing, ~~including the words~~ ~~erased, and the words~~ ~~added~~, and that I have no interest, in said claim, either direct or indirect.

Isaac T. Nichols.
(Signature.)
Notary Public.
(Offical Character.)

WC 506,811
173624
WIDOW'S Claim.
APPLICATION FOR PENSION.
Alice M. Sutton
WIDOW OF
William J. Sutton
Co. L, 12 N. J. Reg't. Vols.
Enrolled 18
Discharged 18
FILED BY
J. W. MORRIS & CO.
(Late Principal Examiner U.S. Pension Office.)
Attorney at Law,
WASHINGTON, D. C.
EAST. DIV.
JUN 6 1904
RECEIVED.

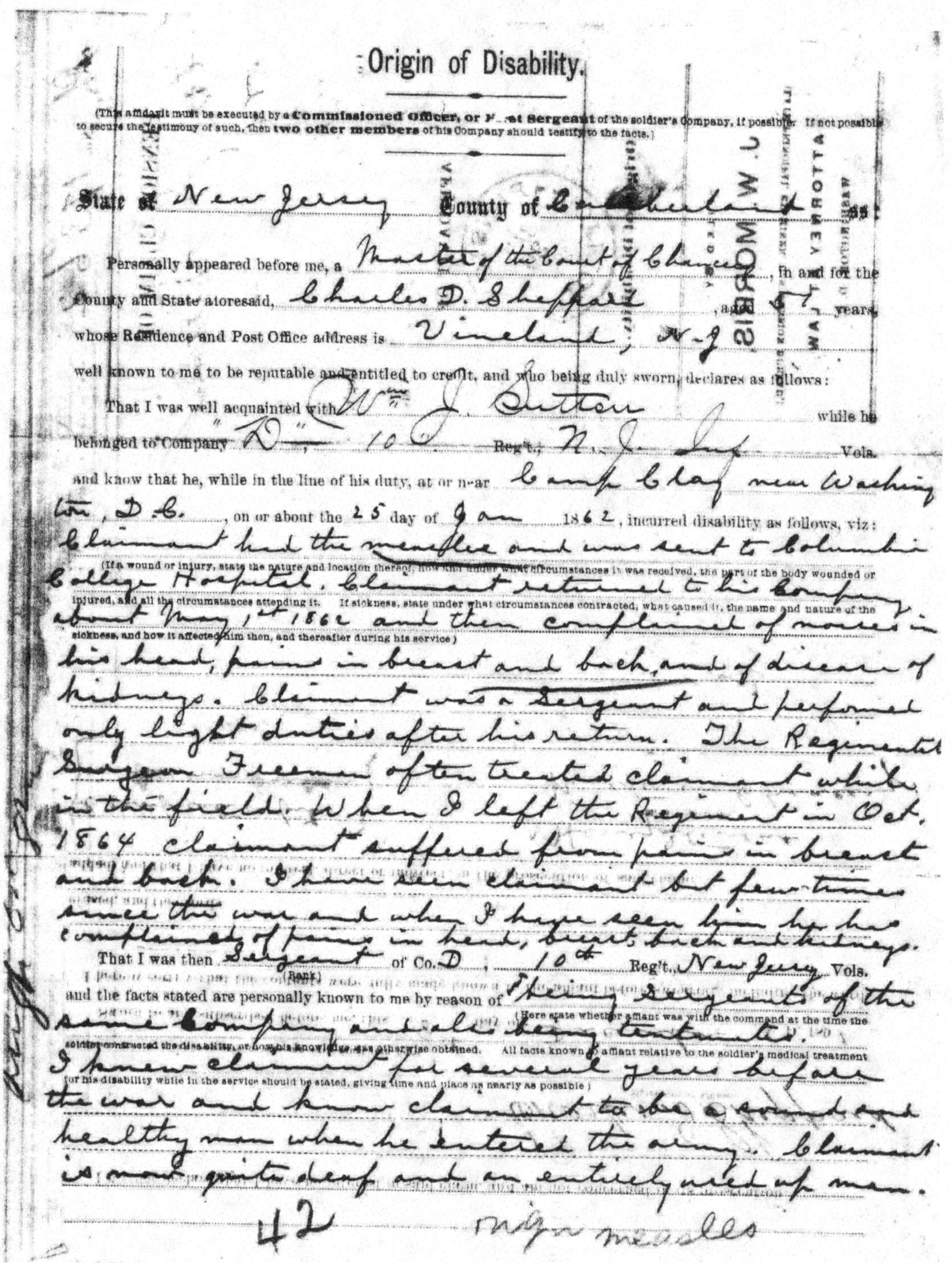

Origin of Disability.

(This affidavit must be executed by a Commissioned Officer, or First Sergeant of the soldier's Company, if possible. If not possible to secure the testimony of such, then two other members of his Company should testify to the facts.)

State of New Jersey County of Cumberland ss:

Personally appeared before me, a Master of the Court of Chancery, in and for the County and State aforesaid, Charles D. Sheppard, aged 51 years, whose Residence and Post Office address is Vineland, N.J. well known to me to be reputable and entitled to credit, and who being duly sworn, declares as follows:

That I was well acquainted with Wm J. Sutton while he belonged to Company "D" 10 Reg't., N.J. Inf Vols. and know that he, while in the line of his duty, at or near Camp Clay near Washington, D.C., on or about the 25 day of Jan 1862, incurred disability as follows, viz: Claimant had the measles and was sent to Columbia College Hospital. Claimant returned to his company about May 1st 1862 and then complained of noises in his head, pains in breast and back, and of disease of kidneys. Claimant was a Sergeant and performed only light duties after his return. The Regimental Surgeon Freeman often treated claimant while in the field. When I left the Regiment in Oct. 1864 claimant suffered from pains in breast and back. I have seen claimant but few times since the war and when I have seen him he has complained of pains in head, breast, back and kidneys.

(If a wound or injury, state the nature and location thereof, how and under what circumstances it was received, the part of the body wounded or injured, and all the circumstances attending it. If sickness, state under what circumstances contracted, what caused it, the name and nature of the sickness, and how it affected him then, and thereafter during his service.)

That I was then Sergeant (Rank) of Co. D, 10th Reg't. New Jersey Vols. and the facts stated are personally known to me by reason of being Sergeants of the same Company and also being tentmates.

(Here state whether affiant was with the command at the time the soldier contracted the disability, or how his knowledge was otherwise obtained. All facts known to affiant relative to the soldier's medical treatment for his disability while in the service should be stated, giving time and place as nearly as possible.)

I knew claimant for several years before the war and knew claimant to be a sound and healthy man when he entered the army. Claimant is now quite deaf and an entirely used up man.

42 M&G measles

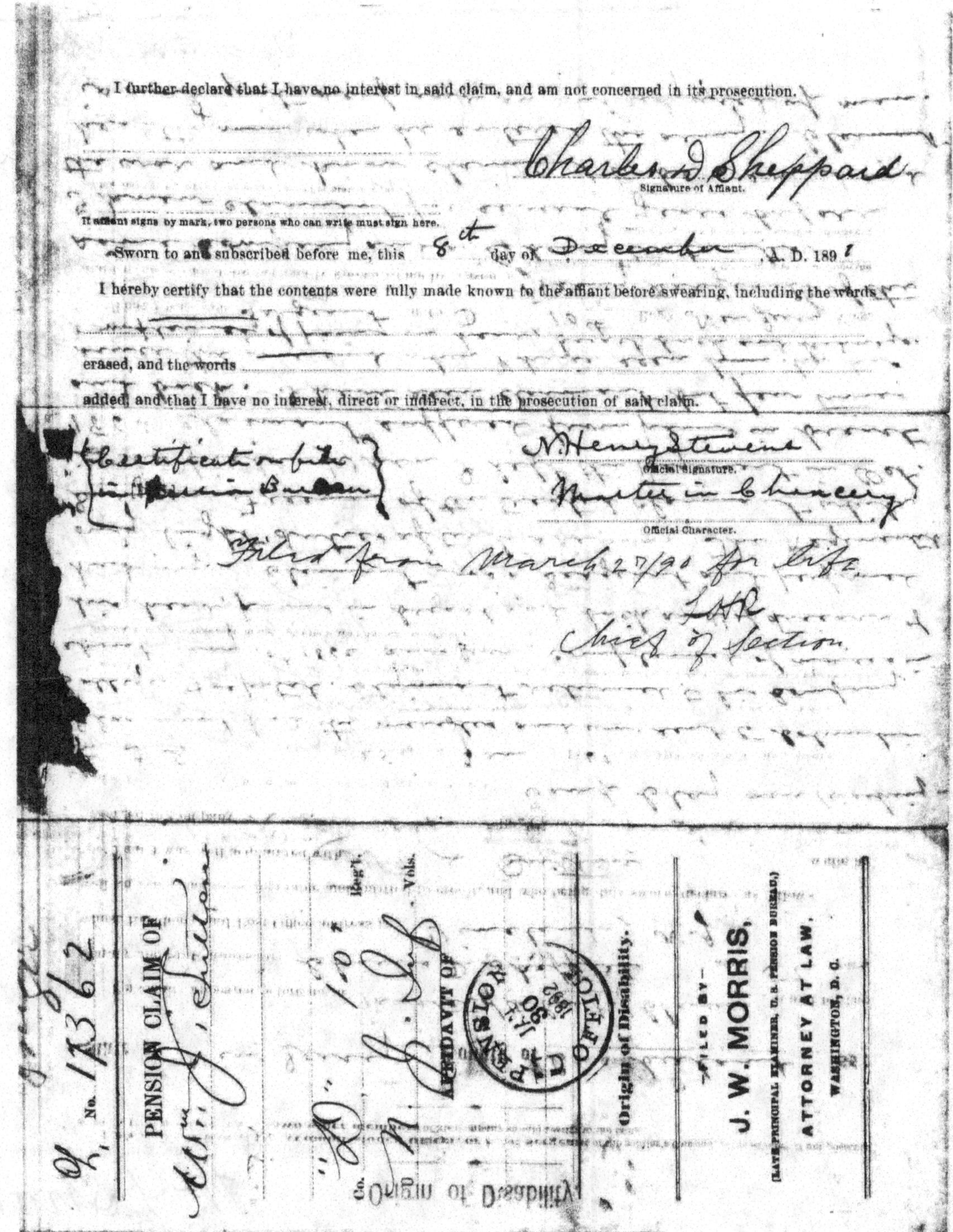
I further declare that I have no interest in said claim, and am not concerned in its prosecution.

Charles D Sheppard
Signature of Affiant.

If affiant signs by mark, two persons who can write must sign here.

Sworn to and subscribed before me, this 8th day of December, A. D. 1891

I hereby certify that the contents were fully made known to the affiant before swearing, including the words

erased, and the words

added, and that I have no interest, direct or indirect, in the prosecution of said claim.

{Certificate on file in Pension Bureau}

N Henry Stevens
Official Signature.

Master in Chancery
Official Character.

Filed from March 27/90 for life
LHR
Chief of Section

No. 17362

PENSION CLAIM OF

AFFIDAVIT OF

Origin of Disability.

FILED BY—
J. W. MORRIS,
(LATE PRINCIPAL EXAMINER, U.S. PENSION BUREAU,)
ATTORNEY AT LAW,
WASHINGTON, D. C.

STATE OF Virginia,
~~County~~ City OF Alexandria } ss.

On this Twenty Second day of March A. D. 1879, before me, a Clerk of Corporation Court in and for the City ~~County~~ and State aforesaid, personally appeared W. H. Snowden a resident of Fairfax County Virginia who, being duly sworn, on oath declares

That he is the person who was Captain of Company "D" of the 10th Regt. N. J. Vols. And well remembers William J. Sutton who was a Sergeant of said Co. "D" 10th N. J. Vols. and afterwards 2d Lieut. of said company.

That said Sutton received a gun-shot wound in action at the battle of the "Wilderness" May 6th A.D. 1864, the ball taking effect in the right hand and causing the loss of the right thumb.

That he states the above from personal knowledge, having been present with said Regt. during said battle.

And that he has no interest herein.

That he states the above from personal knowledge, and has no interest herein.

Witnesses to (x) mark, if made by affiant. }

W. H. Snowden.

Subscribed and sworn before me this 22 day of March A. D. 1879. I hereby certify that the contents of the above have been carefully made known to affiant before execution; that each affiant appears to be a respectable and credible witness; and that I have no interest in any proceeding to which this relates.

[illegible] Morton Marye

24

Affidavit.

State of N Jersey , **County of** Cumberland **ss:**

In the Pension Claim of [illegible]

Company and Regiment of Service, if in the Army; or Vessel and Rank, if in the Navy.

personally came before me, a Justice Peace in and for the County and State aforesaid William J Sutton whose Residence and Post Office address is Seeley Cumberland Co. N J well known to me to be reputable and entitled to credit, and who being duly sworn, declares in relation to aforesaid case as follows:

Affiant should here state all the known facts pertaining to the case, and how a knowledge of them has been obtained.

I believe that the poor physical condition in which I was left from the measles caused me to take sunstroke after which I had great weakness of the head and nervous trembling could not think plain or act as quick felt a loss of something I could not get back the least excitement or worry caused blood to rush to my head causing severe head ache pains running down my back when I lay down from back of my head down neck to shoulders get sore and stiff could not turn my head without turning my body my back is badly affected from ribs down to hips When I am down I cannot rise up without support I can not furnish the medicle evidence called for from the fact that of ten physicians that have treated me since my discharge eight are dead one does not practice my present physician is Dr A Sullivan of Shiloh N J

(Here state by whom, when and where the above testimony was written; whether in the presence of the witness, and from his oral statements only; and whether he was prompted by any printed or written statement or recital prepared or dictated by any other person, and not attached as an exhibit.)

this Statement is prepared and Written by my Self

I further declare that I have no interest, either direct or indirect, in the prosecution of said claim.

William J Sutton
Affiant sign here.

If affiant signs by mark, two persons who can write must sign here.

…f New Jersey—Bureau of Vital Statisti…

CERTIFICATE AND RECORD OF DEATH.

William J. Sutton

[If an infant not named, so state, and give sex.]

Days. | Hours.

6. Last place of residence: ………

(If in a city, give name, street and number; if in township give name

Township - Cumberland Co

and county; if in an institution, so state.)

7. How long resident in this state ………

8. Place of death Staley Deerfield

(If in a city, give name, street and number; if in township give name

Township - Cumberland Co

and county; if in an institution, so state.)

9. Father's name Ozwell Sutton

Country of Birth U.S.

10. Mother's name Keziah Sutton

Country of Birth U.S.

11. I hereby certify that I attended the deceased during the last illness, and that he died on the 30th day of April 1904, and that the cause of death was Pulmonary Abscess

Length of sickness 3 months. See over and particulars.

NAME OF SOLDIER:	Sutton, William J.		
NAME OF DEPENDENT:	Widow,	Sutton, Alice M.	
	Minor,		
SERVICE:	D 10 N J Inf.		

DATE OF FILING.	CLASS.	APPLICATION NO.	CERTIFICATE NO.	STATE FROM WHICH FILED.
	Invalid,			
1904 May 31	Widow,	806811	583872	N.J.
	Minor,			

James C. Sutton m. Elizabeth M. Maul
10/24/1855

Box 31325

Cert. no. 636
Elizabeth M. Sutton now Ayres
formerly widow of
James C. Sutton

Bundle #40

Shiloh, New Jersey, Jan 30th A.D. 19[illegible]

The Hon. Commissioner of Pensions.

Washington D.C.

Mrs Elizabeth K. Ayars of this village who was the identical person named in Pension Certificate No. 636 dated June 3rd 1891. Died January 24th A.D. 1911

Please send to my address what is necessary in such cases, for me, her Executor to collect pension due at the time of death.

She [illegible] to defray funeral expenses.

Yours truly

[illegible], Executor

[illegible]

3—796.

DROP ORDER AND REPORT.

Department of the Interior,
SPECIAL ACT.
BUREAU OF PENSIONS,
FINANCE DIVISION.

Washington, D. C., FEB 4 - 1911, 19

Elizabeth M. Sutton now Ayars
(Pensioner.)

636
(Certificate number.)

WIDOW.
(Class.)

James C.
(Soldier.)

D. 10 N.J. Vol. Inf.
(Service.)

U. S. Pension Agent,
Philadelphia

SIR: You are hereby directed to drop from the roll the name of the above-described pensioner who died January 24, 1911.

J. L. Davenport.
Commissioner.

REPORT.

Commissioner of Pensions.

SIR: The name of the above-described pensioner, who was last paid at $ 12 per month to Nov 4, 1910, has this day been dropped from the roll of this agency.

[signature]
U. S. Pension Agent.

FEB 15 1911, 19

6—833

State of New Jersey }
Cumberland County ss. }

On this thirteenth day of September, A.D. eighteen hundred and sixty two, personally appeared before me Providence Ludlam Clerk of the Court of Common Pleas of the County aforesaid, Elizabeth M. Sutton, a resident of the township of Chancesey in the county of Cumberland, and State of New Jersey, aged thirty one years, who, being first duly sworn according to law, doth on her oath make the following declaration, in order to obtain the benefit of the provision made by the act of Congress approved July 14. 1862: That she is the widow of James C. Sutton, who was a corporal in company D. then commanded by Capt John Evans, now by Capt Wm H. Snowden, in the Tenth Regiment of New Jersey Volunteers in the war of 1861, who died at the Columbia Hospital in the city of Washington D.C. on the seventh day of March 1861, of Measles and inflamation on the lungs. She further declares that she was married to the said James C. Sutton, on the twenty fourth day of October 1855; that her husband, the aforesaid James C. Sutton, died on the day above mentioned, and that she has remained a widow ever since that period, as will more fully appear by reference to the proof hereto annexed

She also declares that she has not in any manner been engaged in, or aided or abetted the rebellion in the United States, and that she has no children.

Elizabeth M Sutton

Also personally appeared Margaret A. Sutton, and Noah Ayars, jr. persons whom I certify to be respectable & entitled to credit, and who reside in the town of Bridgeton, Cumberland county, & state of New Jersey, and who being by me duly sworn say that they were present and saw her sign her name to the foregoing declaration; and they further swear that they have every reason to believe, from the appearance of the applicant and their acquaintance with her, that she is the identical person she represents herself to be, and that they have no interest in the prosecution of this claim.

Margaret Alice Sutton
Noah Ayars jr

Sworn to and subscribed before me this thirteenth day of September A. D 1862. & I do certify that I have no interest direct or indirect in the prosecution of this claim. In witness whereof I, P. Ludlam, Clerk of the Court of Common Pleas of the county of Cumberland New Jersey, have signed my name & affixed the seal of said court the day & year last aforesaid.

P Ludlam Clerk

New Jersey
Cumberland County ss.

On this thirteenth day of September A.D. 1862, personally appeared before the subscriber P. Ludlam, Clerk of the Court of Common Pleas of Cumberland County Margaret A. Sutton and Noah Ayars Jr. whom I do certify to be respectable & entitled to credit & who being by me duly sworn, say that they are well acquainted with Elizabeth M. Sutton, the above named applicant, that her husband was a corporal in Company D. 10th Regiment New Jersey Volunteers, & that he died at the Columbia Hospital in the city of Washington D.C. on or about the 7th day of March A.D. 1862, and that the said applicant still remains a widow.

Margaret Alice Sutton.
Noah Ayars Jr

Sworn & subscribed before me. P. Ludlam Clerk of the Court of Common Pleas of the county of Cumberland, this thirteenth day of September A. D. 1862.

In witness whereof I have hereto set my hand & affixed the seal of said Court the day & year last aforesaid.

P. Ludlam Clerk

over

I. P. Ludlam, Clerk of the Court of Common Pleas, of the county of Cumberland, New Jersey, do certify that as appears by the records of marriages in the Office of said Court, James C. Sutton and Elizabeth M. Maul, were united in marriage according to the laws of New Jersey by the Rev. I. M. Challis, a minister of the Gospel, on the twenty fourth day of October, eighteen hundred and fifty five, the said marriage being duly recorded in book B. of marriage page 162.

In witness whereof I have hereto set my hand and affixed the seal of said court the thirteenth day of September A.D. eighteen hundred & sixty two.

P. Ludlam Clerk

Applicants post office address:

Elizabeth M. Sutton
Bridgeton
Cumberland County
New Jersey.

77

Adjutant General's Office,

Washington D. C.,
November 24th 1862.

Sir:

I have the honor to acknowledge the receipt from your Office of application for Pension No. 2909, and to return it herewith, with such information as is furnished by the files of this Office.

It appears from the Rolls on file in this Office, that James C. Sutton was enrolled at Shiloh N.J. Sep 20/61 in Co. "D", Tenth (10) Regiment of New Jersey Volunteers, and mustered into service as a Corpl. Oct 8th 1861 3 yrs at Philadelphia in Co. "D", Tenth (10) Regiment of New Jersey Volunteers. On the Muster Roll of Co. "D" of that Regiment for the months of March & April, 1862, he is reported as having died at Columbia Hospital March 7th 1862.

I am Sir very respectfully
Your obedient servant
[illegible signature]
Assistant Adjutant General.

The Commissioner of Pensions
Washington D. C.

Memoranda
Name of applicant Elizabeth M. Sutton
Address Bridgeton N.J.
R.B.

I, Isaac T. Thackara, 1st Lieutenant of Co. D. 10th Regiment, New Jersey Volunteers, do hereby certify that James C. Sutton was Corporal in said Company, at the time of his death, on the 7th day of March AD 1862: that the said James first contracted the measles whilst in the service of the United States, & in the line of his duty: & died of the said disease, together with inflammation of the lungs, at the United States Hospital Columbia College, on or about the seventh day of March last.

And I do further certify, that the surgeon then in charge of said Hospital has since left: & that John Evans then the Captain Commanding said Co. D. has been mustered out of the service of the United States,

Dated Feby 13 1863

Lieut. I T Thackray
Co D- 10th Infy N.J. Vols

Shiloh N.J. Jan 25th 1911

Mr Theo F Davis executor of estate of Elizebeth M Ayars decd To
Ruth. A. Gillespie Dr

For nursing said Eliz M. Ayars in her last sickness. from Jan 8th to Jan. 16th A D 1911 $5.00

I hold Theo. F. Davis executor responsible for the payment of above bill.

Ruth. A. Gillespie

3—044.

APPLICATION FOR REIMBURSEMENT.

(This application, when properly executed before some officer having authority to administer oaths for general purposes, should be forwarded, together with the pension certificate and itemized bills of all expenses, to the Commissioner of Pensions, Washington, D. C.)

STATE OF New Jersey
COUNTY OF Cumberland } ss:

On this 15th day of February, A. D. one thousand nine hundred and Eleven personally appeared before me, a Justice of the Peace within and for the County and State aforesaid, Theo F. Davis executor, aged 66 years, a resident of Shiloh, County of Cumberland, State of New Jersey, who, being duly sworn according to law, makes the following declaration in order to obtain reimbursement from the accrued pension for expenses paid (or obligation incurred) by claimant for the last sickness and for the burial of Elizebeth M Ayars, who was a pensioner of the United States by certificate No. 636, on account of the service of James E Sutton Corpl (Name of soldier or sailor.) in Co D. 10 Regt. N. J. Vols Infantry (Describe service by company and regiment, etc., if in the Army, or by the words U. S. Navy, if in the Navy.)

That pension was last paid to Elizebeth M Ayars Nov 4th, 1910, by the U. S. Pension Agent at Phila Pa.

That the answers to questions propounded below are full, complete, and truthful to the best of my knowledge, information, and belief, and that no evidence necessary to a proper adjustment of all claims against the accrued pension is suppressed or withheld.

1. What was the full name of the deceased pensioner? Elizebeth M. Ayars. formerly Elizebeth M Sutton (first husband)

2. In what capacity was decedent pensioned? (As invalid soldier or sailor, or as a widow, minor child, dependent relative, etc.) Widow. I have her Pension Certificate No. 636

3. If decedent was pensioned as an invalid soldier or sailor—
   (a) Was he ever married? (Answer yes or no.)
   (b) How many times, and to whom?
   (c) If married, did his wife survive him? (Answer yes or no.)
   (d) If so, is she still living? (Answer yes or no.)
   (e) If not living, give full names and dates of death of all wives
   (f) Was he ever divorced? (Answer yes or no.)
   (g) If so, is the divorced wife still living? (Answer yes or no.) (If living, a copy of the decree of divorce must be filed.)
   (h) If not living, give her full name and the date of her death

4. Did pensioner leave a child under 16 years of age? (Answer yes or no.) no. She had no children

5. Is any such child still living? (Answer yes or no.)

6. Was there insurance (life, accident, or health) in force on life of pensioner at time of death? (Answer yes or no.) no

7. If so, give the name of each company in which a policy was carried and the amount in which each policy was written

PENSION N FEB 17 1911 U. S. OFFICE

8. Who was the beneficiary named in each policy?

9. What was the relation of each beneficiary to the pensioner?

10. Were the premiums paid by the deceased pensioner?

11. If not paid by the deceased pensioner, state the amount of premiums paid by each person who made payment on that account

12. Was pensioner a member of any society paying sick or death benefits? (Answer yes or no.) no

13. Is there an executor or administrator, or will application be made for appointment of any person as administrator? yes
Theo F. Davis Shiloh N.J. is her executor

14. Did the deceased pensioner leave any money, real estate, or personal property? yes, a little personal.

15. If so, state the character and value of all such property Household Goods not over twenty five dollars, probably not over twenty dollars + Note $60.

16. What was the assessed value (last assessment) of the real estate?

17. How was the pensioner's property disposed of? at private sale.

18. Did pensioner leave an unindorsed pension check? (Answer yes or no.) no

19. What was your relation to the deceased pensioner? none

20. Are you married? (Answer yes or no.) yes

21. What was the cause of pensioner's death? Chronic Diarrhea

22. When did the pensioner's last sickness begin? became helpless about Dec 15th 1910

23. From what date did the pensioner become so ill as to require the regular and daily attendance of another person constantly until death? Dec 15th 1910

24. Give the name and post-office address of each physician who attended the pensioner during last sickness
Herbert H. Fritts M.D. Shiloh N.J.

25. State the names of the persons by whom the pensioner was nursed during the period or any portion of the period of last sickness and the period covered by such service in each instance Ruth Gilespie one week Mrs James Grey three weeks. Bridgeton Hospital one week. neighbors + friends interspersed

26. Where did the pensioner live during last sickness? At Shiloh N.J. and Bridgeton Hospital

27. Where did the pensioner die? At Hospital. Bridgeton Cumb. Co. N.J.

28. When did the pensioner die? January 24th A.D. 1911

29. Where was the pensioner buried? Shiloh. Cumb. Co. N.J. Cemetery

30. Has there been paid, or will application be made for payment to you or any other person, any part of the expenses of the pensioner's last sickness and burial by any State, County, or municipal corporation? (Answer yes or no.) no

31. State below the expenses of the pensioner's last sickness and burial. Write the word *none* where no charge is made in case of any item of expense noted.

(Each charge entered below should be supported by an itemized bill of the person who rendered the service or furnished any supplies for which reimbursement is demanded, and should show, over his signature, by whom paid, or who is held responsible for payment, and contain the name of the pensioner for whom the expense was incurred or service rendered.)

Names.	Nature of Expenses.	State Whether Paid or Unpaid.	Amount.
H. H. Fritts M.D.	Physician	unpaid	31.00
	Medicine	none	
Mrs J. R. Grey and Ruth A. Gillespie	Nursing and care	20. paid	25.00
Pierce + Carll	Undertaker	unpaid	35.00
	Livery	none	
John T. Dixon	Cemetery	unpaid	3.00
	Other expenses and their nature:		
Bridgeton Hospital Association	Hospital	unpaid	8.00
S. V. Davis	Store bill	unpaid	11.82
Theo F. Davis Ex	Executors bill	unpaid	20.00
	Total		$133.82

32. **Is the above a complete list of *all* the expenses of the last sickness and burial of the deceased pensioner?** (Answer yes or no.) yes, as far as I know

That my post-office address is No. ...., on .... street, town or city of Shiloh, County of Cumberland State of New Jersey

(When the claimant for reimbursement is a married woman, she is required to sign the application with her own full name, not using the Christian name or the initials of her husband, and all bills should be receipted to her in her own name.)

6—1572

Theo F. Davis, executor
(Claimant's signature in full.)

Also personally appeared George L. Lykins
and Artis E. Davis, persons whom I certify to be respectable and entitled to credit, and who, being by me duly sworn, say that they were present and saw Theo. F. Davis, the claimant, sign his name (or make mark) to the foregoing application, and that they know the claimant therein; that they have read all the questions, answers, and declarations in said application and believe the facts therein set forth to be true; and that they have no interest, direct or indirect, in this claim.

George L. Lykins
Shiloh N.J.
Artis E. Davis
Shiloh N.J.
(Signatures and post-office addresses of witnesses.)

Subscribed and sworn to before me this 15th day of Feb, A. D. 1911; and I certify that the contents of the foregoing application, etc., were fully made known and explained to the claimant and witnesses before swearing, including the words .... erased and the words .... added; and that I have no interest, direct or indirect, in the prosecution of this claim.

F. S. Gillespie
(Signature.)
Justice of the Peace.
(Official character.)

STATEMENT OF ATTENDING PHYSICIANS.

Give date of the pensioner's death Jan. 24. 1911

Give date of commencement of pensioner's last sickness About Oct. 15, 1910

From what date did the pensioner require the regular and daily attendance of another person constantly until death? Oct. 15, 1910

During what period did you attend the pensioner? Oct. 5. 1909 to Jan. 24. 1911

State nature of disease from which pensioner died A chronic diarrhoea, beginning in summer of 1909 + becoming decidedly worse the middle of Oct. 1910. About Dec. 15. 1910 a broncho pneumonia developed. The asthenia resulting from this + the intractable diarrhoea resulted in her death.

Give name of each person who rendered service as nurse, and who has made or will make a charge for such service Mrs. Jas. Gray
Mrs. Ruth Gillespie

Give name of any other physician who attended the pensioner in last sickness Dr. Leslie Cornwall of Bridgeton N.J. then attending physician at Bridgeton Hospital

Does your bill include a charge for all medicine furnished the pensioner during last sickness? Yes

State whether you have read the questions in the foregoing application, and the claimant's answers thereto, and whether such answers are correct according to your best knowledge, information, and belief? Yes

Mention any other facts within your knowledge which in your opinion would be helpful in adjusting this claim for reimbursement: She was taken to the Bridgeton Hospital Jan. 16, 1911, at which place she died. The charge for nursing there is included in the one charge by the hospital.

I certify that the foregoing statement is correct.

Feb. 11, 1911 — Herbert H. Fritts, M.D.
Attending Physician.

........, 191 ....
Attending Physician.

6—1572

Widow's [illegible] Ctf. H. 636

E. D.

Department of the Interior.

BUREAU OF PENSIONS.

[illegible]

Washington, D.C. April [illegible], 1891

MAY [illegible] 1891

Sir:

Will you please return this letter stating the present post office address of Elizabeth M. [illegible] of [illegible] Co. D, 10th [illegible] who was pensioned under Special Act [illegible] March 3rd [illegible].

Very respectfully,

[illegible]

Commissioner.

Hon. C. A. Bergen,

Trenton,

N. J.

My Dear Sir:- In answer to your above request I have the honor to state that the address of Mrs. Elizabeth M. Ayars is Rosenhayn, Cumberland Co., New Jersey.

Respectfully Yours,

C A Bergen 5/6/91

War of 1861 636

Brief in the case of Elizabeth M. Sutton, widow of James E. Sutton, Cumberland County and State of N.J. Corp'l in Co. D, 10th N.J. Volunteers

Act 14th July 1862.

CLAIM FOR PENSION, Original

PROOF EXHIBITED.

On rolls "died at Columbia Hospital, March 7th 1862." Cause of death and origin of disease shown by certificate of Lieut. of Com'dg. Declaration in form and made before Clerk of Court of Common Pleas. Identity established by testimony of two witnesses. Marriage proven by public record. Deceased soldier left no child.

Admitted Feby 21st 1863, at $8 per month, to date from March 7th 1862.

Claimant's P.O.
Bridgeton
Cumberland Co.
N.J.

Decided by

Hon John T. Nixon H of R. J.H.B.
Name and Residence of Agent.

E. H. Talbott
Examining Clerk.

RECEIPT ACKNOWLEDGED
VP
APR 1 - 1911 Clerk.

Shiloh N.J. March 23/11

The Hon. Commissioner of Pensions
Washington D.C.

Sir:- Your favor of March 20th in regard to the matter of Elizabeth M. Ayars certificate No 636, at hand.
The estate is so small that I concluded it did not warrant me in qualifying as Executor, is the reason it has not been done.
I would prefer to relinquish my claim of $20. for services rather than run the estate to expense. If I am to understand your letter to say that the Bureau will pay the Court charges, I will qualify at once.
Otherwise I can furnish ample proof of all points.

Respectfully yours
Theo F. Davis Executor
Shiloh. N.J.

P.S. I await your reply
T.F.D.

FINANCE DIVISION
MAR 27 1911
BUREAU OF PENSIONS

found in Millers Cemetery
New Gretna, NJ

501 Mohawk Drive
Erie, Penna.
Feb. 6, 1966

Robert Sutton
Hillside Road
New Gretna, N.J.

Dear Mr. Sutton:

What do you know about your ancestors? My great, great grandmother was Elizabeth Sutton, born Mar. 20, 1784 in Burlington Co., N.J. She married, about 1803 to Thomas Brown of Mansfield Twp., Burlington Co. I have been trying to find the names of her parents, but the closest I can get to it, is a tradition given to me by a relative who lived in N.J. all of her life, and that is, that there were three sisters, that the other 2 married and moved to the state of New York!

Then my Aunt told me that her father had always told them, that one of the ancestors was killed in the Revolutionary War. I have eliminated any Brown ancestor that might have been in the Rev. War, so that leaves the Sutton line.

A Robert Sutton was killed in the Revolutionary War as he was on his way to fight the British at Bordentown, or near there. The British ;fired on them from the Delaware River, they returned the fire, and Robert Sutton was killed. He had with him at that time, a son---name unknown. This proves that this Robert Sutton was married, and perhaps had more children than the one son. I have beenn unable to find out anything more about this family.

This Robert Sutton who was killed in the Rev. War was a son of Robert Sutton whose will was made in Burlington Co., on Mar. 30, 1766. His will named 4 sons-Robert, Daniel, James and John, and a daughter Deborah Bird. James Sutton is called "mariner" and he was made administrator of h s father's will. I can't find another word about these children except that the son Robert was killed in the R.W. What happened to them?

Daniel Sutton was the progenitor of these families in Burlington Co. He was a tailor and he came to America on the ship "Endeavor" which landed in Philadelphia on the 29th of the 7th mo., 1683. He is buried in the cemetery of St. Mary Church in Burlington, and he died the 10th day of March, 1711. His will lists 2 sons Daniel and Robert, and 2 daughters Mary Margaret and Susan.

The son Daniel married Mary Jackson and by her had 2 sons- Daniel Jackson Sutton (also buried at St. Mary's, who died aged under 21), and John Jackson Sutton; also 2 daughters Catherine and Mary, & Jane

John Jackson Sutton was married twice, and he moved to Seneca Co., N.Y. about 1800, with some of his children. His wife did not go with him but stayed in N.J. We have found a lot of old letters that this John Jackson Sutton wrote to his son in N.J., also letters that one of his daughters had written to her relatives back in N.J. We also found an old Bible record of his children, which shows that he had a son named Robert Jackson Sutton, born Oct. 10, 1784. This date proves that my Elizabeth Sutton was not his daughter, since he could not have had a daughte born in Mar. and a son b. in Oct. of the same year--- so that eliminates the famil of Daniel Sutton, Jr. and his wife Mary Jackson Sutton, as my ancestors.

That leaves only Robert Sutton, the other son of Daniel Sutton, Sr. as a possibili This Robert is the one whose will was made in 1766, and who was the father of the Robert Sutton who was killed in the Rev. War!

This Robert Sutton was killed on Mar. 10, 1778. His wife's name was Mary and she was given a pension for his service, by the State of N.J., not by the U.S. Government. This pension record gives no other information. She was to receive this pension quarterly, as long as she remained a widow.

I thought I might get some information from somone's DAR papers, but noone has joined the DAR on his service. Neither has any chapter in N. J. marked his grave.

Another story that I got from this relative who lived in N. J. was that she seemd to remember her father, saying that Elizabeth Sutton lived down "on the shore". The fore I thought perhaps there might still be someone of this family still living "on the shore". That is why I am writing to you. There were other Sutton families in N. J. both in Salem Co., and in other counties, which I have not searched, since I am sure that my Elizabeth belonged to the Daniel Sutton family of Burlington Co.

If you have any information about your forebears, I would like to know what you have. If it should be possible that you belong to this same family, I have a lot of information to share with you.

I am getting my records in shape so that I can make stencils and run them off on the mimeograph in the near future. I had hoped that I could get more informatio on the Sutton family before I did this, but I seem to have exhausted all means that I know of to get information. Let me hear from you.

Sincerely,

Rohena B. Cook

Mrs. Harold A. Cook